THE DESTRUCT

THE DESTRUCTORS

The Story of Northern Ireland's Lost Peace Process

MICHAEL KERR
King's College London

IRISH ACADEMIC PRESS
DUBLIN • PORTLAND, OR

First published in 2011 by Irish Academic Press

www.iap.ie

© 2011 Michael Kerr

British Library Cataloguing in Publication Data

ISBN 978 0 7165 3098 5 (cloth)
ISBN 978 0 7165 3099 2 (paper)

Library of Congress Cataloging-in-Publication Data
An entry can be found on request

All rights reserved. Without limiting the rights under copyright reserved alone, no part of this publication may be reproduced, stored in or introduced into a retrieval system, or transmitted, in any form or by any means (electronic, mechanical, photocopying, recording or otherwise) without the prior written permission of both the copyright owner and the above publisher of this book.

Printed by Good News Digital Books, Ongar, Essex

For Julia Kerr,
who breezed through these troubled times

And it may well be that my history will seem less easy to read because of the absence in it of a romantic element. It will be enough for me, however, if these words of mine are judged useful by those who want to understand clearly the events which happened in the past and which (human nature being what it is) will, at some point or other and in much the same ways, be repeated in the future.

Thucydides
The Peloponnesian War

The struggle of man against power is the struggle of memory against forgetting.

Milan Kundera
The Book of Laughter and Forgetting

I know they's a lots of things in a family history that just plain aint so. Any family. The stories gets passed on and the truth gets passed over. As the sayin goes. Which I reckon some would take as meanin that the truth cant compete. But I dont believe that. I think that when the lies are all told and forgot the truth will be there yet. It dont move about from place to place and it dont change from time to time. You cant corrupt it any more than you can salt salt.

Cormac McCarthy
No Country for Old Men

Contents

List of Abbreviations		ix
Dramatis Personae		x
Acknowledgements		xii
Prologue		xiii
Introduction		1

PART I: DIRECT RULE

1	Bringing it All Back Home	19
2	Breaking the Mould	45
3	The Whitelaw Settlement	81
4	A Salesman for Sunningdale	113

PART II: THE POWER-SHARING EXECUTIVE

5	Hands Across the Border	143
6	The Other End of the Bridge	169
7	The Wildcats Strike	201
8	The Triumph of the Destructors	223

PART III: MAJORITY REPORT

9 Responsibility Without Power	251
10 No Direction Home	289
Select Bibliography	331
Index	335

List of Abbreviations

BBC	British Broadcasting Corporation
CBI	Confederation of British Industry
DFA	Department of Foreign Affairs
DUP	Democratic Unionist Party
EEC	European Economic Community
GOC	General Officer Commanding
INLA	Irish National Liberation Army
IRA	Irish Republican Army
NILP	Northern Ireland Labour Party
NIO	Northern Ireland Office
RTÉ	Raidió Teilifís Éireann
RUC	Royal Ulster Constabulary
SDLP	Social Democratic and Labour Party
SIS	Secret Intelligence Service
UDA	Ulster Defence Association
UDR	Ulster Defence Regiment
UFF	Ulster Freedom Fighters
UN	United Nations
UPNI	Unionist Party of Northern Ireland
UWC	Ulster Workers' Council
UUC	Ulster Unionist Council
UUUC	United Ulster Unionist Council
UVF	Ulster Volunteer Force

Dramatis Personae

The British Government
Edward Heath (Prime Minister, Conservative government 1970–4)
William Whitelaw (Northern Ireland Secretary of State 1972–3)
Sir Alec Douglas-Home (Foreign Secretary 1970–4)
Peter Carrington (Minister of Defence 1970–4)
Reginald Maudling (Home Secretary 1970–2)
Harold Wilson (Prime Minister, Labour government 1974–6)
Merlyn Rees (Northern Ireland Secretary of State 1974–6)
Roy Mason (Minister for Defence 1974–6)
Stanley Orme (Minister of State 1974–6)

The Irish Government
Jack Lynch (Taoiseach, Fianna Fáil government 1966–73)
Liam Cosgrave (Taoiseach, Fine Gael–Labour government 1973–7)
Garret FitzGerald (Minister for Foreign Affairs 1973–7)
Conor Cruise O'Brien (Minister for Posts and Telegraphs 1973–7)

The Northern Ireland Executive
Brian Faulkner (Chief Executive, Unionist)
John Baxter (Information)
Roy Bradford (Environment)
Herbert Kirk (Finance)
Basil McIvor (Education)
Leslie Morrell (Agriculture)
Gerry Fitt (Deputy Chief Executive, SDLP)
Austin Currie (Housing, Local Government and Planning)
Paddy Devlin (Health and Social Services)
John Hume (Commerce)
Oliver Napier (Office of Law Reform, Alliance Party)

The United Ulster Unionist Council
Harry West (Official Unionist Party)
John Taylor
John Laird
William Craig (Vanguard)
Glen Barr
Ernest Baird
Ian Paisley (DUP)
William Beattie

Provisional IRA
Dáithí Ó Conaill
Seán Mac Stíofáin

British Officials
Frank Cooper (NIO)
Philip Woodfield (NIO)
Frank Steele (NIO)
Bernard Donoughue (Downing Street)
Frank King (GOC)

Irish Officials
Seán Donlon (DFA)
Dermot Nally (Taoiseach)

Northern Ireland Officials
Ken Bloomfield
Robert Lowry
Maurice Hayes

Acknowledgements

The research for this book was conducted while I was Leverhulme Research Fellow in the International History Department at the London School of Economics (LSE). I wish to thank the Leverhulme Trust and their staff for all their generosity, kindness and support in funding this project.

I must thank my sister Gillian for looking after me through many summers of writing, and Robert, Valerie, Richard, Sonya and Fred for their support and encouragement.

I wish to thank all those at the LSE who helped me, especially Dr Kirsten Schulze, Professor Arne Westad, Professor Nigel Ashton, Professor David Stevenson, Dr Antony Best, Mrs Demetra Frini, my old roommate and friend Dr Paul Keenan, and fellow LSE alumnus Professor Brendan O'Leary.

Professor Rory Miller, Director of the Middle East and Mediterranean Studies Programme at King's College London, assisted me enormously in writing this book. His generosity, kindness, and patience are rare gifts and I am extremely fortunate to have him as a friend and a colleague.

Many thanks to Lisa Hyde at Irish Academic Press. This is our third book together, which speaks volumes about our friendship.

Thanks to all those who shared their recollections and thoughts on the events that took place in Northern Ireland in the 1970s. Thanks to Professor Paul Bew, Professor Adrian Guelke, Dr Simon Prince, Dr Owen McEldowney and Geoff McGimpsey for their comments and criticisms. Thanks Hannah Stewart for all your help and your thoughts on voluntary coalition. Thanks David McClay and Ronan Smyth for occasionally distracting me from the subject of this book. And thank you Daniel for finding it a title.

Prologue

In Graham Greene's nihilistic short story, 'The Destructors', a gang of young boys break into Old Misery's house, hell-bent on destroying it from within. Damaged during the Blitz, from the outside the building appears crippled. On the inside it is a beautiful home with ornate panelled walls unravelling around a corkscrew staircase, built over two hundred years ago by Sir Christopher Wren.

In planning the attack, 'T', Blackie's rival for the leadership of the gang, instructs his companions not to steal anything from the house. He has a better idea. 'We'll pull it down,' he declares, 'we'll destroy it.' And when his friends voice their concerns that such action will attract the attention of the police, he tells them, 'They'd never know. We'd do it from the inside', when Old Misery is away. 'We'd be like worms, don't you see, in an apple. When we came out again there'd be nothing there, no staircase, no panels, nothing but just walls.'

'Driven by pure, simple and altruistic ambition of fame for the gang', Blackie agrees to the plan and the young destroyers set about their assignment, advancing chaos with gusto and working with the fortitude of creators. For destruction, Greene reminds us, is a form of creation.

Looking for 'something special' to mark his ascendancy in the gang, 'T' discovers Old Misery's savings in bundles of pound notes and instructs the boys to burn them, one by one, as a gesture of 'celebration' for their achievement. The next day, when Old Misery returns and disturbs them with their project incomplete, the boys prepare to escape, declaring that their work is almost done anyway. Taking Old Misery captive in his broken home, 'T' tells the gang members, 'Anybody could do this', and compels them to finish the job properly by destroying the walls. 'This,' Greene muses, 'was the shattered house with nothing left but the walls. Yet walls could be preserved. Façades were valuable. They could build inside again more beautifully than before. This could again be a home.'[1]

* * * *

In January 1974, Ulster unionist and Irish nationalist opponents crossed the sectarian divide by forming a power-sharing government at Stormont. This Northern Ireland Executive was short-lived however, destroyed by a very un-British coup in May of that same year. It was the first time since the Second World War that there had been a significant threat to constitutional government in the United Kingdom (UK). An Ulster Workers' Council (UWC) became the focal point for opposition to political reform from within the largely Protestant unionist community. It successfully challenged the authority of the Westminster parliament to determine the form of government that Northern Ireland would have following direct rule in March 1972. Taking control of Northern Ireland's power stations, and bringing the province to the brink of political and economic meltdown through the imposition of a general strike, the UWC undermined the capacity of the Stormont and Westminster administrations to govern the province. Ignoring calls from the Northern Ireland Executive to break the strike in its first days, Labour prime minister Harold Wilson offered no military challenge to the Protestant paramilitary groups that were aligned against it; for had he done so, the British Army might have been exposed to the venom of *both* communities in Northern Ireland. In failing to uphold constitutional government in Northern Ireland, Wilson was rejecting the idea that the British could or should provide a solution to Ireland's ancient troubles, either by imposing power-sharing or through some other form of direct rule from Westminster.

The closure of Northern Ireland's electricity generators would have completely destroyed its economic infrastructure, leaving the province in a state of anarchy with political authority firmly in the hands of its different paramilitary factions. Strike leader Glen Barr confirmed that this was exactly what the UWC intended to do should the British Army or the Royal Ulster Constabulary (RUC) attempt to end the stoppage. We 'would have done it', Barr recalls. The sole objective of the UWC's challenge to the British was 'to destroy' the Northern Ireland Executive, to 'wreck it and bring it down as quickly as possible'.[2] After Conservative

Prime Minister Edward Heath imposed direct rule, his government never doubted it. Eighteen months before the strike, Northern Ireland's first secretary of state, William Whitelaw, warned colleagues that 'sooner or later a major confrontation between the security forces and the Ulster Defence Association was probably inevitable'.[3]

In the event, Wilson simply allowed power to ebb from Stormont to the UWC headquarters in east Belfast, on the Hawthornden Road. With no power to forcibly challenge the growing authority of the UWC, the executive, led by former unionist prime minister Brian Faulkner and Social Democratic and Labour Party (SDLP) leader Gerry Fitt, collapsed a fortnight into the unconstitutional stoppage. However, it was not just their government that the UWC destroyed. The edifice of intercommunal political accommodation based on power-sharing between unionists, nationalists and the centre ground Alliance Party, which Whitelaw had painstakingly constructed in 1973, lay in tatters. So following the events of May 1974, the vehicle for political reform in Northern Ireland that power-sharing between unionists and nationalists had come to represent was severely damaged.

John Hume, Northern Ireland's first nationalist minister for commerce and the SDLP's most influential figure, described the British government's unwillingness to prevent the executive's collapse as 'one of the greatest mistakes in Irish history'.[4] It is perhaps unsurprising, then, that the UWC strike has been all but airbrushed from the narrative of twentieth-century British and Irish political history. Had the power-sharing venture proved successful it would have been of no less significance. It would be lauded as a high point in a decade of decline, one which saw the British government complete its political and economic retreat from empire and struggle to find a post-colonial role on the world stage.

* * * *

This book is neither a survey of political events during the early phases of British direct rule in Northern Ireland nor a historiographical work on what has been written already on why direct rule came about or on why power-sharing failed. This book is not a social history, or a history of the origins of the Northern Ireland troubles, or a study which offers a particular focus on the religious and nationalist ideologies that reinforce divisions within this society. One of the obvious and perhaps quite startling conclusions one may draw from what follows is that ideology acts as a constraining rather than a determining factor in the actions of many of the politicians that were central to the Northern Ireland peace process. That is not to say that ideology is of little significance, but simply that it is of far less significance than one might otherwise have expected. For the most part, in the struggle for power that ensued following direct rule, political realism and opportunism motivated most of Northern Ireland's politicians to shift from, or to altogether abandon, core political principles and beliefs. Reacting to direct rule, almost all the major parties to the conflict made ideological U-turns over Northern Ireland's constitutional future.

This book is the story of the rise and fall of an idea: using power-sharing as a method of regulating Northern Ireland's troubles, distancing its political antagonisms from Westminster, and giving the Irish government a role in its affairs. Told for the first time, it is an historical account of Northern Ireland's lost peace process, centring on the power politics that took place in and over Northern Ireland in the early years of direct rule. The book's starting point is the beginning of direct rule rather than the outbreak of the troubles, as this was when Northern Ireland's first peace process and the idea of using power-sharing began to take shape. The story ends with the collapse of the Northern Ireland Constitutional Convention in early 1976, rather than the collapse of the Northern Ireland Executive in 1974, as this is the point when the idea of using power-sharing was finally vanquished.

It is written purely from official British, Irish and Northern Irish documentary evidence, and from the reflections of key participants in these events who were kind enough to share their views with me over the last decade. As far as is practically possible, it is written using the words, language and thoughts of those participants. As I went through the archival material in preparing this book, it struck me just how honest, accurate and consistent those participants were in their recollections. This is significant, as there remains much debate over the reliability of using oral history in this manner. Nevertheless, I have always taken the view that, where possible, contemporary historians and political scientists should seek to acquaint themselves with the people at the centre of the events that they are writing about, for, as with any fieldwork exercise, it assists one greatly in getting to the heart of the matter.

Writing a historical account of this nature has some obvious shortcomings. The official documentary evidence is almost always incomplete, and some of the key actors in this story were either deceased or unwilling to discuss with me the role they played in these events. Moreover, as anyone who has ever been involved in politics will know, many of the decisions and discussions that shape the nodal points in history are taken in the corridors of power, or in the tearooms and bars that align them, rather than in official negotiations or party talks. No attempt has been made here to colour the available evidence with secondary sources. Furthermore, if the strength of the evidence from which one may draw firm conclusions appears to lack symmetry, at different points, this is because the available evidence upon which one can make sound judgements is more substantial in some places than it is in others.

Northern Ireland's first peace process took place at a frenetic pace, with very little preparation and almost no long-term planning; it was not a seamlessly choreographed political process. Nevertheless, the availability of different official records, taken from the perspective of Belfast, Dublin and London, enables us to closely analyse many issues that might otherwise have fallen between the cracks of intergovernmental negotiations and party political wrangles. Immediately after introducing direct rule, and after the power-sharing executive collapsed, the British government did not have a clear policy on what to do about Northern Ireland. At times, this may blur the picture that is presented here, but the very fact that they did not have a clear policy is important and instructive. Examining how the Heath and Wilson governments sought to construct complementary political and security polices for Northern Ireland – in Wilson's case a policy which was almost the complete reversal of Heath's – and how the Irish parties reacted and responded to these policies, provides us with a rounded and panoramic view of how events took shape.

The cross-examination of sources from Belfast, Dublin and London allows us to understand what power-sharing in Northern Ireland meant to the different parties to the conflict. This is crucial to understanding why power-sharing failed and in what order it failed. It enables us to draw comparative conclusions from these events regarding conflict regulation, civil war, and the external variables that often shape the outcome of conflicts and peace processes in divided societies. Aside from understanding the failure of power-sharing in this period of Northern Ireland's history, for many this will be the primary value of this book, as many of the events described herein will not differ greatly from what occurs in other conflicts over territory in contested states, or multi-national societies, which sit on the fault lines of post-colonial state-building failures.

The question each participant appears to be asking themselves as the Northern Ireland peace process unfolds is of relevance to societies which may experience civil war, revolution or insurgency in the future: in what order have the Heath and Wilson governments decided to abandon the political status quo in Northern Ireland and what political risks are they prepared to take to impose a new order? This is a question of great importance to the study of international relations and the politics of third-party intervention in divided societies in contested regions. In what order does a state decide to abandon a constitutionally formed government, or remove another government from power, and seek to replace it with a form of administration that better serves its interests? How does a state go about preparing a society for regime change and a new system of governance, and what are the limitations of intervention of this nature? The contrasting approaches towards the use of power-sharing in Northern Ireland, taken by the Heath and Wilson governments in the 1970s, offers a compelling example of the complexities of applying consociational democracy to a divided society in which there is no consensus over what the objective of power-sharing is, and where the external parties to the conflict lack the political power or the political will to implement and police it.

* * * *

How divided societies remember civil war is of great importance, not only in terms of conflict resolution and reconciliation, but in shaping and restructuring the identity-forming narratives that set ethno-national conflicts in the hearts and minds of those who inherit them, and those who are socialised into them. In divided societies, peace processes exacerbate and fuel latent religious and ethno-national tensions, but they can also serve to strip bare, deconstruct and challenge the dogmatic and doctrinal myths that are central to conflicts of this nature. This book offers a view of how these processes occurred in Northern

Ireland's first peace process. It examines conflicts between parties who sought to rapidly advance their political objectives through the window of opportunity that direct rule represented and their efforts to force the British to include them in any new political order. It details how, after the British have eliminated the Stormont parliament as an institution through which political reform might be initiated, the struggle begins to build new institutions faster than the opponents of British policy can destroy them.

In *The Book of Laughter and Forgetting*, Milan Kundera suggests that 'the struggle of man against power is the struggle of memory against forgetting'.[5] Power uses memory to its advantage too, but it is still a beautiful formulation. He is referring to the Communist Party's airbrushing of history in Czechoslovakia and the sacking of many Czech historians after the Russian invasion in 1968, which came in response to the Prague Spring. In *The Unbearable Lightness of Being*, Kundera warns of the danger of removing a country's road signs. At first this confused the invading army, but later it enabled the Russians to rename whole towns. If we remove the signposts in a country's history, paper over the cracks and fissures of civil conflict, and airbrush the truth from a nation's historical narrative, we risk losing the struggle to remember and the struggle to learn from past mistakes in societies were violent conflicts very often see history repeat itself.

Northern Ireland's struggle is the struggle to remember the culpability of a state unwilling to enforce the rule of law to support a fairly legitimate government, and to remember how easy it is to unleash partisan wrecking forces against democracy even when a reasonable consensus of opinion can be found.

There is no historical account of the rise and fall of the idea of using power-sharing to regulate Northern Ireland's troubles. This book's aim is to analyse the politics of applying consociational democracy to regulate Northern Ireland's troubles by constructing an accurate narrative of the events that led to its failure in the 1970s, and provide a foundation upon which a historical narrative that reinterprets the troubles may be based, should Northern Ireland's 'attics one day be properly swept'.[6]

NOTES

1. G. Greene, 'The Destructors', in *Complete Short Stories* (London: Penguin Books, 2005), pp.3–18.
2. Interview with Glen Barr, Londonderry, 22 August 2001.
3. Cabinet Office files (CAB) 130/560, cabinet meeting, 10 Downing Street, 9 November 1972.
4. Interview with John Hume, Londonderry, 13 September 2001.
5. M. Kundera, *The Book of Laughter and Forgetting* (London: Faber & Faber, 1996), p.4.
6. K. Salibi, *A House of Many Mansions: The History of Lebanon Reconsidered* (Berkeley, CA: University of California Press, 1988), p.234.

Introduction

In August 1969, British troops arrived on the streets of Belfast after the Northern Ireland government requested the British government's assistance in maintaining law and order. Having failed to prevent pressure for political reform from igniting latent sectarian animosities between the majority Protestant and minority Catholic communities, Northern Ireland's unionist prime minister, James Chichester-Clark, was forced to rely upon the British government to support the Stormont parliament in Belfast. Two years later, with no let-up to the violence in sight, and in efforts to end a republican insurgency against Stormont, his successor Brian Faulkner interned 342 suspected IRA members.

Conservative prime minister Edward Heath neither trusted Faulkner nor had he any faith in him to deliver widespread political reforms from Stormont.[1] The British had been hopeful that Faulkner might bring a fresh approach to government, but as time went by they came to view him as a politician with 'feet of clay'.[2] When Faulkner signalled that he could not continue in office without internment, in August 1971, Heath began to conclude that Northern Ireland's existing governmental structures were not going to last; 'the old Anglo-Irish ascendancy, the cranes and rooks in Northern Ireland, hadn't got much longer to run'.[3]

In Whitehall, internment was viewed as Faulkner's 'last shot' at ending the violence,[4] but it fuelled the conflict it was meant to quash, and its mishandling deeply embarrassed the British on the world stage. It exposed Faulkner's inability to initiate a programme of political reforms which might satisfy both his unionist and nationalist critics, and prevent the British from ending the position of political supremacy his Official Unionist Party had enjoyed since Northern Ireland's devolved parliament was opened in 1921. Moreover, it made it all the more obvious that northern nationalists would never again consent to unionist rule,[5] placing the onerous responsibility for Northern Ireland's troubles, however unwelcome, at Westminster's door.

The Northern Ireland parliament was established by the British after the First World War, but the act of partition, through the Government of Ireland Act 1920,[6] ran against the grain of majority political opinion in both Dublin and London. By pressing their claim for self-determination in six of Ulster's nine counties, Irish unionists, as the British viewed it, succeeded in 'having their cake and eating it'.[7] Partition enabled Ireland's minority Protestant community to both opt out of an Irish Free State, which became all the more Catholic, Gaelic and nationalist in their absence, and secure a great degree of political autonomy from Westminster through the Stormont parliament. So much so that any future British government would find it difficult to release itself from the burden of responsibility for Irish affairs that continued political union with a part of Ireland represented.

Although deeply divided on the issue, for the British, partition was a compromise between the contradictory claims to self-determination that different sections of the Irish population held: the unstoppable force that Irish nationalism represented within Ireland and the unmovable object that Ulster unionism remained within the UK. It was a policy based on realism, for imposing a united Ireland against the will of the unionist community would have involved pitting the British Army against both communities in Northern Ireland and risking civil war within the UK. Nationalists viewed partition as a device by which British colonial rule in Ireland could be continued, and one which prevented the people of Ireland from fully exercising their right to self-determination as a nation. For unionists the Stormont parliament represented a double veto on the nationalist question: it enabled them to resist pressure from Dublin to join a united Ireland in which they would become a minority community; and it provided a buffer against any British government that viewed partition as a temporary expedient to achieving that very end.

Britain and Ireland had changed greatly by the late 1960s, but both governments held simplistic and outdated views towards the contested territory that represented a fissure in the state-building ventures of their ancestors. These attitudes stemmed from the way they each interpreted the Government of Ireland Act: accepting partition and Stormont, the view from London was that it had resolved the Irish question; rejecting partition and Stormont, the view from Dublin was that it was the root of all evil. The political instincts of Ulster unionists towards both the Dublin and Westminster parliaments had changed very little during the half century of one-party rule from Stormont. Unsurprisingly perhaps, as the Irish government had a duty to fulfil its constitutional commitment to bring the six counties of Ireland that remained under British sovereignty into a unitary state. Moreover, the British government would not have been reluctant to see Northern Ireland join such a state, should that become the wish of the majority of its people.

The British government was most displeased at being dragged back into Irish troubles that had lain dormant for almost fifty years. They struggled to comprehend unionists' fears over Irish unity and were exasperated by their refusal to countenance alternative forms of government in Ireland. For the most part they believed that, in the long term, the 'only "solution" in Britain's interests' was to pressure unionists into accepting the reunification of Ireland. One British Foreign Office official in Dublin suggested that 'we are not advocating that they [unionists] be sent to Auschwitz, but reincorporated in a State all of whose spokesmen (even the IRA factions) declare that they would have a full role to play [in government]'. He argued that the only alternative to reunification, again in the long term, was 'an independent Ulster'. The united Ireland solution was presently 'not on', he continued, as there was a high probability that it would lead 'directly to civil war in the north', which would bring further international disgrace upon the government and ever deeper involvement in Irish affairs. Pending a time when uniting Ireland might become a possibility, some form of direct rule from Westminster would have the great advantage of being broadly acceptable to unionists while providing the government with the means to win back the confidence of the minority community by reforming Stormont. If the British gained a favourable response to direct rule from the Catholic community, he concluded, public opinion in the Republic of Ireland would swing against the Irish Republican Army (IRA) and the Irish government might then be more willing to cooperate with the British to defeat its 'hard-core' element.[8]

This realism was not well received in Whitehall, where officials were reluctant to even contemplate the thought of direct rule. It was Heath's determination to impose a form of devolution that was in tune with new realities in Northern Ireland, following a short period of direct rule, which informed the government's decision to suspend the Stormont parliament. On 24 March 1972, Heath initiated this radical intervention. At that time, neither he nor the man who became Northern Ireland's first secretary of state, William Whitelaw, held any firm views on the form of devolution that would eventually replace direct rule. Drawing little distinction between the troublesome Irish factions[9] – Protestant, Catholic or dissenter – Heath simply viewed temporary direct rule as the most realistic means of preventing the Northern Ireland crisis from derailing what was a particularly challenging period in domestic British politics. Although Heath's political intervention was premised on a desire to insulate Britain from the fallout of Northern Ireland's escalating conflict, he had come to view the transfer of responsibility for all security matters to Westminster, and a reformed system of government, as the most viable means of achieving this objective. The British Army, who initially regarded their job 'as very similar to what they had been doing in Cyprus, Aden or Malaysia',[10] would 'put a lid' on the conflict and 'hold the ring'[11] while Whitelaw, acting as a latter-day 'colonial governor',[12] speedily devised and imposed an alternative to one-party rule.

Whitelaw was the obvious choice for what was the most unenviable task in British politics in the early 1970s. A sharp-witted, genial character, he was quick to cast off the shackles of historic Anglo-Irish antagonisms. Although deferential to a prime minister who viewed politics in rather black and white terms, Whitelaw was something of a diplomatic antidote to his aloof political master and, equally, to the distaste with which British intervention created, at different points during his tenure, in both the unionist and nationalist communities. When quizzed by journalists on complex questions of Irish history during his first day in Belfast, Whitelaw replied, 'I always think that it is entirely wrong to prejudge the past.'[13] And given the mission that Heath had set him and the break with unionism that direct rule represented, this was a typically astute, if perhaps unintentional, observation.

Whitelaw's task was to irreversibly 'break the mould' of unionist politics in Northern Ireland, before bringing political moderates from both communities together under a new form of government.[14] Before his arrival, the Foreign Office was examining alternative forms of government that might facilitate compromise in Northern Ireland. One proposal that emerged was to adopt what Brian Faulkner described as constitutional borrowing from Lebanon's 'entrenched government', or power-sharing, as it is otherwise known.[15]

Under the direction of senior intelligence officer Howard Smith, the British government had already established a UK representative office in Northern Ireland, at a picturesque cottage in Cultra, which was aptly named Laneside. Starting from a 'very blank sheet', as one British intelligence officer put it, Laneside operated as an informal political and military intelligence headquarters.[16] Smith's replacement as Whitelaw's political adviser, MI6 officer Frank Steele, boasted that many of his staff had been chosen because of their experience in what was, at the time, pre-civil war Lebanon. Laneside became the 'eyes and ears' of the government,[17] and a useful 'second circuit' of contact for keeping in touch with people 'who weren't immediately relaxed in going to formal meetings at Stormont'.[18] As Heath paved the way for the introduction of direct rule, it served to isolate the Northern Ireland government, as sympathetic intelligence officers drew the SDLP's attention away from Stormont. So much so that Faulkner's staff compared its role to that of the 'Soviet embassy in Budapest' during the Cold War.[19]

* * * *

There was nothing inevitable about the failure of power-sharing in Northern Ireland in the mid-1970s. There is little evidence to suggest that, as a form of government which brought together elected unionist and nationalist representatives, power-sharing was unacceptable to the majority of the Northern Ireland people. More so, the idea of power-sharing was something that the majority of Northern Ireland's elected representatives were neither opposed to on ideological grounds nor on grounds of religious conviction, although some clearly were. Those who, at one time or another, stood in opposition to power-sharing did so, primarily, as a means of augmenting their ambition to attain high office.

Power-sharing in Northern Ireland did not fail simply due to bad timing or the lack of public support for the parties that bravely took office at the beginning of 1974. As a political system, it had begun to successfully regulate Northern Ireland's political divisions, not long after they led to the outbreak of violence in 1969. The executive's success, in this respect, led its permanent secretary Ken Bloomfield to conclude that 'no-one with inside experience would accept the argument that such a system is intrinsically unworkable'.[20] In fact, it was the executive's potential that prompted its unionist opponents to defy the British parliament by resorting to unconstitutional methods, and the IRA to redouble its violent efforts to undermine it. For had it been allowed to take root as a form of government that was acceptable to both communities, then unionist demands for a return to majority rule, and republican efforts to achieve a united Ireland by force of arms, would have been greatly reduced.

The power-sharing idea was finally quashed by Democratic Unionist Party (DUP) leader the Rev. Ian Paisley during negotiations with the SDLP at the Northern Ireland Constitutional Convention in early 1976. He believed, correctly, that the Labour government had neither the power nor the inclination to impose power-sharing between unionists and nationalists. Equally importantly, he believed that entering into a voluntary coalition with Catholics of any political colour would split his party and the Free Presbyterian Church that he led. Just as the Irish government feared that, rather than leading to a united Ireland, power-sharing might actually reinforce partition, Paisley feared that if all of the main Northern Ireland parties accepted power-sharing as a form of government, and it was seen to work over time, then it would be far harder to resist arguments against majority rule in the future.

Power-sharing failed for a number of reasons, all of which are related to the different perceptions that each party to the conflict held over the long-term implications of implementing this form of government in Northern Ireland. These differing views are central to understanding what the British and Irish governments were prepared to do to preserve a power-sharing executive. They also illustrate why a history and a culture of power-sharing are so important to a divided society such as Northern Ireland.

The British government had no ideological interest in taking full governmental control over Northern Ireland after the outbreak of the troubles. It did, however, have strategic and economic interests in Northern Ireland; therefore it had an interest in facing up to its statutory responsibilities there. A single-minded, forceful and brave politician, Heath was the first to recognise this and take firm action. In the face of considerable opposition from within the government, the decision to bring about direct rule was his. By 1972, Heath was convinced that allowing the Northern Ireland government to continue in the face of a sustained IRA insurgency would be more detrimental to UK interests, in the long term, than immediately bringing about direct rule. If the British government did not act, he argued, it might become more permanently involved in the administration of Northern Ireland and a solution to its troubles more difficult to come by.

The timing of the crisis was unfortunate for Heath. The government was struggling to implement a far-reaching monetarist anti-corporate manifesto, during an economic crisis, which was not, in the event, realised until after his successor Margaret Thatcher took office in 1979. These pressures forced him to seek a quick fix to Northern Ireland's troubles, putting time constraints on Whitelaw's mission to deliver a comprehensive settlement. Although he was unsentimental in both his break with unionism and his resolution to establish a new political order, he did set Northern Ireland high on the government's list of priorities.

Unlike Whitelaw, Heath held a rather technocratic view of the troubles, believing that modernisation, socio-economic development, inward investment and urban regeneration could transform the whole atmosphere in Northern Ireland. For Heath, there was little that good management could not solve, and this partly explains his dismissive attitude towards the complexities of Anglo-Irish history in his attempts to reform Northern Ireland. He assumed that the IRA's campaign would eventually 'run out of steam, and that life would go on very much as it had done for fifty years, since 1922'.[21] He overlooked the fact that both subtlety and patience would be required if his government was to successfully regulate Northern Ireland's deep-seated political, cultural and religious divisions.

Heath eventually came to view power-sharing as the most realistic policy to pursue if he were to end direct rule in the short term. He found the idea of creating all-Ireland bodies acceptable, hoping that this would guarantee the Irish government's support for the political initiative and its commitment to combating IRA terrorism on a cross-border basis. This was the value of the policy to Heath and Whitelaw: power-sharing was the most effective means of fulfilling British national interests in Northern Ireland – bringing the security crisis under control and ending direct rule.

Heath certainly viewed the troubles as a distraction from an agenda dominated by Europe and the various economic crises which threatened his premiership during the first years of direct rule. So much so that when Whitelaw brokered a power-sharing agreement in November 1973, Heath had the Anglo-Irish conference which took place at Sunningdale the following month 'written off as a triumph'. The purpose of this conference was to set Whitelaw's settlement in an Anglo-Irish context, prior to the ratification of agreements reached there and the establishment of a Council of Ireland. But Heath viewed it as 'a bit of a sideshow', and, having put the Northern Ireland problem 'back in its box', one that would allow him to concentrate on the government's main priorities.[22]

By the time he left office, Whitelaw had concluded that power-sharing was, in fact, the best and most realistic means of regulating Northern Ireland's political divisions, but this was not a motivating factor in Heath's decision to end one-party rule and break unionism's electoral dominance. The immediate objective of direct rule was to ensure that responsibility for security policy in Northern Ireland was determined by the Westminster parliament alone. The long-term objective was to ensure that Northern Ireland was never again governed by a party that drew its support almost entirely from one community. It was the damage that this system of government had caused to British interests, and to the British government's international reputation, that was the determining factor in Heath's decision to initiate direct rule. However, the short time frame within which Heath demanded a settlement, and his unwillingness to compensate for Faulkner's weakness by supporting him at Sunningdale, led him to accept an imbalanced settlement. In their haste to end direct rule, Heath and Whitelaw badly overestimated both the strength of Faulkner's moderate unionist support base and his ability to sell an uneven accord to a community that was experiencing the end of an era of political dominance in Northern Ireland.[23]

For the Irish government, the prorogation of the Stormont parliament presented an irresistible opportunity to press for Irish unity. Dublin had an ideological territorial interest in Northern Ireland, one which it was constitutionally obliged to pursue. The Republic of Ireland was not prepared for Irish unity, however, and neither the Fianna Fáil government nor the Fine Gael–Labour coalition that succeeded it, in

1973, wanted Irish unity in the short to medium term. British intervention in Northern Ireland, and the concept of power-sharing with an Irish dimension, presented Fianna Fáil leader Jack Lynch a role in the political affairs of Northern Ireland, something which the British government had not previously offered. Through proposals to establish a Council of Ireland, both he and his successor, Liam Cosgrave, pressed for the maximum degree of influence in Northern Ireland's affairs. They sought to establish a pan-Irish tier of government, which would enjoy enough executive power to harmonise the machinery of government between Belfast and Dublin. The question was whether these all-Ireland bodies, if established, would represent one small step towards unity by consent or one giant leap that locked an otherwise unwilling unionist community into a predetermined constitutional settlement which made Irish unity inevitable. Although there were dissenting voices in Cosgrave's coalition, most notably from Labour Party minister Conor Cruise O'Brien, the latter course was overzealously pursued by Irish minister for foreign affairs Garret FitzGerald and the SDLP's John Hume.

The power-sharing proposals represented the first tangible opportunity for nationalists to advance the goal of Irish unity since partition; the British government had broken with the Official Unionist Party and were willing to offer Dublin a significant role in the government of Northern Ireland. This was the primary value of power-sharing to the Irish government. It had no interest in the policy in and of itself, nor did it view power-sharing as the best or most realistic means of governing Northern Ireland in the long term, for this would have legitimised partition. The Irish government viewed it as a means to an end – incrementally bringing about Irish unity by establishing ambitious all-Ireland bodies through a power-sharing settlement between northern nationalists and Ulster unionists.

The Irish government also had strategic and economic interests in Northern Ireland, but it was completely dependent upon the British government to fulfil its statutory commitments to the province. Economically and militarily, it was totally unequipped to deal with the storm brewing in Northern Ireland over the British government's power-sharing proposals or the civil war that would ensue should the British attempt to relinquish their responsibilities and withdraw, which was exactly what Heath's successor had in mind. So there was a contradictory thread running through Irish policy during this period. Pursuing Irish unity through the opportunity that power-sharing presented in the north, in the letter and in the sprit of the Irish constitution, ran against the grain of the government's other national interests.

Bringing Northern Ireland's constitutional nationalists, the SDLP, into the political process was a key aspect of Whitelaw's mission to end unionist hegemony in Northern Ireland. The SDLP were divided over the opportunity that power-sharing with unionists presented the minority community in the north. Some of its leaders would have settled for a reformed Stormont parliament – the east of the River Bann social democrats such as party leader, Gerry Fitt, and Falls MP Paddy Devlin. They took a pragmatic view of the achievement that power-sharing with unionists represented to the Catholic minority. Others were determined to reject this form of compromise – the west of the Bann nationalist ideologues, such as Foyle MP John Hume and East Tyrone MP Austin Currie.

Hume viewed the immediate political interests of northern nationalists as secondary to the overriding imperative of uniting the Irish nation. He saw little or no value in power-sharing in Northern Ireland in and of itself, regardless of the great political advance it represented to his community. If power-sharing proved to be a device which reinforced partition, by locking the SDLP into a Northern Ireland government without the guarantee of powerful all-Ireland bodies, then Hume was prepared to make the ultimate sacrifice and abandon the idea; one was not acceptable without the other.[24]

Both the Official and Provisional wings of the IRA viewed power-sharing between constitutional nationalists and unionists as a threat. During this period, however, a number of IRA leaders grasped the fact that the British government had little interest in remaining in Northern Ireland and sought to further weaken its resolve to maintain the political union. Some of the more farsighted republicans wished to politicise their movement and the British appeared willing to assist them in this endeavour; but divided, militarily weakened, and lacking a solid basis to advance a political strategy following direct rule, they remained unelectable.

Unionists were also divided over the power-sharing proposals, unsurprisingly perhaps, since they were designed to fragment the unionist electoral bloc. Following the imposition of direct rule, a power struggle ensued between those who interpreted it as the end of unionist dominance in Northern Ireland and those who believed that they could force the British government into accepting a return to some form of majority rule. Through Whitelaw's power-sharing proposals, Heath hoped that a new unionist leadership would emerge; one that was strong enough to lead a Northern Ireland Executive, but too weak to dominate it. Faulkner was convinced that Heath had no intention of going back on this policy, so he accepted that power-sharing was the price that unionists would have to pay if they were to maintain Northern Ireland's constitutional link with Britain. Moreover, Whitelaw tempted him to accept this compromise by suggesting that integration with the UK, with an executive layer, would be 'the only solution in the end', and that some form of political pluralism was a step towards that end.[25]

The imposition of direct rule, the split it represented with the British government, the agreements reached at Sunningdale, and the role the British were offering the Irish government in Northern Ireland's political affairs were heavy political defeats for unionism. Without support from either Heath or Whitelaw at Sunningdale, Faulkner was unable to secure a balanced settlement with the Irish government: an agreement which he could sell to his own party, and one which reflected the unionist community's standing as the majority group in Northern Ireland. Nevertheless, the agreements reached at Sunningdale presented Faulkner with what was probably his last opportunity to lead a Northern Ireland administration. Moreover, they offered an opportunity to lock northern nationalists into a power-sharing settlement, with Dublin's consent, which would be largely reliant on his political survival for *its* survival. How that settlement would be implemented, who would receive the blame if it collapsed, and whether it would reinforce partition or pave the way for a united Ireland would be determined by what the British and Irish governments were prepared to do to sustain it.

Many of Faulkner's unionist opponents did not see things this way. They viewed power-sharing as a stepping stone on the road to a united Ireland and the all-Ireland bodies as the instrument by which unity would be achieved without their consent. Official Unionist John Taylor suspected that the underlying objective of direct rule was 'to slowly, by stages, extricate Northern Ireland out of the UK and tie it up more closely with the Republic of Ireland'.[26] All of Faulkner's political rivals viewed direct rule as an opportunity to displace him as the leader of the unionist community. Some sought to position themselves as a moderate force that Heath and Whitelaw could deal with. Many others, and particularly those who had served in the Stormont government, believed that they could regain 'something equally effective' to its parliament 'in stages'.[27] They were convinced that if the power-sharing model was seen to have completely failed, then having endeavoured to please everybody, the British would be forced to revert to a modified version of the old majority rule system. Faulkner's successor as leader of the Official Unionist Party, Harry West, viewed this as a distinct possibility, and James Molyneaux, who in turn succeeded West, argued that 'at a heavy price', unionism 'might get Stormont back'.[28] This was also the view held by an anti-Faulkner ginger group within the Official Unionist Party, Ulster Vanguard, led by William Craig and his supporters Rev. Martin Smyth, Captain Austin Ardill and Ernest Baird.[29] While taking a similar position to Faulkner's political rivals against the power-sharing executive, some Protestant paramilitary leaders hoped that its collapse would see the old unionist establishment figures finally swept aside, allowing them to play a greater role in politics.

* * * *

The imposition of direct rule and the UWC strike were the two most significant events to have occurred in the history of Northern Ireland by the mid-1970s. One ended half a century of government by the party that partitioned Ireland through its claim to self-determination on behalf of the Irish unionist community; the other destroyed a settlement that could have ended the Northern Ireland troubles not long after they had begun – satisfying nationalist demands for an equal role in government and greater Irish unity, while allowing unionists to maintain Northern Ireland's constitutional position within the UK with the consent of those nationalists.

Direct rule came about because Heath considered the Stormont parliament incapable of initiating the sort of political and security policies that might settle the crisis. But after removing Stormont's security powers, his successor failed to protect the executive against the strike, despite the fact that the government had been expecting something of

Introduction 13

this nature for some time. The strike began immediately after Faulkner favourably renegotiated the constitutional aspects of the Sunningdale Communiqué and forced the Irish government to accept a more balanced settlement. In the form it took, the strike was a consequence of the enhanced political instability that Heath's February 1974 general election defeat brought to Northern Ireland.

Heath and Whitelaw had invested too much political capital in Northern Ireland to have allowed the power-sharing settlement to collapse in the face of such unconstitutional unionist opposition. In contrast, Harold Wilson's inertia during the first week of the stoppage spoke volumes about his interpretation of what Britain's responsibilities were towards Northern Ireland and how he should go about meeting them. The available evidence suggests that the UWC would not have garnered enough support within the unionist community, and its elected representatives, to bring down the power-sharing executive if the British government had immediately set out to break the strike, regardless of who was in power at Westminster. To ponder over what might have happened had the government acted would be pure conjecture. But what is clear is that Wilson did not try to save the executive by breaking the strike in its first days. Perhaps the most damning conclusion that can be reached from this is that Wilson's inaction was by design, as he did not believe that power-sharing was the most realistic means of bringing about a united Ireland.

The collapse of the Northern Ireland Executive provided the setting for what Wilson and Northern Ireland secretary of state Merlyn Rees hoped would be the beginning of a period of direct rule in which the government could honourably, albeit uncomfortably, withdraw altogether from Northern Ireland. In their search for such an opening, Rees reversed Whitelaw's policy of building a middle ground coalition and excluding the more extreme and unconstitutional parties to the conflict. By fostering political uncertainty over Northern Ireland's future, isolating its political parties from the government, refusing to play a role in negotiations over the province's future, and politicising Northern Ireland's paramilitary factions, Rees was attempting to force reasonableness upon those who had united to destroy the executive. Through the Constitutional Convention, which opened in 1975, he hoped that the United Ulster Unionist Council (UUUC), which comprised the Official Unionist Party, Vanguard and the DUP, would either accept an emergency coalition with Catholics, as a means of alleviating the security crisis, or press for some form of dominion status or independence.

By abandoning Faulkner, the SDLP and the Alliance Party, Rees promoted the notion that it might be easier to reach agreement between Northern Ireland's extreme factions. Seeking to create the circumstances in which a purely Irish solution to the troubles might materialise, his security policies were designed to fundamentally alter the nature of political violence in Northern Ireland. Rees ended negotiations with the Irish government over the constitutional future of Northern Ireland, and perpetuated the ambiguity that existed over British policy towards Northern Ireland by consistently refusing to dispel the notion that the government was considering withdrawal. Negotiations took place between British officials and the Provisional IRA, the former fomenting the idea that working-class republicans and loyalists could replace the SDLP and the unionist establishment. And as the province edged towards civil war, violence against the state was replaced by sectarian killing.

Although it pushed Northern Ireland to the brink of civil war, the reversal of Whitelaw's polices were not entirely without success. The Provisional IRA ceasefire of 1975 split the republican movement and undermined its capacity to resuscitate its faltering insurgency against the state. Moreover, at one point, UUUC leaders Craig, Paisley and West accepted, in principle, the idea of forming an emergency voluntary coalition on the power-sharing model to alleviate the security crisis. But by abandoning the Constitution Act which had brought the power-sharing executive into existence, and by allowing the constitutional uncertainty over Northern Ireland's future to fester, the British government reinforced Paisley's view that it could be pressured into accepting a return to majority rule. Moreover, the political vacuum that these policies created ensured the ascendancy of a new IRA leadership, one which viewed the ceasefire as an almost fatal mistake. They believed that the British had lured them into a political cul-de-sac through negotiations, in which the pro-ceasefire IRA leaders had grossly overestimated the value to the republican cause of the government's determination to get out of Northern Ireland.

In turn, Wilson's quest to find a policy that would enable his government to withdraw from Northern Ireland led the Irish government to abandon its commitment to power-sharing with an Irish dimension, abandon the SDLP, and prepare for a civil war in the North in which it would have no choice but to intervene. This prompted the SDLP to adopt what was essentially the same position as the IRA – the British government should make a declaration of intent to withdraw from Northern Ireland. The more Dublin sought to distance itself from the crisis in the North, the more desperate the SDLP became for their support. So much so that its leaders actually sought military support from the Irish government to maintain its leadership position over the minority community in the event of civil war.

Thus by 1976, Whitelaw's power-sharing settlement, and the opportunity it represented to allow unionists and nationalists to peaceably coexist in government, appeared to be irretrievably lost.

NOTES

1. Interview with Sir Robin Chichester-Clark, London, 25 June 2008.
2. Interview with Lord Carrington, Knightsbridge, 21 November 2007.
3. Interview with Lord Armstrong, Westminster, 24 October 2007.
4. Interview with Sir Robert Andrew, London, 14 November 2007.
5. Interview with UK Representative Office official.
6. *Government of Ireland Act* (London: HMSO, 1920).
7. Foreign and Commonwealth Office files (FCO) 87/114, Problems with reunification between Northern Ireland and the Republic of Ireland, Blatherwick to Bone, 24 November 1971.
8. Ibid.
9. Interview with Lord Heath, London, 7 February 2001.
10. Institute of Contemporary British History (ICBH), *British Policy on Northern Ireland, 1975–82*, p.15.
11. Interview with NIO official, London, 30 January 2008.
12. Interview with UK Representative Office official.
13. *Guardian*, 2 July 1999.
14. W. Whitelaw, *The Whitelaw Memoirs* (London: Aurum Press, 1989), p.114.
15. B. Faulkner, *Memoirs of a Statesman* (London: Weidenfeld & Nicolson, 1978), p.182; Prime Minister's Office files (PREM) 15/486, Meetings between the prime minister and Mr Lynch, Doc. 14, 3 September 1971; Interview with Kelvin White, Didcot, 13 August 2007; Robert Ramsey, *Ringside Seats: An Insider's View of the Crisis in Northern Ireland* (Dublin: Irish Academic Press, 2009), pp.85–6.
16. Interview with UK Representative Office official.
17. Interview with NIO official London, 30 January 2008.
18. Interview with James Allan, London, 10 December 2007.
19. Interview with Robert Ramsey, Cultra, 6 March 2008.
20. Public Record Office of Northern Ireland (PRONI), Central Secretariat files (CENT) 1/3/24, Constitutional Convention Discussion Paper 1974, 19 July 1974.
21. Interview with Lord Armstrong, Westminster, 24 October 2007.
22. Interview with Lord Howell, Westminster, 17 October 2007.
23. Interview with Sir Oliver Napier, Holywood, 29 December 2000.
24. Interview with Dermot Nally, Dublin, 7 March 2008.

25. Interview with Lord Molyneaux, Westminster, 30 January 2001.
26. Interview with Lord Kilclooney, Westminster, 15 February 2001.
27. Interview with Lord Molyneaux, Westminster, 30 January 2001.
28. H. Patterson and E. Kaufmann, *Unionism and Orangeism in Northern Ireland since 1945: The Decline of the Loyal Family* (Manchester: Manchester University Press, 2007), p.180.
29. Interview with John McColgan, Dublin, 9 August 2007.

PART I
DIRECT RULE

During the first period of direct rule from Westminster, which ran from March 1972 to December 1973, the British government radically altered the allocation of political authority in Northern Ireland by establishing new institutions under which moderate unionist and nationalist parties would share power. This meant going back on the policies of accepting majority rule and denying the Irish government a role in Northern Ireland's affairs. Time was a constraining factor. The British quickly came to view power-sharing with an all-Ireland dimension as the most realistic means of meeting these short-term policy objectives. Whitelaw's mission – to break unionism's electoral dominance, reduce levels of paramilitary violence prior to political negotiations and forge a sustainable power-sharing executive – was to be achieved before the next Westminster general election.

1

Bringing it All Back Home

The last days of Stormont exposed a degree of political naivety on Faulkner's part in his dealings with the British government.[1] On departing from Downing Street, a month prior to the imposition of direct rule, and having ignored warnings that it was imminent from unionist MPs who were far closer to Heath than he was,[2] Faulkner asked the prime minister if he was sure that there was nothing else on his mind. Heath replied that there was not:[3] 'we are in this together,' he said, 'and we'll support you all the way, however long it takes.'[4] In the event, Heath presented Faulkner with a Hobson's choice: the Northern Ireland government could remain in office after all its security powers had been transferred to Westminster, or it could resign, and total responsibility for Northern Ireland would be transferred to Westminster. Unwilling to govern without authority, and not wishing to be forcibly removed from office, Faulkner tendered his government's resignation, taking the course he believed to be the least damaging to the union.

Taken aback by Heath's duplicity, Faulkner had sound reasons for doubting that direct rule was inevitable: Stormont provided a buffer between Westminster and Northern Ireland, and imposing direct rule ran the risk that Westminster would become permanently responsible for administering Northern Ireland's affairs.[5] Direct rule was the 'last thing' the British government wanted,[6] and Heath had considerable difficulty in convincing senior colleagues that a 'discontinuity' of government in Northern Ireland was urgently required.[7] His decision was influenced by the domestic and international pressure he came under to embark on a radical Northern Ireland initiative. Labour Party leader Harold Wilson had embarrassed the government with visits to both parts of Ireland, in November 1971. There he declared that he would neither oppose direct rule nor support calls for the army's withdrawal[8] – before informing parliament that a Labour government would consider 'a constitution of a united Ireland, to be reached by agreement and requiring ratification by all three Parliaments and with enforceable safeguards for minorities, to come into effect fifteen years from the date agreement is reached'.[9]

Senior government ministers such as Peter Carrington at Defence and Alec Douglas-Home at the Foreign Office were very slow in accepting Heath's arguments as to why the government must again take full responsibility for Anglo-Irish problems. Northern Ireland was 'tremendously remote' from British politics, and their view was shared by many Whitehall officials. Psychologically, the Whitehall machine displayed extreme reticence towards the idea that Britain should re-involve itself in Irish affairs. Officials complained, 'here we are again, flogging ourselves to death to replace a small incumbent county council' in a part of Ireland.[10]

Home secretary Reginald Maudling had responsibility for Northern Ireland. His apathetic approach to the crisis, in what he famously described as 'a bloody awful country',[11] epitomised Whitehall's reserve. He offered the starkest exposition of British instincts, during a speech to the House of Commons on 29 November 1971, in which he said: 'I welcome the greatest possible degree of co-operation between North and South in all practical ways, and if, by agreement, the North and the South should at some time decide to come together in a United Ireland, if, by agreement, this should be their wish, then not only would we not obstruct that solution but, I am sure, the whole British people would warmly welcome it.'[12] Yet it was the conditions for bringing Northern Ireland closer to Westminster that ripened over the following months.

Heath used the perception that internment had failed as a wedge issue with which to persuade his colleagues that direct rule was both necessary and inevitable. When the British Army killed thirteen nationalist protesters in Londonderry, on 30 January 1972, in what became known as Bloody Sunday, the incident provided him with a catalyst for this political intervention. Although the British government was widely criticised in the wake of Bloody Sunday, it granted Heath the international legitimacy and domestic support he needed to take a dramatic political initiative in Northern Ireland.

Introduced by the Northern Ireland government against the advice of some of Faulkner's colleagues,[13] and with great reluctance from Westminster,[14] internment had been a concession to the unionist leader. Since there was no alternative to Faulkner, Heath felt that granting internment would 'buy some time so that the issue of direct rule could be studied and agreed'.[15] Although Faulkner was badly damaged by the fact that internment had been aimed almost exclusively at the Catholic community, he used the British Army's security perspective to resist direct rule. Senior army officers wished to preserve internment, despite the fact that its mishandling had given the IRA a boost.[16] They argued that no pool of political activists existed within the prison community that were suitable for release, as all Catholics presently interned were members of the IRA.[17] On balance, however, the security benefits of internment – the reduction of the IRA's operational capacity in certain areas and the generation of much-needed intelligence – no longer outweighed the political damage it was causing both to Faulkner's standing and the British government's international reputation. Moreover, the perception that internment had failed united British, Irish and American voices in their demand that unionist rule must end.

In early February 1972, Heath, Maudling and Whitelaw agreed that the time was right to temporarily suspend the Northern Ireland parliament. Heath aimed to establish a form of 'community government', with places for both 'majority' and 'opposition' parties held 'as of right'.[18] The unionist government monopoly would be broken by fragmenting the Northern Ireland party system through the introduction of proportional representation, and by offering nationalists the opportunity to play a full role in the affairs of the state. The British had no sense, however, that they could simply superimpose some form of compulsory power-sharing system on the existing government machinery. It was understood that Whitelaw would have to create the conditions in which this could occur over the next year or two.[19]

So by the beginning of February 1972, Heath had a loose strategy for constructing some form of power-sharing administration in Northern Ireland under direct rule from Westminster. Given that unionists and nationalists would likely reject 'community government' proposals, he believed that a period of interim direct rule, of between twelve and eighteen months, would necessarily have to precede any such reforms.[20] A border poll would be held on the question of whether or not Northern Ireland should remain a part of the UK and internment would be steadily phased out. The idea of holding a referendum was viewed as a means of reassuring the unionist community that direct rule was not the first step on a road to a united Ireland. Ending internment would draw the SDLP into political negotiations and pave the way for significant cooperation with the Irish government on cross-border security issues.

More radical steps, such as repartition, perhaps coupled with population transfers to the Republic of Ireland, were considered in the context of the government's 'great emergency' plans for the complete breakdown of law and order in Northern Ireland. Contemplating a short, sharp civil war approach to solving Northern Ireland's troubles, the government concluded that in such circumstances it would have to be prepared to be 'completely ruthless in the use of force'.[21] Unsure of Heath's intentions, Faulkner warned him that should any significant change to Northern Ireland's constitution be proposed in the government's plans, he would be risking a 'backlash' from the unionist community, 'the like of which has never been seen or envisaged'.[22]

Heath, Carrington, Douglas-Home and Maudling presented a united front when they met Faulkner at Downing Street on 4 February. They informed him that major concern had been expressed in cabinet over how much longer British forces could remain exposed in Northern Ireland. Hinting at the government's intentions, Carrington said there was increasing impatience in Whitehall with the notion that a solution could just be expected to 'emerge'. Should the security picture worsen, Heath predicted that there would be great pressure for a 'change of course', a view reiterated to varying degrees by Carrington, Maudling and Douglas-Home – none of whom displayed any great sympathy with the unionist prime minister's dilemma. Faulkner told the Conservative Party leaders that if by a 'change of course' this meant the withdrawal of troops from Northern Ireland, then they could expect nothing less than a vast and immediate civil war.[23] Lynch might be playing a dangerous game in the Republic, he warned, allowing the security situation to deteriorate to the extent that the British were forced to intervene in a manner that was favourable to the Irish government's interests.[24]

The governing party in the Republic of Ireland, Fianna Fáil, was deeply split between those favouring, or at least prepared to tolerate, the use of violence in Northern Ireland and those opposed to violence, which included Lynch, who had come to accept the view that there could be no change to Northern Ireland's constitutional status without the consent of the majority of its population.[25] More than that, Lynch was extremely guarded against the 'sneaking regarders' of militant republicanism within

Fianna Fáil who were prepared to use the issue of IRA violence as a means by which to undermine his leadership.[26]

Although the burning of the British embassy in Dublin after the Bloody Sunday killings caused Anglo-Irish relations to deteriorate rapidly, Lynch signalled that a radical change in British policy towards Northern Ireland would be well received by his government. Calling for one-party rule in Northern Ireland to be replaced by some form of power-sharing, he began to privately urge the SDLP to participate in talks with the British.[27] Lynch's government was not secure, however, and having recently lost the support of three Fianna Fáil TDs, Faulkner suspected that he may have allowed the embassy to be burnt down in the hope that the protestors would 'get it out of their system'. He even suggested to Heath that the IRA might take over in Dublin.[28]

Seeking to reassure Faulkner, Heath said that his government would only contemplate direct rule in the event of a total breakdown of law and order in Northern Ireland. He asked the unionist leader why some of his colleagues viewed closer integration with Britain as a threat to their constitutional position. Faulkner reminded him that Stormont's very existence was viewed by the unionist population as a bar against any move that a British government might make to facilitate Irish unification.

The Labour Party, Heath told him, was committed to a policy of transferring law and order powers to Westminster. Faulkner retorted that since the 1920 Government of Ireland Act granted him responsibility for 'peace, order, and good government', the transfer of security powers would strip him of all political credibility, imply that his government could not be trusted, and amount to direct rule in all but name. The question the British government had to consider, Faulkner insisted, was whether or not it wished to maintain a credible government in Northern Ireland.[29] Faulkner insisted that while his government was committed to finding an 'active, permanent and guaranteed' role in government for the minority community, this would not extend to finding a place in cabinet for people who held republican sentiments. Moreover, the transfer of law and order powers, he said, would leave him with no basis for viable government.[30]

Following these discussions, Heath told his cabinet that direct rule could only be avoided if Faulkner implemented radical reforms. Given the present security crisis, and the growing opposition to his leadership of the Official Unionist Party, he did not expect Faulkner to pre-empt direct rule by announcing a satisfactory reform package. The government was divided over whether to announce the introduction of direct rule as a firm policy, or merely to put it forward as part of a set of policy proposals. Three options were open to Heath as to how he might handle Faulkner in this process: he could inform him of the nature of the power-sharing proposals in an effort to keep him onboard; he could force him from the political scene and offer the inducement of a seat in the House of Lords for his compliance; or he could attempt to isolate him completely by splitting the unionists as far as possible and reconstructing a unionist party around another figure, such as DUP leader Ian Paisley. Heath's main priority was to keep Faulkner in office during the transfer of power from Stormont to Westminster, so as to avoid a dangerous political vacuum in which Faulkner might rally unionists in opposition to the Westminster government. Therefore, Heath decided to prorogue rather than dissolve the unionist parliament in the hope that Faulkner would go quickly and go quietly.

In efforts to shift the focus from Stormont, Faulkner declared that his government was determined to 'hold fast' to Northern Ireland's constitutional position and oppose any suspension of its regional parliament, before mounting a scathing attack on Lynch's cross-border security record.[31] Calling for a referendum on the border, Faulkner suggested that if the Irish government recognised Stormont and accepted the principle of consent, then a common law enforcement area could be established, between North and South, with provisions for a joint Irish intergovernmental council to consult on matters of mutual interest.

Persistent rumours that direct rule was imminent increased pressure on Faulkner from within the unionist community. Former home affairs minister William Craig had formed a hardline Vanguard movement within the Official Unionist Party. Its stated objective was to take whatever action it considered necessary 'to preserve majority rule in Northern Ireland'.[32] At the end of February, Faulkner's ability to compromise was further reduced, when the Official IRA killed seven in a bomb attack on Aldershot military barracks and attempted to assassinate home affairs minister John Taylor. But Faulkner was not simply facing opposition from republican militants and the extreme fringes of his own party. Welcoming the prospect of direct rule, development minister Roy Bradford told British officials that a Protestant backlash against its intervention could be avoided if the initiative was handled correctly[33] – while Paisley and a number of other unionist MPs were striking a rather moderate tone at Westminster.

The nationalist community's alienation from the state, and growing international criticism of his government's approach, led Heath to conclude that a solution to the Northern Ireland crisis could not be found by military means alone.[34] After Bloody Sunday, the government was losing the propaganda war over Northern Ireland. The Irish foreign minister was stoking up anti-British sentiment in North America and Europe, causing nervousness within the Foreign Office over the UK's bid to join the European Economic Community (EEC).[35] As highly critical congressional hearings on Northern Ireland took place in the US, Maudling told the cabinet that the UK's 'whole position in the world' was now being seriously affected by the troubles.[36] The dangers posed to the government by continuing with its present policy, he said, were greater than the dangers posed by imposing direct rule and constructing an administration that reserved minority representation in government as of right.

On 25 February Heath set the wheels of direct rule in motion, inviting Faulkner to London, not to inform him of his plans but to test his likely reaction to them. The same day, Faulkner informed his government that Heath was 'playing fair'; no decisions had been taken and, having abandoned the idea of holding inter-party talks with the SDLP, the prime minister was prepared to act on the strength of the Northern Ireland government's proposals.[37] Uncertain as to what Heath would do next, Faulkner indicated that he could not hold talks with the government until it clarified its current policy on Northern Ireland.

On 1 March, in a detailed articulation of the political reforms that his government was prepared to concede, Faulkner linked the question of finding a political role for the minority community to the issue of finding all-Ireland consensus over the future of Northern Ireland. If Northern Ireland's constitutional framework and political institutions were accepted by the Irish government, and it agreed that Irish unity could only come about by consent, then it would be realistic to expect the minority community to cooperate within that framework. Faulkner believed that there needed to be an agreement with the Irish government on the constitutional position of Northern Ireland within the UK and on how that might be changed in the future. His preference was to hold a referendum on the issue, treating Northern Ireland as a single constituency.

Such agreement would enable both governments to find a common policy to defeat terrorism in Ireland, provide for some form of intergovernmental all-Ireland institution, and legislate for the extradition of terror suspects in both jurisdictions.

On the question of the minority community's participation in government, Faulkner argued that a guaranteed permanent place in cabinet for nationalists would be 'wrong in principle and unworkable in practice'. However, his government was prepared to increase parliament's size from fifty-two to eighty members, and a proportional increase in the senate, from twenty-six to about forty. It would consider increasing the number of committees, ensure that ministers consulted with the minister for community relations before making public appointments, and consider introducing a bill of rights.[38] Faulkner indicated that he and his colleagues were in agreement with the police and the army that it would be foolhardy to risk public safety, for the sake of political expediency, by phasing out internment while Northern Ireland faced an existential threat from both IRA factions.

The following day Heath advised his cabinet that the minimalist approach taken by the Northern Ireland government meant that the only remaining course was to initiate a period of temporary direct rule; negotiations would not be necessary.[39] The British government remained divided over the feasibility of Heath's proposals and over whether or not the minority community's representation in government should be guaranteed. Some ministers feared that direct rule might fail to win sufficient support in the nationalist community and add ideological credibility to the IRA in justifying its campaign of violence. Furthermore, it risked alienating the unionist community and losing the support of the Westminster unionist MPs, especially if Faulkner was to forcefully oppose the government. Heath was still undecided as to whether he should tell Faulkner of his intention to proceed immediately to direct rule or merely inform him that he intended to remove Stormont's law and order powers. Fudging the issue, he sent a telegram to Faulkner dismissing detailed media reports of the government's plans to constitutionally reform Northern Ireland[40] as 'pure speculation'.[41] And he urged Faulkner not to take a public position on issues of policy while both governments were still considering the way forward.

Although Faulkner remained unconvinced, there was further evidence that direct rule was imminent. Lynch had begun publicly urging the SDLP to participate in a Northern Ireland government, and Wilson claimed that if internment was ended then nationalists would be able to participate in all-party talks.[42] On 3 March Faulkner vented his frustrations during an Ulster Unionist Council (UUC) meeting, accusing Wilson of playing politics with Northern Ireland, after the Labour Party leader pledged on Irish television that he would revamp his programme for all-Ireland reform if he won the next general election. Compounding Faulkner's isolation, Wilson then suggested that although the Northern Ireland government could remain in office without security powers, this would amount to 'the *de facto* suspension of Stormont'.[43]

On 9 March, chasing the possibility of procuring a republican ceasefire, Wilson held a secret meeting with a group of Provisional IRA leaders at the home of Irish politician John O'Connell.[44] The delegation included Belfast IRA veteran Joe Cahill. He informed Wilson that the Provisionals were willing to end their campaign of violence, and become involved in politics, if the government was prepared to make a declaration of intent to withdraw all British troops from Ireland, abolish Stormont, and grant a complete amnesty for all political prisoners.[45] Having spoken with leaders from both IRA factions, and having sounded out DUP leaders Ian Paisley and Desmond Boal, O'Connell advised the British that if internment was ended, following a thirty-day republican ceasefire, then political talks could take place with IRA representatives.[46] Although the IRA declared a three-day truce, Wilson informed his contact that their conditions for a ceasefire were totally unrealistic, and Heath ignored the matter.[47]

Heath's plan was to create the impression that direct rule had come about as a consequence of Faulkner's refusal to accept the transfer of law and order powers to Westminster. Therefore, he decided to prorogue rather than dissolve the Stormont parliament, and to inform Faulkner of this decision rather than consult with him over it. He believed that postponing rather than abolishing Stormont would considerably reduce the likelihood of incurring a lengthy, bitter and divisive split with a unionist government that clung to office.[48] Ironically, the same day Faulkner met with the Loyalist Association of Workers leadership in efforts to prevent staff from walking out of Belfast's power stations the following week in protest over the government's anticipated political initiative.[49]

The British government remained divided, however, with Carrington and Douglas-Home firm in their conviction that power-sharing in

Northern Ireland would fail. They argued that direct rule would provoke a major IRA campaign in Britain and reduce the government's ability to implement its domestic and international policies – in particular its application to join the EEC.[50] Douglas-Home stressed to Heath that 'the real British interest would I think be served best by pushing them [unionists] towards a United Ireland rather than tying them closer to the United Kingdom'. Therefore, any prorogation of Stormont should have a short timeframe attached, after which, should no agreement be reached, the UK government would impose its own solution.[51] But the fate of Faulkner's government was already sealed. Heath had written to the Queen on 9 March informing her that the events of Bloody Sunday 'might have created a climate in which there was a prospect of making a political initiative which could be acceptable to majority opinion in Northern Ireland and at the same time to a great body of moderate Catholic opinion on both sides of the border'.[52]

As political pressure on Heath to take the initiative reached a point of critical mass, he invited Faulkner to come to Downing Street on Wednesday 22 March to discuss the way forward. Faulkner asked Heath to confirm whether he was being invited for consultations over Northern Ireland's future and whether any decisions would be taken that day. Heath replied that consultations were to precede any announcement on a political initiative, but whether or not there would be decisions for immediate announcement on that day would depend on where they got to in their discussions. Neither the prime minister nor his officials gave Faulkner any indication as to the topics that would be discussed at the meeting. As none of the ideas were 'firm enough' to be put on paper,[53] Heath told Faulkner flatly that they would simply be 'going over the ground'. Faulkner replied that without firm proposals for discussion, he would be able to offer nothing in advance of the reform proposals put forward by his government at the beginning of March.[54] Under increasing pressure from Wilson, Heath publicly defined the two principles which would lie at the heart of his political initiative. He said that the constitutional status of Northern Ireland could not be changed, 'except by consent', and that 'there can be no going back on this', but the minority community 'must be assured of a real and meaningful part in the taking of the decisions which shaped their future'.[55]

On 22 March, having the previous day informed the Stormont parliament that he would 'stand or fall' by his government's judgements,

Faulkner travelled to London, with deputy prime minister Senator Jack Andrews, and met with Heath three times. Before departing from Belfast, Faulkner advised his cabinet that Heath's intention was 'consultation' rather than 'decision', as it would be unrealistic for them to be expected to accept new ideas on the basis of one day's discussions. Bradford took the view that having reached firm conclusions regarding political reform in Northern Ireland, the government could not continue with respect and integrity under substantially different conditions. He pressured Faulkner to widen the Northern Ireland government's delegation beyond two, but the prime minister insisted that a large group of cabinet ministers might be construed as representative of government opinion; therefore it might be expected to take immediate decisions on its behalf. Faulkner thought Heath would propose reforms above and beyond those offered by the Northern Ireland government, thus his cabinet waited for him to return with proposals over which it could negotiate.[56]

As expected, Heath informed Faulkner that the British government viewed his reform proposals as a wholly inadequate basis for a new beginning in Northern Ireland. The British Army had come to the firm conclusion, Heath said, that there could be 'no purely military solution' to Northern Ireland's troubles. More than that, the government's military commitment in Northern Ireland had become such a drain on its resources that it was causing 'massive interference' with its international responsibilities. When measured against the security benefits it delivered, the damage internment was causing to the UK's important international relationships made it a luxury that could no longer be afforded.

Faulkner rejected these arguments, not on the grounds of perception but based on the security facts in Northern Ireland; he both accepted and shared the British Army's view that internment was vital in the fight against terrorism. Defending his government's performance, he argued that the security crisis might have been more severe at the beginning of 1972 had internment not been used. The IRA's operational capacity had been greatly diminished in Belfast, where the security services had removed 700–800 individuals from circulation, dislocating its leadership and communications structures. Faulkner argued that pressure must now be brought to bear on the Irish government to match these successes by arresting the 140 important IRA terrorists that were operating from within its territory.[57]

Heath told Faulkner that in order to bring about a swing in support away from the IRA in both parts of Ireland, what Northern Ireland required was a de-escalation of military force. Although his government would maintain firm pressure on the IRA 'hard men', unwinding internment would play a part in this process, as it would enable Catholics to identify with and participate in the state. Since continuing to pursue a purely military solution to the conflict would require an escalation of force that would make the casualties of 30 January 1972 appear minute, a 'fresh attempt to break through the deadlock' in Northern Ireland was politically imperative.[58]

Heath then made Faulkner an offer he could only refuse. For these changes to be brought about, he said, Westminster must take full responsibility for the provision of law and order in Northern Ireland, including internment. Faulkner's government could remain in office with the double guarantee of the Ireland Act 1949[59] and periodic referendums on the border, with a secretary of state for Northern Ireland facilitating political talks over how the minority community could be given an active, permanent and guaranteed role in government.[60]

Having returned to Stormont and met with his cabinet, Faulkner and Andrews then flew back to Downing Street, on the evening of 23 March, for further talks with Heath. Faulkner offered to compromise on the question of internment and suggested that the attorney generals of both governments could become jointly responsible for criminal prosecutions in Northern Ireland. These proposals were rejected by Heath, and when Faulkner asked whether the decision to transfer security powers was rooted in any conviction that his government had abused its power, he replied that it was not. Boxed in on all sides, Faulkner rejected the opportunity to remain in office, without authority, on the basis of 'vital principle'.[61] He said that the diminution of governmental responsibility implied a fundamental lack of confidence from Westminster in his ability to rule;[62] therefore, without security powers, the Stormont parliament would be 'a mere sham, or a face saving charade'.[63] Faulkner then handed Heath a letter of resignation signed by the Northern Ireland government and, much to Heath's relief, indicated that it would remain in office until parliament had approved the legislation that brought direct rule into effect.[64] The British cabinet then agreed to prorogue the Stormont parliament[65] and Heath telephoned Faulkner to confirm its decision.

On 24 March Heath announced that to enable Northern Ireland to make a 'completely fresh start', all Stormont's executive and legislative powers were being transferred to Westminster.[66] Having concluded that the freely elected parliament of Northern Ireland could not serve as a foundation for widespread political reforms, Heath had successfully forced the resignation of Faulkner's government and avoided the explicit imposition of total direct rule. Half a century of unionist rule had been brought to an end, not through negotiations between the two governments or a dramatic imposition of political power in Northern Ireland, but simply through a *fait accompli* in a day in British politics which Heath described as 'the worst of my life'.[67]

Applauding the British government's initiative as 'a step forward', Lynch returned the Irish ambassador to London, who had been withdrawn after the Bloody Sunday shootings.[68] The SDLP also welcomed direct rule, describing it as the 'first serious step on the road to peace', and promised their 'fullest cooperation' should the British government's 'military repression end'.[69] Accusing Heath of capitulating to IRA terrorism, Faulkner warned the prime minister that his decision to force his resignation 'may have the gravest consequences, the full extent of which cannot now be foreseen'.[70] Leading the protests against direct rule at Stormont, Craig announced that a two-day strike would begin on 27 March, and Faulkner's most senior civil servants[71] warned the government to prepare for the reduction of Northern Ireland's electricity supply.[72] Chastising Whitelaw on his arrival in Belfast, Faulkner said that Northern Ireland was no 'coconut colony', and warned unionists to guard themselves against whatever else crawled out from the 'upturned stone' of Heath's intervention.[73] Expecting widespread unrest, Heath increased troop numbers, set up an advisory commission to assist Whitelaw, and instructed him to ascertain the extent to which the Northern Ireland government was prepared for serious industrial unrest at its main power stations.

Much as Heath predicted, forcing the Northern Ireland government to resign rapidly deepened divisions within the Official Unionist Party. On its second day Craig's strike saw over 60 per cent of shops and factories close their doors. Caught off guard by Heath's initiative,[74] Faulkner's reactions to direct rule were largely framed by Craig's efforts to outflank him as the voice of unionist hostility towards the British government. Distancing himself from Craig's threat to form a provisional government, Paisley called for the total integration of Northern Ireland into the UK, while Bradford set out his stall as a potential leader of moderate unionism, signalling that he was not at all opposed to Whitelaw's arrival.

On 28 March, in what was a display of solidarity and reconciliation with his fiercest critic during the Stormont parliament's last ever sitting, Faulkner appeared alongside Craig at a Vanguard rally. The symbolism of the moment forced graciousness upon Craig, who said, 'whatever our differences, we will stand together to win back Ulster'. Making an address to the 100,000-strong crowd from Stormont's balcony, Faulkner told unionists that although they had been 'betrayed' by the 'undemocratic' actions of Heath's government, their power of veto lay in their numbers, and he used the opportunity to dismiss Craig's notion of an independent Ulster as 'utter nonsense'.[75]

* * * *

The façade of unionist unity and an upsurge in IRA violence made the first few months of direct rule an uncomfortable experience for Whitelaw. Focused on winning nationalist support for direct rule, the new secretary of state released seventy-three detainees, while Faulkner bitterly attacked his handling of the security crisis, charging the government with giving the IRA in Londonderry free rein to police its own 'no-go areas'.[76] This issue was a thorn in Whitelaw's side from the outset of direct rule. To assuage the nationalist community, he had instructed the security forces to keep a 'low profile' in Catholic areas, but this caused a drastic reduction in police and army intelligence on the IRA. Whitelaw felt that if he ordered a military incursion into the Bogside or Creggan areas in Londonderry, the no-go zones that Faulkner was referring to, then this could trigger a second 'Bloody Sunday' incident and guarantee the SDLP's absence from forthcoming political talks.

At the end of April, twenty-three explosions shook the province in one day, and nationalists accused Whitelaw of overseeing a government whitewash when a committee, headed by Lord Widgery, which had been investigating the events of Bloody Sunday, reported that no deaths would have occurred had those organising an illegal march in Londonderry not created a dangerous situation. Finding that gunmen had fired the first shots, Widgery merely questioned the wisdom of the British Army's arrest operation given the obvious risk to civilians.[77]

Heath then asked the Irish government to match the political risks he was taking in Northern Ireland by introducing tough security measures to destroy the IRA cells operating along the border. If the political initiative was to mark a positive turning point in Irish history, he said, then the 'IRA must be hit hard, and hit now'.[78] Lynch responded positively, forging closer cooperation between the Garda Síochána and British security forces operating in border areas. Cross-border security was a very sensitive issue between the two governments. Although Lynch's officials had been collecting evidence in Northern Ireland to support fifteen nationalists who were allegedly tortured by the RUC,[79] Heath hoped that the Irish government might drop its legal case against his government. The case, which was to be heard at the European Court of Human Rights in Strasbourg, held that UK security policies in Northern Ireland breached the European Convention on Human Rights. In return for his cooperation on cross-border security, Lynch sought an official channel of contact with Whitelaw to facilitate discussions on Northern Ireland policy, as a prelude to Irish involvement, as equals, in all-party talks. At this point the British were determined to deny Lynch any such role, although Whitelaw accepted his view that moderate unionists should be encouraged to be more open-minded about the idea of eventual Irish unity. He suggested that Lynch could aid this process by publicly raising the possibility of making changes to the Irish constitution, as a reduction of the Republic of Ireland's irredentist claim to Northern Ireland might diminish the unionist community's hostility towards the idea of Irish unity.[80] And in a speech linking his government's desire to see a united Ireland with its application to join the EEC, Lynch stated that the 'constitution of a new Ireland' must 'not be irksome to any of those who are to live under it'.[81]

Despite Craig's two-day strike, the much-feared Protestant backlash against direct rule failed to materialise, and Whitelaw was greatly relieved by the positive approach taken by the Northern Ireland civil service in facilitating a surprisingly smooth administrative transition to direct rule. Since partition Northern Ireland had been isolated from British politics, therefore administrative continuity was a great advantage to him in overseeing the transfer of Stormont's responsibilities to the newly established Northern Ireland Office (NIO). Prior to direct rule, political links between Belfast and London were virtually non-existent. Given the government's responsibilities there, senior NIO officials admitted that the 'depth of ignorance' in Westminster regarding Northern

Ireland affairs was 'pretty horrific'.[82] This was equally the case in the Irish Department of Foreign Affairs (DFA). With one man working on Northern Ireland 'in his spare time',[83] it had harder information on the Nigerian–Biafran war, from its mission in Lagos, than it did on the events unfolding in Belfast.[84] However, Anglo-Irish relations developed significantly during this period through both the 1965 Anglo-Irish Free Trade Agreement and the joint bid to enter the EEC.[85]

Whitelaw was having difficulty in winning over the SDLP, as they had made the ending of internment a precondition for entering into political talks over Northern Ireland's future. This presented a considerable difficulty, for the IRA was able to maintain a level of violence at which ending internment could not be justified in security terms alone. Having made 200 releases in his first six weeks in office, had Whitelaw maintained this release rate then internment would have ended at the beginning of August 1972. However, there was a hardcore of around 100 among the 600 or so remaining detainees who would present a very serious security threat should they be set free.

Although embroiled in a bitter feud, both IRA factions had regrouped, rearmed and re-established their military capacity to almost pre-internment levels. British estimates put the number of active Official IRA members at 800, compared with 750 prior to internment and 410 at the imposition of direct rule, and the Provisionals strength at 900, compared with 1,300 and 420 for the same period.[86] With widespread violence flaring across the capital and unionist leaders predicting civil war, Whitelaw's honeymoon period was brought to a bloody conclusion in mid-May. Paratroopers struggled to establish a 'peace line' between Protestants and Catholics in Belfast's Springmartin and Ballymurphy estates, while sectarian gun battles claimed lives as the army lost control of Andersonstown. The Provisional IRA fuelled sectarian tensions with attacks in Protestant areas;[87] the British Army prevented the establishment of loyalist 'no-go areas' in Belfast, and Whitelaw appealed for unionists to show restraint.

Whitelaw needed to find a point of balance in his security policies that enabled him to create an atmosphere in which political progress could occur. He sought to do this by reducing both internment and the army's presence in nationalist areas and, at the same time, by robustly suppressing the IRA's campaign of violence in an effort to avoid alienating the entire unionist community. Whitelaw planned to reduce the army's role, gradually replacing it on the streets with the RUC, and establish special interrogation centres at police stations in Castlereagh, Ballykelly and Armagh.[88] A programme of socio-economic reconstruction would complement these security policies and ease the impact of the government's proposals for constitutional reform. New local government structures would be put in place in April 1973, after proportional representation was introduced for local council elections that he planned to hold in October 1972.

The British government was divided over whether it should bite the bullet, end internment and remove the issue as an obstacle to all-party talks. Without a ceasefire, however, ending internment would make political progress more difficult to come by, as it would intensify levels of IRA violence, strengthen Craig's position, and provoke widespread reprisals from Protestant paramilitaries. Taking full advantage of Whitelaw's security problems, Faulkner set up an Official Unionist committee to examine the constitutional future of Northern Ireland, as a foil to Whitelaw's newly established advisory committee, and, in efforts to unite his party, invited Craig to be its first member.

Whitelaw received a boost when 63,000 Catholics in Belfast signed a petition condemning violence, the Official IRA announced a permanent ceasefire on 29 May, and the SDLP relaxed its attitude towards participating in political talks. Reacting to these positive developments, he released another 125 internees, mostly members of the Official IRA, but indicated that internment could not be brought to a complete end until violence was at a complete end.[89] Meanwhile, Lynch proposed the establishment of special courts to combat terrorism and his security forces arrested Provisional IRA leaders Joe Cahill and Ruairí Ó Brádaigh. Although unionist opinion was still enflamed by the fall of Stormont, Whitelaw had achieved a degree of success in reducing the IRA's standing in the Catholic community.[90] In June, he outlined his commitment to brokering 'a square deal' between Northern Ireland's two communities. He gave a 'categorical pledge' to unionists that the border would not be changed against their will, and offered nationalists the opportunity to play a full part in a new Northern Ireland, committing the government to balanced investment and equal job opportunities.[91]

Northern Ireland's largest Protestant paramilitary group, the Ulster Defence Association (UDA), responded to Whitelaw's overtures to the nationalist community by sealing off Belfast with seventy barricades and threatening to establish permanent Protestant 'no-go areas' unless the IRA's strongholds were broken. On 14 June, seeking to avoid a major confrontation between the army and the Protestant paramilitaries, Whitelaw met with the entire UDA leadership. When they complained bitterly about the concessions he had made to the nationalist community since taking office, Whitelaw promised to address the problem of republican 'no-go areas', but only at a time of his choosing. He assured the loyalists that the British Army's low-profile approach in nationalist areas was paying dividends, as the Provisional IRA were coming under increasing pressure from within the Catholic community to call a ceasefire.[92]

The groundwork for the political process that Whitelaw was trying to create was being conducted in secret, at Laneside, where Faulkner, who always arrived alone, was engaged in discussions with the SDLP and the Alliance Party.[93] British officials were also examining the possibility of securing a Provisional IRA ceasefire through secret discussions between its leadership and the SDLP. At first, Whitelaw publicly rejected approaches from the Provisional IRA to hold 'peace talks',[94] but Heath agreed with him that it was desirable to reach some form of understanding with them.[95] Having held talks with IRA leaders Seán Mac Stíofáin and Dáithí Ó Conaill, the SDLP's John Hume and Paddy Devlin convinced Whitelaw that the Provisionals were both willing and able to call an 'immediate and indefinite' truce.[96] In return, the Provisionals required Whitelaw to grant 'political status' to republican prisoners and meet personally with Ó Conaill and detainee Gerry Adams. Although he gave permission for Whitelaw to open discussions with the Provisional IRA, Heath insisted that he must avoid conceding political status to paramilitary prisoners. Whitelaw advised Hume and Devlin that if an agreement was reached which led to an IRA ceasefire, while republican prisoners could not be granted political status, they could expect to be accommodated in a separate compound from other offenders and perhaps be allowed to wear civilian clothing. Although Whitelaw's intervention ended a republican hunger strike in Belfast's Crumlin Road jail, it marked the beginning of a *de facto* 'special category' status for paramilitary prisoners,[97] something which he came to deeply regret.[98]

Optimistic about the prospect of ending republican violence prior to the beginning of all-party talks, Whitelaw sent British officials Frank Steele and Philip Woodfield to meet the IRA men at Ballyarnett, on the Donegal border, on 20 June. He kept Lynch informed of these developments and the taoiseach responded in kind, ensuring that Ó Conaill slipped 'through the dragnet' of an arms sweep that was taking place in Donegal. A hint of cordiality appeared to be creeping into Anglo-Irish relations, as Lynch remarked to the British ambassador in Dublin that 'we must hold by our principles and allow a little elasticity in applying them'.[99]

Ó Conaill and Adams advised the British that an indefinite ceasefire would be forthcoming if the army ceased all harassment of the IRA, 'political status' was granted to republican prisoners, and Whitelaw agreed to meet personally with its leadership. Ó Conaill accepted Whitelaw's compromise on prisoners and Woodfield gave an assurance that the army would not take advantage of the ceasefire by arresting prominent IRA men. The British left the meeting extremely impressed by the sincerity displayed by both IRA men, who they found to be 'reasonable and moderate'. Woodfield informed Whitelaw that there is 'no doubt whatever that these two at least genuinely want a ceasefire and a permanent end to violence'.[100] Steele described Adams as 'extremely bright', noting that 'he's the kind of guy we'd have with us if we could get hold of him'.[101]

Two days later, the Provisional IRA announced that if a 'reciprocal response' was forthcoming from the British Army, then a ceasefire would commence from midnight on 26 June. The IRA suggested that a bilateral suspension of hostilities could lead to 'meaningful talks between the major parties to the conflict' and that they would present their own peace proposals at an appropriate point in the future.[102] Accepting the IRA's gesture, Whitelaw immediately informed parliament that the British Army would 'obviously reciprocate' to any cessation of IRA hostilities, but denied having had any personal contact with its leadership.[103] The Provisional IRA was in the throes of a leadership struggle between the Ó Brádaigh and Ó Conaill factions, and splits over the ceasefire surfaced when prominent Belfast IRA leader Seamus Twomey stated that the campaign of violence would resume with renewed ferocity within a month or two.[104]

Seven members of the security forces were killed during the period between the ceasefire announcement and its implementation, after which calm returned to republican areas of Northern Ireland and some barricades were dismantled in the Bogside and the Creggan. In contrast, the UDA tested the government's resolve in Belfast by attempting to extend its barricades to incorporate areas of mixed population, which caused a confrontation between the army and thousands of uniformed militiamen.[105] The Protestant paramilitaries stepped back from the brink, however, and an agreement was reached whereby soldiers would set up roadblocks in the areas of mixed population and the UDA would patrol the streets behind them.[106]

Happy with the more robust approach taken by Irish security forces, Whitelaw pressed Lynch to match the 'extreme restraint' the British Army was observing in order to preserve the ceasefire.[107] Although terror suspects enjoyed an effective amnesty in Northern Ireland, the British government's arrest policy was ambiguous. The army had been instructed not to 'lift' known IRA leaders for interrogation or detention, but since existing warrants for arrest issued against wanted IRA men could not be revoked, suspects remained on the run and were subject to the law if they were both seen and recognised as falling into this category.[108]

Holding true to his word, Whitelaw held secret talks with the Provisional IRA leadership on 7 July, at minister of state Paul Channon's house in Chelsea. Whitelaw was very reluctant to meet with Seán Mac Stíofáin, who led and dominated a delegation that included Dáithí Ó Conaill, Seamus Twomey, Gerry Adams, Ivor Bell and Martin McGuinness. The cordiality and businesslike approach that Ó Conaill and Adams had taken in their pre-ceasefire meeting with government officials was not replicated on this occasion. Seemingly nonplussed by the Northern Ireland secretary of state's legendary charm, Mac Stíofáin began by reading Whitelaw a list of the IRA's demands. The crucial issue was for the British government to make a 'declaration of intent' to withdraw from Ireland, a disengagement from which all else would follow. Accepting that Whitelaw could not immediately make a public statement to this effect, Mac Stíofáin suggested that a secret commitment to withdraw would be acceptable to the IRA if it was deposited with a third party, such as the general secretary of the United Nations, by 10 July.

Mac Stíofáin's demand left no room for negotiation and Whitelaw told him that he could not possibly respond to this request before 17 July. To have made such a statement would have directly contradicted the British government's statutory commitment not to change Northern Ireland's constitutional status without the consent of its people. This aspect of Mac Stíofáin's negotiating strategy was counterproductive, as

Whitelaw's position on the withdrawal of British forces, and an amnesty for prisoners and wanted terrorists, was that these were issues the British government was prepared to negotiate over.[109]

The IRA leadership in Dublin no longer believed that their aims could be achieved purely by violence, but it had lost ground to the hardliners in the North. Depressed by the encounter, Whitelaw concluded that the IRA faction that had opposed the ceasefire had gained ascendancy over those who had been instrumental in procuring it.[110] While this assessment proved to be true, a significant opportunity was lost and Whitelaw laid the blame for the physical resumption of hostilities squarely with the UDA, which had been stoking sectarian tensions at flashpoints where he had instructed the army to hold the two communities apart.

On 9 July six civilian lives were lost during fierce gun battles between the army and the IRA as its ceasefire collapsed. Whitelaw considered resigning when the IRA leaked details of the secret talks,[111] and he gave a humbling account of his actions to the House of Commons.[112] Although extremely controversial, the meeting with the IRA was a calculated risk wholly in keeping with Whitelaw's tactic of being seen to be talking to everyone, and of going to great lengths to make political progress before excluding any of the parties to the conflict from the government's plans. Power-sharing in Northern Ireland was to have a very narrow base, but Whitelaw wanted to create the impression, both domestically and internationally, that those who would not share power were excluding themselves.

The collapse of the truce paved the way for a dramatic shift in British security policy. Troop levels were increased to 17,000 and general officer commanding (GOC) in Northern Ireland, Harry Tuzo, presented the government with plans for an assault against the IRA which would crush it as a fighting force. Whitelaw resisted pressure to implement these extreme security measures on the grounds that they would undermine his political strategy by completely alienating the Catholic community. Moreover, there remained a glimmer of hope that the IRA might reinstate its ceasefire.[113] The British received a message from Provisional IRA leaders in Dublin which indicated that the ceasefire could be reinstated if Heath was willing to make a declaration of intent, at some future point, along the Mac Stíofáin lines.[114] The following day, Wilson and Northern Ireland opposition spokesman Merlyn Rees met again with a group of Provisional IRA leaders,[115] but Mac Stíofáin's position had not softened and the Labour leader concluded that nothing could be gained from any further contact with the Provisionals at this point.[116]

The Protestant paramilitaries represented an armed confederation of about 25,000 men, allied to a 100,000-strong Protestant trade union movement, the Loyalist Association of Workers, which weighed heavily on the government's security considerations. The UDA and a smaller Protestant paramilitary group, the Ulster Volunteer Force (UVF), were waging a campaign of sectarian murder and intimidation against the Catholic community, casting themselves as defenders of a besieged Protestant population, and purposefully opposing the security forces as they sought to defend the Catholic population from attack. British intelligence suggested that not only were Protestant paramilitary leaders determined to remove republican no-go areas, they were preparing to defy parliament by pressing for the restoration of Stormont or, failing that, make a unilateral declaration of independence. With the UDA taking the law into their own hands on the streets of Northern Ireland, Whitelaw was concerned that the army might be drawn into a military confrontation in which it was 'fighting on two fronts against extremists of both factions' that were independently challenging the authority of the state.[117]

At its present strength, the British Army could not cope with a militant revolt in Northern Ireland from within both communities. The government believed that in the event of such a confrontation, elements within the RUC and the local auxiliary force, the Ulster Defence Regiment (UDR), who were sympathetic to the UDA's demands, would pose considerable difficulties.[118] This was part of a wider problem facing the British. RUC reform was long overdue in 1972, but it would take years to reconstruct the force to the point were it could act as the civil authority applying the civil power in Northern Ireland. Devastated following the outbreak of the troubles, senior NIO officials viewed it as a shattered police force that was 'not merely dismembered', but in a state of 'total collapse'.[119]

Following the fiasco with Mac Stíofáin, Whitelaw came under pressure from Conservative backbenchers and unionists to resign,[120] while senior army officers were urging him to immediately end his 'softly softly' approach towards the IRA.[121] Whitelaw needed to reduce the level of violence for talks between unionists and the SDLP to succeed, and although he was against sanctioning a full-scale assault on the IRA, he was equally reluctant to face the 'embarrassment of being forced back onto the Faulkner government's policy of search, arrest, interrogation and internment'.[122] Without internment, however, it was practically impossible to convict the IRA leaders who were directing the violence, as they organised attacks but generally refrained from participation. Furthermore, given the army's low profile in nationalist areas, the police had precious little evidence with which to pin a conviction on IRA ringleaders, and anyone willing to testify against them risked assassination. From a security perspective internment remained the only way of getting them off the streets; therefore Whitelaw hoped to introduce 'preventative detention' through the use of special tribunals that could convict terrorist suspects of proscribed offences, such as membership of a paramilitary organisation.

On 21 July, which became known as Bloody Friday, a terrorist outrage provided Whitelaw with an opportunity to initiate a military surge at a moment when there was widespread frustration within the army and almost universal revulsion towards the IRA. The Provisional IRA exploded twenty-six bombs in Belfast in the space of an hour and a quarter, killing nine civilians and injuring 130. Horrific television scenes showed police officers shovelling body parts into translucent plastic bags from the rubble that had once been Belfast's Oxford Street bus station. The IRA blitz on the capital prompted the government to reinforce troop levels by 4,000 and implement the British Army's plan to clear the 'no-go areas' in the Bogside and Creggan, along with UDA strongholds.[123] Whitelaw sought to limit the incursions to Londonderry,[124] but arguments put forward by the army, and the enormous political pressure he was under to seize the military initiative, forced him to take a political risk on which both his leadership and the success of the Northern Ireland political process would hinge.[125]

On the morning of 31 July, launching the largest armoured manoeuvre of British forces since Suez, codenamed 'Operation Motorman', Whitelaw set out to 'destroy the capacity of the Provisional IRA to terrorise the community', and provide 'a new basis for the administration of Northern Ireland in which the minority will have a true part to play'.[126] The military assault saw the mobilisation of 21,000 British and 15,000 local forces, with company commanders authorised to use 'heavy weapons (such as Carl Gustav [rifles])' against positions in which there was sustained hostile firing.[127] The UDA accepted the army's assistance in dismantling its barricades, while Steele ensured that the IRA offered no resistance.[128] In the event, only two civilian lives were lost before the army triumphantly declared that 'the Bogside and Creggan are breached'.[129] And when Whitelaw was woken at around 5am that morning and informed that 'all had gone well' in the Londonderry surge, the secretary of state's 'sigh of relief could be heard rumbling around Hillsborough Castle'.[130]

NOTES

1. Interview with Sir Ken Bloomfield, Craigavad, 19 December 2007; Interview with Sir Robin Chichester-Clark, London, 25 June 2008.
2. Interview with Stratton Mills, Belfast, 21 December 2007; Interview with Robin Chichester-Clark, London, 25 June 2008.
3. *The Times*, 2 March 1973.
4. Ramsey, *Ringside Seats*, p.101.
5. Ibid., pp.99–101.
6. Interview with senior NIO official.
7. Interview with Sir Ken Bloomfield, Craigavad, 19 December 2007.
8. PREM15/1022, Visit to Northern Ireland by the Leader of the Opposition, 15–18 November 1971.
9. Hansard, vol. 826, cols 1571–93, 25 November 1971.
10. Interview with Keith McDowall, London, 8 January 2008.
11. *BBC News Online*, 6 January 2006.
12. Hansard, vol. 827, cols 32–40, 29 November 1971.
13. Interview with Sir Robin Chichester-Clark, London, 25 June 2008.
14. Interview with Lord Armstrong, Westminster, 24 October 2007; Interview with Sir Robert Andrew, London, 14 November 2007.
15. Interview with Lord Armstrong, Westminster, 24 October 2007.
16. Interview with UK Representative Office official.
17. PREM15/1002, Smith to Woodfield, 17 February 1972.
18. PREM15/1002, Burke Trend to Edward Heath, 14 February 1972.
19. Interview with senior NIO official.
20. CAB130/560, Cabinet meeting, 10 Downing Street, 16 February 1972.
21. CAB130/561, Contingency Planning, Gen 79 (72) 28, 6 December 1972.
22. *The Times*, 5 January 1972.
23. PRONI, CAB/9R/238/7, Meeting between Heath and Faulkner, Downing Street, 4 February 1972.
24. PRONI, CAB/9R/238/7, Meeting between Heath and Faulkner, Downing Street, 4 February 1972.
25. Interview with Seán Donlon, Limerick, 25 September 2007.
26. Interview with Muiris Mac Conghail, Dublin, 24 July 2007.
27. Department of the Taoiseach files (DT) 2003/16/472, Lynch's Fianna Fáil Ard Fheis Speech, 19 February 1972.
28. PRONI, CAB/9R/238/7, Meeting between Heath and Faulkner, Downing Street, 4 February 1972.
29. Ibid.
30. PREM15/1002, Faulkner to Heath, 16 February 1972.
31. PREM15/1003, Speech by Brian Faulkner to the Mid-Antrim Unionist Association, 29 February 1972.
32. *The Times*, 13 February 1972.
33. PREM15/1003, Smith to Woodfield, 28 February 1972.

Bringing it All Back Home 43

34. CAB130/560, Cabinet meeting, 10 Downing Street, 9 February 1972.
35. PRONI, CAB/9R/238/7, Meeting between Heath and Faulkner, Downing Street, 4 February 1972; Ramsey, *Ringside Seats*, pp.103–5.
36. CAB130/561, Memo by Home Secretary, 29 February 1972.
37. PRONI, CAB/9R/238/7, Meeting of the Northern Ireland Cabinet, Stormont, 25 February 1972.
38. PREM15/1003, Faulkner to Heath, 1 March 1972.
39. CAB130/560, Cabinet meeting, 10 Downing Street, 2 March 1972.
40. *Daily Mail*, 1 March 1972.
41. PREM15/1003, Heath to Faulkner, 2 March 1972.
42. *The Times*, 4 March 1972.
43. PREM15/1022, Peck to Steele, 14 March 1972.
44. PREM15/1022, Peck to White, 16 March 1972.
45. PREM15/1004, IRA Peace Proposals, 9 March 1972; Armstrong to Angel, 10 March 1972.
46. PREM15/1004, Note of a meeting with Dr O'Connell, G.L. Angel, 27 January 1972.
47. *Telegraph*, 11 March 1972.
48. CAB130/560, Cabinet meeting, 10 Downing Street, 8 March 1972.
49. PRONI, CAB/4/1643/12, Meeting of the Northern Ireland Government, 7 March 1972.
50. CAB130/560, Cabinet meeting, 10 Downing Street, 10 March 1972.
51. PREM15/1004, Douglas-Home to Heath, 13 March 1972.
52. PREM15/1004, Edward Heath to Queen Elizabeth II, 9 March 1972.
53. PRONI, CAB/4/1646/16, Meeting of the Northern Ireland Government, 21 March 1972.
54. PREM15/1004, Telephone Conversation between Faulkner and Heath, 15 March 1972.
55. *Financial Times*, 17 March 1972.
56. PRONI, CAB/4/1646/16, Meeting of the Northern Ireland Government, 21 March 1972.
57. PRONI, CAB/4/1646/13, Memo by Faulkner on internment, 18 February 1972.
58. PRONI, CAB/4/1647/14, Points made by Heath at Downing Street Meeting, 22 March 1972.
59. *Ireland Act 1949* (London: HMSO, 1949).
60. PRONI, CAB/4/1647/13, Later statement made by Heath at Downing Street Meeting, 22 March 1972.
61. *The Times*, 25 March 1972.
62. PREM15/1005, Faulkner to Heath, 23 March 1972.
63. PRONI, CAB/4/1649/13, Statement by Brian Faulkner, 24 March 1972.
64. PRONI, CAB/4/1648/13, Meeting of the Northern Ireland Cabinet, Stormont, 24 March 1972.
65. CAB130/560, Cabinet meeting, 10 Downing Street, 23 March 1972.
66. *Belfast Telegraph*, 25 March 1972.
67. Interview with Sir Robin Chichester-Clark, London, 25 June 2008.
68. *The Times*, 25 March 1972.
69. SDLP statement, 25 March 1972; PREM15/1006, Political Summary, 24–28 March 1972.
70. PRONI, CAB/4/1649/13, Statement by Brian Faulkner, 24 March 1972.
71. PREM15/1005, Burke Trend to Heath, 24 March 1972.
72. CAB130/560, Cabinet meeting, 10 Downing Street, 24 March 1972.
73. *The Times*, 28 March 1972.
74. Interview with Sir Robin Chichester-Clark, London, 25 June 2008.
75. *The Times*, 29 March 1972.
76. PREM15/1007, Faulkner to Heath, 17 March 1972.
77. *The Times*, 20 April 1972.
78. PREM15/1007, Heath to Lynch, 24 April 1972.
79. PREM15/1007, Alexander to Gregson, 4 May 1972.
80. PREM15/1007, Meeting between Whitelaw and Hillery, London, 27 April 1972.
81. PREM15/1007, Speech by Lynch at Ballybofey, 30 April 1972.
82. ICBH, *British Policy on Northern Ireland, 1970–4*, p.26.
83. Interview with Dermot Nally, Dublin, 7 March 2008.
84. Interview with Seán Donlon, Limerick, 25 September 2007.
85. Interview with Lord Armstrong, Westminster, 24 October 2007.
86. CAB130/560, Cabinet meeting, 10 Downing Street, 25 May 1972.

87. Hansard, vol. 837, cols 698–700, 18 May 1972.
88. CAB130/560, Cabinet meeting, 10 Downing Street, 10 August 1972.
89. *The Times*, 8 June 1972.
90. Hansard, vol. 838, cols 1739–40, 15 June 1972.
91. *The Times*, 17 June 1972.
92. PREM15/1009, Meeting between Whitelaw and the UDA, Stormont, 14 June 1972.
93. Interview with UK Representative Office official.
94. *The Times*, 14 June 1972.
95. CAB130/560, Cabinet meeting, 10 Downing Street, 16 June 1972.
96. CJ4/136, Meeting between Whitelaw, Hume and Devlin, 18 June 1972.
97. PREM15/1009, Meetings between Whitelaw, Devlin and Hume, Laneside, 18 & 19 June 1972.
98. Whitelaw, *The Whitelaw Memoirs*.
99. FCO87/74, Attitude of SDLP towards meetings between Whitelaw and Provisional IRA, Dublin to UKREP [United Kingdom Representative] Belfast, 19 June 1972.
100. PREM15/1009, Note of a meeting with representatives of the Provisional IRA, Philip Woodfield, 21 June 1972.
101. Interview with UK Representative Office official.
102. *The Times*, 23 June 1972.
103. Hansard, vol. 839, cols 722–9, 22 June 1972.
104. *Irish Press*, 23 June 1972.
105. *The Times*, 4 July 1972.
106. PRONI, CAB/9G/27/6/3, Conclusion of Morning Meeting, Stormont, 4 July 1972.
107. CAB130/560, Cabinet meeting, 10 Downing Street, 22 June 1972.
108. Northern Ireland Office files, CJ4/458, White to Trevelyan, 21 June 1972; Security forces' reactions to a ceasefire, 27 June 1972.
109. PREM15/1010, Note of a meeting between Whitelaw and the Provisional IRA, 7 July 1972.
110. CAB130/560, Cabinet meeting, 10 Downing Street, 10 July 1972.
111. Interview with Keith McDowall, London, 8 January 2008.
112. Hansard, vol. 840, cols 1179–90, 10 July 1972.
113. *The Times*, 11 July 1972.
114. CJ4/134, Meeting between Channon and O'Connell, London, 17 July 1972.
115. *The Times*, 19 July 1972.
116. PREM15/1010, Nield to Trend, Peck to White, 19 July 1972; Note for the Record, Discussion between Heath, Whitelaw, Carrington and General Sir Michael Carver, 20 July 1972.
117. CAB130/560, Cabinet meeting, 10 Downing Street, 10 July 1972.
118. PREM15/1010, Nield to Trend, 10 July 1972.
119. ICBH, *British Policy in Northern Ireland, 1970–4*, p.27.
120. *The Times*, 19 July 1972.
121. PREM15/1010, Note for the Record, Discussion between Heath, Whitelaw, Carrington and Carver, 20 July 1972.
122. PREM15/1011, Nield to Trend, 27 July 1972.
123. CAB130/560, Cabinet meeting, 10 Downing Street, 21 July 1972.
124. PREM15/1011, Trend to Heath, 26 July 1972.
125. CAB130/560, Cabinet meeting, 10 Downing Street, 21 July 1972.
126. Hansard, vol. 841, cols 1326–31, 24 July 1972.
127. PREM15/1011, Draft message from GOC to Brigade Commanders, 27 July 1972.
128. Confidential source.
129. *The Times*, 1 August 1972.
130. Interview with Keith McDowall, London, 8 January 2008.

2

Breaking the Mould

The decision to initiate Operation Motorman in favour of the far more drastic contingency plan, Operation Folklore, marked a turning point in Whitelaw's search for a political solution to Northern Ireland's troubles. The IRA detonated three car bombs in the town of Claudy, killing nine civilians, on the day the military surge took place, but its attacks became sporadic and less coordinated over the following months. The establishment of British Army bases in republican 'no-go areas' hastened Whitelaw's political recovery from the Mac Stíofáin incident. More importantly, the breach created momentum for the implementation of an evenly balanced political-security policy, one which might allow him to deliver a settlement within a fairly short space of time. Although the republican movement was discredited, divided and subdued, Whitelaw knew that he would also have to confront the Protestant paramilitaries if his efforts to broker a settlement were to succeed.

In the Republic of Ireland, Lynch responded to Operation Motorman, calling for immediate political progress from which the 'door to Irish unity, by agreement, must be unlocked'.[1] He suggested a surprising 'horse trade' with the British, offering to drop his government's case at Strasbourg in return for the release of the remaining internees.[2] Lynch believed that the unionist community's refusal to consider Irish unification was set in stone by the British government's guarantee to maintain Northern Ireland's present constitutional status. He felt that the persistent threat of a Protestant backlash had stiffened debate in Whitehall over Northern Ireland policy. Hume, whose views on Northern Ireland held considerable sway in Dublin, argued that these problems would be reduced considerably if the British government openly declared that it had 'no national interest which opposes the reunification of Ireland'.[3] This was not a view shared by Heath, who told Lynch that 'the door is certainly not locked and we do not want to lock it: but it must be for the people of Northern Ireland to decide whether and when they want to come through it'.[4] Should the time come when the people of Northern Ireland wish to enter into a united Ireland, Heath stressed that the British government 'would not stand in their way', but warned that it would be counterproductive to frame a solution in Hume's simplistic nationalist terms. Once the people of Northern Ireland, as a whole, had decided upon a form of government by which they could peaceably coexist within the EEC, Heath believed that the importance of the border would diminish organically.[5] As leader of Fianna Fáil, Lynch naturally wanted to control the nationalist position in the forthcoming talks over Northern Ireland's future. His relations with the SDLP were not warm and, endeavouring to keep them apart, the British believed that granting Lynch access to all-party talks at this stage would make a settlement more difficult to come by in the short term and a united Ireland less likely to occur in the long term.[6]

Conscious that all-party talks might not lead to agreement, Heath tasked Whitelaw with formulating proposals to 'impose some form of constitutional settlement', so as to ensure that direct rule could be ended abruptly. With this in place, he wanted the government to be in a position to legislate before the existing temporary statutory arrangements expired on 24 March 1973.[7] Radical plans, such as redrawing the Northern Ireland border and population transfers to the Republic, were discussed in Downing Street in the context of a loss of British control. To some, these plans were 'in harmony' with the nature of Operation Motorman, but they were certainly not in harmony with Whitelaw's plan to reconcile both communities to a power-sharing settlement.[8] As an alternative means of relieving Westminster of the burden of Northern Ireland's legislative process, Whitelaw hoped to deliver the 'greatest possible degree of devolution consistent with the responsibilities of HMG'.[9] The idea of reserving places for the minority community in government as a prerequisite for a settlement was not set in stone.[10] A regional assembly modelled on the Greater London Council was considered, which would be elected by proportional representation and have committee chairmanships reserved for opposition parties.

On 7 August, when Whitelaw met the SDLP leaders at Laneside for talks about talks, the nationalists stuck firmly to the position that they could not attend an all-party conference until internment had been discontinued. If the SDLP were unable to achieve this, then, in the eyes of the nationalist community they 'would have achieved nothing'. Fitt argued that by sanctioning Operation Motorman Whitelaw had created a 'state of euphoria' within the unionist community, while the UDA threatened to enforce a twenty-four-hour stoppage at one of Belfast's power-stations. He urged the secretary of state to strike while the iron was still hot and have the guts to link Operation Motorman's success to the termination of internment.[11] Accusing Whitelaw of bowing to loyalist pressure, the SDLP described the reintroduction of tough security policies as a knee-jerk reaction to the antagonism that his *détente* with the nationalist community had provoked within the unionist community. They argued that Operation Motorman, the pledge to hold a plebiscite, and the exclusion of the Irish government from the planned talks were all major concessions to the unionist community, while the SDLP's constituents lay interned and Protestant paramilitary gangs were literally getting away with murder.

By the time their discussions resumed the following day Whitelaw had signed release papers for forty-seven internees, adding to the 700 releases he had made from a total of 1,000. The SDLP leaders dismissed this as a 'totally insufficient' political gesture, and although these meetings were unproductive, they confirmed Whitelaw's view that the chances of bringing the Northern Ireland parties to agreement in the short term were remote. Remaining in opposition mode, the nationalist party's attitude towards political reform in Northern Ireland seemed to be, 'we want to go into government, but at no cost to ourselves'.[12] Although Whitelaw was keen to build up the SDLP as a political force, he was aware that bringing such a fragmented and inexperienced group of tempestuous individuals into serious negotiations was not going to be easy.[13]

As a reward for maintaining their ceasefire and having largely abandoned violence, Whitelaw released the last eighteen Official IRA internees, before inviting the Northern Ireland parties to participate in roundtable discussions. Whitelaw was desperate to find a credible alternative to internment: a security policy which was acceptable to moderate nationalism, but which also satisfied the British Army's desire to continue detaining the Provisional IRA's leaders, if not by internment then by some other means. At the same time, he hoped to make it politically viable for the SDLP to participate in a constitutional conference by ending internment in September, just as new legislation brought special tribunals into effect. Whitelaw rejected the SDLP's suggestion that he should set a date by which internment would end, as the IRA would only increase levels of violence to make it impossible for him to meet his own deadline. In propaganda terms, the ending of internment would be a setback for the Provisionals and a political triumph for the SDLP. However, if Whitelaw released the remaining internees in the absence of a Provisional IRA ceasefire, then this would certainly heighten the level of violence. He was not aided in these security dilemmas by US senator Edward Kennedy who, on 9 August – the first anniversary of the introduction of internment – declared that 'British justice is a farce in Northern Ireland today' as 'no nation that calls itself a democracy can justify' the 'cruel and repressive policy of internment'.[14]

Heath was considering setting up the 'formal machinery' necessary for 'special consultation' between the British and Irish governments on as many Northern Ireland interests as possible.[15] He met Lynch on the fringes of the Olympic Games in Munich for what was their first discussion since the imposition of direct rule. But the two premiers clashed publicly after a sour and testy encounter, with Heath rebuffing Lynch's suggestion that the Irish government could be directly involved in talks over Northern Ireland's constitutional future.

Before the first official round of talks commenced at Darlington, between the Alliance Party, the Northern Ireland Labour Party (NILP) and the Official Unionists, Faulkner warned that it would be 'a fatal mistake' to 'use internment as a political bargaining counter' to draw in the SDLP.[16] At Chequers, on 12 September, Heath and Whitelaw did make last-ditch efforts to persuade the northern nationalists to participate in the conference. At what was their first meeting with a British prime minister, the SDLP promised Heath that ending internment would allow them to participate and deliver 'a knock out blow' to the Provisional IRA.[17] Given the security threat the remaining internees presented and the negative reactions that wholesale releases would provoke from both the security forces and the unionist community, Whitelaw told the SDLP that he could not end internment in the absence of something to replace it with. Moreover, the SDLP were correct in their suspicion that Whitelaw's 'something' would essentially be another form of detention; and although they were divided on the issue, the nationalists rejected the invitation to enter talks at this point.

The SDLP published a policy document, entitled *Towards a New*

Ireland, which called for the British to declare that Irish unity was in the 'best interests' of all parties concerned, before establishing a form of joint sovereignty with the Republic of Ireland over Northern Ireland as an interim step towards that end.[18] The document set out Lynch's bottom line in the political process: the SDLP could not accept a purely 'internal solution'; therefore some form of all-Ireland institutions were 'absolutely necessary' for it to participate at government level. The SDLP remained split, however, between nationalists from the western counties of Northern Ireland who hoped that the border would one day shift slightly upwards to include them in a southern state, and the Belfast-centric socialists who had long since recognised 'that they were not going to be part of any all-Ireland state', as Austin Currie put it, and 'had come to terms with it'.[19]

Whitelaw planned to dismantle the Special Powers Act,[20] strengthen the government's intelligence operations in Northern Ireland and reinforce the RUC. With respect to internment, the decision to detain someone could be removed from the executive authority, ordinary courts convicting people on suspicion of membership of illegal organisations. Terrorists would also be tried through temporary special tribunals where the normal process of criminal law proved insufficient. These policies were designed to end internment without releasing the 100 Provisional IRA detainees that posed the greatest security threat, by processing them directly through special tribunals. Whitelaw had accepted that the short-term side effect of this policy would be the SDLP's absence from the first round of political discussions. But he viewed this as a price worth paying to prevent a significant escalation of IRA violence during a crucial phase in the political process. Since Operation Motorman, 127 people had been charged with terrorist-related offences and, while this new security policy amounted to internment in all but name, he was determined to keep as many Provisional IRA members incarcerated as was possible, without departing too far from the normal processes of law. Whitelaw actually favoured introducing a special court system with Nuremburg-style trials – the Nazi SS had been convicted as an organisation as constituting a conspiracy to murder – but he was forced to accept a less powerful tribunal system, under which individual members of illegal organisations could be tried with planning murder.[21]

* * * *

The Darlington talks, which ran from 25–27 September, made public the secret political process that had been taking place at Laneside. Politically, they also marked the end of the first phase of direct rule, during which Whitelaw had tried to 'redress the balance between the two communities'.[22] In what would be the penultimate and final phases of total direct rule, Whitelaw planned to bring the parties closer together through consultations, before delivering a new constitutional framework through parliament which would allow him to implement a power-sharing settlement. Anxious to avoid the impression that he was imposing a settlement with an Irish dimension, Whitelaw was keen to manage this in such a way that the government's ideas appeared to have emerged, having been stimulated by a broad-based public consultation process over Northern Ireland's constitutional future. The inter-party talks at Darlington were intended to initiate this public discourse.[23] Following assembly elections, if the unionist representatives who refused to relinquish their right to govern Northern Ireland without consensus outnumbered those who supported the government's proposals, Whitelaw would be forced to abandon his peace process and impose a settlement that was acceptable to the British government. In such circumstances, it would be impossible to present a settlement as having been endorsed by a broad section of Northern Ireland opinion.

In the event of Whitelaw failing to achieve some form of consensus government, and having ruled out both British military withdrawal and Irish unification as serious policy options, Heath thought that imposed integration was the most likely outcome. Although integration would make agreed unification more difficult to come by in the long run, Heath hoped that the threat of integration might be used at an opportune moment to dash nationalist aspirations and reduce the determination of unionists to force a return to majority rule. Although this further illustrated Heath's pragmatic approach, the inherent problem with this policy was that for many unionists total integration was the most preferable alternative to some form of devolution.[24]

When Whitelaw brought the permanent secretaries of the Northern Ireland civil service into his consultation process, splits were evident over the available constitutional options. Some favoured a form of integrated government in which the Northern Ireland civil service would retain a strong role within the UK civil service. For them, retaining powers akin to those of a local council was a way of taking advantage of the crisis, by establishing a 'real union between Great Britain and Northern Ireland'. In opposition to integration were officials such as Ken Bloomfield, who advocated introducing a strong devolved executive to govern on a power-sharing basis.[25] This process exacerbated existing tensions between the Northern Ireland civil service and the NIO – the two sets of officials were segregated to the extent that the former was kept 'out of the loop' over security and political decision-making[26] – as integration amounted to a form of permanent direct rule, which was an unpalatable option to most Whitehall mandarins. Nevertheless, a discussion paper incorporating the concept of 'The Irish Dimension'[27] was eventually endorsed unanimously by the Northern Ireland civil service heads.[28] This paper formed the basis for Whitelaw's consultation process from which the government's white paper proposals would emerge on 20 March 1973.

At Darlington, Whitelaw frustrated Faulkner's efforts to draw him on the question of the British government's long-term policy objectives in Northern Ireland. Sticking to his self-defined role as independent arbitrator, Whitelaw listened and collated views from the three parties, and without the power and authority of the unionist government behind him, Faulkner's discomfort was palpable. Although dominating the proceedings, Faulkner's voice was merely one of three and his position a minority one which drew precious little support from Whitelaw. Unwilling to compromise on almost any point, he blamed Whitelaw for the 'deterioration in the security situation' in Northern Ireland following the imposition of direct rule.[29] However, he raised little objection at Darlington to the idea of establishing an all-Ireland body.

On 26 September the parties focused on the forms of executive authority a future Northern Ireland Assembly might have. Alliance and the NILP joining forces against Faulkner, who insisted that the Official Unionist Party was only prepared to consider a 'two-tier' system of 'advisory committees' and 'executive ministers', in what amounted to a return to Stormont government with limited reforms.[30] Whitelaw used the conference to spell out to Faulkner that, having reflected on the mistakes of unionist rule and the 1920 Government of Ireland Act,[31] putting 'Humpty Dumpty' back on the Stormont wall was not on his agenda.[32] Thus the Darlington talks marked a radical departure for unionism and provided Whitelaw with a taste of how difficult it might be to prise Faulkner from some of his more intransigent colleagues.

Whitelaw emphasised to the parties that any solution to Northern Ireland's troubles would have to take into consideration the interests of the UK as a whole. He stressed that he did not believe that 'in the modern world any country', or 'any part of any country', could 'live in isolation from the world as a whole'.[33] His message to moderate unionism was clear. A political consensus in Northern Ireland had to be reached, not just between unionists and nationalists, but also between Belfast and Westminster; therefore the sooner unionists adjusted to this new reality the better the outcome would be for all concerned.

Hume went further, advising the British that unionists would adjust to new realities much quicker if they brought them 'down to earth' with 'a nudge towards union' with the Republic of Ireland; an approach, he suggested, that a future Labour government would not be reluctant to adopt.[34] He was concerned, however, that a change of Northern Ireland secretary of state was much more likely than a change of government, for despite boycotting the Darlington talks, Hume was extremely pleased at Whitelaw's success in reducing the influence of the Provisional IRA in Londonderry.

Away from Darlington, Faulkner's opponents suspected that what lay beneath Whitelaw's reform proposals was a British design to prod them towards a united Ireland. They interpreted Wilson's remarks at the Labour Party conference as a commitment to bring about a united Ireland within fifteen years. Voicing unionist fears over the Conservative Party's long-term intentions, John Taylor said that there no longer seemed to be 'any major political party in Great Britain' which had it as part of its policy to 'strengthen' the union with Northern Ireland.[35] This reinforced Craig's view that if a restored Stormont parliament was out of the question then a negotiated independence was preferable to all other alternatives. But having set out to eliminate these options at Darlington, Whitelaw hoped that Taylor and others could be detached from Craig's bandwagon.

Craig struggled to control himself, at times slipping into a 'Mussoliniesque' mode,[36] and his increasingly militant outbursts certainly aided Faulkner's political rehabilitation. On 19 October the Vanguard leader stunned the right-wing Monday Club in the House of Commons when he announced that he was 'prepared to kill' to defend the province from being sold 'down the drain' by the British.[37] Faulkner asked unionists to carefully consider who exactly Vanguard would be fighting against when Craig claimed to have the support of 80,000 men who would 'shoot to kill'.[38] So flagrant had his speeches become that the British actually considered charging him with sedition, treason or incitement to commit a criminal offence.[39] And with Faulkner shifting away from Craig and his paramilitary supporters, Whitelaw sought to isolate the unionist and republican extremes from their moderate counterparts and diminish the capacity of all paramilitary groups to increase levels of violence.

Cross-border violence remained a major problem and Faulkner kept up the pressure on Heath by demanding action to 'prevent the Republic being used as a harbour for gunmen' in their terror campaign against the Northern Ireland people.[40] The nature of violence in Northern Ireland had significantly changed, however, as a large part of it was being directed against the Catholic community by Protestant paramilitaries who were regularly challenging the authority of the army in loyalist strongholds. Relations between the British Army and the UDA had deteriorated in Belfast. When two UDA supporters died after being struck by military vehicles during rioting, running gun battles ensued between the two sides. The UDA issued a 'declaration of war' against the army which read: 'To hell with the British army ... The British army and the British government are now our enemies.'[41] These developments led the government to conclude that 'Protestant extremists now represent a mirror image of the IRA before Motorman'.[42] With loyalist violence reaching unprecedented levels, Whitelaw advised the British cabinet that sooner or later 'a major confrontation between the security forces and the UDA was probably inevitable'. Given the army's present security commitments, he warned the government that in such circumstances it might have to accept a reduction of pressure on the IRA. More than that, since the UDA-backed Loyalist Association of Workers could control Northern Ireland's power-generating and switching stations, the possibility, he said, of the government having 'to fight our way through' could not be excluded.[43]

A related security headache was the degree of association that existed between the UDR and the UDA which, unlike the UVF, was not an illegal organisation. It would have been politically difficult for Whitelaw to have dismissed large numbers of UDR men simply on suspicion of paramilitary association,[44] and some of his officials viewed it as 'a problem to be managed' rather than 'a contribution to operational effectiveness' in the fight against terrorism.[45] Although the army in turn viewed the UDA as a channel for negative Protestant energies, it had become a powerful organisation with a province-wide working-class support base, which included a rump of terrorists who were conducting a blatantly sectarian assassination campaign against the Catholic community in coordination with the UVF.

The levels of violence in Northern Ireland soared in 1972, with 470 deaths and over 12,000 shooting and bombing incidents. Of these fatalities, 148 were members of the security forces and 322 civilians, of which 122 were recorded as sectarian assassinations with twice as many Catholic victims as Protestant. In July alone, ninety-five people died as a result of bombings, gun battles, sectarian assassinations and politically motivated violence. Nevertheless, Northern Ireland had experienced a period of direct rule during which the IRA threat had been reduced, raising public expectations that Whitelaw would broker a political settlement in early 1973.

At the end of October, the government published a discussion paper entitled *The Future of Northern Ireland*, which introduced the concept of an 'Irish dimension' to the public discourse and hinted that power-sharing between unionists and nationalists would be the outcome most favourable to the British government from further inter-party talks. It said, 'there are strong arguments that the objective of real participation should be achieved by giving minority interests a share in the exercise of executive power'.[46] Officials in Whitehall were busy studying consociational practices in other divided societies such as Canada, Cyprus, Belgium, Lebanon and Switzerland. And in what was a significant shift in the Irish government's public position towards the North, Lynch welcomed the proposals and made no calls for immediate Irish unity or intergovernmental talks. He said that 'one essential part of the search for peace is the need to find a political structure which can command the consent of the separate communities in the North', and achieving this end would require 'major changes in attitudes, behaviour and institutions ... both north and south' [47] – precisely the sort of constructive response to the initiative the British were aiming for.

Security permitting, Whitelaw intended to guide the plebiscite bill through the UK parliament, as he still viewed this as an essential ingredient for getting 'the neurosis of the border out of the systems of the majority community'. He would then publish a white paper and introduce constitutional legislation, before proceeding to negotiations in search of a settlement before the anniversary of direct rule, on 24 March 1973. From that point, he would implement an 'evolving' solution to Northern Ireland's troubles. He was aware, however, that holding Northern Ireland Assembly elections might produce an 'obstinate polarisation of views', at the very moment he was presented with an opportunity to push through a settlement.[48]

* * * *

Attempting to inject a sense of urgency into the political process, Heath travelled to Northern Ireland on 16 November. Drawing first blood, at what was their first meeting since Stormont had been prorogued, Faulkner told the prime minister that 'one of the tragic results of direct rule' was that power had moved away from government and onto the streets of Northern Ireland. When Faulkner asked Heath for his view on how an all-Ireland body might function, the prime minister assured him that it would focus on matters of common interest such as 'power supplies, transport and tourism'.[49] Insisting that the plebiscite should precede the white paper, Faulkner warned that unless the government's proposals were broadly acceptable there would be no let up to the violence. The underlying purpose of Heath's visit was to survey Northern Ireland's barren landscape for new unionist leadership and Faulkner wasted no time in highlighting that the alternatives to him were all far worse. Heath concluded from his trip, however, that if moderate leadership of 'adequate calibre' was not forthcoming, and although such measures would be extremely unwelcome, then 'there might be little alternative to the complete integration of the province within the United Kingdom'.[50]

When Heath met Lynch, on 24 November, the establishment of evolving all-Ireland institutions topped the Irish government's agenda. Mac Stíofáin was being sentenced in Dublin as they spoke, and the British signalled their appreciation of Lynch's efforts to tighten security measures against the IRA. The taoiseach declared that a multidimensional Council of Ireland, operating at both official and parliamentary levels, with a full-time secretariat, would be a deal-maker for nationalists in any forthcoming settlement. For the white paper proposals to be acceptable to his government, Lynch said that there would also have to be 'a measure of discussion and consultation in advance'. Heath saw no great difficulty with moderate opinion in Northern Ireland accepting the establishment of a Council of Ireland, but he emphasised that while he was prepared to discuss and consult with Lynch, there was no question of the two governments negotiating over future arrangements for Northern Ireland.[51]

On 1 December the Irish parliament held a critical debate on the Offences against the State (Amendment) Bill, which proposed that persons suspected of membership of a proscribed organisation could be convicted on the word of a senior police officer. On his return to Dublin Lynch narrowly avoided being forced to call a general election when, at the last minute, Fine Gael dropped its opposition to the controversial anti-terrorism legislation. As the debate was taking place news filtered through the chamber that Dublin had been hit twice by UVF car bombs, which killed two and injured over a hundred people. Denying responsibility, the UDA suggested that although this sort of thing was 'bound to happen in Dublin', it 'may do some good' in the long run.[52] The attack certainly heightened the Irish parliament's awareness of the threat posed by cross-border terrorism and, fearing a crackdown was imminent from Lynch, many IRA members who had fled Northern Ireland prior to or as a consequence of Operation Motorman sought shelter in the North. The British were quick to offer Lynch operational support in reducing cross-border attacks from either direction,[53] and Heath personally sent an intelligence dossier on the IRA to assist his efforts. He also considered bringing British legislation into line with the law in both parts of Ireland, where membership of the IRA was an offence. This would prevent mainland Britain, as British home secretary Robert Carr put it, from becoming 'the haven for IRA extremists that Southern Ireland has been hitherto'.[54]

The Irish government's preferred short-term outcome from Northern Ireland's political process was a condominium, along the lines of the SDLP's proposals. More realistically, they hoped that the British might facilitate the joint administration of local security forces by participating in a Council of Ireland, if this was seen as a step to eventual disengagement. The Irish were also considering the viability of an Anglo-Irish Council with representatives from Belfast, Dublin and Westminster, as a means of preventing unionists from actively 'stonewalling' the all-Ireland bodies. Moreover, they thought that a Council of the Isles might enable the British to push unionists towards a united Ireland and facilitate the smooth transfer of British sovereignty to the Republic.[55] Not wanting to be presented with a *fait accompli* by the British, and having taken security measures to show that his actions spoke louder than his government's rhetoric, Lynch requested immediate consultation, at official level, to discuss the Council of Ireland proposals that would be put forward in the white paper. Prior to this point, the British government had never consulted with the Irish government on any aspect of Northern Ireland affairs and, while seeking to stall the process, Heath indicated that discreet meetings could occur as soon as Whitelaw had concluded his ongoing round of consultations. Anglo-Irish relations had advanced considerably from the bad-tempered teething problems that were evident in Munich. The two governments were beginning to row in the same direction on Northern Ireland, although not towards the same short-term goals.

Lynch's new security legislation eased the introduction of Whitelaw's measures to replace internment; parliament approved the Detention of Terrorists Order 1972 and, offering no alternative to detention, the Diplock Commission's report, published on 20 December, recommended trial without jury for suspected terrorist offenders.[56] Londonderry Provisional IRA leader Martin McGuinness was arrested in Donegal and a County Clare court ruled that two men wanted in connection with firearms offences should be extradited to Northern Ireland. Lynch was testing the waters on the sensitive issue of extradition, as this was the first case of its kind since July 1971. The RUC had been unsuccessful in the thirty-eight extradition warrants forwarded to the Irish during that period,[57] while the Irish had presented thirty extradition requests to the UK, of which nineteen had been successful.[58] Irish Labour Party deputy Conor Cruise O'Brien did not think that Lynch's security measures went far enough, describing them as mere 'window dressing'. 'It is not a question of legislation but whether or not the government wants to act against the IRA,' he said, which 'is a political not a legal matter'.[59] Nevertheless, Lynch was even upsetting the 'other Irish', denouncing the Irish Northern Aid Committee in the US as a front for the Provisional IRA.[60]

Whitelaw set up an anti-assassination police squad and considered redeploying the army from the Catholic areas in which there had been a drastic reduction in IRA activity into the Protestant areas from which the sectarian murder gangs were operating. Considerably weakened by the failure of their summer ceasefire, a number of Provisional IRA leaders, on both sides of the border, again put out peace feelers to the British. Despite the collapse of the IRA ceasefire, the British had maintained its backchannel of communication with the Provisionals. The outcome of a meeting of the IRA's military and political leadership in late November indicated that republicans wanted peace and could deliver a sustainable ceasefire. Even with Mac Stíofáin in jail and possibly favouring such a move, the British were unconvinced of the Provisional IRA's ability to maintain a ceasefire, the sincerity of their yearning for peace and the desirability of relinquishing the army's military advantage by giving them the breathing space to regroup.[61] The British took the position that if the Provisional IRA wanted a ceasefire then all it had to do was ceasefire.

In mid-December, Whitelaw held discussions with various parties over the formation of a Northern Ireland Executive and the establishment of an all-Ireland body. Faulkner told him that the question of whether or not unionists would accept the establishment of a Council of Ireland was entirely dependent on the Irish government's attitude towards Northern Ireland. If it 'recognised Northern Ireland's right to run its own affairs' then the Official Unionists would have 'no objection' to a council that consisted of representatives from the two Irish governments. This issue was not the focus of Faulkner's fire. Determined to win back some control over local security powers, he dismissed Whitelaw's notions of executive power-sharing: unionists would accept nothing more radical than his party's proposals for minority representation through a committee system. Faulkner warned Whitelaw that if the British pushed him too far, he would be ousted and replaced by something more extreme.[62] This was not dissimilar to the SDLP's stance. Entrenching their position with calls for joint sovereignty and the disestablishment of the RUC, they argued that if internment was not ended, then they would be swept away by an extreme form of republicanism. More than that, they told Whitelaw that the Northern Ireland political process required 'the long-term certainty of political union by 1980 within the context of the EEC'.[63]

Although disappointed by his failure to detach either the SDLP or the Official Unionists from their zero-sum positions, Whitelaw was now determined to form a power-sharing executive that included moderate unionists and nationalists following constituent assembly elections. He was in two minds as to whether he should announce the powers that would be delegated to a Northern Ireland Executive. Making such a statement before holding assembly elections might tempt strong candidates from both communities to take the bait and compete for places in government, but doing so would reveal his hand. He made it clear to all the Northern Ireland parties that the white paper would disappoint both sides, as many Catholics wanted a united Ireland and many Protestants still sought a return to one-party rule. He was encouraged that Faulkner appeared to appreciate this better than many of his colleagues; unionists would 'be forced to *thole* some things' that they did not like.[64]

The government intended to rule out a number of different constitutional options in the white paper: a united Ireland could not be achieved by force, there would be no return to one-party rule at Stormont, and Craig's idea of an independent Ulster would not be acceptable to parliament. More so than Heath, Whitelaw was against the full integration of Northern Ireland into the UK, given the legislative burden this would place on the Westminster parliament and the opposition it would provoke in Britain, both parts of Ireland and the US. His primary objective was to initiate a process of rolling or evolving devolution. Of all the options open to him, Whitelaw believed that this was not only the most realistic policy, but the course of action that was most likely to be acceptable to moderate political opinion in both communities. In the short to medium term, this meant maintaining direct rule and incrementally devolving power to an executive body at Stormont, in two or three stages, over the next eighteen months. With security powers reserved, Whitelaw accepted that his plans would require an increase in the number of Northern Ireland's MPs from twelve to eighteen, which would create parity within the UK and allow for the diminution of power at Stormont. Positive safeguards against the abuse or monopolisation of power would be institutionalised, but Whitelaw remained undecided over whether he would guarantee the minority community a number of seats on the executive. Worried that a mixed executive, or even a system that juxtaposed 'majority' heads of departments with 'minority' heads of committees, might be a recipe for deadlock, he favoured a system of departmental committees that mirrored party strengths in the assembly. Once the committees had scrutinised legislative and executive actions the assembly might then approve measures by weighted majorities of 70 or 75 per cent. Whitelaw liked the idea of an executive comprised of political figures, acceptable to both communities, who had been approved by the assembly in exactly the same way. Fleshing out the functions of a Council of Ireland should be left until after the nature of the constitutional settlement had been agreed. In contrast, Heath argued that until they had decided what functions might be exercised jointly, or in cooperation with the Republic of Ireland, the government could not be clear about the powers that would be devolved to a Northern Ireland Executive.[65]

The timing of the referendum remained a particular headache for Whitelaw. By the end of November it was clear that administrative and legislative difficulties would delay it until March and, consequently, the publication of the white paper would also be delayed. Lynch had made the nationalist case for publishing it ahead of the plebiscite, if the poll had to be held at all, on the grounds that the people of Northern Ireland would then be voting in full knowledge of the constitutional options available to them. Whitelaw was totally opposed to this idea, as a post-white paper poll could become a rallying point for all his opponents. There was no reason to believe that an early border poll would not actually harden unionist opinion should the SDLP boycott it. More than that, delaying the white paper until after the poll made the extension of direct rule inevitable and threw Whitelaw's devolution timetable completely off course. Whether holding a poll sooner rather than later would make it easier for Faulkner to rally moderate unionist support was the critical factor, as it had been promised in the first place as a means of augmenting his support base. At this point, Heath and Whitelaw had not invested all their political capital in Faulkner's leadership of the unionist community, and while he remained at odds with Craig, the unionist leader also appeared to be keeping his options open.

Whitelaw was increasingly concerned that after the white paper's publication loyalist paramilitaries could pose a considerable threat to Northern Ireland's electricity grid. Northern Ireland's business leaders had served a warning to him that 'an electricity strike could have a crippling effect on industry and seriously inconvenience domestic users'. They urged the government to ensure that the burden of any industrial strike was shared with domestic users so as to increase pressure on those imposing the stoppage.[66] Moreover, Northern Ireland's trade union leaders warned Whitelaw that the size and strength of the Loyalist Association of Workers was insignificant, as a determined 10 to 15 per cent of the workforce could close any particular plant through intimidation.[67]

Noting these developments, Whitelaw initiated a review of Operation Folklore, the government's secret military plan to 'saturate the critical areas of the province and disarm the population'. Operation Folklore detailed how the security forces would use overwhelming force to crush loyalist and republican paramilitary factions, maintain essential services and use internment to prevent further offensive action. It envisaged a massive increase in the number of major infantry units, from eighteen to forty within seven days and rising to forty-seven with further support units over the following days.[68] If implemented, this military initiative would have formidable repercussions, but it was held in reserve as a doomsday plan to be unleashed only in the event of a deterioration of the security situation to the point at which the government was on the brink of losing control over Northern Ireland.

The present security threat was 'not quite the FOLKLORE situation',[69] but Whitelaw sought to ensure that secret military, legislative and administrative planning for a major confrontation with the unionist community was as advanced as was practically possible at this time. Existing plans for the maintenance of essential services were insufficient and unsatisfactory, but Whitelaw's attempts to revise them were frustrated. For if the government acted to significantly improve its emergency plans then this would reveal something of their nature to the Northern Ireland civil service, widening the small group of officials that were aware of Operation Folklore.[70] Consequently, there was no move at this point to secure the power stations from either intimidation or attack.

* * * *

By January 1973, having consulted with all sections of Northern Ireland society, Whitelaw concluded that the establishment of a basis for a lasting settlement, between the moderate parties, was going to require considerable time and patience. He did not believe that direct rule could be ended in 1973. This was the opposite of what Heath wanted to hear. Concurring with Whitelaw, however, officials in Downing Street advised Heath that, should a general election take place, as was expected in the Autumn of 1974, then considering the challenges that restoring political stability to Northern Ireland presented, an eighteen-month interval was 'not a day too long'.[71] Given administrative setbacks, and the intransigent positions that both Faulkner and the SDLP remained wedded to, Whitelaw dispelled any notion that a quick retreat from direct rule in Northern Ireland was even a remote possibility. A secretary of state would have to police Northern Ireland's new institutions, initiate new legislation from Westminster, and act as a mentor to the new executive with ultimate sanction against the abuse of power. Although not objecting to this, Faulkner stressed his concern to Whitelaw that if any future secretary of state was seen as a 'final arbitrator' then this would undermine the executive; anti-unionist and anti-government parties would be inclined to 'go above their heads' in much the same way as had occurred through the UK representative at Laneside prior to direct rule.[72]

On New Year's Day 1973 British and Irish officials held the first in a series of meetings, from which Whitelaw remained aloof, to discuss the proposed all-Ireland structures. From the outset of the negotiations, the Irish government's strategy was to seize the moment and push for the absolute maximum that could be attained on the all-Ireland structures, firm in their conviction that the British could and should herd unionism in their direction. The British stressed the point that overly ambitious proposals would likely be rejected in Northern Ireland, which underscored the impracticality of imposing them on the unionist community.[73] They warned that trying to force unionists to participate in a Council of Ireland with strong powers would be counterproductive and not something that Westminster could impose. The British favoured an all-Ireland council that operated at official level, with scope to evolve as confidence in the political process evolved. The Irish did not agree, contending that if there was to be a 'courageous solution' to the troubles, then making the evolution of a Council of Ireland dependent on a change of unionist heart was hardly a practical way to proceed.[74] The British countered this argument by flagging up the thorny issue of recognition, which could be a deal breaker for moderate unionism.

The Irish were most dismayed by what they viewed as British reticence, and left the talks assuming that this was perhaps just a negotiating ploy. But following the meeting, Whitelaw sought to dampen their expectations further. No one should expect an all-encompassing Council of Ireland to be established 'overnight', he said, but if one emerged that dealt with 'matters of mutual economic interest', then that would be 'a useful start'.[75] The Irish feared being drawn into supporting a Northern Ireland settlement, only for the British to retreat from the Council of Ireland proposals and drive a wedge between them and the SDLP. Furthermore, if the unionists were granted an institutional veto on the council, then the Irish government would be tied into an all-Ireland body that could be permanently held hostage to the whims of the unionist community. There was a clear distinction, however, between the overzealous line taken by DFA officials and some of their political masters, who took a more realistic view of how the Irish dimension might evolve.[76]

Whitelaw informed the British cabinet of proposals to create a new Northern Ireland Assembly, with a multi-party executive emerging through consultation with elected representatives to which health, education and transport powers would be devolved. Success would be determined by whether the 'great mass of moderate opinion' in both communities found the proposals acceptable and were prepared to work them.[77] The great advantage in the 'evolving settlement' approach, he argued, was that it would not have the appearance of being completely imposed. Admittedly, it ran the risk of enabling Faulkner, or one of his rivals, to establish a unionist majority within the assembly and stand in opposition to the government, but this could be avoided provided unionism remained divided. The alternative option was to present a 'cut and dried' solution in the white paper and implement a settlement in one decisive act. Taking such a course would certainly unite unionism around Faulkner or a more extreme figure and make the imposition of a settlement extremely tricky. Unimpressed by Whitelaw's logic, Heath held to the conclusion he had formed during his visit to Northern Ireland: the government's priority must be to immediately remove the existing uncertainty over its constitutional future. Whitelaw's proposals left far 'too many uncertainties and loopholes' for Heath's liking, maximising the potential for protest from those who were hell bent on destroying them, and prolonging the period in which disaffection could fester in the unionist community.[78] The prime minister favoured putting specific proposals on the formation of an executive in the white paper, seeing no reason to make

Whitelaw's step-by-step approach to ending direct rule any more long and drawn out than was absolutely necessary.

Heath and Whitelaw faced a serious dilemma concerning the unionist electoral bloc. Their plan was to ensure that the white paper caused further splits within unionism, but this ran the risk that if Faulkner was replaced by Craig as Official Unionist leader, Whitelaw would then have to decide which one he recognised as the voice of moderate unionism. The secretary of state was completely opposed to a Craig leadership, yet he remained suspicious enough of Faulkner to dismiss the idea of taking him into his confidence over the government's proposals prior to the white paper's publication. The threat of severing the link between the Conservative and Official Unionist parties at Westminster, he suggested, might sober some of Faulkner's more moderate colleagues and help him bring them to the negotiating table. Increasing the number of Northern Ireland MPs could be held in stock as a further political carrot. Should Craig oust Faulkner, Whitelaw believed that the link between their parties would have to be broken anyway; given the severity of his split with the government, working with the Vanguard leader would be extremely risky.

So after almost a year of direct rule, Faulkner, 'the devil they knew', presented the safest bet for Heath and Whitelaw.[79] Yet Northern Ireland's last prime minister was loathed by the nationalist community and many of its political representatives, distrusted by the liberal unionist elite that Whitelaw was nurturing, and equally out of sorts with the emerging cross-community representatives with whom he would be expected to form an executive. Notably, Oliver Napier of the Alliance Party warned Whitelaw that giving power back to Faulkner would be akin to going back on the very initiative that ended fifty years of unionist domination.[80] Napier was part of a 'centre group' that comprised liberal unionists such as Robin Bailie, Robin Chichester-Clark and Stratton Mills. These moderates hoped to emerge as an electoral force should the Official Unionist Party disintegrate after the white paper's publication. They pressed Whitelaw to definitively spell out the method of power-sharing that would form the basis of a future Northern Ireland Executive, face down the Protestant backlash that this would undoubtedly provoke, and provide them with a sound electoral platform from which to emerge. Ever the realist, Whitelaw was weary of taking such a provocative approach, but agreed with them that the key to delivering radical constitutional reforms lay in preventing unionist unity[81] and separating the 'moderate Protestants from the extremists' among them. Whitelaw's aim was to 'find a point of balance' in his proposals where moderates on each side felt that they could comfortably compromise and coexist, despite the fact that the proposals would fall short of the maximal preferences of their core supporters.[82]

Seeking to reinforce division among the unionist factions, Whitelaw had a number of UDA/UVF men arrested on suspicion of perpetuating a recent spate of sectarian murders. Detention was finally being employed against Protestant militiamen and Heath advised his cabinet to be prepared for a confrontation with the forces of militant unionism.[83] Without consulting Craig, the Loyalist Association of Workers responded by announcing that a one-day strike would be held on 7 February. Craig immediately asked Whitelaw to reverse his detention policy, so as to provide him with the means of preventing the strike.[84] Whitelaw pressed Craig to cool the situation himself, reminding the Vanguard leader that it was he who had actually proscribed the UVF in the first place, when he was a government minister at Stormont. Ignoring Faulkner's request for them to remain at the power stations, electricity workers went home early on 6 February, in anticipation of the strike. With nowhere to turn, Craig threw his weight behind the strike, heeding a warning from the loyalist paramilitaries that the old unionist elite would be 'swept aside' if they did not unite.[85]

The strike quickly descended into a day of chaotic rioting, intimidation and raging gun battles between the security forces and the Protestant paramilitaries, with mobs rampaging across the streets of Belfast, Bangor, Larne and Portadown. Some parts of the province experienced electricity blackouts, schools closing as a result, and widespread intimidation forced shop closures and severed transport links. Criticising what he described as the 'low profile posture' taken by the army towards the strike, Northern Ireland opposition spokesman Merlyn Rees asked Whitelaw if he was aware that the intimidation of managers in Northern Ireland's power stations had resulted in a reduction of generated power being fed into the grid.[86] Whitelaw confirmed that a deal had been struck between the strikers and the power station management whereby the electricity supply would be reduced. He told Rees that while the RUC had been reluctant to engage loyalist paramilitaries in areas where they themselves lived, government security forces would meet the challenge of loyalist violence.[87] The danger of Protestant militia-led violence derailing Whitelaw's peace process was now at least as serious as the threat posed previously by the Provisional IRA. In light of recent events, Faulkner concluded that he was not being overly optimistic in assuming that the penny was beginning to drop in Westminster; if the government wanted a reasonable organisation to deal with in Northern Ireland then there was no alternative to his.[88]

Declaring a snap election in the Republic of Ireland, on 28 February, Lynch sought to batten down the hatches in Dublin and gain a 'clear and decisive mandate' from the electorate on national security issues with which to weather the storm brewing in the North.[89] In Belfast, as the unionist community reacted angrily against loyalist violence, Faulkner seized the initiative by attempting to unify moderate opinion against Craig and the malevolent forces he relied upon. Capitalising on middle-class revulsion towards the strikers' violent methods, Faulkner forged a security pact with Phelim O'Neill, Ian Paisley and Vivian Simpson – the leaders of the three pro-union parties, Alliance, DUP and NILP. Taking Faulkner's lead, they informed Whitelaw that they were willing to jointly support 'across the board' initiatives to bring an end to violence if he was prepared to act upon their security advice. Paisley suggested that if the detention policy was to be pursued against the Protestant paramilitaries then a 'once-and-for-all swoop' would be preferable to a 'long-term policy of erosion'.[90] Although Whitelaw was expecting a resurgent campaign from the Provisional IRA, which was keen to exploit the British Army's confrontation with the loyalist paramilitaries, he did not fully swallow Faulkner's bait, merely thanking the 'alternative' moderate centre ground leaders for their support.

Having burnt his bridges with Craig, Faulkner then made his move, condemning the Vanguard leader for his long and dangerous flirtation with loyalist militias. Ridiculing the idea of an independent Ulster he cast Craig out, declaring him 'no longer a unionist' and 'no longer ... a member of the Official Unionists'.[91] Isolated, and attempting to shake off his association with the loyalist strike, Craig made a dramatic U-turn, calling for a Protestant and Catholic 'Dominion of Ulster', only for his UDA colleagues to reject the notion of holding talks with the SDLP.[92]

Whitelaw's pledge to hold a border poll continued to trouble him, as intelligence sources suggested that Protestant paramilitaries planned to protest against the white paper regardless of its timing and would use its result to foster opposition to the government's proposals. Decision time was fast approaching and he put his case to Heath, at Chequers, on 10 February, for the adoption of an evolutionary approach to carving out a devolved settlement with the Northern Ireland parties. His gradualist arguments against imposing a detailed constitutional settlement were reinforced by the fact that, should the latter fail, then the government had no fallback position other than the maintenance of direct rule. In contrast, Whitelaw argued that his evolving approach afforded the greatest degree of flexibility in devising a settlement that might, in time, deliver the greatest degree of support from both communities. Admittedly, it ran the risk of producing a deadlocked assembly, which in turn could drift towards the sort of one-party rule system that the imposition of direct rule had brought to an end. Although his arguments held sway, it was agreed that, should the evolutionary approach be adopted, then the white paper had to detail principles for a form of power-sharing that were both acceptable to moderate unionist opinion and, at the same time, regarded by Lynch as a watertight guarantee that the minority community would be represented in government.[93] Heath viewed Lynch's response to the white paper as critical and he was now prepared to consult with him over the proposals, as his response to them would determine the level of force he was prepared to exert against the IRA in the South. This was an essential ingredient for the long-term success of the political process in the North. Furthermore, Heath and Whitelaw agreed that there was little point in proceeding with the Irish government's demand for a Council of Ireland that held executive powers from the outset, as it would tip the balance in favour of the unionist rejectionists.

Whitelaw faced a dilemma over how to comprise an executive of roughly seven members and accommodate a minority that lacked a solid political representative structure and was sectarian by definition. With the principle objective of breaking the unionist stranglehold on Northern Ireland's electoral process, and thereby making power-sharing appear logical, assembly elections would be held by the single transferable vote (STV) system in multi-member constituencies. This approach helped maintain bipartisanship at Westminster, but the government was divided between those who favoured reserving places in an executive for parties that met a certain quota of seats in the assembly and those who supported Whitelaw's proposal to form an executive by agreement with the support of weighted majorities in the assembly. Explicitly guaranteeing places for Catholics on the executive was not favoured, especially given Faulkner's recent détente with Whitelaw.[94] Moreover, institutionalising sectarianism in such an overt manner would be bitterly resisted by the Alliance Party and the NILP.

Whitelaw's concern was to ensure that the minority community was represented and he was frustrated that no single recognised leader of that community had yet emerged. Given the inflexibility and inexperience that the SDLP leaders had displayed since direct rule, he did not view them as the only Catholic representatives capable of binding the minority community to new institutions. Moreover, Whitelaw intended to preside over a voluntary coalition government, formed through consultation with representatives of an interim assembly, rather than impose a coalition whose composition was determined on the basis of a sectarian headcount. This left open the possibility of a unionist leader forming a coalition with a non-nationalist party that included Catholic representatives, such as Alliance, but he was aware that this would hardly satisfy Lynch. The government decided not to commit itself to any particular form of power-sharing, as the composition of the assembly would have a significant bearing on the option that appeared most viable, and this advanced Whitelaw's gradualist arguments.[95]

* * * *

On 2 March Lynch conceded defeat in the general election and a Fine Gael–Labour coalition government took power, headed by Liam Cosgrave, who played the role of 'chairman' in this political marriage.[96] Lynch's electoral strategy had backfired. Focusing effectively on bread and butter issues, the coalition partners largely ignored the Northern Ireland political process, forcing Lynch to make a mid-campaign switch from constitutional to economic issues, and with disastrous consequences. Cosgrave's coalition brought together the equally brilliant, but sharply contrasting, political talents of Garret FitzGerald and Conor Cruise O'Brien. They both took a keen interest in the North and were to clash constantly over how the government's policy towards it was shaped. The British viewed Cosgrave as a more practical and forward-looking leader than Lynch. But knowing little of Northern Ireland affairs, and influenced by his father's experience of heading the Irish Free State during the Irish Civil War in 1922–3, his main concern in office would be maintaining the stability of the twenty-six counties of the Irish Republic.[97] Moreover, he lacked the power and authority of his predecessor, who had not kept him abreast of any of the political developments on the North.[98]

In contrast to Lynch, Faulkner had bounced back politically in Belfast. He appeared revived, invigorated and recovered from the trauma of March 1972 and the rudderless post-Stormont period of direct rule that had seen him aligned with Craig, sniping at the heels of Whitelaw, and struggling to reinvent himself. Reeling from the disastrous loyalist strike, Craig was charting uncertain waters by holding talks with the SDLP and signalling his preference for the establishment of an ultra-Protestant party. Faulkner had repositioned himself at the centre of not just moderate unionist opinion, but of the moderate political ground that Whitelaw was nurturing. Paisley's newfound support for a committee system with nationalist representatives that unionists could comprehensively control[99] was a measure of Faulkner's political resurrection.[100] The critical question was whether Whitelaw would act decisively to put all the government's eggs in the Faulkner basket. The secretary of state was undecided as to whether Northern Ireland's last unionist prime minister, should he become the chief executive of its first power-sharing administration, would be 'the leader of a new order or a salvager of the old'.[101]

Given the considerable progress that had been made in Anglo-Irish relations during the first year of direct rule, and the fact that neither Fine Gael nor Labour had been in office since 1957, Lynch's electoral defeat was met with considerable apprehension in Whitehall. His departure greatly diminished the possibility of the Irish government risking a referendum on the introduction of changes to the Irish constitution as a means of consolidating a Northern Ireland settlement. On 8 March the Provisional IRA detonated car bombs outside government buildings in central London, killing one and injuring hundreds.[102] The same day, a well-observed nationalist boycott of the border poll delivered unfettered unionist support for the maintenance of the UK link, with only 6,463 people voting in favour of a united Ireland.[103] Interestingly, 591,820 voted positively for the union, which was a significantly higher figure than those voting for unionist candidates in the subsequent council, assembly and general elections.

Seeking a smooth transition, Heath met Cosgrave on 9 March, before he had formed his government. He warned Cosgrave that should Whitelaw's constitutional proposals fail, then, regrettably, the complete integration of Northern Ireland into the UK would be the only realistic option left open to the British. They agreed that a tripartite conference between representatives of the two governments and the Northern Ireland Executive should negotiate the details of a Council of Ireland. Cosgrave insisted that this should only be composed of representatives from the North and South of Ireland, as Anglo-Irish matters should remain separate. He suggested that a great deal of acrimony in the future would be avoided if the white paper set out the functions that would come under its remit. Heath agreed that it should be bipartite, but rejected the idea that the proposed Northern Ireland Assembly should have no say in the formation of a Council of Ireland. He also explained that should the British government be excluded from the council, then the body would have no business discussing a wide range of matters, from Northern Ireland's security to its financial affairs.[104] Moreover, the Alliance Party had made the argument that the unionist community's fear that a Council of Ireland would act as a Trojan horse in the furtive delivery of a united Ireland could easily be allayed if an Anglo-Irish Council was established instead.[105]

Heath found the coalition leaders more practical in their outlook than Lynch, but, nevertheless, he subjected them to a rough introduction to the ongoing security wrangles that were a regular feature of all Anglo-Irish diplomatic encounters. The British, he said, would 'fight them every inch of the way' at Strasbourg if they persisted with the allegations that his security forces practised torture against terror suspects. Security remained Heath's main concern and he told Cosgrave that so long as the troubles persisted, his government would 'never again contemplate sharing responsibility' for security with 'any representative body in Northern Ireland'.[106] The white paper, Heath assured him, would establish that no executive would be acceptable to parliament that drew its support virtually or entirely from one side of Northern Ireland's divided society. He joked that one-party rule was still acceptable to his government, but only if Alliance triumphed at the polls. When Cosgrave wondered how old unionist and nationalist foes would share power in Northern Ireland, Heath told him flatly that they would be bound like any other working coalition to support each other's policies. A bill of rights would be introduced to eliminate discrimination in all sectors of society and a secretary of state would maintain a veto with which to police the agreement.[107]

Whitelaw had no specific intelligence with which to confirm that Craig's supporters intended to initiate a second strike the moment the white paper came off the shelves. Given Craig's lack of middle-of-the-road unionist support, Whitelaw doubted his ability to force a deterioration of the security situation to the proportions envisaged in Operation Folklore and survive politically. In case a one-day industrial strike required the government to maintain essential services,[108] the army garrison was increased to twenty major units, with eight more placed on three days' notice, and Whitelaw used his detention powers to get certain militants out of the way at this critical time.[109]

On 20 March a white paper entitled *Northern Ireland Constitutional Proposals* introduced the idea of an executive form of government for Northern Ireland: 'which can no longer be solely based upon any single party, if that party draws its support and its elected representation virtually entirely from only one section of a divided community'. This opened the door of government to those who sought a united Ireland by constitutional means, but who were also prepared to work for the good of Northern Ireland. Nationalists would have the 'opportunity to play no less a part in the life and public affairs of Northern Ireland than is open to their fellow citizens'.[110] Although it did not use the phrase power-sharing, it was implicit that the establishment of a multi-party executive based on the principles of consensus government was Whitelaw's objective. Once an executive designate was formed, he would end the temporary expedient of direct rule by devolving power to Northern Ireland.

Both wings of the IRA rejected the proposals, but Dáithí Ó Conaill hinted publicly that the republican movement intended to take a more political approach in the future. The SDLP was not as positive in its endorsement as the Irish government, stating simply that it would contest elections to a new assembly and participate in government if internment was ended. Craig sounded the most extreme unionist reaction, while Faulkner described the white paper as a 'reasonable document'.[111] Papering over deep fissures within the Official Unionists, he maintained his leadership of the party when defeating a motion to reject the proposals on the UUC on 27 March, by 348 to 231.[112]

This victory precipitated a permanent split with Craig, who finally quit and formed the Vanguard Unionist Progressive Party three days later. But it was Paisley who Whitelaw had come to view as the 'greatest danger' to the success of his constitutional proposals,[113] as he was 'stoking it up' and 'not at all helpful from a security point of view'.[114]

Public opinion towards the proposals was on the whole positive. Polling taken in May 1973 indicated that 82 per cent of those surveyed were prepared to accept the idea of power-sharing in an executive. Vanguard supporters displayed greater opposition to this suggestion than their DUP counterparts, but a majority of both sets of unionists appeared willing to accept it regardless of party policy. Unionism was completely split over the proposals, which were rejected by 9 per cent of Official Unionists, 38 per cent of DUP supporters and 63 per cent of Craig's followers. For unionists, the Irish dimension was by far the most unpopular aspect, and of those west of the Bann more markedly so, with only 41 per cent of Protestants accepting the idea and a majority of Faulkner's own supporters opposing it.[115]

With the unionist bloc crumbling according to plan, Whitelaw was confident that Faulkner would deliver the moderate elements of his party, who appeared to have accepted that if the proposals were not implemented by March 1974, 'the continued willingness of British public opinion to accept political and military involvement in the affairs of Northern Ireland could not necessarily be assumed'.[116] Having largely reduced the IRA campaign to spasmodic acts of violence, Whitelaw pressed ahead with an intense legislative schedule in preparation for the Northern Ireland Assembly and a Constitution Act that would underpin any power-sharing settlement.

Faulkner sought clarification from Whitelaw over whether the executive could be comprised of members of one party if that party contained representatives from both communities. Whitelaw said it could, provided that the party did not draw its 'elected representatives <u>and its support</u> virtually entirely from one section of a divided community'.[117] The Official Unionists were not opposed to the concept of power-sharing, but against a power-sharing system which was 'designed to reconcile irreconcilables in government', which was precisely what Whitelaw had in mind.[118] Faulkner was also concerned that republican members could be appointed to the executive against the wishes of a majority in the assembly and Whitelaw offered only that 'no person can be acceptable as a member of the Executive who is not prepared to work together with its other members by peaceful means for the benefit of the community'. Faulkner queried whether holding a conference on North–South relations would be contingent on the Irish government recognising Northern Ireland and treating the executive as equals. Whitelaw said he hoped for all practical purposes that they would be treated as equals, indicating that the acceptance of Northern Ireland's constitutional status was one of a number of 'inter-related matters' to be discussed at a conference.[119] Faulkner imagined North–South relations developing in three stages: the first dealing with the constitutional issue of 'the acceptance by the South of the right of the people of the North to self determination'; the second engaging in a thorough review of the extradition arrangements in Ireland; and the third establishing an intergovernmental conference drawn equally from each government to discuss socio-economic cooperation.[120]

The predicted Protestant backlash against the proposals did not materialise, but the three-way split that unionism was experiencing deepened over the proposals: Craig called for the creation of an independent Ulster; the DUP took a more integrationist approach; and Faulkner fudged the issue of power-sharing and held his party together by signalling that Official Unionist candidates in the assembly election would be 'pledged' to make that assembly a worthwhile and effective instrument of government.[121] Faulkner's leadership position was again under threat from Taylor and West, and previously dependable unionist constituency associations had begun to side with the Craig–Paisley loyalist opposition that was taking shape. Craig's appeal was limited, however, by both his hostility towards the British government and his apparent willingness to end the union. Consequently, many of Faulkner's critics chose to oppose the white paper from within the Official Unionist Party and others actually rejoined from Vanguard.[122] Faulkner's party was also splitting in the opposite direction. After he derailed efforts from liberal elements to force a split with Craig's Vanguard movement the previous December,[123] Westminster MP Stratton Mills resigned and Alliance gained its first MP when he joined the centre party, at the end of April, with fellow former Official Unionist Robin Bailie.[124]

Without consulting Faulkner, on 22 May six of the seven Official Unionist Westminster MPs ignored party policy and tabled a motion to defeat Whitelaw's Constitution Bill in parliament.[125] This incident epitomised the lack of political coordination that existed between the Official Unionist Party's headquarters in Glengall Street and its Westminster parliamentary party. Faulkner had a poor relationship with most of these MPs, including those who were sympathetic to the government's reforms, such as Robin Chichester-Clark, who Heath had actually asked to accompany Whitelaw as a minister when direct rule was introduced.[126] At best, they did not act as Faulkner's eyes and ears at Westminster, while others, such as James Kilfedder, were actively working against him.

Aware of the administrative disarray that the Official Unionist Party was in, Whitelaw sought to aid Faulkner in restructuring and coordinating its Westminster and Northern Ireland offices. With unionism split, the secretary of state was confident that no single party would have a majority in the assembly. Although he had successfully divided the Official Unionists, Whitelaw would be reliant on Faulkner's 'pledged' candidates, Alliance and the SDLP gaining a convincing majority between them in the elections. Faulkner then toughened his stance on the idea of power-sharing with nationalists, stating that his party 'will not be prepared to participate in government with any whose primary objective is to break the union with Great Britain'.[127]

In the district council elections held by STV on 30 May, the Official Unionists took 41.4 per cent of the vote, Alliance and the SDLP both made an impact with 13.7 per cent and 13.4 per cent respectively, the NILP vote collapsed at 2.5 per cent, and unionist opposition candidates gained just over 14 per cent between them. Prior to the elections, Whitelaw had dangled the bait of a speedy return to office in front of the Official Unionists. Although not explicitly saying so, he indicated that if Faulkner led unionism into a settlement with Alliance, and possibly the NILP, then 'this might be the basis of power-sharing' in a new executive.[128] This was not entirely fanciful thinking as Alliance received more first preference votes than the SDLP, who remained tied to their hardline proposals.

Elections to a new seventy-eight member Northern Ireland Assembly were held by proportional representation on 28 June 1973. For the first time in Northern Ireland's history, no single party was returned to Stormont with an absolute majority. The Official Unionists won thirty-two seats with 37.8 per cent, the SDLP nineteen seats with 22.1 per cent, Alliance eight seats with 9.2 per cent, and the NILP one seat with only 2.6 per cent. On the eve of the poll the psychopathic killing of prominent SDLP man Paddy Wilson, who died with his Protestant girlfriend as they sat in his Mini car in a quarry outside Belfast – shot and stabbed fifty-one times between them, Wilson having his throat slashed by assailant John White – served as a gruesome reminder of the gulf that stood between Whitelaw's opponents and those pledged to support his reforms. White immediately claimed responsibility on behalf of a UDA assassination squad, the Ulster Freedom Fighters (UFF), in a phone call to the *Belfast News Letter*. Lamenting Wilson's passing, Faulkner described him as 'one of the most human and good natured men' he had ever met at Stormont. Paisley was not so generous. 'To blame Protestants for this dastardly crime on the strength of a phone call', he said, was 'highly irresponsible'.[129]

Twenty-three of the Official Unionists who entered the assembly had 'pledged' to work the white paper proposals, eight were elected 'unpledged' and in opposition to them, while pro-white paper candidate Leslie Morrell lifted Faulkner's support base to twenty-four having simply refused to sign the 'pledge'. He believed Faulkner was 'very foolish' to introduce a mechanism that enabled his rivals to challenge his leadership from within.[130] Former Community Relations Minister Basil McIvor went further; he argued that Faulkner had deliberately split the candidates after deciding to appeal for change within unionism over the heads of those bitter rivals.[131] This was the price Faulkner paid for binding the majority of his party to the proposals, and the 'unpledged' members joined the eight DUP, seven Vanguard and three Loyalist Coalition anti-white paper members, leaving him without a unionist majority in the assembly and with less supporters than the combined total of Alliance, the NILP and the SDLP. Although the anti-white paper unionists had twenty-seven seats, they could be outvoted by the SDLP and the centre parties or, more convincingly, by Faulkner and the centre parties. The result complicated Whitelaw's efforts to form a coalition between the Official Unionists and the SDLP, as the 'pledged' group had attracted less than half the unionist vote. And after reflecting on the results, Heath conceded that an executive would need time to acquire a 'unity of purpose' before it was exposed to the difficulties of a tripartite conference.[132] Whitelaw's task was to establish this without precipitating an exodus from Faulkner's ranks, for it was clear at this point that up to four of his members would object to going into government with the SDLP.[133]

Following the election, Fitt told Whitelaw that the SDLP were willing to form an executive, but that it would be easier for his party to do so if it was not headed by Faulkner.[134] Napier insisted that the appointment of either Faulkner or Hume as chief executive would totally alienate either the Catholic or Protestant members of Alliance respectively.[135] Despite his unpopularity, the Irish government went to great pains to persuade the SDLP that reinstating Faulkner as the head of Northern Ireland's executive authority was the only realistic course to follow.[136]

When Whitelaw told Faulkner that he considered it essential that the SDLP participated in government at executive level, the unionist leader was not opposed. He suggested that his colleagues might be prepared to sit in government with nationalists, such as Gerry Fitt or Eddie McGrady, if they accepted the Constitution Act and ended the 'rent and rates' strike that the SDLP had launched against the introduction of internment in 1971. He stressed, however, that sharing power with John Hume or Austin Currie would be a bridge too far for some. Preferring not to think in terms of a 'last chance', Whitelaw warned Faulkner that, given recent developments in British politics, should an executive not be formed by the end of September then it was unlikely to be formed at all.[137] The Labour Party took an altogether different view to that of the government of developments in Northern Ireland politics. Shadow foreign secretary Jim Callaghan had sent a warning shot across the unionist bow during a parliamentary debate on the Constitution Bill, stressing that 'Britain cannot bleed forever'; if unionists defy the will of parliament by sabotaging the Northern Ireland Assembly then the British government should reconsider its position there.[138] Faulkner understood Whitelaw's message; despite having imposed direct rule, unionists were fortunate that the Conservative Party were both in office and willing to give them a second chance to run their own affairs.

Reiterating these warnings during a bruising encounter with Craig, Whitelaw told him that should the constitutional bill be rejected, while the British government 'would not unilaterally abandon its obligations … it was not clear what the future of Northern Ireland would be if it left the United Kingdom'. If the UK link was broken, he said, then 'those responsible would have to consider the consequences'. Stating his preference for an independent Ulster state, Craig retorted that the 'people of Ulster would have to consider whether they accepted the terms for membership' of the UK. Describing this as a 'policy of despair', Whitelaw told him emphatically that independence was 'totally unrealistic'. Should the will of the British parliament be frustrated, bi-partisanship at Westminster would almost certainly collapse, the campaign for the withdrawal of British troops would be advanced, and this could precipitate a conflict with repercussions throughout the world. Craig replied that in such circumstances the sooner the army withdrew from Northern Ireland the better; civil war was inevitable and a 'scorched earth' was better than an unsatisfactory political solution. Whitelaw's proposals for a power-sharing executive, he said, contained the 'seeds of its own destruction'. Rejecting the concept of 'enforced power-sharing', Craig told Whitelaw that his constitutional proposals were nothing more than a 'timetable for rebellion' in Northern Ireland. Whitelaw implored him to reconsider how a 'satisfactory compromise could be reached without the Armageddon to which he had referred'. In parting, Craig left him in no doubt as to the threat he posed to his power-sharing venture: 'Sometimes,' the Vanguard leader said, 'it is necessary to destroy before thought could be given to re-building.'[139]

NOTES

1. PREM15/1012, Peck to UKREP, 1 August 1972.
2. PREM15/1011, Peck to UKREP, 31 July 1972.
3. FCO87/114, Memo, O'Sullivan to Whitelaw, 28 July 1972.
4. PREM15/1012, Heath to Lynch, 10 August 1972.
5. FCO87/73, Meeting between the Irish Ambassador and the Prime Minister, 2 August 1972.
6. PREM15/1012, Platt to Heath, 2 August 1972.
7. PREM15/1012, Heath to Whitelaw, 3 August 1972.
8. PREM15/1010, Redrawing the border and population transfer.
9. CJ4/136, Round Table Conference on Northern Ireland, Long-term strategy, June 1972.
10. PREM15/1012, Note of a meeting between Heath and Whitelaw, 4 August 1972.
11. PREM15/1012, Meetings between Whitelaw and the SDLP, Laneside, 7/8 August 1972.
12. Interview with Muiris Mac Conghail, Dublin, 24 July 2007.
13. PREM15/1012, Meetings between Whitelaw and the SDLP, Laneside, 7/8 August 1972.
14. US Senate Debates, 9 August 1972; PREM15/1012, Tebbit to UKREP, 11 August 1972.
15. PREM15/1012, Heath to Whitelaw, 14 August 1972.
16. PREM15/1025, Faulkner to Heath, 11 September 1972.
17. PREM15/1025, Meeting between Heath, Whitelaw and the SDLP, Chequers, 12 September 1972.
18. Towards a New Ireland: Proposals by the SDLP, 20 September 1972.
19. Interview with Austin Currie, Dublin, 5 January 2001.
20. *The Civil Authorities (Special Powers) Act (Northern Ireland)* (London: HMSO, 1922).
21. CAB130/560, Cabinet meeting, 10 Downing Street, 11 September 1972.
22. CAB130/561, Cabinet Memo, GEN 79 (72) 18, 7 September 1972.

23. CJ4/136, Meeting between Whitelaw and Faulkner, 20 June 1972.
24. *Fortnight*, 21 May 1973, p.7. Poll conducted by Carrick James Market Research, with a sample of 950 voters, was drawn from six areas: two groups from Belfast; two from Antrim and Down; and two from Tyrone, Fermanagh, Armagh, and Londonderry. The samples were representative of religion, sex, age and class.
25. CJ4/136, A Devolutionary Solution, 7 August 1972.
26. Interview with NIO official, 30 January 2008.
27. K. Bloomfield, *Stormont in Crisis: A Memoir* (Belfast: Blackstaff Press, 1994), pp.177–9.
28. CAB130/561, Views of the Northern Ireland Officials, GEN 79 (72) 23, 3 October 1972.
29. CJ4/138, GEN 79 – Draft speaking note for the Secretary of State, 28 September 1972.
30. FCO87/73, Telegram: White to Dublin, 26 September 1972.
31. *Government of Ireland Act 1920* (London: HMSO, 1920).
32. CAB130/561, The Essential Requirements of a Constitutional Settlement in Northern Ireland, Gen 79 (72) 23, 3 October 1972.
33. CJ4/311, Darlington Conference on Northern Ireland 1972 – Final Record of proceedings.
34. FCO87/83, Conversation with John Hume at Laneside, 4 October 1972.
35. *Irish Times*, 17 July 1972.
36. ICBH, *British Policy on Northern Ireland, 1975–82*, p.6.
37. *Time Magazine*, 30 October 1972.
38. *The Times*, 28 October 1972.
39. PREM15/1015, Rawlinson to Heath, 21 November 1972.
40. PREM15/1033, Faulkner to Heath, 29 September 1972.
41. *Time Magazine*, 30 October 1972.
42. CAB130/561, Review of Position in Northern Ireland, Gen 79 (72) 26, 7 November 1972.
43. PREM15/1016, Meeting between Heath, Wilson, Whitelaw and Rees, House of Commons, 29 November 1972.
44. CAB130/560, Cabinet meeting, 10 Downing Street, 9 November 1972.
45. Interview with NIO official, 30 January 2008.
46. *The Future of Northern Ireland: A Paper for Discussion* (London: HMSO, 30 October 1972).
47. PREM15/1015, Peck to UKREP, 4 November 1972.
48. CAB130/561, Review of Position in Northern Ireland, Gen 79 (72) 26, 7 November 1972.
49. PREM15/1015, Meeting between Heath and the Official Unionists, Stormont, 16 November 1972.
50. CAB130/560, Cabinet meeting, 10 Downing Street, 22 November 1972.
51. PREM15/1015, Meeting between Heath and Lynch, 10 Downing Street, 24 November 1972.
52. *The Times*, 2 December 1972.
53. PREM15/1016, Whitelaw to Heath, 4 December 1972.
54. PREM15/1016, Robert Carr to Heath, 5 December 1972.
55. DT2004/21/3, Council of Ireland brief, December 1972.
56. *Report of the Commission to Consider Legal Procedures to deal with Terrorist Activities in Northern Ireland* (London: HMSO, 1972).
57. *The Times*, 6 December 1972.
58. PREM15/1695, Meeting between Heath and Cosgrave, Baldonnel, 17 September 1973.
59. PREM15/1016, Political Summary, 8–14 December 1972.
60. *The Times*, 9 January 1973.
61. PREM15/1016, Steele to Peck, 28 November 1972.
62. PREM15/1016, Meeting between Whitelaw and the Official Unionists, Stormont, 12 December 1972.
63. PREM15/1016, Meeting between Whitelaw and the SDLP, Stormont, 12 December 1972.
64. ICBH, *British Policy on Northern Ireland, 1975–82*, p.8.
65. CAB130/560, Cabinet meeting, 10 Downing Street, 14 December 1972.
66. PREM15/1016, Meeting between Whitelaw and the CBI [Confederation of British Industry, Northern Ireland], Stormont, 5 December 1972.
67. PREM15/1016, Meeting between Whitelaw and Northern Ireland Committee of the Irish Congress of Trade Unions, Stormont, 12 December 1972.

68. CAB130/561, Contingency Planning, Gen 79 (72) 28, 6 December 1972.
69. PREM15/1016, Burke to Heath, Northern Ireland – Contingency Planning, 12 December 1972.
70. CAB130/560, Cabinet meeting, 10 Downing Street, 14 December 1972.
71. PREM15/1689, Trend to Heath, 9 February 1973.
72. PRONI/D3591/6 Box 2, 'General criteria against which final proposals should be judged', March 1973; Whitelaw to Faulkner, 22 March 1973.
73. PREM15/1689, Douglas-Home to Peck, 2 January 1973.
74. DT2004/21/3, Meeting between British and Irish officials, London, 1 January 1973.
75. *Boston Globe*, 7 January 1973.
76. PREM15/1689, Peck to Douglas-Home, 4 January 1973.
77. CAB130/633, Gen79 (73) 1, Whitelaw Memo: New Institutions for Northern Ireland, 11 January 1973.
78. PREM15/1689, Meeting between Heath and Whitelaw, 11 January 1973.
79. Interview with Sir Robin Chichester-Clark, London, 25 June 2008.
80. PREM15/1689, Meeting between Whitelaw and the centre group, Stormont, 2 February 1973.
81. PREM15/1689, Meeting between Whitelaw and the centre group, Stormont, 2 February 1973.
82. PREM15/1689, Northern Ireland Cabinet Meeting, Chequers, 10 February 1973.
83. CAB128/51, Cabinet Conclusions, 8 February 1973.
84. *The Times*, 9 February 1973.
85. *The Times*, 22 January 1973.
86. Hansard, vol. 850, cols 646–55, 8 February 1973.
87. PREM15/1689, Meeting between Heath, Whitelaw, Wilson and Rees, Westminster, 8 February 1973.
88. PRONI/D3591/8/K Box 2, Faulkner to Sir Harry Jones, 12 February 1973.
89. *The Irish Times*, 6 February 1973.
90. PREM15/1689, Meeting between Whitelaw, Faulkner, Paisley, Phelim O'Neill and Vivian Simpson, Stormont, 9 February 1973.
91. *The Times*, 13 February 1973.
92. *The Times*, 16 February 1973.
93. PREM15/1689, Northern Ireland Cabinet Meeting, Chequers, 10 February 1973.
94. CAB130/633, Gen79(73)6, Whitelaw Memo: A New Executive, 15 February 1973.
95. CAB130/633, Northern Ireland Cabinet Meeting, Chequers, 19 February 1973.
96. Interview with Dermot Nally, Dublin, 7 March 2008.
97. Interview with Wally Kirwan, Dublin, 7 March 2008.
98. Interview with Noel Dorr, Dublin, 12 July 2007; Interview with Muiris Mac Conghail, Dublin, 24 July 2007.
99. PREM15/1691, Meeting between Whitelaw and the DUP, Stormont, 13 March 1973.
100. PRONI/D3591/6 Box 2, 'General criteria against which final proposals should be judged', March 1973.
101. *The Times*, 2 March 1973.
102. *The Times*, 9 March 1973.
103. *The Times*, 10 March 1973.
104. PREM15/1691, Meeting between Heath and Cosgrave, 10 Downing Street, 9 March 1973.
105. PREM15/1691, Meeting between Whitelaw and the Alliance Party, Stormont, 14 March 1973.
106. PREM15/1691, Meeting between Heath and Cosgrave, 10 Downing Street, 9 March 1973.
107. PREM15/1690, Meeting between Heath and Cosgrave, 10 Downing Street, 8 March 1973.
108. CAB130/633, GEN 79 (73) 14, Contingency Planning, 13 March 1973.
109. PREM15/1691, Meeting between Whitelaw and the United Loyalist Council, Stormont, 14 March 1973.
110. *Northern Ireland Constitutional Proposals* (London: HMSO, 1973).
111. *The Times*, 21 March 1973.
112. *The Times*, 28 March 1973.
113. CAB128/51, Cabinet Conclusions, 22 March 1973.
114. Interview with UK Representative Office official.

115. Poll conducted by Carrick James Market Research, with a sample representative of religion, sex, age and class from 950 voters. See *Fortnight*, 21 May 1973, p 7.
116. CAB128/52, Cabinet Conclusions, 3 May 1973.
117. PRONI/D/3591/6 Box 2, Whitelaw to Faulkner, 22 March 1973.
118. PRONI/D/3591/6 Box 2, Commentary on White Paper: Pros and Cons, March 1973.
119. PRONI/D/3591/6 Box 2, Whitelaw to Faulkner, 22 March 1973.
120. PRONI/D/3591/6 Box 2, Draft/Unionist proposals, March 1973.
121. *The Times*, 13 April 1973.
122. *The Times*, 5 May 1973.
123. *The Times*, 12 December 1972.
124. Interview with Stratton Mills, Belfast, 21 December 2007.
125. *The Times*, 23 May 1973.
126. Interview with Sir Robin Chichester-Clark, London, 25 June 2008.
127. *The Times*, 9 May 1973.
128. PRONI/D/3591/7 Box 3, Meeting between Whitelaw and Tughan, Stormont, April 1973.
129. D. McKittrick, S. Kelters, B. Feeney and C. Thornton, *Lost Lives: The Stories of the Men, Women and Children who Died as a Result of the Northern Ireland Troubles* (Edinburgh: Mainstream Publishing, 1999), pp.371–4.
130. Interview with Leslie Morrell, Belfast, 4 January 2001.
131. Interview with Basil McIvor, Spa, 24 August 2001.
132. PREM15/1694, Heath to Cosgrave, 4 August 1973.
133. CAB130/633 (GEN 79), Cabinet Meeting, Downing Street, 12 July 1973.
134. PREM15/1694, Meeting between Whitelaw and Fitt, Stormont, 10 July 1973.
135. PREM15/1694, Meeting between Whitelaw and Napier, Stormont, 11 July 1973.
136. CAB128/52, Cabinet Conclusions, 26 July 1973.
137. PREM15/1694, Meeting between Whitelaw and Faulkner, Stormont, 10 July 1973.
138. Hansard, vol. 857, cols 1750–1, 14 June 1973.
139. PREM15/1694, Meeting between Whitelaw and Craig, Stormont, 11 July 1973.

The Whitelaw Settlement

On 31 July 1973 the Northern Ireland Assembly's first sitting ended in fiasco. After 'pledged unionist' Nat Minford was elected to act as the assembly's presiding officer, by thirty-one votes to twenty-six, Paisley and his supporters took over the chamber and installed one of their own members in Minford's chair.[1] Despite Paisley's disruptive antics, only Vanguard refused to participate in the drafting of the assembly's standing orders and Faulkner was encouraged by signals from the SDLP that they had no difficulty in accepting Whitelaw's Constitution Act. More than that, Fitt indicated that his party would not insist on holding talks on the Council of Ireland proposals prior to the formation of a Northern Ireland Executive, nor did he think the question of recognising the RUC would be a real stumbling block in the political talks process.[2] Following a meeting between the SDLP leadership and the Irish government, Fitt backtracked, telling the British that his party could not join an executive without policing being addressed in an all-Ireland context.[3] Hume believed that Cosgrave would place the Garda Síochána under the control of a Council of Ireland[4] and he wanted the RUC's name changed to the Northern Ireland Police Service. Although Fitt had recently been unanimously elected as SDLP leader, the Dublin–Derry axis largely determined party policy, and the charismatic West Belfast MP was completely out of step with its thinking.

Hume exercised considerable influence in shaping Irish government policy towards Northern Ireland during this period, and he himself described the SDLP's 'influence in those days' as 'total'.[5] To say the Hume tail at all times wagged the Fine Gael–Labour dog would be an exaggeration. His ideological outlook was symmetrical to that of Dublin's roving diplomat in Northern Ireland, Seán Donlon, who was the government's principle source of intelligence there. Consequently, the

DFA's policy line strongly reflected Hume's views.[6] More than that, 'very much reliant on the SDLP and Donlon',[7] the Irish government feared that if it departed too far from the SDLP line, then the northern nationalists might publicly criticise its approach and Fianna Fáil would fall in behind them.[8] This was a significant factor. Those within Fianna Fáil who viewed their party as the 'keepers of the holy grail', in Irish nationalist terms, viewed the coalition as 'an illegitimate government', and one that lacked the 'moral authority' to negotiate with the British over the future of Ireland.[9] This was something that the new government was acutely aware of, and tensions over this issue were ever-present between FitzGerald and O'Brien. O'Brien believed that the DFA was yielding to pressure from Hume far more than was necessary, correct, or prudent, for the SDLP's interests were not the same as those of the Irish government. Hume was working for immediate Irish unity. Although the Irish government 'wanted Irish unity in theory', and was constitutionally obliged to pursue this goal, it also was obliged to take into consideration the political, economic and military impact that unity would have on the Republic.[10]

O'Brien's instincts were not idiosyncratic. Wilson was shocked by the response he received when he pooled the idea of uniting Ireland in approximately ten years to members of the Irish government in 1971. Wilson's public relations chief Joe Haines recalls that if Lynch 'could have caused the floor to open up and dropped us through it, he would have done so', as 'it was quite clearly something that they didn't want'. So much so that the British came away with the impression that while the Irish were happy to have 'the grievance' of partition, they did not want 'a solution'.[11]

The imposition of direct rule had shattered the old Conservative and Unionist Party alliance in the UK. In contrast, Hume found it relatively easy to carve out 'a common negotiating position' with the Fine Gael–Labour coalition government and, for a time, create a unity of purpose between southern and northern nationalists. Lynch would not have been so pliable. And critical of the new Irish government's 'soft' attitude towards unionism, the SDLP leaders argued that if their demands were presented with a 'strong and firm' enough line from Dublin, then they could be accepted. The SDLP identified policing as the crunch issue on which the whole process hinged; therefore they would demand a Council of Ireland with jurisdiction over policing in

Northern Ireland. Seeking to reassure the coalition government, the SDLP leaders argued that should tripartite negotiations succeed, the IRA were so weak that they might disappear altogether.[12] Hume linked committing the SDLP to join an executive in the future with securing an early tripartite conference to discuss the Council of Ireland proposals with the British. Furthermore, the Irish government hinted to the British that progress of this sort might result in a friendly settlement to the Strasbourg case.[13]

On 17 September 1973 Heath met Cosgrave at Casement Airport, Baldonnel, for what was the first meeting of its kind to take place on Irish soil. Heath told Cosgrave that the time had passed for 'fancy ideas' such as the SDLP's notion of having the RUC abolished. Faulkner's pledged unionists, the SDLP and Alliance would form an executive on the basis of the Northern Ireland Constitution Act 1973.[14] The two governments, he said, should commit firmly to holding a tripartite conference after, rather than before, the executive was formed, otherwise Craig and Paisley would have to be invited and agreement would not be reached.

The Irish took quite the opposite view. Cosgrave argued that a tripartite conference must seek to reach agreement on a 'package basis', addressing the formation of the executive, police reform and the Council of Ireland proposals together. He suggested that it might be possible to hold such a conference after the executive had been formed, but before it actually took office as Northern Ireland's devolved government.[15] Heath told Cosgrave that his priority in Northern Ireland was to end direct rule within a defined time period. British public opinion would not tolerate a further period of 'uncertainty or temporary direct rule'; therefore executive formation would take place between the Northern Ireland parties and the secretary of state alone. Failure to form an executive would greatly increase pressure from unionist quarters for 'permanent direct rule and full integration of Northern Ireland into the UK'. The SDLP, he said, were wrong to imagine that the British government would impose an executive on the unionists, and he implored Cosgrave to stop them from overplaying their hand, especially at a time when Faulkner's flank was exposed.

The Council of Ireland was the issue of paramount importance for the Irish government in the forthcoming negotiations; the establishment of a power-sharing executive was simply a means by which it might realise this objective. They were determined to prevent the negotiations over the Council of Ireland proposals from being sidelined by the negotiations over executive formation and, equally, to prevent the SDLP from being distracted by the allure of power-sharing in the North. Irish officials argued that reaching agreement at a conference on the all-Ireland bodies would make it easier for the SDLP to cooperate on executive formation. The British government's focus was entirely different. With the exception of security, Heath's primary objective was to see every aspect of administering Northern Ireland devolved from Westminster as quickly as was practicably possible. If a conference on the Council of Ireland proposals was held prior to the Northern Ireland Executive's formation, he argued, then the SDLP would make its participation in government conditional on the establishment of an all-Ireland body with executive functions and a powerful structure. Such a move would further exacerbate Faulkner's difficulties and diminish the prospect of procuring a power-sharing settlement.

Heath inadvertently summed up the gulf that existed between the two governments over how they perceived the Northern Ireland troubles. As long as the Northern Ireland parties 'looked to external powers to take decisions', he said, 'they would never come to grips with responsibility'.[16] This was not at all how the Irish government viewed itself, or the future role it envisaged the SDLP playing in a Northern Ireland government. They stressed that the SDLP might boycott the executive should prior agreement on a Council of Ireland's functions, as part of a package deal that included police reform, not be forthcoming. The British ambassador to Ireland, Arthur Galsworthy, advised the Irish that both Fitt and Hume had recently informed him that they would be prepared to form an executive if there was a firm commitment to convene a tripartite conference on the Council of Ireland within one month. Cosgrave retorted that the SDLP would find itself in 'an impossible position' should it enter into an executive 'without a firm commitment to a Council of Ireland with executive functions'. Galsworthy said that if the executive was formed after a tripartite conference, then the SDLP would use this to extract every last concession on their wish list and leave Faulkner in an 'impossible position'. Heath concluded that the two parties had to face 'political reality and learn to live together'; the more they looked to the British and Irish governments for their cue, 'the less likelihood there is that they will get to live together'.[17]

So frustrated was Heath by this tetchy encounter that he took it upon himself to publicly reiterate remarks he had made privately to Cosgrave. Should the government's constitutional proposals not be successfully implemented by March 1974, he said, Northern Ireland would experience a new form of direct rule. This would be 'arranged on an integrated UK basis', as it would be more desirable to 'create a fresh form of government' than return to a form of direct rule on a 'temporary basis'.[18] These comments drew consternation from Wilson,[19] forcing Heath to state that there had been no change in the government's policy on Northern Ireland.[20] Whitelaw was livid, as he knew all too well that, given the choice of full integration or a power-sharing executive with a Council of Ireland, Faulkner's opponents would attempt to reconcile the unionist population with the former to ensure that the latter was stillborn. Moreover, there was speculation that Whitelaw would soon be moving to the Department of Employment to address the government's worsening relations with the trade unions. And buoyed by Heath's gaff, Craig stated publicly, on 28 September, what he had told Whitelaw in private: 'if the new constitution act is the price of peace, then war is preferable and ... if this constitution is Britain's price for maintaining the union, then independence is preferable.'[21]

Caught out playing the British government off against the Irish government, the SDLP leaders reacted furiously to Galsworthy's apparent misrepresentation of their position to the Irish, and used it as a further excuse to drag their feet over agreeing to all-party talks.[22] Severely criticised by Dublin for seemingly having abandoned their joint approach, Hume and Fitt vehemently denied Galsworthy's assertions.[23] They emphasised that there had been no change to the SDLP's basic position: there had to be a firm and detailed commitment to a Council of Ireland with visible movement on the issues of internment and policing. Back on message, Hume argued that the SDLP should not commit itself to an executive until they had seen the shape of the total package. While Faulkner was at his weakest, he argued, it was imperative to ensure that unionism was inextricably tied to a fully negotiated and agreed Council of Ireland prior to the formal establishment of a power-sharing administration. If the executive was established first, he said, Faulkner would not be able to agree to a Council of Ireland and the pressure he faced from London to do so would be 'turned down, if not off'.[24] Conversely, if the executive was frozen pending agreement on a comprehensive package, the British would be very keen to conclude proceedings and, in such circumstances, would make concessions on a Council of Ireland. Currie agreed with Hume. He too had no faith that Faulkner would honour anything that he agreed to in all-party talks without pressure from London and Dublin. Moreover, Bradford was doing his utmost to convince Currie that the SDLP would 'be better off with him as leader than Faulkner'.[25] Although they did not think his chances of leading the Official Unionists into an executive were particularly strong, Hume certainly preferred him to Faulkner.[26] Faulkner was prepared for talks with the SDLP over executive formation, but insisted that should they refuse to accept the Constitution Act, then his party would withdraw from the negotiations. He expected the northern nationalists to abandon the rent and rates strike, accept the RUC as Northern Ireland's police force and acknowledge that the release of detainees should take place in line with decreasing levels of violence.

* * * *

On 5 October 1973 Whitelaw began a series of intensive negotiations at Stormont Castle with the parties he hoped would form a power-sharing executive – Faulkner's pledged unionists, the SDLP and the Alliance Party. At the start of the talks, Whitelaw raised Heath's notion of integrating Northern Ireland into the UK, only to shoot it down as a policy option that lay outside the rubric of his thinking. By entering the castle talks, the SDLP were relinquishing the nationalist objective of achieving a united Ireland as of right, and the Official Unionists the right to govern Northern Ireland through majority rule. The talks got off to an uncontroversial start, the parties reaching agreement on a number of socio-economic issues, and this served as a first step towards building trust between Faulkner and the SDLP. When the nationalist negotiators met Donlon for a debriefing in County Louth, they reported that of the three 'contentious' issues raised by Whitelaw – policing, detention and the Council of Ireland – the last of these appeared to be the least problematic for Faulkner and that 'rent and rates' could also be added to the list.[27]

The same day, another round of Anglo-Irish talks over the Council of Ireland proposals took place. The Irish stated that a mere 'talking shop council' would be unacceptable to both their government and the nationalist minority in Northern Ireland. Although they appreciated that significant all-Ireland bodies would require 'careful selling to the unionists', this could be achieved as the Irish government's participation in any such entity implicitly carried with it 'an acceptance by Dublin of the Northern Ireland institutions'.[28] The British relayed Faulkner's negative reaction to the idea of an all-Ireland consultative assembly; unionists feared that it might turn out to be an all-Ireland parliament in embryo. The basic question facing the Irish government was whether to ignore unionist concerns and negotiate towards a council that would itself form the heart of a future government, or recognise those concerns and opt for an administrative forum for bringing the two governments together. Under the former approach the Irish envisaged a council that would initially act on the principle of unanimity, prior to evolutionary developments. For the most part, the British described their position on the issue as one of 'benevolent neutrality', their interest being 'contingent rather than direct'. Thus the Council of Ireland proposals were essentially something for politicians from both jurisdictions in Ireland to agree upon among themselves. Having no 'theological problems' with the concept of devolving executive power, or power that might be devolved at some future point on reserved matters, the British would not block agreements reached between North and South. Since the ministerial executive body would be the most important component of a Council of Ireland, they felt that the formation of a consultative assembly should be negotiable. Policing and security powers were not going to be devolved and the British were adamant that the RUC would not come under the remit of any all-Ireland body, unless the Irish were considering devolving the responsibilities of the Garda Síochána.

The Irish were encouraged that the British saw 'nothing repugnant' in their 'long-term conviction that a Council of Ireland will eventually be a government of Ireland'. However, the British did not want to appear to be 'pushing the unionists into everything', thus it was important to 'carefully consider how best to bring the unionists along'.[29] To enable a spirit of cooperation to develop, the British recommended that the council should begin by considering relatively minor and non-controversial subjects. The Irish flatly rejected this approach as it amounted to the mere institutionalisation of existing methods of cooperation in an all-Ireland framework. Their principle objective was to 'set up an institution which could evolve into an all-Ireland government, elected by and responsible to an all-Ireland electorate'. Achieving this aim would require a ministerial, parliamentary and administrative council with membership proportionate to the population, North and South, with approximately twenty and forty members respectively, and with a five-sixths weighted majority required for important decisions. British officials made the point that the Irish plan 'outlined exactly what the unionists feared about the Republic's proposals – that the council would become the precursor of an all-Ireland government' in which they would constitute little more than a significant minority. They were firmly of the view that if the council was to get off the ground then the Irish should 'play down this aspect of their plans' and 'cut down' the length, if not the substance, of the ambitious list of functions that they had drawn up for a Council of Ireland.[30]

Anxious to enhance their role and status in the negotiations, the Irish implored the British to make progress on the Council of Ireland while the Northern Ireland parties were preoccupied with the talks process. However, the British viewed progress at Stormont as a means of reducing Dublin's influence, either indirectly through the SDLP or directly through the Anglo-Irish talks – 'bringing the Irish into play if they are a helpful factor, and keeping them at arm's length when (as so often, and as now) they are likely to disturb things'. Thus the British remained keen to delay tripartite discussions over the Council of Ireland proposals until after the executive had been formed. They believed that this would make it more difficult for the Irish to play the 'SDLP card', and that it might result in the emergence of a less ambitious all-Ireland body. These were the precise reasons why the Irish were fixed on holding the talks prior to executive formation.[31]

On the thorny question of recognising Northern Ireland's constitutional status, the Irish took the view that they would almost certainly lose a referendum on the question of whether to abolish or amend Articles 2 and 3 of the Irish constitution. Interestingly, Heath recalls Cosgrave telling him that he 'was prepared to change the constitution', but then dropped the idea completely.[32] Changes to these articles were being considered in the context of a rewriting of the constitution with reference to the position of Northern Ireland and the EEC, steps which FitzGerald seemingly favoured. The Irish were mindful that during tripartite talks, any announcement on the question of its status regarding the acceptance rather than recognition of Northern Ireland's constitutional position should be made as an oral declaration. A written international agreement of this sort might leave the government open to legal challenge as being *ultra vires* of Article 2 of its constitution. The civil service college at Sunningdale was suggested as a venue for the tripartite talks, which would be chaired by the secretary of state and last for three to four days. The Irish wanted a rotating chairman or a neutral third-party representative to oversee the negotiations. The British rejected this idea as it would be difficult for Faulkner to compromise on sensitive issues if, for example, FitzGerald was in the chair. Moreover, it would be counterproductive to have an arbitrator who had not been privy to the complex negotiations between the three Northern Ireland parties.

In Blackpool, Wilson found himself out of step with developments in British politics. In reference to Heath's slender parliamentary majority, and the prospect of a hung parliament following an election, he remarked that Labour would not be sharing power with anybody. Taking a similar line, Heath dismissed suggestions that he should include maverick Conservative MP Enoch Powell in his cabinet. If his party was to maintain 'firm government', he retorted, it was impractical to openly invite disunity over policy. Whitelaw countered these inauspicious British instincts towards the concept of sharing political authority, arguing that power-sharing between unionists and nationalists was workable; Faulkner's unionists and the SDLP both accepted the Constitution Act, under which they would work for the good of Northern Ireland as a whole with its position within the UK safeguarded.

During the first two weeks of talks disagreements between the parties were, more often than not, over ideological points of principle concerning the executive's socio-economic programme rather than sectarian in nature. Devlin accused Bradford of 'acting like a civil servant' during a dispute over public housing targets, and the manner in which the latter was deserted by his liberal unionist colleagues during these debates epitomised the healthy political relationships that were blossoming between the three parties. Agreement soon fell foul to unionist party politics, however, when Faulkner reneged on promises he had made to the SDLP over controversial issues such as having a mace and a sergeant-at-arms in the new Northern Ireland Assembly.[33] Cognisant of Faulkner's need to score political points on issues that were only of symbolic importance to Irish nationalists, the SDLP men swallowed defeat on the matter. Although it was a sign of the SDLP's growing political maturity,[34] it illustrated just how tenuous Faulkner's position was at the outset of the negotiations; there was practically no aspect of the political process on which he could be certain of carrying his party's full support.

The SDLP maintained pressure on the more substantive issues in the talks. When Faulkner's assembly group was diminished by the death of David McCarthy, and through the election of Nat Minford as assembly speaker, Devlin challenged his self-declared right to lead an executive and threatened to nominate Fitt for the position of chief executive.[35] On 23 October the Official Unionist standing committee further reduced Faulkner's margin for error, backing his stance in the talks by 132 votes to 105, and party rebels West and Taylor threatened to call a meeting of the UUC to debate the matter further.[36] Unsure of whether he could presently secure a majority, Faulkner was desperate to avoid a debate on his party's ruling body until it was clear that an executive would be formed and that he would have a majority on it. More than that, he hoped that the Orange Order would quit the party altogether, for the absence of its representatives on the UUC would provide him with a more secure footing.

On 16 October, when Whitelaw presented policing proposals to the parties, the SDLP were so dissatisfied by what the British were prepared to offer that they considered boycotting the next meeting. Although the RUC's name and uniform presented difficulties for the party, Hume conceded that he did not wish to see the 'present police force broken up in any way', simply the removal of certain officers who had been involved in improper practices. Donlon advised the British that as part of a package of security reforms, the SDLP might be persuaded to stick with the name RUC. He made it clear that the Irish government would face real difficulties in handing authority for the Garda Síochána over to an all-Ireland policing authority. Whitelaw insisted that the RUC would remain the police service of Northern Ireland, a number of assembly members would be brought onto a reconstituted police authority, and independent police inquiry procedures would be introduced. Moreover, the SDLP pressed for the Northern Ireland civil service recruitment procedures to be reformed; given the lack of Catholic representatives in its senior ranks, they said that nationalists regarded it as a Protestant preserve.

Faulkner's assembly group were beginning to see the potential benefits that joint-security initiatives might deliver under a Council of

Ireland. Bradford suggested introducing 'a mechanism to formalise co-operation on policing between the North and the South',[37] and Faulkner agreed with his rival, provided that both sovereign governments retained a power of veto over all proposals.[38] The 'pledged unionists' had not yet grasped the significance of the Council of Ireland proposals to the Irish government, nor had they recognised the determination of both FitzGerald and Hume to make them the centrepiece of any Anglo-Irish agreement that emerged following the castle talks. 'Pledged unionist' Basil McIvor admitted that they simply did not view the proposals as 'a very big issue'. More than that, this was an aspect of the political process which Faulkner regarded as 'a red herring'.[39] His unionist opponents, however, were quick to realise that the idea of a Council of Ireland could be used as a wedge issue with which to oppose Whitelaw's reforms, reject power-sharing and press for a return of the old Stormont regime. As Austin Currie put it, the Council of Ireland was identified at an early stage 'as a symbol to those who were opposed to it as well as those who were in favour of agreement'.[40]

By mid-October the atmosphere in the talks had dramatically changed. The SDLP were convinced of Faulkner's commitment to reaching a settlement and making power-sharing work, while the Irish government had established secret contacts with the unionist leader. On 26 October Dermot Nally of the Taoiseach's Office travelled with Donlon to Faulkner's home to set out their government's thinking on the possible functions and structures that a Council of Ireland might be expected to have. Faulkner did not inform his colleagues of their visit, but he relayed unionist fears that a consultative assembly might impede all-Ireland progress at ministerial level; 'wreckers' on both sides might use a parliamentary forum to disrupt executive decision-making. He told his guests that he could accept a ministerial council with executive powers, if it was required to refer agreed decisions back to the parliaments in Belfast and Dublin for ratification. Moreover, the Irish government's use of the grandiose term 'Council of Ireland' and the word 'reconciliation' – which was doublespeak for reunification in unionist phraseology – was not helping him sell these ideas. And when he learned that FitzGerald was planning to visit Northern Ireland at the end of the month, Faulkner warned the Officials that this would be a totally counterproductive exercise at what was a critical juncture in the negotiations, for unionists would assume that a takeover by Dublin was already underway.[41]

On the 30 October, when the castle talks focused on the question of detention, Alliance and the SDLP took the position that the formation of an executive should be preceded by large-scale prisoner releases and a government statement indicating that internment would be brought to an end by a specific date. Napier argued that the only way to restore faith in the judicial process was to release the detainees all at once. Rejecting this suggestion, Faulkner argued that releases must only take place on the basis of the security threat that each detainee posed. He agreed, however, that the sooner detainees not deemed to be a security threat were released the better. Internment was not simply a security issue and, with the exception of Bloody Sunday, Hume said that it remained the most significant factor in the IRA's ability to attract new recruits. Moreover, the SDLP could not guarantee the Catholic community's support for the police in the absence of considerable movement on this issue. Currie reminded his new colleagues that the SDLP were currently associated with the 'poachers' in Northern Ireland, whereas Faulkner remained on the side of the 'gamekeepers'.[42] Therefore, the SDLP felt that their position would be damaged if an executive were established prior to the ending of internment, as then they would be acquiescing in the continuity of the government's detention policy. The fact that only thirty of the current detainees were loyalists, while loyalists were responsible for the recent escalation of sectarian murders, reinforced the nationalist negotiator's concerns.

Despite Faulkner's protestations, FitzGerald made his presence felt during the negotiations over the Council of Ireland proposals by making an unannounced visit to Northern Ireland. Whitelaw was particularly vexed as the unionists saw it for what it was – the Irish government arriving in Belfast to reinforce the SDLP's position from outside the talks. Paisley exerted further pressure on Whitelaw, requesting a meeting with Heath to discuss the 'reserved' issues of policing and detention.[43] Paisley demanded to know why the voices of twenty-seven unionist assembly members who opposed the white paper were going unrepresented in the talks. If the British continued its policy of exclusion, he warned, unionist leaders might be unable to prevent their supporters from 'taking to the streets'. The government, he said, was forcing constitutional loyalists into taking unconstitutional action.[44]

Inside the talks, the parties were divided over four issues: whether a Council of Ireland should have executive functions; whether it should have a policing role; whether it should have a permanent secretariat; and whether it should have the potential to evolve over time. Faulkner wanted an all-Ireland body that was purely consultative in its functions, whereas the SDLP and Alliance favoured a body that had an independent governmental tier, executive powers and scope for further enlargement. The British were keen for a Council of Ireland to operate at an intergovernmental level, between the assembly and the Irish parliament, on the basis of equal representation, and without an Anglo-Irish tier. The SDLP's Council of Ireland proposals were simply a distilled version of the Irish government's proposals: they wanted a body that enjoyed 'exclusive executive functions in certain fields' and 'powers to harmonise structures, laws and services in both parts of Ireland', with consultative and advisory mechanisms administered by a secretariat that constituted its own civil service. Its executive functions should include tourism, electricity, transport, regional planning in border areas, law enforcement and policing. Furthermore, they wanted an all-Ireland court attached to the council, with functions relating to its law enforcement role.

Focusing on what he wanted in return for his party's agreement to establish a Council of Ireland, Faulkner stated that the Irish government must recognise the right of the people of Northern Ireland to determine their own affairs. More than that, the first priority of any all-Ireland body must be to coordinate law enforcement provisions against cross-border terrorism. Unionists could accept an all-Ireland council that enjoyed equal representation from the assembly and the Irish parliament, if it operated under unanimous decision-making procedures with weighted majorities required from both houses on all issues of policy. This would lack the executive authority to override either the Belfast or Dublin governments and operate without a consultative assembly. If there was to be such an assembly, both Faulkner and Alliance opposed the suggestion that the ministerial tier should be accountable to it, stressing that this was more than the unionist community could accept. The SDLP stuck to the Hume–FitzGerald line. The Council of Ireland proposals could not be detached from the negotiations over internment and policing; therefore a tripartite conference must establish consensus between all the parties on a package prior to executive formation. Whitelaw warned the SDLP that if the executive was not even formed 'in embryo' before that point, it might not be possible to exclude from a conference those parties who were completely opposed to the establishment of any all-Ireland institutions and who might wish to disrupt them.[45] Hume stressed that the SDLP was unwilling to compromise on the timing of the tripartite conference, but Whitelaw's threat to include the anti-white paper unionists had its desired effect on Currie and Fitt, who promised to consider the proposals put forward by the government.

Faulkner's ability to sell the idea of establishing a Council of Ireland to mainstream unionism depended on the degree to which he was successful in securing significant gains on security issues and on the broader constitutional relationships between the UK and the Republic of Ireland. This meant ending the Irish government's irredentist constitutional claim to the territory of Northern Ireland or, failing that, having its present status recognised in a treaty, between the Westminster and Dublin parliaments, which acknowledged that Northern Ireland's status could only be altered by the consent of its people through a referendum. Facing threats to his leadership of the unionist community from within his own negotiating team, the wider Official Unionist Party, Vanguard, and the DUP, there was scant possibility of Faulkner maintaining his position should he agree to attend a tripartite conference prior to the formation of an executive. Internally, Bradford was leaking information about both the negotiations and unionist party meetings to the press, so much so that the British were considering whether he could be 'bought off'.[46] Taylor and West were mounting a leadership challenge from the 'unpledged' camp, while Craig and Paisley both sought to force the British into dealing with them by destroying Faulkner.[47] Although the British were well aware of Faulkner's frailties, they had failed to either alter the Irish government's stance on the tripartite conference or completely separate the SDLP from that position, as FitzGerald's intervention illustrated.

Facing a bye-election in Monaghan on 27 November, the Fine Gael–Labour coalition could ill afford to be publicly at odds with the SDLP as the negotiations unfolded in Belfast. Relations between Dublin and the SDLP remained 'close and continuous', and while it was a matter for speculation 'which is the dog and which is the tail at any one moment',[48] the British assumed the SDLP tail had the initiative at this point, as FitzGerald's interference had strained relations within the nationalist camp. Hume and Devlin felt that by exuding such confidence in the North, FitzGerald was fanning the flames of loyalist opposition and giving the impression that the SDLP were on the verge of agreeing to enter an executive without having secured anything on internment and policing.

On 5 November Faulkner raised the possibility of the British government becoming involved in a Council of Ireland and he poured scorn on the idea of establishing all-Ireland judicial institutions; given that both jurisdictions operated under completely separate legal systems, the impracticality of such measures was self-evident. He warned the SDLP that if all-Ireland bodies were to be accepted by and enjoy the support of the Protestant community, pragmatism and practicality, rather than political and ideological adventurism, must be the logic behind their establishment. Again attempting to place the Council of Ireland proposals in an Anglo-Irish context, Faulkner suggested that rather than establishing an assembly on top of a council of ministers, which would give unionists the impression that it was an all-Ireland parliament in waiting, a separate parliamentary body, made up of Northern Ireland Assembly members and representatives from the Dublin and Westminster parliaments, should be established. Since legislation from any Council of Ireland would require the 'consent' of the Westminster parliament, it would therefore be practical to have British MPs sitting on it. Although the idea ran against the grain of British instincts, Whitelaw accepted that it would both allay unionist fears and potentially attract some of Faulkner's critics. More than that, Whitelaw drew a parallel with the Consultative Assembly of the Council of Europe, which the UK had participated in long before joining the European Union.[49]

*   *   *   *

At Westminster, Heath succumbed to pressure and met with Paisley and Official Unionist MP James Kilfedder on 6 November. Paisley stated that had he been aware that Whitelaw would be using the castle talks to address reserved matters such as RUC reform and detention, the DUP would have participated in relation to those matters and 'keep silent when the executive was discussed'. Heath told him bluntly that 'it was not really possible' for him 'to have it both ways'; the issues were being discussed collectively because once the executive was formed it would be acting as an advisory committee to the secretary of state on those reserved matters. Kilfedder then asked Heath what the government's position would be if the envisaged Northern Ireland Executive were to collapse. The prime minister reminded him that the Constitution Act provided for the continuation of direct rule in any such event. Acknowledging that in such circumstances a lot of people would press for the complete integration of Northern Ireland into the UK, Heath stressed that this did not mean that the British government shared this aspiration. Since the government appeared to have already decided that 'there could in no circumstances be total integration', Paisley asked Heath to state this publicly so that the people of Northern Ireland could 'face the reality' of the limited constitutional options that were available to them. Emphasising that he 'did not want to see Northern Ireland wracked by loyalist violence', Paisley warned that 'if the loyalists were not given the safety valve of talks with the secretary of state', then 'there was a danger of violence'.[50]

Back at Stormont, Whitelaw announced that devolution should take place on 1 January 1974. Expecting this deadline to be met, Heath stalled a cabinet reshuffle, fuelling speculation that Whitelaw's time in Northern Ireland was drawing to a close.[51] Having decided that Faulkner would lead a twelve-man executive with a unionist majority, Whitelaw pressured the SDLP to soften its approach over the timing of a tripartite conference and drop its demand for equal representation on the executive.[52] Faulkner's unionists would have six seats, the SDLP four, and the Alliance Party one member with executive voting rights and one member without. The Constitution Act lacked a provision for the appointment of non-voting members who might form part of an overall administration but not sit on the executive itself. Whitelaw could appoint persons to hold non-executive office, however, if the executive was made up of less than twelve; therefore any deviation from this would have to be reached by a one-off informal agreement between the parties, which would last for the duration of the assembly's term.

Faulkner's main problem in this respect was that whichever way Whitelaw configured the executive, in electoral terms, it was impossible to support the political logic that it had to have a unionist majority if it was to consist only of members of the pledged unionists, SDLP and Alliance. There were three possible ways to calculate executive seats in proportion to support: the strength of each party as measured by its number of supporters in the assembly; the strength of each party as measured by the number of first preference votes cast for each of its supporters elected to the assembly; and the strength of each party as indicated by the number of first preference votes cast for its candidates, irrespective of whether or not they were elected. None of these formulas pulled Faulkner over the 50 per cent threshold, nor did any of them grant him a majority of seats in an executive made up of between nine and twelve members. He was at best entitled to half the seats and he did not have the combined weight of the Alliance Party and the SDLP, who held twenty-six seats between them.[53] There was an argument to be made that Faulkner enjoyed the support of many unionist voters that elected 'unpledged' unionist candidates. But given that most of them were, at best, openly unsupportive of the idea of power-sharing, Faulkner was reduced to making what was essentially a nationalist argument; he had to have a majority on the executive as the Constitution Act provided for a power-sharing government that 'is likely to be widely accepted throughout the community'.[54]

In London, Whitelaw informed the cabinet that concessions would have to be made to the SDLP if he was to ensure that Faulkner gained a majority on the executive.[55] He would announce a firm commitment to the idea of establishing all-Ireland bodies, consult with the Irish government and 'all the Northern Ireland parties present on a Council of Ireland' at the end of November, before holding a tripartite conference within a month of forming the executive. In a further attempt to move the negotiations into a conclusive phase, Whitelaw made it clear to FitzGerald that Faulkner 'had very little more to give and, on some issues, could not make any further concessions'. Agreement was 'dependent on the unionists having a majority' on the executive, which, he said, was a reality that neither the SDLP nor the Irish government appeared to be cognisant of. The unionist leader could 'not survive' a name change to the police, and there was absolutely 'no hope' of executive formation taking place without his leadership. Unrelenting as ever, FitzGerald pressed for the establishment of a common law enforcement area through a Council of Ireland, as a means of giving the minority community something in return for accepting that the RUC's name would remain unchanged. Whitelaw warned FitzGerald not to underestimate the 'fears which unionists had about power-sharing'; if Faulkner fell, then the unionist community could become unified in opposition to the Constitution Act.[56]

Faulkner needed the Alliance Party and the SDLP to agree to a unionist majority on the executive before he addressed the UUC on 20 November. This became Whitelaw's unofficial deadline for agreement, as he was set to announce a settlement to the House of Commons two days later. Heath was also aware of Faulkner's precarious position. 'There is no doubt,' Whitelaw told him, 'and the SDLP can be brought reluctantly to acknowledge this – that he must be kept afloat if an executive is to be formed.' Whitelaw conceded, however, that as a 'quid pro quo' for gaining a unionist majority it would be 'advisable to lean towards the SDLP position' on the Council of Ireland proposals. Whitelaw believed that Faulkner could 'go a long way on this' issue, provided that he gained an overall majority on the executive. Given his time constraints, Whitelaw's 'way out' was to hold preliminary inclusive consultations in England between the two governments and all the Northern Ireland parties. This would put Paisley and Craig to the test over their claim to be the representatives of 'excluded' unionism and, at the same time, satisfy the Irish government.[57] The week prior to Faulkner's crucial UUC meeting, in response to an increase in violence designed to derail the talks, Whitelaw proscribed the UFF and their Belfast-based allies the Red Hand Commando, and instructed the security forces to arrest a number of their members as quickly as possible. On 12 November, with Whitelaw eager to reach agreement before the parties could drift apart, substantive talks on executive formation and the Council of Ireland got underway. Having received the message from his party that unionists would view a consultative assembly as an all-Ireland parliament in embryo, Faulkner reiterated his preference for an inter-parliamentary union of the British Isles. Whitelaw backed the SDLP on the necessity of establishing a consultative all-Ireland assembly. He argued that it would enable politicians to meet and discuss common issues in exactly the same fashion as the Council of Europe, and that it would have no real power anyway.

When the discussions turned to executive formation, Fitt mounted a withering attack on Faulkner's position. It was 'ridiculous to demand a unionist majority', he said; all nineteen SDLP and eight Alliance members had pledged their support for the executive, yet it was doubtful whether Faulkner, who 'did not carry his party', could even muster nineteen 'signatures on a pledge of this sort'. Devlin argued that the Catholic community would view it as a complete 'sell-out' if Faulkner's

The Whitelaw Settlement

unionists were given a majority on the executive. Alliance backed the SDLP, insisting that the distribution of executive seats had to be proportional to the support each party carried in the assembly. Faulkner defended his position on the basis of the border poll result and the fact that in the assembly there were fifty-nine pro-union members and only nineteen anti-union. The Alliance negotiators argued that since the fifty-nine members Faulkner had referred to as pro-union included their eight members, then there was 'bound to be a pro-union majority' on the executive. Intervening at this point, Whitelaw stressed that although the phrase 'widely accepted throughout the community' had been inserted in the Constitution Act to protect the minority community, it was 'impossible to ignore its application to the current situation'.

At the end of a very difficult meeting, Faulkner demanded seven seats on the executive, while the SDLP–Alliance negotiators insisted on a five-five-two formula. Linking the issue to the wider negotiations, Hume argued that if Faulkner was granted a majority this would be viewed as a 'defeat for the SDLP', for the media's attention was focused on which party would win the numbers game.[58] The talks broke down without agreement. Whitelaw promised to consult with each party leader over the distribution of seats, but Faulkner was clearly going to pay a high price for the divisions within his ranks and within the unionist community as a whole. Faulkner's fate would depend on how high the SDLP were prepared to raise the stakes before they accepted a unionist majority, and on what Whitelaw was willing and able to do, in the limited time he had available, to rescue the unionist position. During dinner that evening Whitelaw warned the three party leaders that if agreement was not reached then he would invite an outsider to sit on the executive. Moreover, prior to the next round of negotiations scheduled for 19 November, he would decide which executive posts the three parties would occupy.

The following morning Whitelaw met individually with each party leader in efforts to break the deadlock. Faulkner advised him that the only part of an agreement which would carry him through his UUC meeting on 20 November was an overall unionist majority of no less than seven ministers and he was 'in no position to bargain over this'. Whether or not the rest of the 'package' would be helpful to him depended on what it contained. Faulkner believed that the SDLP would attempt to negate the concession that accepting a unionist majority represented to its ideologues, by demanding an agreed package on detention and policing. Although he was surprised by the strength of opposition from within his assembly party to the idea of an all-Ireland assembly, Faulkner thought that this might be reduced if an overall majority was assured. Agreeing that there should be a unionist majority, Whitelaw suggested that the SDLP might accept a six-four-one balance with a fifth SDLP member appointed from outside the executive. This was permissible under Section 8(3) of the Constitution Act. Faulkner indicated that his party had been unaware of this possibility and, in such favourable circumstances, Independent Unionist Anne Dickson and a number of the 'unpledged unionists' might offer their support. Moreover, if Fitt assumed the position of deputy chief executive then his second choice would be the Department of Commerce.[59]

When Whitelaw met with Fitt, the SDLP leader suggested that his party might accept the formula that he had proposed to Faulkner, provided agreement was reached as a package settlement which included policing and detention. If this was possible, Fitt indicated that he would act as deputy chief executive, so long as the three remaining SDLP voting members headed departments of Manpower, Finance, and Health and Social Services, with Ivan Cooper or Eddie McGrady occupying the party's non-executive post.[60] When Whitelaw put this proposal to the Alliance Party leader, Napier insisted that, given his party's lack of trust in the unionists and of Faulkner in particular, if there was an overall unionist majority then its members would not sit on the executive.[61] The British stressed that Faulkner could not control a power-sharing executive, even with a unionist majority, as it had to work collectively. If decisions on a week-to-week basis required a vote and the unionists used their majority to overrule the other two parties, then the power-sharing venture would be very short-lived.

As the government's dispute with the trade unions in Britain worsened, Heath became ever more desperate for Whitelaw to return to frontline politics at Westminster. In the assembly, Craig announced that he was prepared to 'shoulder arms' if Heath attempted to impose an 'undemocratic coalition' government in Northern Ireland.[62] At the Ulster Reform Club the previous day, Whitelaw had issued a rebuke to unionists who might be considering unconstitutional opposition to any agreement that emerged from the castle talks. The British government 'cannot be bullied or coerced', he said, and it 'was not a threat' to say that should the Constitution Act lapse then a very difficult situation would arise in which he, personally, could not imagine that government producing 'any solution more acceptable to the broad mass of opinion in Northern Ireland'.[63] The following day in the House of Commons, Whitelaw challenged Paisley and Craig to 'completely, utterly and totally disassociate themselves from violence and unconstitutional methods'. He said those who sought to 'blur the distinction that exists' between constitutional and unconstitutional opposition were deplorable.[64]

* * * *

November 19 was 'make or break' day for Whitelaw with agreement on a package settlement required by sundown. He would either be returning to Westminster in triumph, his mission accomplished, or he would be recalled by Heath, having brought the parties to the cusp of agreement, only for the Northern Ireland peace process to take second place to the wider electoral considerations of the Conservative Party.[65] Before lunch, Whitelaw presented the negotiators with an 'Inter-Party Talks' heads of agreement paper, setting out the six-four-one executive formula. The SDLP leaders were furious that he had not allocated time for them to discuss the document with their assembly group. Many of them had already read about the paper in the media and Hume accused Whitelaw of leaking it to *The Times* in order to create a pressure cooker atmosphere on the last day of the talks. The paper gave the SDLP something to negotiate away from and Fitt spoke of the 'great concession' his party had already made in accepting that the 'weakest man in the team' would become chief executive. Any renegotiation of the document, he argued, would now be viewed as having been made as a concession to the SDLP. He also complained bitterly about the allocation of ministries outlined in the document. All of the posts designated to the unionists were 'full-scale departments' of considerable importance, whereas the SDLP portfolios, he argued, with the exception of Commerce, had all been split from other departments.[66] Whitelaw feigned complete surprise at the SDLP's angry reaction. He insisted that Commerce was the most important department, which was exactly what he had told Faulkner about Finance the previous week. It offered 'genuine freedom of action' when compared with Finance, he said, which remained subservient to decision-making at Westminster.

When the SDLP again demanded details on the number of detainees that would be released, with the specific dates on which releases would occur, Whitelaw's legendary temper erupted. It would be absolutely disastrous for the executive, he snapped, for him to set a specific release date and then for the paramilitaries to step up their campaign of violence to meet it.[67] Whitelaw appeared to have had little forewarning of just how detached Fitt's private assurances actually were from the SDLP's negotiating position. He noted that when speaking to Fitt in future, the British should never automatically take his view as being that of his party.

Faulkner objected to the SDLP's insistence on a Council of Ireland having its own secretariat and to the holding of preliminary talks ahead of a tripartite conference. Whitelaw told him that an administrative secretariat was necessary for the all-Ireland bodies to function and, given the difficulties that excluding Craig and Paisley posed, intergovernmental talks were required, if only to isolate them.[68] Fitt stressed that the SDLP could not accept preliminary talks at which Craig and Paisley were given a platform. Whitelaw retorted that it was surely in everyone's interests to 'defuse and debunk' Faulkner's opponents in front of the Irish government.[69]

When the negotiations resumed that afternoon, much to Whitelaw's fury, Napier completely rejected the document as a basis for discussion, as there was no place on the executive for Alliance Party assembly member Robert Cooper. Having erroneously assumed that Cooper was qualified to act in a legal capacity to the executive, Whitelaw's document stated that an Alliance member would fill this role. When it transpired that Alliance assembly member Basil Glass was suitably qualified, Cooper took this to mean that the British were offering Napier and Glass a position each at his expense. Having already stated that this aspect of the agreement was non-negotiable, Whitelaw conceded that there could be some further discussion over the allocation of departmental offices. But his patience had finally cracked with the Alliance Party's 'not an inch' position on the six-four-one formula; he was prepared to dispense with them entirely unless they 'more or less' accepted what was on offer.[70] Faulkner demanded a concrete guarantee from Whitelaw that no future change could be made to the unionist majority on the executive as was set out in the heads of agreement paper. Faulkner had also promised the Commerce position to Bradford, while Herbert Kirk was expecting the Finance position, having held it in the last Stormont government. Bradford, however, was willing to accept the Environment ministry on the proviso that it provided him with a 'European outlet' by transferring from Finance the role of coordinating environmental matters with the EEC.[71]

No specific release date would be set for detainees, but under the rubric of a Council of Ireland Whitelaw would consider a common law enforcement area, new extradition procedures and the possibility of coordinating border policing. Returning to the numbers game, he reiterated that a unionist majority on the executive was the government's bottom line; therefore should agreement falter on this point, Alliance and the SDLP would lose everything that they had negotiated. Hume concluded that if this was the case then no agreement could be reached, since the SDLP had gained nothing on the executive's balance, nothing on reserved security issues and nothing on the Council of Ireland proposals. The talks ended in deadlock with Hume accusing Fitt of striking a private deal with Whitelaw at an earlier point in the negotiations. The SDLP leader had been holding out for a departmental post on top of the post of deputy chief executive. Hume opposed this, not least because he already held numerous party positions including Westminster, assembly and local council seats. Nevertheless, having accepted that gaining parity with the unionists on the executive was out of the question, Fitt attempted to distance his party from the numbers game, indicating that the SDLP would compromise if the British moved on the three issues raised by Hume.[72] Fitt and Hume both wanted a position on the administration for SDLP assembly member Ivan Cooper, as they feared that with such a large Provisional IRA following in his Mid-Ulster constituency, he might set himself up as the 'conscience of the party' if he was excluded.[73]

Taking a much firmer line than the SDLP, FitzGerald described Whitelaw's draft agreement as representing 'a number of steps backwards' in the political process and 'unsatisfactory to a dangerous degree'.[74] The Irish had decided not to attend preliminary consultations in England, and he warned Whitelaw not to announce any proposals which concerned his government without first reaching prior agreement.[75] The decision to include Craig and Paisley in preliminary discussions over a Council of Ireland was an 'astonishing turn around' which, he said, would undermine the proposed tripartite conference.

Whitelaw took the opposite view. Openly inviting Craig and Paisley to discussions would flush out the extremist unionist position prior to, and without damaging, the 'real tripartite conference'.[76] Dismayed that the British were determined to form an executive ahead of the tripartite conference,[77] FitzGerald feared that the SDLP would be split from their agreed negotiating position with the Irish government prior to the Council of Ireland negotiations, for the British had already partly achieved this by excluding FitzGerald from the castle talks. He wanted to ensure that the Northern Ireland parties did not have the authority of a Northern Ireland government at the Anglo-Irish negotiations. Moreover, FitzGerald was so enraged at Whitelaw for not having consulted him about the statement he was preparing to make to parliament that he threatened to return immediately from a trip to Copenhagen to meet with him in London or Belfast. Fearing another untimely and disruptive visit, the British firmly rejected this suggestion in the hope that FitzGerald would return to Dublin and be restrained by 'more moderate colleagues'.[78]

With a unionist majority on the executive secured, Faulkner won the argument for participating in a power-sharing executive at the UUC meeting on 20 November, at which 379 delegates voted in favour of the proposal and 369 against.[79] With his party split, Faulkner set out four conditions for entering government with the SDLP: a unionist majority on the executive; an end to the SDLP's support for the rent and rates strike; SDLP support for the police; and binding decision-making on the executive to ensure that the SDLP members on a Council of Ireland could not combine forces with the Irish government to outvote the unionists and act independently.[80]

In another attempt to break the deadlock, Whitelaw presented a fifteen-man executive formula to each of the parties, and gave the SDLP a commitment that the sections of the agreement relating to detention and policing could be enhanced. Whitelaw accepted the SDLP's view that it might be easier to work an executive if, of the 678 persons currently detained, the last 104 people to have been interned by Faulkner were released.[81] The new formula envisaged nine departments in an overall administration comprising fifteen posts: eleven executive members in total – Faulkner and Fitt acting as ministers without portfolio – with four non-voting members outside of the executive.[82] Two non-executive positions – the head of a legal affairs bureau and the head of an information bureau – would be allocated to Alliance who had, in fact, tabled the compromise. The other two positions, EEC Affairs and chief whip of the assembly, would go to the SDLP. These four non-voting members would sit on the executive for meetings of which they were concerned. Delighted with this conciliatory approach, the SDLP emerged in euphoric spirits from their meeting with Whitelaw having accepted the fifteen-man compromise.

Providing a selective account of his discussions with the other two parties, Whitelaw then attempted to sell this compromise to Faulkner after he returned alone from the UUC meeting. Whitelaw informed him that, having finally abandoned their zero-sum approach to the question of a unionist majority, the SDLP and Alliance were prepared to form a fifteen-man executive. Faulkner was sceptical, insisting that if the other parties had requested seats outside the executive, then he would have to do likewise. His party was split down the middle over the process; therefore he could not get away with any more 'fiddling' over numbers. If no compromise could be found, and this was simply a contrivance to satisfy the Alliance Party, Faulkner indicated that he could live with an executive made up of six Official Unionists and five SDLP ministers, conceding only that the six-four-one formula would be attractive if each party held one non-voting member.[83]

Outside the talks, the British complained to FitzGerald about the influence Donlon was exerting over the SDLP, stressing that it was considerably damaging to Anglo-Irish relations if everything that the British embassy told the DFA in confidence was then immediately relayed to the SDLP via their roving intelligence officer in the North.[84] FitzGerald remained insistent that a neutral chairman should be appointed to preside over the Anglo-Irish conference, and suggested that invitations should be issued jointly by the two sovereign governments to the Northern Ireland parties. Having already announced that a tripartite conference would be held, the British argued that this would unnecessarily ruffle unionist feathers at a critical moment in the negotiations. Frustrated that the British government intended to invite 'extremists' such as Craig and Paisley to a preliminary conference, he gave a hostile response to its proposals. British officials stressed to FitzGerald that Whitelaw believed that he had 'pushed the unionist community to the uttermost'. More than that, 'no British government had ever before put so much pressure on the unionists as the present government had'.

When they enquired whether the Irish government would attend if the three Northern Ireland parties agreed to hold a preliminary conference, FitzGerald replied that, 'based on his government's present thinking the answer must be negative'.[85] Irish officials then constrained his room for manoeuvre, leaking details to the press of his split with the British and suggesting that the Irish government would boycott the intergovernmental talks.

On 21 November Whitelaw presented a new document to the parties, setting out a more lenient approach to running down detention, offering around a hundred selective releases and indicating that policing would be discussed if a common law enforcement area was created. Whitelaw stressed, however, that there was no question of the RUC becoming in any way responsible to a Council of Ireland. The British were secretly planning to reduce troop levels from eighteen to fourteen major units by the end of the year and to twelve by Easter 1974.[86] The establishment of a common law enforcement area was the main attraction for the British government in the Council of Ireland proposals, as it held the potential to significantly reduce its military commitments in Northern Ireland. This caused FitzGerald to conclude that he might extract 'a rather higher price' for his government's cooperation than had previously seemed possible. This notion stemmed from a remark which Whitelaw had apparently made to Hume, suggesting that if the present talks failed then the immediate prospect was a 'return to direct rule plus a Council of Ireland'.[87]

In order to secure a Council of Ireland which might organically evolve into a united Ireland, FitzGerald intended to use the common law enforcement issue as a bargaining chip by which to ensure that the all-Ireland bodies had evolutionary powers enshrined in the initial British legislation that brought them into existence. If stages by which they would evolve were not detailed and written into this legislation, then it might prove difficult for a Council of Ireland to act as the formative parliamentary institution through which a united Ireland could be achieved by consent. Consequently, FitzGerald recommended in cabinet that the Irish government should seek to establish a Council of Ireland with the 'powers, responsibilities and financial resources' to enable it to 'evolve, by consent, towards the long-term objective of reintegration'.[88]

Back at Stormont Castle, Hume indicated that the SDLP could agree to form a 'provisional executive' before the tripartite conference and it was agreed that preliminary talks would precede a tripartite conference with the delegates attending as an 'executive designate'.[89] The three parties to a provisional executive would be free to represent their own party positions during preliminary intergovernmental discussions and then form an executive having agreed a common policy. When Whitelaw raised the possibility of inviting the anti-agreement duo to the preliminary conference on the Council of Ireland, admitting that this was a question of political judgement, he suggested to the three parties that it might be easier to defuse loyalist violence if Paisley was kept within the political arena. He argued that while Paisley would probably accept an invitation, Craig would almost certainly refuse to participate and this might drive a wedge between them. He felt that it would be good for the Irish government to have a taste of what it was like to deal with Paisley and learn the hard way that he was not the 'saviour of Ireland'.[90] Bradford thought that if Paisley accepted Whitelaw's invitation, then his opposition to power-sharing would be compromised and he would have implicitly acknowledged the existence of an Irish dimension. Faulkner argued that it was safer not to have a conference until the executive had been formed, as the government would then be able to legitimately shut Craig and Paisley out. Heath also favoured excluding Craig and Paisley from the conference as they were 'quite open' about their intention to 'break it up',[91] thus any participation would only be 'a wrecking participation'.[92] Furthermore, Whitelaw was not formally committed to inviting them to the talks, as the white paper only committed him to consult with leaders of Northern Ireland opinion. But he had promised to hold wide-ranging discussions with Paisley, regarding the Council of Ireland and other matters, before the preliminary discussions occurred.

When the parties returned to the question of executive formation, Napier and Fitt retreated to the position that nothing other than an executive consisting of five unionists, five SDLP and two Alliance members would be acceptable to their parties. The debate went around in circles. Exhausted, Whitelaw told the SDLP that it would be 'a pity' to throw away the 'great advance' of power-sharing that they had gained for the minority community simply by attempting to win a concession that no leader of the unionist community could possibly concede. Emphasising the point, Faulkner reminded them how remarkable it was that the minority community had been offered such a 'strong place in government', for the first time in fifty years, when fifty of the seventy-eight assembly seats were filled by unionists of one shade of opinion or another.

If Whitelaw was to hold to his tight parliamentary schedule, then the executive designate had to be agreed that day. In a last-ditch effort to break the deadlock, he suggested that the Constitution Act could be amended to allow for more than twelve executive posts. The SDLP and Alliance would not budge. Although they accepted that Faulkner should have a unionist majority on the executive, they refused to grant him the same provision on the administration as a whole. Agreement was finally reached on the formation of a two-tier administration, comprised of first- and second-class seats, when the parties accepted Whitelaw's six-four-one formation, after he agreed to appoint four non-voting members who would not be heads of departments. This left the final distribution of seats on the administration at seven-six-two. By shifting the office of manpower services off the executive, Napier had found a position for Robert Cooper on the administration, and Alliance also gained the position of deputy chief whip in the assembly, which was outside of the administration. This meant Napier himself would fill the Office of Law Reform as a department within the executive, which reassured those who wanted to restrain the workings of a Council of Ireland in harmonising the law in the North and South as a prelude to unification. It was bizarre, however, that having finally given up his demand for a second executive position, Napier did not insist on a significant department for himself.

With Whitelaw's helicopter waiting on the lawn, Faulkner agreed to take the ministries of Agriculture, Education, Environment, Finance and Information Services, and the SDLP the positions of Commerce, Health and Social Services, and Housing, Local Government and Planning. Faulkner and Fitt would be chief executive and deputy chief executive respectively, without portfolio. The unionists gained the position of chief whip, with Faulkner acting as leader of the assembly, and the SDLP took the non-executive offices of Community Relations and Executive Planning and Coordination.[93] Changing the Constitution Act to reduce the executive from twelve to eleven seats meant that Whitelaw or his successor would not be able to appoint a 'twelfth man' at some future point, but of course this did not rule out the possibility of Paisley, one of the 'unpledged' unionists, or even Craig, joining the executive in the future. While Faulkner had attained a majority of voting members on the executive, and although Whitelaw had backed him in this respect, the SDLP and the Alliance Party had succeeded in denying him an overall majority in the administration. Out-negotiated, Faulkner agreed that a Council of Ireland should have executive and consultative powers with harmonising functions that enabled it to evolve. Abandoning him on this point, Whitelaw told the unionist leader that there was nothing in it; the harmonisation of the law between North and South would simply allow chartered accountants or solicitors to keep their books in much the same way. Faulkner had focused all his energies on securing a unionist majority, and Minister for Agriculture designate Leslie Morrell stressed that he 'never saw any great problem with the Council of Ireland as long as it was under the control of the assembly'.[94]

After seven weeks of intense and, at times, fraught negotiations, Whitelaw flew off to London 'with tears rolling down his cheeks' to present his unlikely accomplishment to parliament in what was to be his last and most significant speech as secretary of state for Northern Ireland.[95] On 22 November Whitelaw told the House of Commons that he had succeeded in his endeavour to bring the three parties to indicate their willingness to search for a basis on which an executive might be formed within the provisions of the Constitution Act. Therefore, a preliminary conference with the Irish government should lead to the formal appointment of a Northern Ireland Executive. Holding an olive branch to Paisley and Craig, Whitelaw insisted that a Council of Ireland 'must operate with the consent of both majority and minority opinion in Northern Ireland who have a right to prior consultation and involvement in determining its form, functions and procedure'. With the exception of reserved matters, the British government would not be represented on a Council of Ireland, but he stressed that all-Ireland governmental decision-making must take place on the basis of unanimity with mutually reinforcing vetoes enshrined in its legislation from the outset. He warned parliament that this was not a time for 'self-congratulation' as this was merely the beginning of a 'very difficult operation' to regulate Northern Ireland's troubles.[96] And at his humble best, Whitelaw appeared sad and apologetic in departing, at this most untimely and precarious moment, from the role that he had so skilfully played as Ulster's supremo.

Before leaving office, Whitelaw indicated that he would not be consulting with the 'unpledged' Official Unionist members, as Faulkner would be making representations on behalf of his party. Aware that Paisley was scheduled to be in the US until 30 November, he invited Craig and Paisley to put their views to him, individually, on 27 November. They jointly rejected this invitation the following day, describing it as an 'unsatisfactory and futile' means of 'effectively representing majority opinion'.[97] Paisley accused Heath of failing to honour the white paper's pledge to invite 'leaders of majority elected opinion to the Conference on Northern Ireland' which, he said, would have the 'most serious consequences'. Those consequences, he warned Heath, 'will be your responsibility'.[98] The white paper did not actually commit the government to any such thing, as it merely referred to 'the leaders of the elected representatives of Northern Ireland opinion'.[99] Good to their word, Craig and Paisley caused chaos in the assembly the following day, in efforts to whip up a sense of public disaffection with the political process which, at this point, was evidently lacking.

Reaching out to the unionist community by committing his government to do everything within its power to make power-sharing work, Cosgrave told parliament that a settlement in Northern Ireland meant 'agreeing to differ about our long-term aspirations'.[100] Hume was given a hero's welcome by the SDLP assembly members at the alcohol-fuelled celebrations that followed Whitelaw's departure. Devlin told his colleagues that he was 'going home to cry',[101] but they joked that another precedent had that night been set in the history of Northern Ireland, for it was 'the first time Faulkner had been in the bar'.[102] Not everyone shared their sense of excitement and elation over the agreement to form Northern Ireland's first power-sharing executive. The Provisional IRA promised to 'smash it',[103] while Paisley called for the creation of a loyalist coalition of the DUP, Vanguard and the 'unpledged' unionists to destroy it.[104]

NOTES

1. *The Times*, 1 August 1973.
2. PREM15/1695, Cooper to Whitelaw, 5 September 1973.
3. PREM15/1695, Allan to Cooper, 6 September 1973.
4. PREM15/1695, Cooper to Whitelaw, 12 September 1973.
5. Interview with John Hume, Londonderry, 13 September 2001.
6. Interview with Wally Kirwan, Dublin, 7 March 2008.
7. Interview with Declan Costello, Dublin, 23 July 2007.
8. Interview with Dermot Nally, Dublin, 7 March 2008.

The Whitelaw Settlement

9. Interview with Muiris Mac Conghail, Dublin, 24 July 2007.
10. Interview with Dermot Nally, Dublin, 7 March 2008.
11. Interview with Joe Haines, Tunbridge Wells, 19 February 2008.
12. DT2004/21/624, Report on Meetings with the SDLP, Declan Costello, 28 & 29 July 1973.
13. PREM15/1694, Galsworthy to Cooper, 23 July 1973.
14. DT2004/21/624, Meeting between Cosgrave and Heath, Dublin, 17 September 1973.
15. PREM15/1695, Meeting between Heath and Cosgrave, Baldonnel, 17 September 1973.
16. CJ4/468, Meeting between Heath and Cosgrave, Baldonnel, 17 September 1973.
17. DT2004/21/624, Meeting between Cosgrave and Heath, Dublin, 17 September 1973.
18. *Irish Press*, 18 September 1973.
19. CJ4/468, Wilson to Heath, 20 September 1973.
20. *The Times*, 20 September 1973.
21. CJ4/330 GEN 79 (73), Political Developments in Northern Ireland.
22. CJ4/330, Note of meeting between Frank Cooper, Fitt and Devlin, 25 September 1973.
23. DT2004/21/624, Note on Council of Ireland, 25 September 1973.
24. DT2004/21/626, Note of meetings with SDLP members, Donlon, 24 September 1973.
25. Interview with Austin Currie, Dublin, 5 January 2001.
26. DT2004/21/626, Note of meetings with SDLP members, Donlon, 24 September 1973.
27. DT2004/21/624, Meeting between Donlon and SDLP, Ballymascanlon, 6 October 1973.
28. DT2004/21/624, Meeting between British and Irish officials, London, 5 October 1973.
29. DT2004/21/624, Meeting between British and Irish officials, London, 5 October 1973.
30. CJ4/292, Meeting between British and Irish Officials, London, 5 October 1973.
31. CJ4/292, White to Arthur, 26 October 1973.
32. Interview with Lord Heath, London, 4 April 2001.
33. *Belfast News Letter*, 10 October 1973.
34. DT2004/21/624, Meeting between Donlon, Hume and Devlin, Belfast, 17 October 1973.
35. *Guardian*, 11 October 1973.
36. *Financial Times*, 24 October 1973.
37. DT2004/21/624, Meeting between Donlon, Hume and Devlin, Belfast, 17 October 1973.
38. CJ4/331, Meeting between Whitelaw, Alliance, SDLP and the Official Unionists at Stormont Castle, 16 October 1973.
39. Interview with Basil McIvor, Spa, 24 August 2001.
40. Interview with Austin Currie, Dublin, 5 January 2001.
41. DT2004/21/265, Meeting between Donlon, Nally and Faulkner, Downpatrick, 26 October 1973.
42. CJ4/332, Meeting between Whitelaw, Alliance, SDLP and the Official Unionists at Stormont Castle, 30 October 1973.
43. *Guardian*, 1 November 1973.
44. CJ4/332, Paisley's request for a meeting, 31 October 1973.
45. CJ4/332, Meeting between Whitelaw, Alliance, SDLP and the Official Unionists at Stormont Castle, 31 October 1973.
46. PREM15/1695, Hunt to Heath, 1 November 1973.
47. CJ4/332, Note of meeting with Peter McLachlan, 1 November 1973.
48. CJ4/488, Galsworthy to Arthur, 13 November 1973.
49. CJ4/332, Meeting between Whitelaw, Alliance, SDLP and the Official Unionists at Stormont Castle, 5 November 1973.
50. CJ4/332, Meeting between Heath, Paisley and Kilfedder, Westminster, 6 November 1973.
51. *The Times*, 7 November 1973.
52. CJ4/332, Note on meeting between Cooper and SDLP, Laneside, 6 November 1973.
53. CJ4/332, Burns to Trevelyan, 8 November 1973.
54. *Northern Ireland Constitution Act 1973*, Section 2.1 (b) (London: HMSO, 1973).
55. CAB130/633, Cabinet Meeting, Downing Street, 14 November 1973.
56. CJ4/332, Meeting between Whitelaw and FitzGerald, London, 8 November 1973.
57. CJ4/332, Whitelaw to Heath, 9 November 1973.
58. CJ4/332, Meeting between Whitelaw, Alliance, SDLP and the Official Unionists at Stormont Castle, 12 November 1973.

59. CJ4/488, Meeting between Whitelaw and Faulkner, Stormont Castle, 13 November 1973.
60. CJ4/488, Meeting between Whitelaw and Fitt, Stormont Castle, 13 November 1973.
61. CJ4/488, Meeting between Whitelaw and Napier, Stormont Castle, 13 November 1973.
62. *Irish Independent*, 15 November 1973.
63. CJ4/488, Speech at Private Lunch (Draft), Ulster Reform Club, 13 November 1973.
64. Hansard, vol. 864, cols 641–4, 15 November 1973.
65. Interview with Lord Carrington, Knightsbridge, 21 November 2007.
66. CJ4/488, Meeting between Whitelaw and the SDLP, Stormont Castle, 19 November 1973.
67. DT2004/21/625, Donlon to Nally, 20 November 1973.
68. CJ4/488, Meeting between Whitelaw, Alliance, SDLP and the Official Unionists, Stormont Castle, 19 November 1973.
69. CJ4/488, Meeting between Whitelaw and the SDLP, Stormont Castle, 19 November 1973.
70. DT2004/21/625, Donlon to Nally, 20 November 1973.
71. PRONI/D3591/8 Box 1, File B, Bradford to Faulkner, 24 November 1973.
72. CJ4/488, Bob Friend: Interview with Gerry Fitt, 19 November 1973.
73. CJ4/488, Meeting between Allan and Donlon, Laneside, 20 November 1973.
74. CJ4/488, Tel. No. 491, Copenhagen to Dublin and Belfast, 20 November 1973.
75. DT2004/21/625, Cabinet Minutes, 20 November 1973.
76. DT2004/21/625, Donlon to Nally, 20 November 1973.
77. CJ4/488, Tel. No. 491, Copenhagen to Dublin and Belfast, 20 November 1973.
78. CJ4/488, Tel. No. 269, FCO to Dublin, Belfast and Copenhagen, 20 November 1973.
79. Faulkner, *Memoirs of a Statesman*, p.221.
80. *Financial Times*, 21 November 1973.
81. CJ4/488, Meeting between Whitelaw and SDLP, Stormont Castle, 20 November 1973.
82. CJ4/488, Meeting between Whitelaw and Alliance, Stormont Castle, 20 November 1973.
83. CJ4/488, Meeting between Whitelaw and Faulkner, Stormont Castle, 20 November 1973.
84. CJ4/488, Tel. No. 617, Dublin to Belfast, 21 November 1973.
85. CJ4/488, Tel. No. 616, Dublin to Belfast, 21 November 1973.
86. PREM15/1695, Carrington to Heath, 19 September 1973.
87. DT2004/21/624, Donlon to Nally, 6 November 1973.
88. DT2004/21/624, Memo for the Government, 9 November 1973.
89. CJ4/488, Meeting between Whitelaw, Alliance, SDLP and the Official Unionists, Stormont Castle, 21 November 1973.
90. DT2004/21/625, Donlon to Nally, 21 November.
91. Interview with Glen Barr, Londonderry, 22 August 2001.
92. Interview with Lord Heath, London, 4 April 2001.
93. CJ4/488, Meeting between Whitelaw, Alliance, SDLP and the Official Unionists, Stormont Castle, 21 November 1973.
94. Interview with Leslie Morrell, Belfast, 4 January 2001.
95. Interview with Basil McIvor, Spa, 24 August 2001.
96. Hansard, vol. 864, cols 1574–8, 22 November 1973.
97. CJ4/292, Craig/Paisley to Whitelaw, 28 November 1973.
98. CJ4/292, Telegram, Paisley to Heath, 29 November 1973.
99. *White Paper on the Northern Ireland Constitutional Proposals* (London: HMSO, 1973).
100. *Dáil Debates*, 22 November 1973.
101. DT2004/21/626, Note on SDLP meeting, Donlon, 22 November 1973.
102. Interview with Sir Oliver Napier, Holywood, 29 December 2000.
103. *Irish News*, 23 November 1973.
104. *Irish Times*, 23 November 1973.

4

A Salesman for Sunningdale

The 'gloves are off, the friendship is dead' and the 'fire is burning'. This was Paisley's parting shot to Whitelaw's successor, Francis Pym, on the eve of Sunningdale, after the unionist opposition had all but been excluded from the negotiations over Northern Ireland's constitutional future.[1] Storming out of his first meeting with the new Northern Ireland secretary of state, on 4 December, Paisley threatened not only to obstruct the assembly, but to destroy it should he and Craig not be invited to the talks.[2] Pym did invite them both at the eleventh hour, individually, to attend the conference and present their views to its first plenary session.[3] But Paisley exploded with fury at this suggestion, giving Pym a baptism of fire down the phone, frustrated that his plan to lead a delegation of the 'excluded' to challenge the two governments had been thwarted. The only thing the British government understood was violence, Paisley told him, chiding his new adversary with the suggestion that 'the more violent you are, the more Her Majesty's Government listens'. When Pym replied that he appeared to be advocating violence against the state, the DUP leader retorted that the British government no longer allowed him 'to be a good constitutionalist', promising dire consequences in Northern Ireland if the wishes of '300,000 Ulstermen' were ignored.[4]

Whitelaw's transfer to the Department of Employment two days earlier meant that the Sunningdale conference took place without the anchorman who had constructed the framework for the settlement that would bring together unionist and nationalist political representatives in a power-sharing government. Whitelaw was completely opposed to the reshuffle and the prime minister's decision left his colleagues and officials equally aghast.[5] Ken Bloomfield compared Whitelaw's peace process to the construction of a bridge: 'you needed to put the coping stone into the arch and the coping stone was going to be the discussions at Sunningdale', yet 'at precisely that moment', Heath withdrew the politician who had engineered the whole process and took centre stage.[6] Others went further, suggesting that it seemed all too convenient for Heath to redeploy the 'architect of Sunningdale' – a rising star in a cabinet beset by escalating domestic crises – to confront the National Union of Mineworkers and thereby 'get the kudos' for all his achievements.[7] However, it would have been quite out of character for Heath to have acted in this way.[8] It is more realistic to conclude that Heath's reshuffle, and his own absence from large parts of the negotiations, were simply an indication that the government's other priorities had taken precedence over Northern Ireland's peace process. Although Sunningdale was the most important Anglo-Irish summit to take place for half a century, Heath believed that Whitelaw 'had achieved what he wanted'; therefore deploying his diplomatic skills elsewhere was of 'paramount' importance to the government's chances of being re-elected.[9] Moreover, Heath believed that the purpose of the Sunningdale conference was to bring the Irish parties to agreement over the minutiae of a settlement that Whitelaw had already 'fixed'.[10] Heath went there simply 'to tie it all up in a bundle, neatly'.[11]

Heath's belief that Sunningdale was the endgame in Northern Ireland's political process was to have significant repercussions. Whitelaw knew only too well that getting the parties to Sunningdale was just the beginning of what would be a lengthy procedure of reconciliation and conflict management. Therefore his departure was a major turning point in Northern Ireland's peace process, and Heath's decision to replace him was not taken without considerable recrimination. Exhausted and excluded, Whitelaw was left feeling deeply aggrieved.[12] Frank Cooper remarked that by moving Whitelaw, when he was at the height of his powers, Heath caused 'the biggest argument' in the NIO during his time.[13] He might have resigned over the issue and challenged Heath for the leadership of the Conservative Party following an election, but this would have been out of character. Whitelaw had a 'military approach' to politics and an 'old style loyalty' to Heath, as one of his senior officials put it, so 'if he was told to go and deal with the trade unions, [then] he would go and deal with the trade unions'.[14]

At Westminster, the Conservative Party's 1922 Committee cautioned Heath against putting Faulkner under undue pressure in the Sunningdale negotiations.[15] Dispelling any suggestion that his role was to prop up any of the Irish parties, Heath travelled to Sunningdale with the clear objective of protecting British interests, believing Faulkner to be in a 'strong position'.[16] This was not entirely dissimilar to Cosgrave's approach to the negotiations, as his government's primary objective was to achieve 'the maximum position, from a nationalist point of view, without taking account of the Northern Ireland position'.[17] Nevertheless, some of the unionists had not drawn appropriate conclusions from their recent disjuncture with the Conservative government. As they made their way to Sunningdale, Bradford advised Currie that while Heath had 'been against us in the past ... he was going to make up for it now'.[18] Bradford's political outlook was normally a fairly accurate barometer of which way the political winds were blowing in Northern Ireland, but in this instance he could not have been more wrong. Whitelaw's absence not only deprived the unionists of much-needed support, it left them isolated, for there was no senior British politician at the conference who fully appreciated the difficulties that they were going to face in selling a settlement to the unionist community.

In terms of political participation the tripartite conference, which ran from 6–9 December 1973, was nothing of the sort, for the Irish government had succeeded in its objective to enter negotiations with the British prior to the formation of a Northern Ireland Executive. The conference began with a grand plenary session, before breaking into small subgroups for substantive negotiations on specific subjects. These groups reported back to regular plenary sessions, where their conclusions were either discussed and agreed or set aside for further negotiation. The three Northern Ireland parties shared the view that the five parties to the talks should be represented at every substantive negotiation. But before the conference broke into subgroups, Heath told the delegates that his government's 'major interest' at Sunningdale lay in the aspects of governing Northern Ireland that would be reserved at Westminster, the most important of which was policing and justice. Consequently, some issues were primarily for discussion between the Northern Ireland parties and the Irish government. At the top of Heath's agenda was to ensure that the British Army would never again be damaged by security commitments forced upon it by a subordinate UK administration. FitzGerald recalls that Heath disclosed to him, in private discussions, that this 'was a British agenda which was totally at variance' with Faulkner's objectives. Moreover, from the prime minister's perspective, it was one that was non-negotiable.[19]

The purpose of the conference was to agree on a package settlement that would be ratified at a second conference. But there was nothing preliminary about the agenda that Heath presented to the parties concerning the future of Northern Ireland. The Sunningdale conference was rightly perceived by political commentators as the most important negotiations to occur between British and Irish politicians since Michael Collins signed the Anglo-Irish Treaty, on 6 December 1921, a year before the Irish Free State was established. All parties at Sunningdale were aware that if they reached a settlement, and it was subsequently implemented, they would be breathing life into an all-Ireland institution which partition had left stillborn. But those excluded from the negotiations were determined to see history repeat itself; Paisley and Craig sought to ensure that domestic Irish divisions would once again destroy an Anglo-Irish agreement that had been reached on the British mainland.

The Irish delegation travelled to Sunningdale with the ancestral memory of Éamon de Valera staying at home during the 1921 Anglo-Irish Treaty negotiations and the civil war which subsequently erupted. Taoiseach Liam Cosgrave was accompanied by Brendan Corish (Tánaiste), James Tully (Minister for Local Justice), Richie Ryan (Minister for Finance), Garret FitzGerald (Minister for Foreign Affairs), Conor Cruise O'Brien (Minister for Posts and Telegraphs), Paddy Cooney (Minister for Justice) and Declan Costello (Attorney General). This was of course a coalition government and many of these ministers expected to have a future role to play in a Council of Ireland.

In Whitelaw's absence the only senior British politicians that accompanied Heath were Sir Alec Douglas-Home (Foreign Secretary), who attended until lunchtime the following day, and Sir Peter Rawlinson (Attorney General). The Northern Ireland Office team was headed by Frank Cooper, with David Howell (Minister of State) and senior officials Philip Woodfield and Dennis Trevelyan. Northern Ireland was represented by the fifteen men who would form its first power-sharing administration: Brian Faulkner (Chief Executive) and Official Unionist ministers John Baxter (Information), Roy Bradford (Environment), Herbert Kirk (Finance), Basil McIvor (Education), Leslie Morrell (Agriculture), Gerry Fitt (Deputy Chief Executive) and SDLP ministers Austin Currie (Housing, Local Government and Planning), Paddy Devlin (Health and Social Services) and John Hume (Commerce); and Oliver Napier of the Alliance Party (Legal Minister and Head of the Office of Law Reform); with non-executive SDLP ministers Ivan Cooper (Community Relations) and Eddie McGrady (Planning and Co-ordination), Robert Cooper of the Alliance Party (Manpower Services) and Official Unionist Lloyd Hall-Thompson (Chief Whip).

They were supported by the head of the Northern Ireland civil service, David Holden, and Ken Bloomfield, who was to become permanent secretary to the executive. The Northern Ireland political representatives attended Sunningdale as delegates of the Alliance Party, the SDLP and the Official Unionist Party. They were not there as representatives of a Northern Ireland government nor would they negotiate as an executive designate. At the Irish government's insistence, they represented the interests of their respective political parties and negotiated separately on their behalf.[20]

The British were the only party that kept detailed minutes of Sunningdale's plenary secessions.[21] Heath chaired the talks, having dismissed FitzGerald's last-minute pleas to have Luxembourg's foreign minister, Gaston Thorn, installed as a neutral figure. FitzGerald opposed Heath on this issue until the eleventh hour, insisting that his government would even object if Whitelaw took the chair, despite the fact that he was 'the least unacceptable of Englishmen to any Irishman'.[22] But he dropped these protests when he understood that Heath had travelled to Sunningdale in order to defend British rather than Northern Irish interests.[23] This was significant because the Irish expected the conference to be another major negotiation between the British and the Irish, much like the Anglo-Irish Treaty negotiations of 1921.[24] But it was not. And they found Heath to be a fairly benevolent and impartial chairman, as 'he seemed willing to endorse and accept whatever the Northern Ireland parties and Dublin could agree on'.[25]

* * * *

Opening the conference, Heath reminded delegates that they met under the continued threat of violence in Northern Ireland, and whether or not that violence would carry on being a daily reality for the people living there would very much depend on the outcome of the conference's proceedings. To ensure that this violence ceased to be a reality the delegates faced an onerous task in forging a stable power-sharing government on the basis of Northern Ireland's constitutional status within the UK. Paying tribute to Whitelaw, Heath described the Sunningdale conference as both a beginning and an end from which an executive would rise, with a three-tier Council of Ireland heralding a new dawn in Irish politics. He emphasised, however, that there would be no Anglo-Irish agreement at Sunningdale that did not account for and protect the British government's interests in Northern Ireland.

Cosgrave followed Heath's sober reflections with a more emotional presentation, speaking of the historic opportunity that Sunningdale represented. Irishmen had gathered to build institutions that would 'promote trust and cooperation', ending an era of conflict and marking a new beginning. Ireland's political representatives, he said, should 'cease for the moment trying to determine for our children, and our children's children, the exact kind of political institutions they will wish to live under in their day – especially since our past attempts to do so have seemed to promise only new difficulties for them'. The Irish government would be pragmatic and realistic in its approach to achieving those aims and reaching political consensus. Each Irish community was insecure, he said, because each community in Ireland knew that its political aspirations remained in question: both unionists and nationalists feared a settlement that would establish them as a permanent minority – the Catholic community in Northern Ireland and the Protestant community in a unitary Irish state. Ireland required institutions that nurtured consensus between the two communities on issues of common interest and provided scope from within for their mutually antagonistic constitutional aspirations to develop.[26]

Getting straight down to the point, Faulkner reminded delegates that prior to the negotiations the Official Unionists had spelt out three prerequisites for agreeing to sit in a power-sharing executive with a two-tier Council of Ireland. The Republic of Ireland must: end its constitutional claim to the territory of Northern Ireland; recognise that Northern Ireland's present constitutional status within the UK could only be changed democratically through the consent of its people; and agree on extradition measures to bring terrorists operating in both jurisdictions to justice. Faulkner said that a Council of Ireland would only recast relations between Northern Ireland and the Republic of Ireland if its institutions were constituted on the Irish government's acceptance that the people of Northern Ireland had a right to self-determination. Every unionist feared that a Council of Ireland might represent 'a half-way house to a united Ireland'; therefore enshrining their 'right to self determination' in any settlement was of 'paramount importance'. Unionists had of late made all the sacrifices in the political process and had 'no room left for change'. The political development that power-sharing represented had not been widely accepted in Northern Ireland, and 'even to conceive of a Council of Ireland' was 'one hundred times more difficult for unionists to accept than a power-sharing executive'. Only once power-sharing was fully accepted, he said, could 'any other form of cooperation between north and south begin'.[27]

Striking an optimistic note, however, Faulkner told the delegates that the progress unionists and nationalists could achieve in a Northern Ireland Executive would be cause for the governments in Dublin and London to 'look to your laurels'.[28] He reminded the Irish government that 'urgent improvement in the areas of extradition and common law enforcement' were essential for both creating confidence in its all-Ireland proposals and improving relations between Belfast and Dublin.[29] Unionist attitudes towards those proposals would, to a large extent, be determined by the Republic of Ireland's attitude to Northern Ireland's constitutional status at the conclusion of the conference's proceedings. Taking a similar stance to Faulkner, Napier urged the delegates to discuss and find a solution to the outlier issue of the Republic of Ireland's irredentist claim to Northern Ireland, reminding them of the deep resentment this, and the lack of movement on extradition, caused people in Northern Ireland. Sticking to FitzGerald's script, Fitt marked out policing as the key issue for the SDLP at the negotiations. For his party to enter into an executive, a Council of Ireland must have a role to play in the formation of security policy in an all-Ireland context. More than that, for the police force of Northern Ireland to be acceptable to all sections of society, and for nationalists to be able to positively identity with that force, a Council of Ireland must have active policing responsibilities in a common law enforcement area on an all-Ireland basis.

This first plenary session lasted all day, before the delegates travelled to 10 Downing Street for evening dinner. During the afternoon, Heath had focused the discussions on areas where broad consensus could be reached easily, such as the need for the establishment of a Council of Ireland, before highlighting issues for detailed negotiation where there remained significant disagreement. Faulkner had suggested taking the opposite approach, but the Irish government rejected his proposal. Furthermore, it was quickly agreed that the ministerial body of a

Council of Ireland would have equal representation, with five members attending from each administration and other members attending when necessary. Faulkner indicated that he had 'no strong feelings' on this issue, but the question of whether there should be equal representation on an all-Ireland assembly was set aside for further discussion.

There were a number of different ways in which a Council of Ireland could be structured. The Irish government wanted a largely autonomous three-tier parliamentary body that had evolutionary powers from the outset. An assembly would be required to put recommendations to the executive body, which would have the authority in certain areas to act on behalf of the administrations in Belfast and Dublin. A less powerful alternative envisaged a council taking decisions on certain issues of mutual concern, before referring back to Belfast and Dublin for approval, where the ultimate powers of executive decision-making would be retained. A third option was a two-tier council with a consultative assembly, executive powers being delegated from Belfast and Dublin, restricted to certain areas of common interest and carried out by officials on an all-Ireland basis. A variation of that model was a ministerial system served by officials with no assembly at all. And a fifth option was a one-tier consultative assembly that discussed issues of mutual concern and reported back to the administrations in Belfast and Dublin, which could then take unilateral or joint action as they saw fit. It had been provisionally agreed in the plenary session that there would be a three-tier council with a set of permanent members, an advisory council and a secretariat. Furthermore, it was agreed that the council would initially be funded by grants with administrative expenses shared equally between Belfast and Dublin. Therefore, only the details of the structure and functions of this model remained to be negotiated.

It was agreed that the assembly should provide a consultative function for the governing body of a Council of Ireland; all ministerial decision-making had to be unanimous and supported by a majority in the assembly. A Council of Ireland would therefore logically require the full support of the Northern Ireland Executive, as its decision-making process would be based on the principle of unanimity. FitzGerald pressed for an assembly with the power to make decisions by majority voting on issues that related to the evolution and development of the all-Ireland bodies and this was generally agreed. Heath said that decisions concerning the evolution of a Council of Ireland would require unanimous support, with the British government retaining a veto on decisions that impinged upon wider UK interests, as was implicit in the Constitution Act.[30]

All-Ireland assembly members would be chosen by the Northern Ireland Assembly and the Dáil respectively through the single transferable vote system, increasing the scope for small parties to be represented. In the event of the DUP and Vanguard boycotting the election to the assembly, Faulkner suggested allocating their seats to other parties. It was agreed that they would lie empty only if they took part in the electoral process and then instructed their members not to attend. Faulkner argued that it was unnecessary to create a permanent and full-time secretariat to service a Council of Ireland's institutions and perform executive functions; adequate resources could be drawn from the two existing civil services to fulfil this role. The unionists were forced to concede on this point however, and it was agreed that there would be a separate secretariat similar to that serving the EEC. It was important, Faulkner stressed, that a Council of Ireland was unable to impose its will on either the Northern Ireland Assembly or the Dáil; therefore it should be dependent on the existing departments in each administration and unable to diminish the executive authority of either in any way. All the other parties emphasised the need for harmonising and executive functions which, FitzGerald stressed, had to be present from the outset.

The question of where the council would sit was left for the Northern Ireland delegates to decide at a later stage; Faulkner suggesting that its location should alternate between North and South, the SDLP favouring Armagh as it had both Catholic and Protestant cathedrals. The minutiae of the workings of a Council of Ireland were not the central focus of Faulkner's negotiating strategy at Sunningdale. His aim was to concentrate unionist energies on securing significant movement on the issues of status and security. Succeeding on these two fronts, he felt, would leave him in a very strong position to carry the majority of the unionist community with a power-sharing agreement and a Council of Ireland.

At Faulkner's request, the conference then considered Northern Ireland's future constitutional status and the question of the Irish government's recognition of its current status. On the one hand, unionists wanted a declaration on status from the Irish government which did not mention its aspiration to end partition and, on the other hand, the SDLP felt that it was equally important that a declaration should recognise the two conflicting national aspirations that divided the island of Ireland.

O'Brien made it clear that his government would have great difficulty in delivering constitutional reforms; therefore holding a referendum on the question of deleting Articles 2 and 3 of the Irish constitution might prove counterproductive, as it was unlikely that a majority of the population would support such measures. Recent press reports had suggested the Irish government was considering the possibility of putting an amended constitution to the electorate in a referendum, in 1974.[31] FitzGerald had weathered a storm in the Dáil over these rumours, three times denying that this was the case. Amendments to Articles 2 and 3 of the constitution, he contended, 'had not arisen in the course of the discussions with the British Government at any time'.[32] O'Brien accepted that aspects of the 1937 constitution were widely regarded as archaic, but he implored unionists not to focus on this delicate issue at this particular time.

If amendments were out of the question, Faulkner told him that unionists would require a pledge from the Irish government that the constitution would be changed at some point in the future. Bradford went further, suggesting that if there was no movement on Article 2 then his party might reject the Council of Ireland proposals altogether and leave the executive stillborn. Heath suggested that it might be useful if the Irish government's declaration was lodged with the UN. And concluding the discussion, Cosgrave indicated that he was prepared to offer a declaration at the end of the conference's proceedings which would illustrate his government's willingness to cooperate with the political institutions of Northern Ireland. The content of this, however, would be determined by whether or not there was a suitable declaration by the British to match it.

Turning to law and order, the Irish suggested that Anglo-Irish extradition problems could be avoided through the establishment of a special court system, appointed by a Council of Ireland and consisting of three or five judges, which would try terrorists for scheduled offences anywhere in Ireland. The unionists felt that a joint court system might make extradition even more difficult to achieve than was already the case. Basil McIvor argued that reconciling two completely different legal systems would pose an enormous task, and summoning witnesses from different jurisdictions would prove equally difficult. Pym reminded the delegates that since the beginning of Northern Ireland's troubles, no fewer than 355 terrorist incidents had occurred near the border and twenty-four members of the British security forces had been killed within a ten-mile radius of it. In comparison to Northern Ireland, he said, the South was a safe haven for terrorists and a Council of Ireland must undoubtedly address this problem. The British argued that it would be far simpler if the Irish government amended its existing extradition legislation to exclude firearms and explosives offences from its definition of a 'political offence' and use the existing court structure to deal with cross-border offenders. FitzGerald told him that, due to the Republic of Ireland's written constitution, his government could not make an 'offence which is political, not a political offence', simply by saying something to that effect in a piece of legislation.

The nub of the problem was that no formal extradition treaty existed between the UK and the Republic of Ireland. A warrant system was used whereby the Irish courts decided if the accused should be surrendered on the basis of whether or not a political offence had been committed, as set out in the European Convention on Extradition 1957, to which the Irish were a signatory and the British were not. This required Irish courts to decline to surrender somebody accused of an offence connected with a 'political offence', which was as broadly or narrowly defined as the court saw fit. It was an issue of great sensitivity between the two parts of Ireland: unionists suspected that people extradited to the Republic of Ireland on this basis would escape justice or receive a sympathetic hearing; nationalists suspected that those handed over to the British authorities by the Irish Republic would receive rough justice. What cooperation the Irish government had in mind was not clear; it was clear however that the degree to which it was prepared to cooperate with the British security forces would be determined by the extent to which this cooperation might damage the government's domestic standing. The British suggested that both police forces might be given the power to arrest in 'hot pursuit' situations on each side of the border, but the Irish indicated that this proposal was totally unacceptable. They envisaged fairly limited and uncontroversial joint policing arrangements as a first stage in the development of cross-border security cooperation.[33]

In contrast, the British viewed a common law enforcement area as the best means of securing advances in its current extraction arrangements with the Irish government, who maintained that established international precedent created major difficulties in extraditing suspects who claimed to have been involved in politically motivated crimes. The Irish wanted to establish a clear link between a Council of Ireland and a police authority in both jurisdictions but, since the RUC was to remain the police force of Northern Ireland, the British indicated that they would not accept a 'common form of policing' for the whole of Ireland.[34] They wanted to see the 'harmonisation' of policing by liaison between two new policing authorities under the aegis of a Council of Ireland. The Irish stressed that this would not meet the SDLP's requirement for the police to enjoy the confidence of the minority community. This could only be brought about if a Council of Ireland exercised a degree of 'political control' over policing – something which the British believed Faulkner was unlikely to agree to and survive as Official Unionist leader.[35]

The Irish government suggested that if the Northern Ireland police authority was appointed by the Council of Ireland then the nationalist community would be more confident in accepting that the RUC was a police force that represented both communities in Northern Ireland. Faulkner said that it would be impossible for the unionist community to accept this, but Hume stressed that the SDLP had agreed, with the greatest of reluctance, that no name change to the RUC would be made. Associating the police authority with the Council of Ireland, he said, was the only way to ensure that republican strongholds, such as the Bogside and the Creggan, became accessible to that force. More than that, if the Council of Ireland enjoyed a strong policing role, Currie stressed that the SDLP would then be willing to turn to its constituents and say: this 'is our police force you are throwing stones at'.[36] Although the British government offered no objection to the idea of two police authorities working together, it intended to remain centrally involved in appointments to the Northern Ireland policing authority, as future appointments would be made from the Northern Ireland Assembly. However, Heath emphasised that even if a Council of Ireland had a role in relation to the hiring and firing of police authorities, it would have no control over the RUC.

When the conference broke for tea, the Irish government disclosed full details to the press of the agreements that had been reached over the ministerial tier of a Council of Ireland. In doing so, they broke an agreement that had been reached between all of the delegates, at the beginning of the conference, neither to leak information nor to engage in unilateral discussions with the media. Acting on O'Brien's instructions, the Irish press officer had fully briefed journalists on the afternoon's deliberations over the all-Ireland bodies.[37] This was rather ironic, for O'Brien had insisted on acting as the Irish government's sole ministerial spokesman at

Sunningdale, so as to ensure that it spoke with a single voice. This was due to his concern that the reaction of the Irish media to 'British leaks and inspired stories' would be 'unpredictable'.[38] The Irish record states that the agreement not to speak to the press individually, or for delegations to place their spin, piece by piece, on what was taking place inside the conference, had not been reached at that stage. Although the British version contradicts this assertion, O'Brien certainly had no desire to damage the talks or create a bad atmosphere at the first plenary session. Nevertheless, the incident illustrated that the Irish government was far more concerned about how its achievements would be perceived by Fianna Fáil, in Dublin, than it was over how they would be interpreted both by Faulkner's supporters and detractors in Belfast.[39] Faulkner was almost physically overcome with anger when the Northern Ireland parties learned of the disclosure at 6 pm, as the breach made it clear that he had agreed to detailed structural provisions for a Council of Ireland without first having negotiated any of his publicly stated prerequisites for a settlement.

The delegates then travelled by coach to Whitehall. Heath had organised a programme of Irish music to accompany dinner, which began with 'If You're Irish, Come into the Parlour' and concluded with 'When Irish Eyes are Smiling'. The occasion marked a turning point in Anglo-Irish relations which, as Heath's private secretary Robert Armstrong noted, 'had entered a new era'. It was indeed an historic occasion for a British prime minister to be offering hospitality to political representatives from both parts of Ireland. And when his guests rose to their feet when Heath proposed a toast to 'the president of Ireland', he quickly proposed a second toast to 'the queen' before any of them could sit down. On the return journey to Sunningdale, Devlin crowned the festivities with a rendition of the Ulster Protestant anthem 'The Sash my Father Wore', other SDLP members providing a 'kick the pope' refrain, and Hume himself conceded, 'it's a great song'.[40]

* * * *

The second session of the Sunningdale negotiations began in acrimony at midday, on 7 December. Faulkner informed the delegates that he could no longer abide by the previous day's agreement on the number of representatives that would sit on a Council of Ireland. He demanded that the figure should be altered in order to contradict the Irish government's press briefing. The conference agreed to this and the figure was raised to seven members from each jurisdiction and further progress was made on the functions that a Council of Ireland executive would have. Faulkner complained that no acceptable suggestions had yet been made on the deadlock-breaker issues of Northern Ireland's status and a common law enforcement area.

That evening it was established that the agreements reached in the individual working groups would then be subject to comprehensive agreement on all the issues under discussion in the subgroups. Nothing would be agreed at Sunningdale until everything was agreed and presented in one document at the conclusion of the conference. The delegates tasked with negotiating over the Council of Ireland proposals were FitzGerald, Bloomfield (in the unusual position of representing the British government), Morrell, Devlin and Glass. Dominating the Irish delegation at Sunningdale, FitzGerald attempted to set the agenda for these negotiations by presenting the unionist delegates with a list of potential executive functions. He insisted that a list of the functions that the council could undertake independently of the Belfast and Dublin administrations had to be included in the final agreement. Devlin was furious when he arrived typically late to find FitzGerald and the unionists halfway through the list. Without sitting down, the soon-to-be Northern Ireland minister for health exclaimed, 'Well Garrett, you can keep your hands off my bloody ambulances for a start!'[41] The matter was left for further discussion, but when the conference reconvened late that night, FitzGerald reported that they were 'within five minutes of agreement'.

This was another example of the Irish government's determination to prevent the Northern Ireland Executive designate from forging any common political position. Even Hume complained that the SDLP had not been represented at a meeting on policing which had taken place that morning. At a second round of discussions, the unionist negotiators argued that it would be politically difficult for them to agree in advance on a list of functions that would be devolved to a council of ministers. In an act of executive unity, the SDLP backed Faulkner to a certain degree, which was precisely what the Irish had been seeking to avoid. FitzGerald was particularly 'hard nosed' in these negotiations,[42] so much so that the unionists gave Devlin much credit for cosmetically reducing the Irish foreign minister's list of executive functions by half. FitzGerald conceded that by eliminating some things and amalgamating others, Devlin had managed to diminish 'the total content somewhat, but reduced the visible content even more'. Acknowledging that his government 'pushed' the Council of Ireland proposals too far, FitzGerald admitted that the SDLP were willing to compromise on this issue as many of them 'weren't at that time that interested in it'.[43]

The issues of policing and common law enforcement were negotiated separately. On policing, Pym, Cooper and Trevelyan represented the British, Cooney and Donlon the Irish, with two negotiators each from the three Northern Ireland teams – Bradford and Baxter for the Official Unionists, Currie and advisor Michael Canavan for the SDLP and Robert Cooper and advisor Ivor Canavan for Alliance. The parties were at loggerheads from the outset. The unionists could not accept any operational control of the RUC being placed under a Council of Ireland; the SDLP negotiators insisted that this was a prerequisite for them to accept the present security regime in Northern Ireland. The unionists were prepared to consider any form of association between the RUC and the Garda Síochána or future police authorities, and if a Council of Ireland was to be the means by which such cooperation would to be arranged, then they could live with this. Bradford argued that the SDLP's difficulty was simply one of symbolic identification. Moreover, if the British government immediately devolved control over the RUC to the executive, nationalist ministers would be playing a full part in policing matters anyway. Currie rejected this suggestion, sticking to the party line that the hiring and firing of the police authorities, the chief constable and the police commissioner should all fall under the remit of a Council of Ireland. Pym insisted that, short of a miraculous improvement in the security situation, there was absolutely no possibility of his government devolving policing powers to the executive. Therefore the SDLP men reiterated their demand for some operational control over policing to be devolved to a Council of Ireland. In response to the SDLP's pressure on the unionists, the Irish government backtracked on its previous position, indicating that it was prepared to see a Council of Ireland assume some authority over the Garda Síochána. It soon became clear, however, that they had no intention of seriously pressing this point, given the domestic political upheaval that sanctioning official Garda Síochána cooperation with the RUC would cause the coalition government.[44]

At the same time, O'Brien, Faulkner, Napier and Hume negotiated over the thorny issue of status with British officials Philip Woodfield and Kelvin White. The British linked finding agreement on the Council of Ireland proposals to the Irish government's acceptance of Northern Ireland's present constitutional status. To secure a Council of Ireland the Irish agreed to recognise Northern Ireland at the end of the conference but, given the constitutional difficulties recognition entailed, they hoped to formulate a statement in terms of accepting Northern Ireland's status rather than granting the overt political recognition that Faulkner was asking for. Having interpreted Cosgrave's recent remarks as forward looking, the British were expecting significant movement on this issue. On 21 June 1973, at Blackrock, in Dublin, the taoiseach had indicated that in dealing with the tangled problem of division in Ireland, and indeed in Anglo-Irish relations more generally, what was needed was 'a willingness to accept, and work forward from, existing realities, rather than a concern with abstract legalistic or constitutional definitions'.[45] The British took this to mean that not only had the Irish government accepted the existence of Northern Ireland, but that Cosgrave was appealing to his fellow countrymen not to focus on Article 2 of their constitution. Equally, it could have been interpreted as an appeal to the unionist community to completely ignore the constitution and accept the Irish government's willingness to work with a Northern Ireland Executive, on an equal footing, and accept this as a sufficient mark of political recognition.

The DFA's refusal to negotiate with the Northern Ireland parties, on an equal footing as an executive designate, considerably weakened Faulkner's hand in this aspect of the discussions. FitzGerald argued that an Irish declaration on status would create a constitutional anomaly. When questioned some months earlier over Northern Ireland's status, at Chatham House in London, the Irish foreign minister had dismissed this issue, suggesting that it would be improper for the Irish government to recognise Northern Ireland since it was part of the UK.[46] But in the days before Sunningdale, he conceded that his government would have to make a declaration on status, but insisted that this should be matched by a declaration from the British which indicated that they favoured Irish unity. In tying all the loose ends of his settlement together before he left Belfast, Whitelaw had forced Faulkner to go well beyond his own party supporters on the Council of Ireland proposals. When he raised the issue of status with FitzGerald on 30 November, Whitelaw emphasised that if a declaration on recognition was agreed between the Irish, at a very early stage, this would 'literally' provide Faulkner with the key to unlocking the numerous doors that might lead the Northern Ireland parties to an enduring settlement.[47]

Undoubtedly, if the status issue could be resolved at Sunningdale, this would enable Faulkner to return to Belfast having secured an enormous victory for unionism, and one which would be central to his efforts to convince his party that a power-sharing settlement was in its interests. Whitelaw's officials did press the Irish to accept the right of the people of Northern Ireland not to be as Irish as the Irish constitution says they should be. But as with the negotiations over the Council of Ireland proposals, it was not an issue on which Heath was prepared to intervene, leaving the Irish negotiators to play their hand with the unionists, regardless of the fact that the two parties were not on an equal footing. Had Whitelaw led the British negotiating team, given the support he had shown to Faulkner as his party political position steadily deteriorated, it is most unlikely that he would have remained aloof from the negotiations on this issue.

From the perspective of the British, what the Irish had to say on Northern Ireland's status remained the bone of contention. Moreover, no significant debate had taken place in Whitehall over whether Heath should build on the British government's previous statements on the issue.[48] The Irish wanted something more from the British, to develop the assertion made by Heath in a speech at the Guild Hall prior to the imposition of direct rule, that he did 'not believe any British Government would stand in the way'[49] of Irish unity, and Maudling's less subtle declaration that 'the whole British people would warmly welcome it'.[50] Prior to this meeting, the British had agreed to this by stating that: 'If in the future the majority of the people of Northern Ireland should indicate a wish to become part of a united Ireland, the British Government would support that wish.'[51]

In the absence of constitutional amendments to Articles 2 and 3, the two governments faced a significant presentational problem on this issue. The Irish government could not contradict its constitution by signing a treaty under the title of United Kingdom of Great Britain and Northern Ireland and the British government could not accept anything less. Up until this point, the two governments had never signed any agreed bilateral text of any treaty. They avoided the problem by presenting two texts, identical except in title, with each side signing its own version and keeping a Xerox copy of the other. The Irish government could grant *de jure* recognition of Northern Ireland's status at the conclusion to the conference, leaving the Irish constitution alone for the time being, but this would leave it open to legal challenge if a joint declaration employed the correct British title.

On the morning of 7 December, at least six separate drafts of a joint declaration were in circulation and by 4 pm the number had risen to fifty.[52] The British statement satisfied the Irish in the sense that it went further than Heath's Guild Hall speech, committing the British government to 'support' the wish of the majority should it decide in favour of unity. Appreciating that the Irish government could not commit to a public declaration that contradicted its written constitution, a compromise was forged in the early hours of Saturday morning. O'Brien presented Frank Cooper with a draft on which there was much agreement, suggesting that two parallel declarations could be presented in a joint communiqué. Cooper then produced two declarations, side by side, setting out the positions of the two governments on status using the terms 'British Government' and 'Irish Government'. O'Brien accepted the fudge with the proviso that the Irish statement would appear on the left-hand side of the page, so as not to infer any agreement with the British declaration by following it,[53] or appear subordinate to it.[54] Cooper then pointed out that a draft with the two parallel statements had already been shown to the unionists in which the British declaration was in the left-hand margin. Furthermore, when the draft was presented to the conference that evening, the Irish declaration omitted the explicit phrase: 'the present status of Northern Ireland is that it is part of the United Kingdom'. The unionists rejected this, some threatening to pack their bags and return to Belfast if it was not included. Faulkner stressed that it was the words 'is part of the United Kingdom' that he wished to see in the text, and these were eventually included in the British statement on Hume's suggestion.

Early drafts of the communiqué referred to 'Her Majesty's Government' and 'the Government of the Republic of Ireland', but Cosgrave requested that this be replaced with 'Irish Government'. Faulkner then remarked that the communiqué should stick to formal titles and enquired if 'Irish Government' was the formal title. FitzGerald retorted that 'Irish Government' was a colloquialism and that the correct and formal title was 'Government of Ireland', i.e. the government of the entire island. With the declarations all but agreed, falling feet first into FitzGerald's trap, Faulkner unwittingly reopened the whole question of designation and status with it. As the session ended, British officials told their Irish counterparts that if they insisted on 'Government of Ireland' then they would revert to 'the Government of the United Kingdom and Northern Ireland', which would publicly reopen the debate by presenting two contradictory assertions in the same paragraph.[55] They could not both claim to be the government of Northern Ireland and the official Irish title, as articulated by FitzGerald, did just that. After a minor row, with the Irish threatening to issue a separate communiqué, identical to the British one save for the government's title, a compromise was agreed to revert to the mutually ambiguous colloquialisms of 'British' and 'Irish' governments.[56] In terms of recognition, the agreement fell far short of what Faulkner required. As Napier put it, 'two stupid statements on recognition in different languages' presented little more than an obvious fudge on one of the most important issues that needed to be addressed at Sunningdale.[57]

* * * *

The conference had been scheduled to conclude on Friday evening or, at the very latest, Saturday morning. Heath had a lunch appointment with the Italian prime minister at Chequers on 8 December, which he missed, sending Carrington in his place. In the subgroup on extradition and human rights, which sat on Friday and Saturday, with extreme difficulty a final draft of what became paragraphs ten and eleven of the Sunningdale Communiqué was agreed. The group comprised the two attorney generals, Costello and Rawlinson, British and Irish officials and, of the Northern Ireland parties, Basil McIvor, Ivan Cooper and Oliver Napier. Rawlinson left the SDLP considerably disgruntled. Rejecting calls for an all-Ireland human rights court, he argued that it would be better instead to ensure that human rights principles were followed in both jurisdictions. Costello and Cooper argued for a common law enforcement area, while Napier and McIvor insisted on a commitment from the Irish government to introduce firm extradition legislation. In the middle, the British held the ring and, at times, tilted towards the unionist position when their interests converged.

Some progress was made when Costello admitted that the extradition problem was neither legal nor constitutional, but one of fundamental party political concern. He argued that the government would 'run into grave constitutional difficulties' if it accepted what the unionists wanted.[58] It could not command a majority in the Dáil or maintain public support for amendments to existing extradition legislation; therefore this issue was non-negotiable.[59] Putting great pressure on Costello,[60] Napier and McIvor argued that extradition was a deal-breaker issue in an overall settlement for their supporters. The British then fudged the issue, convincing Costello to enter into a firm commitment with them to take positive action against those engaged in political violence. This entailed setting up a law commission to examine potential solutions to the extradition problem, which would report back to the two governments within a certain timeframe. A great deal of animosity and harsh exchanges occurred when the usually placid McIvor, with tears in his eyes, launched a fierce attack on Costello. Rejecting the proposal and threatening to walk out of the talks, Napier and McIvor argued that there could be no agreement at Sunningdale which did not guarantee immediate action by the Irish government to deal with IRA killers in Northern Ireland. Shaken by their resolve, Costello returned with a proposal to revive the Offences against the Person Act 1861 as a means by which the Republic of Ireland could try fugitive murderers in its courts, and gave an undertaking that this would be enacted with immediate effect.[61]

The Irish delegation met with Currie, Fitt and Hume after lunch on 8 December, explaining that there could be no change in the law on extradition. Hume informed them that the SDLP could not shift from its demand for a Council of Ireland to have a role in policing; therefore they needed something 'to get them off the hook' of the policing issue in particular. Hume said that if the SDLP could not support the forces of law and order in Northern Ireland it would not be entering government at all.

The parties reconvened at 3 pm, Heath meeting the SDLP men in efforts to broker a last-minute compromise on policing. The British had drawn up a document detailing the SDLP's gains in the political process, which Heath presented to the northern nationalists. These included the suspension of the Stormont parliament; the introduction of proportional representation; and the introduction of power-sharing arrangements under which they held the position of deputy chief executive and other departments within an administration that lacked a unionist majority.

Also included were the establishment of a multi-tier Council of Ireland with executive and harmonising functions; the negotiation of these matters prior to executive formation; and an advisory role for the executive on all matters relating to participation on a reformed police authority. Furthermore, selective releases of detainees before Christmas had been agreed and a pledge to end internment when the security situation prevailed, as well as advances in the field of human rights. Nevertheless, Hume and Currie argued movingly for the establishment of a new policing system in Northern Ireland – one which the minority community could not only identify with but one which it could support – before Heath was forced to leave for Chequers at 3.45 pm.

At 6 pm the subgroup on policing found a possible solution. By order in council the British would devolve the power to appoint a police authority and its members to the Northern Ireland Executive. In this way, the unionists would gain some general control over policy in relation to policing, while the SDLP would achieve an aspect of what it wanted on a Council of Ireland. But when it came to the crunch, neither the British government nor the SDLP were keen for the executive to have policy control over policing, while the Irish were particularly keen to avoid engaging in overt Garda Síochána cooperation with the RUC.

Heath returned from his meeting with the Italian prime minister late that evening and presented a new document to the conference for the delegates to consider. This contained all the agreed passages, as a 'package', prompting Devlin to enquire whether he had received 'advice from Rome'.[62] Agreement had been reached on the status of Northern Ireland, the structure and functions of a Council of Ireland, human rights, and the powers that would be devolved to the assembly, and it had been established that these agreements would be ratified at a second conference. However, attitudes between the two sides hardened again over policing, and Heath formed a new subgroup, consisting of two senior representatives from each delegation, to resolve the outstanding issues.

Heath and Pym negotiated for the British government, FitzGerald and Cooney for the Irish, Faulkner and Bradford for the unionists, Hume and Currie alternating for the SDLP, and Napier and Cooper for the Alliance Party. Bradford wanted the British government to consider devolving responsibility for the RUC to the Northern Ireland Executive, within twelve months, with absolutely no control of the force being relinquished to a Council of Ireland. Unsympathetic to their demands,

Heath reminded Faulkner and Bradford that 'less than two years ago the British Government had had to remove power over the police from a Unionist Government' which had lost control over Northern Ireland.[63] Currie had been instructed 'not to agree to anything on policing' until the extent to which it could be 'linked in with the Council of Ireland' became clear.[64] And this provoked a clash with the Irish government, who had by this stage moved away from the SDLP – 'dropping out' of the negotiations between the Northern Ireland parties over policing in an all-Ireland context,[65] and merely registering a desire to see 'some role for the council' on this issue.[66]

During the night, Heath and Frank Cooper went from party to party, harrying the negotiators to reach a compromise. Much to the prime minister's annoyance, Napier stuck tightly with Faulkner over the issue of devolving policing powers to the executive, both negotiators hoping to cancel out the SDLP's insistence on securing a policing role for the Council of Ireland. During these meetings, Heath brought considerable pressure to bear on Faulkner and the Alliance duo to reach agreement, threatening them each with the blame should the talks collapse at the eleventh hour. Napier recalls that when Heath learned that the unionist and Alliance negotiators were considering 'going home in the morning ... to think out their positions', he 'went through the roof' and 'terrorised' Faulkner into submission.[67] Substantiating this view, FitzGerald noted also that while Faulkner certainly 'wasn't throwing punches that day', the Alliance members were actually 'tougher than the unionists in some ways', and had a 'better sense of some of the dangers' they faced.[68] Others believed that Faulkner had in fact failed to grasp the strength of the position he was in at Sunningdale. When he heard that Heath was twisting Faulkner's arm as the conference dragged on, Official Unionist MP Rafton Pounder quipped, 'What if it is made of Indian rubber?'[69] But although Faulkner was 'overawed' by Heath at Sunningdale, Bradford argued that the real reason he would not stand up to the prime minister was his belief that having entered into the negotiations at Sunningdale he was 'in the last chance saloon'.[70] Whereas Bloomfield contends that the prime minister simply 'bullied' him into submission.[71]

No agreement was reached, and fearful that they would be returning to Northern Ireland with nothing, the unionists played for time by arguing that they could not work on a Sunday. At 5.55 am, Hume and Currie came to the Irish delegation in a state of severe agitation, declaring that 'they have decided to wreck it … we are in real trouble'. Moreover, the SDLP men accused the British of having no stamina in the negotiations, arguing that the demands the unionists were making over policing were 'in contravention of the Constitution Act'.[72]

The negotiations continued until after 7 am, when Hume requested a break until 3 pm, exhaustion having become an obstacle to making further progress. After dropping their opposition to working on a Sunday, the unionists produced a more moderate proposal on the devolution of policing, before entering into negotiations with the SDLP for the remainder of the afternoon. By 6.30 pm, with agreement in sight, the subgroup reconvened to consider an Official Unionist–SDLP draft agreement, the unionists finally accepting a commitment from Heath to merely discuss the devolution of policing powers at a later date. Morrell suggests that this was all they could achieve, as Faulkner 'didn't have the sympathy of Heath', who would have sold the unionist position for 'sixpence if he could'. 'We were there on our own,' he said, 'and had to fight our own corner.'[73]

The SDLP's desire for appointments to be made to the police authority, under the aegis of a Council of Ireland, was the outstanding unresolved issue. At 7.15 pm, Heath proposed a compromise and the Irish delegation then pressured Hume to accept the unionists' demand that appointments to the Northern Ireland police authority should be made only after consultation with the executive. The impasse was finally broken at 7.50 pm, when Faulkner was heard to say, 'Yes, prime minister, we can accept that.' All eyes then focused on Hume, who in turn nodded his consent and everyone shook hands. The agreed paragraph read: 'With a view to improving policing throughout the island and developing community identification with and support for the police services, the governments concerned will cooperate under the auspices of a Council of Ireland through their respective police authorities.' This entailed a commitment on the part of the Irish government to create a police authority, 'appointments to which would be made after consultation with the Council of Ministers', and in the case of the Northern Ireland Police Authority, 'appointments would be made after consultation with the Northern Ireland Executive which would consult with the Council of Ministers of the Council of Ireland'.[74] At 8.20 pm, the Irish government delegates met and accepted, to the taoiseach's satisfaction, the document entitled 'Agreed Communiqué'.

* * * *

After four days of negotiations, at 8.30 pm on Sunday evening, Heath announced that the Sunningdale conference had reached a successful conclusion and presented the communiqué to the delegates. The Northern Ireland party leaders each paid tribute to Whitelaw for his valiant and unrelenting efforts and to Frank Cooper, his right-hand man, but for whose tireless diplomacy no agreement could have been reached. Fitt concluded the proceeding by addressing Heath: 'A hundred years ago, Prime Minister, Mr Gladstone said that his mission was to pacify Ireland. He failed. But by what you have achieved at this conference, I believe that you have succeeded.'[75] At 9 pm, the negotiators emerged to a hungry press pack and publicly signed the agreement the communiqué represented – to make a formal agreement ratifying the proposals it incorporated at a second tripartite conference and to register this at the UN. There was no time to copy-type duplicates of the communiqué, so the party leaders had to accept and sign a Xerox copy. This produced a sigh of relief from the Irish as the machine could not reproduce the British royal cipher embossed on the original blue-crested paper.[76]

Since the Council of Ireland proposals had largely been agreed prior to the negotiations, it was the second 'head to head' between Heath and Faulkner over who would control Northern Ireland's security forces, that caused the conference to drag on so long. Following a confrontation between the two leaders in the small hours of the morning, browbeaten by his prime minister, isolated and defeated in the negotiations, Faulkner backed down for the second time.[77] Bradford had warned him that if they did not return from the negotiations having gained something on security, then the Official Unionist Party would 'tear our arms out'. Seemingly resigned to his fate on the UUC, Faulkner replied that 'Heath was determined. He would not shift.'[78] Hume confirms this view, reflecting that quite a bit of Sunningdale was 'imposed by Heath', who was, it seemed, more influenced by the SDLP than Northern Ireland's last unionist prime minister.[79]

It was the Irish government's non-negotiable stance on the Council of Ireland proposals, and Faulkner's ambivalence towards them, which led Devlin, Napier and O'Brien to conclude, at Sunningdale, that the unionist leader had gone 'far too far' and would not be able to carry his community with its agreements.[80] Although this was the position that O'Brien took at Sunningdale, Currie stressed that it did not have 'much effect even on the Labour members of the [Irish government's] negotiating team'.[81] They raised the question of Faulkner's vulnerability in a meeting with Cosgrave, FitzGerald and Hume. And while the taoiseach was sympathetic to the view that Faulkner had gone too far, Fitzgerald 'blew up' at the suggestion, arguing that with twenty-four years in politics, and as the leader of the Official Unionist Party, Faulkner was best placed to know what he could and could not sell to his own community.[82] This position 'couldn't be moved', Napier recalls; 'Hume and Garret were singing from the same hymn sheet ... like limpets ... they were as tough as tough can be [and] they weren't changing one inch'. He contends that some members of the SDLP team wanted to move closer to the Official Unionist–Alliance position; 'Devlin very much so', and 'Currie would have moved' too. Fitt, on the other hand, Napier reflects, was so unconcerned about the all-Ireland bodies that he 'sat with a glass in his hand and a cigarette in his mouth, in front of a large open fire, and every time I walked past, he said, "have we reached agreement yet?"' However, 'Hume was adamant,' Napier said, 'it was his show, but the problem was the southern government had decided in advance what they were and weren't going to agree to.' Had the Official Unionist and Alliance delegates walked out then they 'weren't going to be called back in on the way to the airport. The only possibility of putting humpty-dumpty back together would have been a week later, after the southern government had had a cabinet meeting and had changed their *tied* agreed cabinet approach.'[83]

FitzGerald blamed Faulkner's failings at Sunningdale on the weakness of his negotiating team, arguing that this led to an agreement in which the Irish government 'got too much and they [the unionists] got too little'.[84] Heath did not act in concert with Faulkner, and while the Irish government had assumed he would,[85] he certainly did not view it as his role to ensure that Faulkner was not forced into accepting a deal that he could not comfortably sell in Northern Ireland. Consequently, the agreements reached at Sunningdale were heavily influenced by this disequilibrium and the inability or unwillingness of FitzGerald and Hume to resist the urge to over-negotiate on almost every issue. It is in this respect that the significance of Whitelaw's absence from Sunningdale should be measured. Whitelaw intervened at every stage of the castle talks to ensure that no one party came away having gained little and lost a lot. Thus, it seems highly probable that he would have taken a similar approach had he chaired the negotiations at Sunningdale, for he was cognisant of FitzGerald's intention to consume Faulkner's energies on the red herring issue of policing in an all-Ireland context. More than that, having created the peace process, Whitelaw would have viewed it as in his own interest to ensure that the unionist leader returned to Northern Ireland with a deal that was at least palatable to his own supporters.

From an electoral point of view, almost all of Faulkner's colleagues believed his performance at Sunningdale to have been 'well below par',[86] and FitzGerald reflects that 'he was not as tough as he should have been', nor did he 'get as much as he could have' in the negotiations.[87] The first part of this statement is undoubtedly true, but it is very hard to see how, with the resources he had available to him and the opposition he faced in FitzGerald, Heath and Hume, Faulkner could have succeeded on one or all of his prerequisites for agreement. Moreover, Frank Cooper recalled that as the conference unfolded, Faulkner became 'more and more worried' about what he had already conceded on the Council of Ireland.[88]

Of the Irish delegates at the talks, O'Brien was 'the most realistic'. He 'correctly calculated the negative impact' the all-Ireland proposals would have, as they stood, and was 'firmest in the view that the unionists had lost too much'.[89] After thirty hours of negotiations, while walking in the gardens of Sunningdale, O'Brien warned Faulkner, 'You are never going to sell this to the loyalists.'[90] Given his political weakness, it seemed that all Faulkner could achieve at Sunningdale, without risking the wrath of Heath by walking out, was to re-establish himself at the centre of government, where all the parties to the settlement would be dependent on his survival for its implementation. And with 'an air of resignation about him',[91] as the conference gathered for the last time, Faulkner remarked that while all the delegates would need to be 'salesmen' of the Sunningdale Communiqué, it was he who would have to be 'a super-salesman' for the settlement that they had all agreed to.[92]

A Salesman for Sunningdale

NOTES

1. CJ4/292, Record of telephone conversation between Pym and Paisley, 5 December 1973.
2. PRONI/CENT1/3/40, Meeting between Pym and Paisley, 4 December 1973.
3. CJ4/292, Pym to Paisley, 5 December 1973.
4. CJ4/292, Record of telephone conversation between Pym and Paisley, 5 December 1973.
5. Interview with Sir Robin Chichester-Clark, London, 25 June 2008.
6. Interview with Sir Ken Bloomfield, Craigavad, 19 December 2007.
7. Interview with Keith McDowall, London, 8 January 2008.
8. Interview with Sir Robin Chichester-Clark, London, 25 June 2008.
9. Interview with Lord Heath, London, 4 April 2001.
10. Interview with Lord Carrington, Knightsbridge, 21 November 2007.
11. Interview with Lord Howell, Westminster, 17 October 2007.
12. Interview with Sir Robin Chichester-Clark, London, 25 June 2008; M. Garnett and I. Aitken, *Splendid! Splendid! The Authorised Biography of Willie Whitelaw* (London: Pimlico, 2002), p.171.
13. Frank Cooper Papers, King's College London; Interview with Frank Cooper, Susan Higgins, 2 April 1998.
14. Interview with senior NIO official.
15. Interview with Lord Molyneaux, Westminster, 30 January 2001.
16. Interview with Lord Heath, London, 4 April 2001.
17. Interview with Seán Donlon, Limerick, 25 September 2007.
18. Interview with Austin Currie, Dublin, 5 January 2001.
19. Interview with Garret FitzGerald, Dublin, 12 September 2001.
20. Party advisors at the conference were Peter McLachlan, Reginald Magee and Professor Harry Calvert (Official Unionist); Paddy O'Hanlon, Michael Cavanan and Patrick Duffy (SDLP); and Ivor Cavanan and Liam McCollun (Alliance).
21. CJ4/474, Note of the Conference at Sunningdale, 6–9 December 1973. There is no verbatim transcript as was agreed between the two governments before the conference. British officials subsequently submitted notes for the record on aspects of the negotiations to which they contributed. Of the Irish delegates, Dermot Nally of the Taoiseach's Department took notes on both the sub-group discussions that the Irish delegation were party to and the plenary sessions. There appears to be no other official records of what took place at Sunningdale. It seems likely that the Irish had only Nally's record, as they subsequently requested copies of the British government's records but were only provided with an abridged version.
22. CJ4/488, Tel. No. 618, Dublin to Belfast, 21 November 1973.
23. Interview with Garret FitzGerald, Dublin, 12 September 2001.
24. Interview with Muiris Mac Conghail, Dublin, 24 July 2007.
25. Interview with Noel Dorr, Dublin, 12 July 2007.
26. CJ4/292, Opening speech by Cosgrave, Sunningdale, 6 December 1973.
27. CJ4/292, Opening speech by Faulkner, Sunningdale, 6 December 1973.
28. DT2005/7/626, Sunningdale Conference, 15 February 1974.
29. CJ4/292, Opening speech by Faulkner, Sunningdale, 6 December 1973.
30. CJ4/474, Note of the Conference at Sunningdale, 6–9 December 1973.
31. *Financial Times*, 22 November 1973.
32. *Dáil Debates*, Oral Questions, 218, 21 November 1973.
33. CJ4/292, Meeting between British and Irish officials, 26 November 1973.
34. DT2004/21/626, Summary of talks between British and Irish officials, 28 & 29 November 1973.
35. *Financial Times*, 30 November 1973.
36. DT2005/7/626, Sunningdale Conference, 15 February 1974.
37. *Irish Times*, 17 December 1973.
38. DT2004/21/626, O'Brien to Cosgrave, 29 November 1973.
39. Interview with Muiris Mac Conghail, Dublin, 24 July 2007.
40. CJ4/474, The Sunningdale Conference, note by Robert Armstrong, 1 March 1974.

41. Interview with Sir Ken Bloomfield, Craigavad, 19 December 2007.
42. Interview with Leslie Morrell, Belfast, 4 January 2001.
43. Interview with Garret FitzGerald, Dublin, 12 September 2001.
44. CJ4/474, Note on the Subgroup on Policing, Denis Trevelyan.
45. CJ4/293, Speech by Cosgrave, Blackrock, 21 June 1973.
46. CJ4/293, Brief on Status and Recognition for Tripartite Talks.
47. DT2004/21/626, Meeting between FitzGerald and Whitelaw, 30 November 1973.
48. Interview with Kelvin White, Didcot, 13 August 2008.
49. Guildhall speech, 15 November 1971.
50. Hansard, vol. 827, cols 32–183, 29 November 1971.
51. *The Sunningdale Communiqué*, paragraph 5 (London: HMSO, 1973).
52. DT2005/7/626, Sunningdale Conference, 15 February 1974.
53. CJ4/474, Note on the Subgroup on Status, by Philip Woodfield, 18 February 1974.
54. Interview with Noel Dorr, Dublin, 12 July 2007.
55. CJ4/292, White to Bloomfield, 12 December 1973.
56. CJ4/474, Note on the Subgroup on Status, by Kelvin White, 13 February 1974.
57. Interview with Sir Oliver Napier, Holywood, 29 December 2000.
58. Interview with Declan Costello, Dublin, 23 July 2007.
59. Interview with Mahon Hayes, Dublin, 24 July 2007.
60. Interview with Declan Costello, Dublin, 23 July 2007.
61. CJ4/474, Note of the meetings of the Subgroup on Extradition and Human Rights, by G.W. Watson, 14 February 1974.
62. CJ4/474, The Sunningdale Conference, note by Robert Armstrong, 1 March 1974.
63. *Irish Times*, 17 December 1973.
64. Interview with Austin Currie, Dublin, 5 January 2001.
65. Interview with Noel Dorr, Dublin, 12 July 2007.
66. DT2005/7/626, Sunningdale Conference, 15 February 1974.
67. Interview with Sir Oliver Napier, Holywood, 29 December 2000.
68. Interview with Garret FitzGerald, Dublin, 12 September 2001.
69. Interview with David Smyth, London, 18 February 2008.
70. ICBH, *British Policy in Northern Ireland, 1970–4*, p.50.
71. Interview with Sir Ken Bloomfield, Craigavad, 19 December 2007.
72. DT2005/7/626, Sunningdale Conference, 15 February 1974.
73. Interview with Leslie Morrell, Belfast, 4 January 2001.
74. The Sunningdale Communiqué, paragraph 15 (London: HMSO, 1973).
75. CJ4/474, The Sunningdale Conference, note by Robert Armstrong, 1 March 1974.
76. CJ4/292, White to Bloomfield, 12 December 1973.
77. Interview with Leslie Morrell, Belfast, 4 January 2001.
78. ICBH, *British Policy in Northern Ireland, 1970–4*, p.50.
79. Interview with John Hume, Londonderry, 13 September 2001.
80. Interview with Sir Oliver Napier, Holywood, 29 December 2000.
81. Interview with Austin Currie, Dublin, 5 January 2001.
82. Interview with Sir Oliver Napier, Holywood, 29 December 2000.
83. Ibid.
84. Interview with Garret FitzGerald, Dublin, 12 September 2001.
85. Interview with Seán Donlon, Limerick, 25 September 2007.
86. Interview with Sir Oliver Napier, Holywood, 29 December 2000.
87. Interview with Garret FitzGerald, Dublin, 12 September 2001.
88. ICBH, *British Policy on Northern Ireland, 1970–4*, p.46.
89. Interview with Garret FitzGerald, Dublin, 12 September 2001.
90. Interview with Basil McIvor, Spa, 24 August 2001.
91. Interview with Lord Howell, Westminster, 17 October 2007.
92. DT2005/7/626, Sunningdale Conference, 15 February 1974.

PART II
THE POWER-SHARING EXECUTIVE

By the time the Northern Ireland Executive was formed, the British government was no longer secure in office and Whitelaw had been relieved of his duties as Northern Ireland's secretary of state. The opponents of British policy in Northern Ireland – the paramilitary organisations and the unionist politicians who had not been central to Whitelaw's power-sharing plans – were determined to ensure that it failed. Heath's defeat in the February 1974 Westminster general election presented those opponents with an opportunity to test the two governments' commitment to Northern Ireland's fledgling power-sharing institutions. They sought to efface the power-sharing model from the constitutional options that would be open to Northern Ireland in the event of the executive's collapse. If Faulkner and his colleagues were to establish power-sharing as a form of government that was acceptable to both communities, then they needed to stabilise and legitimise Stormont's new institutions through a balanced implementation of the agreements reached at the Sunningdale conference. The executive, however, was largely reliant on the two governments to secure it from the unconstitutional forces that were plotting its destruction.

Hands Across the Border

On Tuesday 1 January 1974, Brian Faulkner became head of a Northern Ireland government for the second time in his political career, bringing twenty-one months of British direct rule to an end. Faulkner had never met with the approval of the establishment figures of the Official Unionist Party, the Anglo-Irish aristocrats, landowners and army officers who had governed Northern Ireland since partition. Gerry Fitt often joked that when he first entered Stormont, 'he didn't know whether to salute or to shake hands'.[1] And Faulkner too understood what it felt like to be an outsider inside Stormont, as he was the first Official Unionist leader to have emerged from grassroots, from the business and commerce sectors of Northern Ireland society.[2] A private man, Faulkner stood out among his peers as a pragmatic and tactical career politician, and one who was 'never chippy about the south'.[3] Predisposed to playing a lone hand in politics for these reasons, the remarkable political rehabilitation he experienced following his split with Heath in 1972 typified the overwhelming determination he possessed to again lead a Northern Ireland government.

On New Year's Eve, Pym had bestowed the first government in the history of Northern Ireland to consist of both unionists and nationalists with their official seals of office. The first decision taken by this executive was to share power on the basis of unanimity and collective responsibility.[4] It was also suggested that the assembly should require a two-thirds majority to pass legislation; anything failing to reach that level of support would be referred to Westminster for further consideration. Central to the administrative transformation Northern Ireland was experiencing, it came as a surprise to no one when Ken Bloomfield was appointed to act as permanent secretary to the executive. Maurice Hayes, his most senior and able Catholic colleague, filled the position of assistant secretary to the executive, adding symbolic balance to the upper echelons of a secretariat that had hitherto been a unionist preserve. Upon taking office, Hayes joked that he had probably only been appointed to 'look after' Gerry Fitt and advise Faulkner on how to pronounce 'taoiseach' and 'Oireachtas'.[5] But his remark certainly demonstrated the sense of disbelief that he, and the nationalist ministers he would serve, felt at having finally arrived in government at Stormont. So together, Faulkner and his former political adversaries embarked on 'a very radical experiment, launched into a very narrow window' at a time of great political crisis.[6]

Praising the 'genius' of Whitelaw and recommending that he be nominated for the Nobel Peace Prize for bringing the parties to accord, Edward Kennedy paraphrased Winston Churchill during the Second World War when he said that Northern Ireland had reached 'the end of the beginning' of its troubles.[7] The Irish government was also delighted by the sweeping advance it had made into the political affairs of Northern Ireland; securing a Council of Ireland with evolutionary powers, without having made any reciprocal commitment to amend the Irish constitution. As one Irish official put it, agreement was reached because the 'unionist neck, represented by Faulkner, had been thrust forward towards us' having been 'boxed in on every other side'.[8] Overjoyed by his success at the Sunningdale conference, FitzGerald believed that the agreements reached there might be a stepping stone on the road to a united Ireland. He was disappointed, however, by the lack of progress that had been made towards the creation of a common law enforcement area, and blamed the British for not producing detailed proposals at the negotiations. Conceding that Articles 2 and 3 of the Irish constitution were non-negotiable at Sunningdale, he suggested that his government was now free to look, as a matter of urgency, at what constitutional changes might be necessary to move the process forward.

Although Lynch was upset at Cosgrave for not having consulted with him prior to or during the Sunningdale conference, he gave a cautious welcome to the government's achievements at the historic Anglo-Irish summit. The Irish delegates had left Sunningdale feeling deeply anxious however, worried that they would be returning to 'a very disgruntled home territory', as Fianna Fáil had attacked them over the weekend in the Irish media for having achieved less than they had set out to. This was despite the fact that the coalition government was 'not giving anything away at all', as one Irish official put it, but merely attempting to put nationalists into government in Northern Ireland 'with Brian Faulkner's consent'.[9]

Maintaining a cautious approach, Cosgrave declared that Sunningdale was a morally binding rather than a legally binding agreement; therefore it did not need to be formally ratified in the Dáil. A 'working understanding of the centre' had been established, he told parliament, which represented the sensible elements of political opinion throughout Ireland. However, Fianna Fáil hardliners were not generous in their assessment of that understanding, taking the view that it represented an implicit and an explicit recognition of partition. Mavericks such as Neil Blaney viewed the Sunningdale Communiqué as the 'greatest sell-out' in Irish history.[10] Blaney had been expelled from the parliamentary party in 1971 following an illegal arms-smuggling scandal which Lynch exploited by removing the more 'radically green element' of Fianna Fáil.[11] And when a parliamentary debate on the communiqué ended in acrimony, with Paddy Cooney accusing Fianna Fáil of taking a 'carping, small and mean' approach to the settlement, Cosgrave became even more worried that Lynch might not fall into that centre.

Although he was generally supportive, Lynch indicated that Fianna Fáil had difficulties with section five of the communiqué, questioning the extent to which it 'impinged' on Article 2 of the Irish constitution.[12] Contesting Cosgrave's moralistic reading of the communiqué, he argued that as it had been agreed that it would be lodged with the UN after its agreements were ratified, then it must first gain the Irish parliament's approval. Since the communiqué entailed the charge of public funds, Lynch contended that there was a constitutional requirement for it to pass through the Dáil at some stage.[13] Moreover, the establishment of a Council of Ireland would require significant legislation and possibly constitutional amendments as well.[14]

During the Northern Ireland Executive's first meeting, Faulkner suggested that it should 'keep the door open' in making every effort to persuade the unionist opposition to become involved with and participate in government. By calling for an executive with a 'much broader party base', Bradford had already raised this idea in the assembly. Furthermore, he suggested that in the short-term it 'might not be impossible to involve those other groups who at the present moment feel that they cannot in conscience participate'.[15] However, Faulkner's proposal met with 'solid resistance' on the executive,[16] a response which Bloomfield described as having an 'air of greediness about it'.[17] For the majority of Faulkner's colleagues, the new power-sharing 'shop was clearly closed'. In his retrospective journal, Bradford found the executive guilty from the outset of 'repeating past unionist mistakes'. The power-sharing 'club was to remain an exclusive preserve with disastrous results', for only Fitt, 'to his eternal credit', joined him in support for Faulkner's proposal.[18]

There was neither a honeymoon period for the new Northern Ireland government nor any respite from the ongoing power struggle within unionism. Taylor tabled a motion on the UUC to 'reject the proposed all Ireland Council settlement'.[19] And after being defeated on his party's ruling body the previous Friday, by fifty-three votes, Faulkner resigned as the leader of the Official Unionist Party on Monday 7 January. This collapse greatly reduced the credibility of his claim to represent majority unionist opinion on the executive. In departing from Glengall Street, Faulkner was effectively severing his ties with the 'unpledged' unionist faction, as his thoughts turned to forming his own party.[20]

Some of Faulkner's allies believed that he could have played harder to get at Sunningdale and 'failed tactically' due to his eagerness to return to office.[21] Others blamed this collapse on his own unshakable sense of self-belief, reflecting that his attitude at the time was, 'I can sell it, get me back into power and I'll sell it'.[22] But having failed to carry his support base with the Whitelaw settlement and, equally, on the course that his own personal ambition had driven him, Faulkner was now wholly dependent on the power-sharing executive for his political survival. This was a highly significant failing, for many of the 'unpledged' group did not differ from their 'pledged' colleagues on major issues of policy – they were simply against Faulkner. Nevertheless, Northern Ireland's first power-sharing administration set sail with Whitelaw's unionist anchorman at the helm, but without the political vessel that had carried unionism from Irish home rule to British direct rule.

In response to the establishment of the Northern Ireland Executive, Craig and Paisley launched their joint campaign to destroy it, with a 'Save Ulster' rally in Lisburn, at which they pledged that power-sharing 'would be broken' when the assembly met on 22 January. 'Faulkner may say hands across the border,' the DUP leader told his supporters, 'but

I say shots across the border.'[23] Expecting widespread street disturbances, Heath put Northern Ireland's security forces on alert and pressured Cosgrave to take decisive action against the IRA in the South.[24] In the event, the anti-Sunningdale rally attracted a crowd of only 1,000, which was some indication of the uphill struggle facing Craig and Paisley if they were to arouse an apathetic Protestant population in protest against Northern Ireland's new political order.

On 2 January, Cosgrave had instructed the Garda Síochána to arrest fifteen men on suspicion of being in the IRA, but all but one was released after it became clear that they had apprehended the wrong people. The raid was timed to give Faulkner a political bounce as he defended the Sunningdale Communiqué to the UUC. However, the IRA had been tipped off in advance and the fiasco left Faulkner politically 'castrated',[25] forcing Cosgrave to apologise personally to the Northern Ireland chief executive for the damage it had caused to his position. Humiliated, Faulkner complained bitterly to Cosgrave that what the executive needed was the arrest of high-profile IRA leaders; 'one Martin McGuinness', he said, was worth 'six unknowns'.[26] However, it was a remark that Cosgrave made after the Sunningdale conference which had precipitated Faulkner's defeat on the UUC.[27] Trying to quell domestic opposition to the communiqué, Cosgrave announced that there was no question of his government changing the Irish constitution with regard 'to our claim of sovereignty over all of Ireland'.[28] Many of Faulkner's colleagues had therefore taken the Irish government's declaration on status in the Sunningdale Communiqué to be meaningless. To unionists, Cosgrave's comment seemed to suggest that the Irish government 'didn't really recognise them at all'. It was not what was in the communiqué that they could not accept, but what was absent from it, as Napier put it; 'the *quid pro quo*' on status, recognition and extradition 'that didn't exist'.[29]

Faulkner wanted the taoiseach to repair the damage which this had caused to the executive by unequivocally stating that the Sunningdale Communiqué represented a *de jure* acceptance of Northern Ireland's constitutional position within the UK. But having weathered a tetchy parliamentary debate on this issue, Cosgrave's government was facing a constitutional court case from a disgruntled former Fianna Fáil politician, Kevin Boland, who had resigned from Lynch's cabinet over the arms scandal in 1970. So it seemed that the most Faulkner could expect from

Dublin, in such circumstances, was an assertion that the communiqué represented a *de facto* acceptance of Northern Ireland's constitutional status, which in itself might cause the Irish government further difficulties.

In the absence of Herbert Whitten and with the dissent of James Stronge, Faulkner's unionist assembly group backed a motion of confidence in his leadership and set out to rally moderate unionist opinion.[30] But after only a week in government, it was clear that Faulkner would not be able to maintain his position purely on the basis of the agreements that had been reached at Sunningdale. In what was his first step in efforts to renegotiate those accords prior to their ratification and implementation, Faulkner told Cosgrave that he could not agree to his request for an intergovernmental meeting until the 'political dust' had settled in Belfast. Critical of the Irish government's reticent approach towards challenging the IRA in the Republic, he warned the taoiseach that if the arrangements envisaged at Sunningdale did not come into operation with 'general public confidence and support', then they would be 'still-born'.[31] Moreover, Bradford stressed that if the Irish government failed to produce security measures which aided the executive in its fight against terrorism, then it would be immensely difficult to sell Sunningdale's agreements to the unionist community. Hume backed Faulkner on this point, signalling that the executive was 'interested in results', and not simply in being seen to call for them.[32] As did Heath, who wrote to Cosgrave complaining that statements made by his government, which suggested that there was neither the possibility of constitutional change nor the introduction of new extradition legislation, had 'seriously reduced the value to Faulkner of the Sunningdale Agreement'.[33] Ignoring Faulkner's criticisms and blaming the British for allowing momentum on the Council of Ireland proposals to slip,[34] Cosgrave requested that the Sunningdale Communiqué be ratified, in early February, at a second tripartite conference in Dublin.[35] Faulkner put the brakes on this political process, arguing that phased and visible movement on the agreement as a whole was required prior to ratification.

At Stormont, the SDLP were experiencing some rather unorthodox problems in sharing power with unionists. Currie and Devlin voiced concern to the Irish government about the cordial relationship that was developing between Faulkner and Fitt as they settled into adjoining offices. The nationalist leaders pressured the Irish to pressure the British to force Faulkner to proceed immediately with Sunningdale's formal stage. They argued that the unionist leader's defeat on the UUC was no reflection of the 'solid' support that he enjoyed within the Protestant community.[36] Having been concerned that their accession to ministerial office at Stormont might diminish the SDLP men's appetite to press for the establishment of a strong Council of Ireland, this was exactly what the DFA wanted to hear.[37]

On 14 January, Boland's legal case against the Irish government reached Dublin's High Court. He contended that the Irish government's declaration in the Sunningdale Communiqué contradicted the Irish constitution. Napier called for the Irish government to draw up a constitution that corresponded with the 'declaration of recognition' it had granted Northern Ireland in the Sunningdale Communiqué which, he argued, had effectively rendered Articles 2 and 3 redundant.[38] But his remarks reinforced Boland's argument and tightened Cosgrave's room for manoeuvre, as opposition to Sunningdale within Fianna Fáil hardened around former minister Charles Haughey, who Lynch had also sacked for his involvement in the arms scandal.

Responding to the continuing security crisis in Northern Ireland, Faulkner and Cosgrave held talks in Dublin, on 16 January, as Cooney announced an operation to remove the 'blight' of republican terrorism 'from the Irish nation'.[39] Faulkner saw no hope of ratifying Sunningdale with the question of status hanging 'in the air'; he would 'resign from the executive' if a tripartite meeting was scheduled before the issue had been satisfactorily resolved. At Sunningdale, unionists had consented to the Council of Ireland proposals; but unless the Irish government threw a lifebelt to Stormont by making reciprocal concessions on the issues of status and security, the executive would not survive its implementation. SDLP assembly member Hugh Logue confirmed unionist suspicions and added to Cosgrave's woes when he described the Council of Ireland as a vehicle that would 'trundle us into a united Ireland'.[40] And with unionist confidence in Sunningdale 'completely eroded', Faulkner warned Cosgrave that should the Irish insist on rushing its implementation, then they would be responsible for smashing 'the whole thing' up.[41]

Cosgrave explained to Faulkner, who he got on with very well,[42] that with Boland's case pending he could not presently clarify his government's position on Northern Ireland's status. Although he expected to win the case, his government was 'tongue-tied' with respect to making a statement on status while the proceedings remained open, as it might be viewed as a legally prejudicial intervention.[43] Cosgrave pointed out that his government's defence did not include any denial that the joint declaration in the Sunningdale Communiqué meant that Northern Ireland could not be integrated with the Republic of Ireland until, and unless, a majority of its people indicated their desire for unification. This was a subtlety lost on the unionist press, he said, as it actually denied that there had been any agreement to acknowledge Northern Ireland's constitutional position in the UK, as Sunningdale contained two separate declarations. Bloomfield retorted that this ambiguity itself lay at the very heart of the problem, as the parallel presentation of the two government declarations made it practically impossible to identify precisely what status, if any, the Irish government was recognising.[44] Therefore, if the Irish government won the case on the basis that the declaration was constitutionally meaningless, then, from a unionist perspective, the Sunningdale Communiqué was a worthless document with respect to the question of status. For Faulkner, the only positive aspect to this argument was that if the government actually lost the case and the communiqué was struck down as unconstitutional, then the damage to the executive's standing would be even greater. Moreover, FitzGerald later conceded that his government's entire defence of the case actually 'involved demolishing the entire political position' it had built prior to Sunningdale.[45]

Faulkner emphasised to Cosgrave that the executive was actually working with 'a sense of purpose', more so than any institution that he had ever been part of in his entire political career.[46] But to 'revalue' its declaration at Sunningdale, he insisted that the Irish government should state clearly that it accepted that the 'status of Northern Ireland' could only be changed by consent, and he urged Cosgrave to consider holding a referendum on Articles 2 and 3. Cosgrave felt that holding a referendum might compound these difficulties; therefore the question should be left to an all-party committee which might recommend that a new constitution should be drawn up to assuage the unionist community's concerns. With nothing more to offer, Cosgrave's words in parting exposed both the taoiseach's sincerity and frustration; he told Faulkner: 'We accept you as you are, and that's that.'[47]

The following day Boland lost his case, the court ruling that the Sunningdale Communiqué did not contradict the Irish constitution as it represented a statement of government policy, which could not affect the legal rights of any citizen in its acceptance of the current *'de facto'* constitutional status of Northern Ireland.[48] Nevertheless, Faulkner's political survival depended on his ability to exploit the inherent weakness in his position and claw back some of the political territory that unionism had conceded prior to and at Sunningdale. He sought from Cosgrave an unequivocal declaration on status and a commitment to implement tough security measures against the IRA. In response to Faulkner's call for clarification on status, Fianna Fáil backbenchers urged Lynch to abandon his cautious support approach to the government's Northern Ireland policy.[49]

* * * *

By 22 January, the Northern Ireland Executive was beginning to split over the Council of Ireland proposals. The Law Commission had met on 16 January, and Faulkner told his colleagues that Sunningdale could not be ratified, nor the all-Ireland bodies established, in the absence of conclusive evidence that the Irish government were prepared to act firmly against the IRA. The SDLP rejected this, sticking to the position that the establishment of a Council of Ireland was part and parcel of an agreed package, which must be implemented immediately.[50] The same day, Harry West was elected leader of the Official Unionists and Paisley orchestrated another riot in the assembly. This time opposition members completely disgraced themselves, physically assaulting the unionist ministers, before eighteen of them, including the DUP leader, were hauled from the chamber by the RUC. Paisley and his supporters then arrived, uninvited, at the doors of Stormont Castle, and engaged in a bitter exchange with Pym. The DUP leader complained that in posting hostile army and RUC contingents at Stormont, the government was forcing the assembly to meet 'at the point of a bayonet'. Paisley told the new secretary of state that he would break his government's 'dunderhead policy'; it is the opposition 'who control the Protestant people in this Province' and 'if you want a confrontation', he warned him, 'my God we can produce it'.[51]

On 28 January, when the executive examined the functions that it might delegate to a Council of Ireland, there was no enthusiasm from any minister to dilute his departmental responsibilities by devolving powers to an all-Ireland body. Taking a minimalist view, Bradford described most of the Department of the Environment's services as 'essentially inward looking', suggesting there was no great scope for cooperative relations on this front. Joint decisions, he said, could lead to joint action through existing channels of government on cross-border roads, rail links and waterways. Morrell referred to current cross-border cooperation on a number of agricultural issues, which took place on a 'commonsense rather than a doctrinaire basis'. Of the SDLP ministers, Devlin presented 'no firm proposals' for devolution, in the fields of Health, Social Welfare and Social Security, as 'there was nothing of intrinsic importance to place on the agenda of a Council of Ireland at present'.[52] Hume was also reluctant to diminish his ministerial brief, arguing that since Commerce was limited to Northern Ireland, 'there's really nothing that I have that can be transferred over'.[53] In contrast, an interdepartmental unit met in Dublin to discuss the transfer of functions to a Council of Ireland. It concluded that the relocation of approximately 'six thousand civil servants and six thousand four hundred other employees' would be required, with an expenditure of £62m per year.[54] But Irish civil servants were in line with their northern counterparts,[55] showing 'no desire whatever to hand over things to some other all-Ireland body'; more than that, 'they were deeply opposed to it'.[56]

The executive was close to agreement on the position it would take towards the ongoing 'rent and rates' civil disobedience campaign. Although there was to be no amnesty, efforts would be made to persuade people to come off the strike before the executive imposed harsher measures against them.[57] Faulkner was impressed by the industry and ability of the SDLP ministers, and many civil servants found their enthusiasm for the job and their interest in departmental matters a refreshing change from the Stormont era. The SDLP men did not, however, find any passion for the Council of Ireland proposals among those civil servants, who were in fact very conscious of the political difficulties that lay ahead.[58] Hayes believed that the all-Ireland bodies would have to begin by operating at a very low key level, and he advised the Irish government not to insist on executive action or decision-making from the outset. Delay could be tolerated, he argued, as it was still the issue of internment that caused northern nationalists the most concern.[59] Since taking office the SDLP ministers had kept their distance from Dublin, and Devlin was beginning to share Fitt's view that Hume should adopt a less doctrinal position on the Council of Ireland proposals. Nevertheless, they requested a secret meeting with Cosgrave to coordinate their approach towards the list of areas where executive functions might be appropriate.[60]

When it met with the Irish government for the first time, at Hillsborough on 1 February, the executive took a unified approach to their discussions over the Council of Ireland proposals and security. Setting the tone, Faulkner declared that he could 'not move a further inch on ratifying the Sunningdale Agreement' without a concrete assurance from the Irish government that it accepted the status of Northern Ireland within the UK and accepted that this status could not be changed without the consent of a majority of the people of Northern Ireland. Cosgrave promised to formulate a statement after Boland's case had been fully resolved in the Irish Supreme Court. The unionists insisted that it must contain the words 'Northern Ireland is within the UK'. More than that, if the executive was to successfully sell the agreements reached at Sunningdale, then the Irish government must address the question of extradition and introduce tougher security measures to reduce the number of IRA units that were presently operating from within its territory. This sparked an angry exchange. The unionists argued that security along the border was the price their constituents demanded in return for the establishment of a Council of Ireland and Bradford insisted that it could not be established without first finding a solution to the extradition problem.

The executive was united in its conviction that delegating too much power too quickly to a Council of Ireland would destroy the power-sharing agreement. It was agreed that a steering group would conduct joint studies on its potential functions and report within twenty-one days. Ever focused, Hume suggested setting a date for Sunningdale's ratification and asking the Law Commission to report before that deadline. Admitting that this issue had already become a 'festering sore', Faulkner agreed that ratification should not be dragged out as long it was concluded as a 'complete, acceptable package'.[61]

On 5 February, Faulkner defended the power-sharing agreement and the all-Ireland dimension to the settlement in the Northern Ireland

Assembly. It had been suggested, he said, that the Irish government's declaration on Northern Ireland's status was nothing more than a statement of policy, which could be revoked by any subsequent government. But Northern Ireland's consent to cooperate in the machinery of an all-Ireland council, he argued, hangs upon the Irish government's consent to acknowledge 'our right to self-determination, and a withdrawal of the one at any time in the future will necessarily and directly lead to a withdrawal of the other'.[62]

Faulkner immediately wrote to Cosgrave, urging him to grasp the nettle and make a fresh statement on status. Sunningdale committed the executive to the establishment of a 'two-tier' Council of Ireland, but to bring the second tier into existence, at this stage, might 'prejudice acceptance of the whole system'. It would be a 'great pity', he said, 'to see the whole project founder because of an insistence upon creating the entire structure at once'.[63] Cosgrave reminded the unionist leader that the concept of a 'consultative body' predated the Sunningdale conference; therefore postponing it at this late stage 'would cause a dangerous and perhaps fatal loss of credibility in the Sunningdale package'.[64] Against O'Brien's advice, FitzGerald and Hume stepped up their pressure to have Sunningdale's agreements ratified, in Dublin, before 17 March. Hume believed that Faulkner was using the issues of status and security as an excuse to put the Council of Ireland proposals on the long finger, in the hope that 'the finger would eventually drop off or contract an incurable disease'.[65]

In London, Irish ambassador Donal O'Sullivan asked the British to ensure that the Law Commission's report was produced by 22 February and, on Fitzgerald's request, enquired whether investigations had been made into the recent allegations of RUC brutality that his government had brought to their attention. Philip Woodfield told the ambassador that Donlon's visits to Northern Ireland to collect this sort of information were at best unorthodox. How would the Irish government respond, he asked him, if a member of the British diplomatic service was to tour the Republic collecting allegations against the Garda Síochána, and if the Irish ambassador was then summoned by the British foreign secretary and asked to produce an almost instant explanation to those allegations.[66]

Cosgrave finally took Lynch into his confidence over Sunningdale, in what was a belated effort to maintain bipartisanship over Northern

Ireland in the Dáil. Restive Fianna Fáil backbenchers prompted Lynch to firmly oppose any derogation from the Republic of Ireland's constitutional claim to Northern Ireland at his party's annual convention. But in an attempt to take some ownership of the settlement, he reminded the party faithful that the 'road to Sunningdale' was a path long chartered by Fianna Fáil in government, and this meant that the Northern Ireland Executive must be given 'every chance to work'.[67]

Two days before a Westminster general election which Heath had called against Whitelaw's advice,[68] Cosgrave informed parliament that a Council of Ireland should not be 'a way of achieving unity either by stealth' or against the wishes of the majority community in Northern Ireland.[69] Blaney tabled a motion calling for parliament to reaffirm a resolution that had been passed unanimously in the Dáil on 10 May 1949, rejecting the British legislation that endorsed partition and reiterating the 'indefensible right of the Irish nation to the unity and integrity of the national territory'.[70] Cosgrave tabled an amendment to the motion, asserting that the aspiration to Irish unity could only be achieved 'by peaceful means and with the consent of a majority of the people of Northern Ireland'.[71] When the government survived a division in the chamber by five votes, this raised further doubts over Lynch's ability to support the Sunningdale Communiqué. Moreover, Fianna Fáil rejected the taoiseach's inference that the people of Northern Ireland had a legal right to 'maintain the Partition of Ireland by opting out at all times of a United Ireland'. Criticising Cosgrave's failure to resolve the ambiguities over Northern Ireland's status in the communiqué, Lynch voted against the spirit of Sunningdale, having failed to temper opposition to the settlement from within his own party.[72] Although opposition to Sunningdale from within Fianna Fáil was predictable, Cosgrave was paying a price for having refused to take Lynch into his confidence during the Anglo-Irish negotiations that preceded the Sunningdale conference. The Irish government had not done enough to pave the way for the safe passage of its achievements in the Irish parliament. More than that, FitzGerald suggested that it 'may have missed an opportunity' to alter the Irish constitution, as reliable Fianna Fáil sources informed him that Lynch would have supported movement on Articles 2 and 3.[73]

* * * *

In the general election on 28 February, Fitt was the only Northern Ireland candidate returned to Westminster on a pro-Sunningdale ticket.[74] Campaigning under the banner of 'Dublin is just a Sunningdale away', the United Ulster Unionist Council (UUUC) triumphed at the poll, winning eleven seats and just over 51 per cent of the votes. If non-unionist anti-Sunningdale candidates were added to the new loyalist coalition's tally, opposition to the executive reached almost 60 per cent. The election, which took place against a background of well-orchestrated violence, was widely regarded as a litmus test on the executive's capacity to marshal broad-based cross-community support. Faulkner's unionists and the Alliance Party performed particularly badly, winning 13.1 and 3.2 per cent of the vote respectively. The SDLP slightly increased its share from the 1973 assembly election, with 22.4 per cent, suggesting that solid support existed within the nationalist community for its recent achievements.

Prior to the election, the three parties to the executive neither entered into an electoral pact nor coordinated their electoral strategies. In South Belfast, Alliance stood against outgoing pro-assembly unionist MP, which helped ensure a comfortable victory for the UUUC's candidate. The loyalist troika brought together Craig's Vanguard Unionist Loyalist Coalition, Paisley's DUP and West's Official Unionists, in what was a rather uneven and uncomfortable partnership. As John Taylor noted, Paisley's 'overbearing presence', coupled with his simmering rivalry with Craig, made the alliance particularly 'difficult to work'.[75] Reflecting on the election results, Frank Cooper believed that if the government managed to deflate the DUP leader then this, in turn, would deflate the UUUC. Sooner or later, he concluded, the unionist community was going to have to be presented with a stark choice: it could either back Faulkner the moderate or side with Paisley the malevolent 'wrecker' and 'hate merchant'.[76]

Having miscalled the election, Heath resigned as prime minister on 4 March, before Labour Party leader Harold Wilson formed a minority government. Merlyn Rees became Northern Ireland's third secretary of state, with Stan Orme and Lord Jack Donaldson joining him as minister of state and parliamentary under-secretary of state respectively. Frank Cooper retained his position and, being an old friend of Rees from their RAF days during the Second World War, enhanced his pervasive influence over the administration of Northern Ireland. The

SDLP were the only Irish party that were glad to see Wilson return to power.[77] Although he had maintained bipartisanship over Northern Ireland in opposition, his return to Downing Street did not bode well for the power-sharing executive. He did not have the strength of commitment to Stormont or unionism that the Conservative Party did, nor to the Whitelaw settlement. Wilson re-entered government under the assumption that the UUUC's success meant that power-sharing had failed as a method of regulating the Northern Ireland troubles; therefore he 'began to think about other approaches'.[78] More than that, his private secretary, Robert Armstrong, stressed that Wilson 'didn't have any investment in the Sunningdale Agreement, it wasn't his achievement, it was somebody else's'.[79] So having been sprung back into office during a global economic crisis, and finding himself seventeen seats short of an overall majority, Wilson was inclined to 'put a lid on' Northern Ireland[80] and concentrate on winning a second general election in 1974.[81] That is what he did. Furthermore, Wilson's closest political confidants, Bernard Donoughue and Joe Haines, both contend that, due to his deteriorating mental health, he only planned to be in office until 1976.[82] Donoughue stresses that Wilson 'didn't take any initiatives on anything because he knew he was going',[83] and of the issues that he wanted to address in that time, Haines admits that 'Northern Ireland was not at the top of the pile'.[84]

Wilson had never made any secret of his anti-unionist sentiments, but having involved himself in discussions with the IRA in 1972, he was as distrusted by the ruling elite in Dublin as he was by the leaders of Stormont's old order in Belfast.[85] In opposition, Rees and Orme had also expressed their contempt for unionism. Rees viewed Craig as the most 'evil' politician Ireland had produced 'in 150 years', which was saying something given the Welshman's rather idiosyncratic reading of Irish history.[86] Like Whitelaw, Rees was emotionally affected by his involvement in Northern Ireland but, unlike his predecessor, he found himself befuddled by the irreconcilable national antagonisms at the heart of its troubles and out of his depth in the ever-shifting sands of its political process. As secretary of state, he was neither able to distance himself from events nor take firm decisions and stick with them. And he often appeared tormented by the righteousness of different points of view or swayed into reactionary decision-making by rapidly-changing events, all of which left him hopelessly ineffective and consistently unable to provide firm leadership.

* * * *

On Friday 1 March the Irish Supreme Court rejected Boland's appeal, concluding that the Irish government's declaration did not acknowledge that Northern Ireland was part of the UK: 'Clause 5 of the communiqué, containing British and Irish declarations distinct from each other, is in no sense an agreement on fact or principle.' The court ruled that 'the status of Northern Ireland' and the acceptance of it by the Irish government were merely a reference to the '*de facto* position of Northern Ireland, and nothing else, and the respective declarations are no more than assertions of the policies of the respective governments, matters clearly within their respective executive functions'.[87]

Following discussions with his pro-assembly group, which had been reduced to seventeen members after officially losing the support of Whitten and Stronge, Faulkner issued a statement that ruled out any further discussion or cooperation with the Irish government unless it agreed to 'accept the right of the people of Northern Ireland to determine their own future'.[88] Talks between the pro-assembly unionists and the Irish government over a Council of Ireland, he said, were being put into cold storage. Having suffered a humiliating electoral defeat at the hands of James Kilfedder in North Down, Bradford had proposed this measure in efforts to weaken Faulkner's position on the executive.[89] At this point, Faulkner was certain of the support of roughly half of his assembly group; even his closest supporters felt there was presently no bargain on offer that could politically justify his acquiescence in the establishment of a Council of Ireland. Nevertheless, Lynch criticised the unionist minority in Ireland for their 'intransigent insistence' that the majority should acknowledge their aspiration to maintain the link with Britain as a '*de jure* right'.[90] And Cosgrave, who was preparing to make a statement to the Dáil on the question of Northern Ireland's status, postponed his speech to avoid creating the impression that he was capitulating to Faulkner's demands.[91]

On 5 March, Faulkner told an anxious executive that the general election result was a 'clear warning' from the unionist community; therefore their priority, from this point onwards, must be to preserve Northern Ireland's power-sharing arrangements. Hume attacked Bradford for publicly stating that the executive's base should be broadened and criticised Faulkner for issuing a statement that ruled out further cooperation with the Irish government without having consulted with either the SDLP or the executive. Hume said that the public had taken Faulkner's message to mean that the all-Ireland bodies had been put on ice. If this was the case, he said, 'his party would go' and Northern Ireland would be 'back in the hands of the extremists'.[92]

No progress had been made on extradition and the executive was aware that the Law Commission's findings would be wholly inadequate, given the Irish government's continued reticence towards cross-border security cooperation. Currie urged his colleagues not to panic. Morrell suggested that the executive should 'rock back to some degree', blaming Dublin and not each other for the predicament they were in. Not panicking, Hume argued that when power-sharing was first proposed there had been a general degree of opposition to the concept, but the idea now seemed to have been generally accepted. In similar circumstances, he said, if the Council of Ireland was pushed through quickly, then the public's reaction would be the same.[93] But the circumstances were not at all the same. The executive had been badly thrown off course by the general election result and Faulkner had broken with the SDLP. Moreover, the Irish government's defence in the Boland case, and FitzGerald's recent announcement that new extradition legislation was out of the question, had also damaged the executive.

The unionists defended Faulkner's actions. Had he not issued the statement, they argued, the executive would no longer enjoy the support of his unionist assembly group. Bradford told the nationalist ministers that unionists could not see how cooperation with the Irish government was benefiting Northern Ireland in any way. Faulkner suggested issuing a statement to reassure the public that the executive 'stood firmly together' and was 'not going to rush into Sunningdale'. He convinced the SDLP ministers that it was now the Irish government's turn to take the necessary political risks for Sunningdale's agreements to be implemented. Hume proposed a compromise: 'the executive are united on policy but agree that its successful implementation will demand not only resolution and determination by them, but a delivery, in the letter and spirit, of those commitments entered into by the British and Irish Governments'.[94]

After only nine weeks in office, the power-sharing executive had become so unstable that the parties to it were appealing, over the heads of their own supporters, to the two governments to provide political support to ensure that it did not collapse. Faulkner had telephoned

Cosgrave earlier in the day to inform him that should the executive ignore the general election result and go 'ahead blindly' towards ratification then it would lose the backing of his entire assembly group. Those members had thus far supported the executive without departing from the agreements reached at Sunningdale, but they would go no further without reciprocal moves from Dublin on the issues of status, extradition and joint action to combat terrorism in Northern Ireland. Cosgrave reminded Faulkner that the Law Commission was not going to reach agreement and, making a remark that should have alerted the unionist leader to the Irish government's present thinking, questioned the attitude of Wilson's government towards the power-sharing settlement.[95]

On 6 March, Rees declared that he did not believe that the Sunningdale Communiqué, like 'any bit of paper', represented 'the last word' on the Irish question,[96] which seemed to suggest that his government was keeping its options open over whether or not it should back the executive. Faulkner was further deflated by rumours that Heath had been tempted to remain in office with the support of the seven Official Unionist Westminster MPs, after the Liberals rejected his offer to form a coalition. Had the unionists taken the Conservative Party whip this would have split the UUUC, but it would have been very damaging to the settlement that Whitelaw had constructed. Faulkner contends that the Tory whip was accepted, only for Captain Orr to withdraw it, on 4 March, under pressure from Paisley, on the one hand, and fervent opposition from Whitelaw and Pym on the other. When they met in London Faulkner warned Rees that in the absence of any movement from the Irish government on the issues of status and security, he did not possess 'a single card to play' in the Northern Ireland political process.[97] And the following day Rees notified FitzGerald that Faulkner's supporters felt that all was lost, with Bradford suggesting that they would 'have to look in other directions'.[98]

Unsympathetic to Faulkner's predicament, FitzGerald told Rees that the unionist leader was simply 'wilting under pressure', having 'not been brought up in the tough tradition of Irish politics'.[99] Faulkner was simply attempting to reinterpret agreements that he had accepted at Sunningdale; therefore this made it all the more important that the two governments ratified them before matters went further adrift. Frank Cooper argued that what Faulkner actually needed was for the Irish government to take tough action against the IRA. Moreover, should Cosgrave make a 'major impact' declaration on status, he said, and should he follow it up with reinforcing statements, then this would have a substantial impact on the unionist community. Concerned that his government's position would be 'whittled away with nothing in return', FitzGerald stressed that he was reluctant to let Faulkner off the hook by taking unilateral action before ratifying a package agreement.[100] When he pressed the British to make progress on their commitment to run down internment, Cooper contended that the unionist community was presently 'incapable of taking wholesale releases'.[101] Following the meeting FitzGerald complained bitterly that the British found inadequacy in any declaration the Irish made on status which fell short of addressing the need for future constitutional change.[102] Moreover, he criticised the government for creating a sense of inertia in the Northern Ireland political process by stalling the settlement's ratification.[103]

The SDLP leaders were divided over how to respond to the crisis on the executive. The unionist ministers were demanding a massive clampdown on the IRA, and Currie, Devlin and Fitt agreed with them that this was urgently required. More than that, Devlin appeared to share Faulkner's view that ratification could not take place until effective security action had been taken, which might delay a second conference until May or June. The IRA had recently obliterated the town centres of Dungannon, Omagh and Strabane, leaving the SDLP men confident in their assertion that stringent security measures would be well received by the vast majority of people in Northern Ireland. And they clashed with the Irish government for failing to prevent 'flying columns' of rotating IRA teams from launching cross-border attacks from Monaghan into Armagh and Tyrone. Arresting and trying high-profile leaders such as Dáithí Ó Conaill or Séamus Twomey, the SDLP argued, would have a tremendous effect on unionist opinion. The government's response was that it would be easier if offenders were arrested and charged when and where they committed their offences. Dismissing the government's concern that taking 'effective action' might lead to a 'shooting war' between the IRA and Irish security forces, Devlin retorted that it might very well come to that.[104] Moreover, the fact that the IRA army council had narrowly voted in favour of boycotting the recent elections suggested that some of its members were again looking for a way out of the cycle of violence.[105]

Even if Cosgrave made a declaration on status along the lines agreed at Hillsborough, the SDLP ministers were no longer confident that this would fully satisfy Faulkner. They believed that he was hoping to cut a deal whereby unionists would accept the wholesale release of detainees and, in return, the SDLP would abandon its attachment to the Council of Ireland proposals. Hume advised the Irish government that it should show Faulkner an advance copy of its statement on status so as to avoid making a concession only for the unionist leader to reject it on the grounds that it was inadequate. Hume had formed a completely different analysis of recent events to that of the other SDLP ministers. Having moved too fast for even his own moderate supporters, he believed that Faulkner had 'seen the writing on the wall' and now wanted to 'abandon the Sunningdale Agreement', having concluded that it was unlikely to ever be implemented. Consequently, the unionist leader's current actions were designed to ensure that when it all came crashing down, 'the blame for the breakdown will be laid at Dublin's door'. Faulkner's primary aim was to establish the principle of power-sharing with the SDLP and, regardless of what the Irish delivered on status, extradition or security, Hume was convinced that he would find reason to break the agreement over the Council of Ireland proposals. He took the view that the Irish government would be 'ill-advised' to make further concessions to Faulkner 'in any major way'. A gesture should be made, he argued, if only to show goodwill to the new Labour government and tease out Faulkner's intentions. And he urged Donlon to ensure that Cosgrave went no further in his statement than had roughly been agreed at Hillsborough.[106]

On the basis of these discussions Donlon advised his political masters that having made a concession to Faulkner, a deadline in March should be set for Sunningdale's ratification. If Faulkner refused to meet that deadline, then the SDLP would consider how it might withdraw from the power-sharing executive and the agreements it had reached at Sunningdale. In Hume's view, if the reduction of the Council of Ireland proposals was the price to be paid for keeping Faulkner in office, then power-sharing had to be sacrificed.[107] This was certainly not a view shared by all the SDLP ministers or assembly members, most notably Devlin and Fitt. But it was Hume's view that carried the most weight in Dublin and London. And the following day his analysis was relayed to Cosgrave, and then to Rees when he met FitzGerald on 7 March.[108]

Hume's analysis skewed the negotiating positions of both the SDLP and the Irish government. Significantly ahead of northern nationalist opinion, which viewed power-sharing as a great advance, his negotiating position diminished the prospect of it becoming established as a stable form of government in Northern Ireland which was acceptable to both unionists and nationalists. People in Northern Ireland were sickened by the ruthless and indiscriminate escalation of Provisional IRA violence that the peace process had provoked. Moreover, it was clear from the attitudes of many SDLP assembly members that the vast majority of nationalists would accept and support effective action from the security forces, on both sides of the border, against the IRA.

The Council of Ireland proposals were no more a deal breaker issue for SDLP voters than they were for most unionists. The SDLP's supporters were far more concerned with ending internment, reducing violence and the day-to-day problems of employment and housing. Public opinion was evenly split on the issue: 41 per cent of people thought the Council of Ireland proposals were a good idea in principle, 37 per cent viewed them in a negative light, while over two in ten people had either never heard of them or did not state a view as to whether they were good or bad. Two-thirds of those who viewed the proposals in a favourable light were Catholic, and two-thirds were of the opinion that if a Council of Ireland was set up, then it should have responsibility for the suppression of terrorism throughout the island, with only 15 per cent opposed to this idea.[109] And when Donlon suggested to a group of Currie's constituents that a security role for the council might help end political violence, they told him bluntly that instead of waiting for Godot, the Irish government would be better off rounding up the IRA along the border and putting them in prison. One woman present told him that there was not much point in nationalists having the 'guts to lock our doors at night if the boys can hop over the border, not only to safe beds but to a hero's welcome'.[110] Such dispatches must have made awkward reading in the DFA, as they totally contradicted Hume's doctrinal nationalist view of where a settlement to the Northern Ireland troubles lay. Nevertheless, while the executive in Belfast was functioning as an administrative governmental body, the Irish government had not psychologically accepted its existence, continuing instead to deal with the three parties to it on an individual basis.

* * * *

Despite the election result, neither of the two governments nor the parties to the executive had completely given up on Sunningdale's agreements. What each party was prepared to do to implement these accords, however, was uncertain. What was certain was that Wilson was not replicating Heath's approach to political reform in Northern Ireland. No less than Heath, he was searching for a policy that would reduce the British military commitment in Northern Ireland and end direct rule. Wilson was preoccupied with the economic, political and social problems that he had inherited from Heath, and focused on his party's preparations for a second general election that year. His officials, however, were considering the international legal, political, economic and military implications of a complete disengagement from and constitutional break with Northern Ireland. The Foreign Office view was that the fallout from a complete disengagement could make Britain 'significantly less attractive' to other states as an ally, as a political or economic partner, or as a place to invest in or lend money to. More than that, they informed the prime minister that abandoning Northern Ireland to civil war might be viewed abroad as constituting an act of 'international delinquency' in itself.[111]

Making a 'solemn declaration' to a packed Dáil on 13 March, Cosgrave put into words the *de facto* recognition that his predecessor, Seán Lemass, had bestowed upon Northern Ireland by his actions, when he became the first taoiseach to visit Stormont in 1965. The Sunningdale Communiqué, Cosgrave said, referred to 'the *de facto* status of Northern Ireland', that is to say 'the factual position of Northern Ireland is that it is within the United Kingdom and my Government accept this as a fact'. With the support of Fianna Fáil, Cosgrave conveyed almost the exact wording that Bradford had requested from the Irish government at Hillsborough. And although he refrained from explicitly reiterating his government's aspiration for Irish unity, seemingly heeding Hume's advice, he omitted any reference to constitutional change, security or terrorism.[112]

Signalling to his critics that 'realism in politics is the art of ever recurring renegotiation', Bradford again called for the executive's base to be broadened. Describing the Irish government's reserve over the question of status as a 'matter of legal semantics', he said that the electorate's 'howl of protest' on 28 February was a 'clear cut message to go into reverse'; therefore unionists must 'slam the breaks' on Sunningdale until Dublin agreed to extradite fugitive offenders.[113] Paisley was even more scornful, telling unionists that all Cosgrave had done was 'recognise his own agreement' at Sunningdale in a 'vain attempt to bail out Faulkner'.[114] Unlike the 'Republican Unionists' on the executive, Paisley promised that the UUUC would not undermine Northern Ireland's constitutional integrity just to ensure 'Éire' fulfilled its moral obligation to extradite terrorists to the UK.[115] The DUP leader's criticisms must have stung the coalition in Dublin, as Irish senator Billy Fox had just been murdered by the IRA near Clones in County Monaghan. And bitterness remained at the heart of the debate, with Paisley interrupting tributes to Fox in the assembly to complain that the house did not show the same remorse when members of the RUC and UDR were murdered by the very same terrorists.[116]

Two days earlier, Donlon and Nally had travelled to Belfast to consult with both Rees and Faulkner over the wording of the Irish government's statement, but the unionist leader had departed from Stormont by the time they arrived. When Bloomfield relayed Cosgrave's message by telephone, Faulkner described it as the 'first concrete' step that the Irish government had taken since the Sunningdale conference. He voiced his concern, however, that Cosgrave might regard this as all that was required from his side before the Sunningdale Communiqué was ratified. Bloomfield articulated his personal view, that the general election result represented a 'howl of rage' from the unionist community against what it perceived as an imbalanced agreement. Cosgrave's statement, he said, should not be looked upon as 'necessarily getting us out of the wood'. Nally pointed out that 30 per cent of the population had not even bothered to vote and, of those who did, around 42 per cent favoured pro-Sunningdale parties; therefore the Ulster eleven had gained an altogether disproportionate return for their votes. Bloomfield reiterated his analysis to the Irish officials. There was a real danger, he said, that should the Council of Ireland idea be pushed too hard, without the consent of a large part of the unionist community, then they might find there to be no Protestant 'at the other end of the bridge'.[117]

NOTES

1. Interview with Sir Oliver Napier, Holywood, 29 December 2000.
2. Interview with Lord Kilclooney, Westminster, 15 February 2001.
3. Interview with Robert Ramsey, Cultra, 6 March 2008.
4. Interview with Sir Ken Bloomfield, Craigavad, 19 December 2007.
5. DT2005/7/627, Visit to Northern Ireland, Donlon, 28 February/1 March 1974.
6. ICBH, *British Policy in Northern Ireland, 1970–4*, p.66.
7. DT2005/7/625, Statement by Edward Kennedy, 10 December 1973.
8. DT2004/21/627, Note at the conclusion of Sunningdale, Noel Dorr, 9 December 1973.
9. Interview with Muiris Mac Conghail, Dublin, 24 July 2007.
10. DT2004/21/627, Statement by Neil Blaney, 11 December 1973.
11. Interview with Noel Dorr, Dublin, 12 July 2007.
12. *Dáil Debates*, 12 December 1973.
13. *Dáil Debates*, col. 1579, 12 December 1973.
14. Interview with Mahon Hayes, Dublin, 24 July 2007.
15. Northern Ireland Assembly, vol. 1, cols 166–7, 16 October 1973.
16. PRONI/D4211/4/1/23, Roy Bradford Papers, Executive Diary, 8 January 1974.
17. Interview with Sir Ken Bloomfield, Craigavad, 19 December 2007.
18. D4211/4/1/23, Roy Bradford Papers, Executive Diary, 8 January 1974.
19. *Irish Times*, 4 January 1974.
20. CJ4/470, Allan to Trevelyan, 2 January 1974.
21. Interview with Robert Ramsey, Cultra, 6 March 2008.
22. Interview with David Smyth, London, 18 February 2008.
23. CJ4/470, Save Ulster Rally, Lisburn, 5 January 1974.
24. CJ4/470, Heath to Cosgrave, 10 January 1974.
25. DT2005/7/624, Peter McLachlan phone call, 4 January 1974.
26. Minutes of the Northern Ireland Executive, OE2/3, Minutes of Executive Meeting held at Stormont, 17 January 1974.
27. Interview with Sir Ken Bloomfield, Craigavad, 19 December 2007.
28. *Sunday Press*, 16 December 1973.
29. Interview with Sir Oliver Napier, 29 December 2000.
30. McIvor Papers, PRONI, D/2962/1/12/8, Ardill to McIvor, 4 January 1974.
31. CJ4/470, Faulkner to Cosgrave, 10 January 1974.
32. OE1/2/1, Minutes of the Northern Ireland Executive, Stormont, 8 January 1973.
33. PREM15/2142, Heath to Cosgrave, 10 January 1974.
34. CJ4/470, Meeting between Pym and O'Sullivan, London, 11 January 1974.
35. CJ4/470, Cosgrave to Heath, 14 January 1973.
36. DT2005/7/624, Visit to Belfast, Donlon, 9 January 1974.
37. DT2005/7/624, Nally to Cosgrave, 9 January 1974.
38. *Irish Times*, 28 December 1973.
39. CJ4/470, Tel. No. 34, Galsworthy to FCO, 16 January 1974.
40. Speech by SDLP Assembly member Hugh Logue at Trinity College Dublin, 17 January 1974.
41. DT2005/7/625, Meeting between Cosgrave and Faulkner, 16 January 1974.
42. Interview with Declan Costello, Dublin, 23 July 2007.
43. Interview with Noel Dorr, Dublin, 12 July 2007.
44. DT2005/7/625, Meeting between Cosgrave and Faulkner, 16 January 1974.
45. ICBH, *British Policy in Northern Ireland, 1970–4*, p.48.
46. Interview with Dermot Nally, Dublin, 7 March 2008.
47. OE1/35, Meeting between Faulkner and Cosgrave, Baldonnel, 16 January 1974.
48. *Irish Times*, 18 January 1974.
49. *Irish Times*, 23 January 1974.
50. OE2/4, Minutes of the Northern Ireland Executive, Stormont, 22 January 1974.
51. PREM15/2142, Confrontation with Dr Paisley, 22 January 1974.
52. OE2/6, Minutes of the Northern Ireland Executive, Stormont, 28 January 1974.

Hands Across the Border

53. Interview with Sir Oliver Napier, Holywood, 29 December 2000.
54. DT2005/7/625, Nally to Cosgrave, 25 January 1974; Interview with Dermot Nally, Dublin, 10 May 2001.
55. Interview with Mahon Hayes, Dublin, 24 July 2007.
56. Interview with Garret FitzGerald, Dublin, 12 September 2001.
57. OE2/8, Minutes of the Northern Ireland Executive, Stormont, 5 February 1974.
58. Interview with Wally Kirwan, Dublin, 7 March 2008.
59. DT2005/7/627, Visit to Northern Ireland, Donlon, 28 February/1 March 1974.
60. DT2005/7/625, SDLP delegation, 25 January 1974.
61. DT2005/7/626, Meeting between the Irish Government and the Northern Ireland Executive, Hillsborough, 1 February 1974.
62. Northern Ireland Assembly, vol.2, col. 551, 5 February 1974.
63. OE1/35, Faulkner to Cosgrave, 6 February 1974.
64. OE1/35, Cosgrave to Faulkner, 13 February 1974.
65. DT2005/7/627, Visit to Northern Ireland, Donlon, 28 February/1 March 1974.
66. CJ4/470, Meeting between Woodfield, Trevelyan and O'Sullivan, 7 February 1974.
67. *The Times*, 17 February 1974.
68. Interview with Sir Robin Chichester-Clark, London, 25 June 2008.
69. *Dáil Debates*, Col. 1538, 26 February 1974.
70. *Dáil Debates*, Col. 1521, 26 February 1974.
71. *Dáil Debates*, Col. 1533, 26 February 1974.
72. *Dáil Debates*, Col. 1550, 26 February 1974.
73. Interview with Garret FitzGerald, Dublin, 12 September 2001.
74. *Irish Times*, 1 March 1974.
75. Interview with Lord Kilclooney, Westminster, 15 February 2001.
76. DT2005/7/628, Visit to Northern Ireland, Donlon, 21/22 March 1974.
77. Interview with Noel Dorr, Dublin, 12 July 2007.
78. ICBH, *British Policy in Northern Ireland, 1970–4*, p.56.
79. Interview with Lord Armstrong, Westminster, 24 October 2007.
80. Interview with Lord McNally, Westminster, 9 June 2008.
81. Interview with Lord Armstrong, Westminster, 24 October 2007.
82. Interview with Lord Donoughue, Westminster, 27 February 2007.
83. Ibid.
84. Interview with Joe Haines, Tunbridge Wells, 19 February 2008.
85. Interview with John McColgan, Dublin, 9 August 2007.
86. London School of Economics, Merlyn Rees Papers, Rees1/4, *Northern Ireland*, p.5; see also M. Rees, *Northern Ireland: A Personal Perspective* (London: Methuen, 1985).
87. The Supreme Court, Boland v An Taoiseach and Others, 1 March 1974.
88. *Irish Times*, 5 March 1974.
89. DT2005/7/627, Visit to Belfast, Donlon, 6 March 1974.
90. *Irish Times*, 5 March 1974.
91. CJ4/471, Tel. No. 114, Galsworthy to White, 5 March 1974.
92. OE2/10, Minutes of the Northern Ireland Executive, Stormont, 5 March 1974.
93. Ibid.
94. Ibid.
95. OE1/35, Telephone conversation between Faulkner and Cosgrave, 5 March 1974.
96. *Irish Times*, 7 March 1974.
97. CJ4/786, Meeting between Rees and Faulkner, Stormont, 6 March 1974.
98. DT2005/7/627, Meeting between FitzGerald and Rees, London, 7 March 1974.
99. DT2005/7/629, Meeting between Cosgrave and Wilson, London, 5 April 1974.
100. CJ4/471, Meeting between Rees and FitzGerald, London, 7 March 1974.
101. DT2005/7/627, Meeting between FitzGerald and Rees, London, 7 March 1974.
102. *Financial Times*, 8 March 1974.
103. DT2005/7/627, FitzGerald to Rees, 11 March 1974.
104. DT2005/7/627, Meeting between SDLP and Irish Government, Dublin, 8 March 1974.

105. PREM15/2142, Douglas-Home to Galsworthy, 18 February 1974.
106. DT2005/7/627, Visit to Northern Ireland, Donlon, 6 March 1974.
107. Ibid.
108. DT2005/7/627, Meeting between FitzGerald and Rees, London, 7 March 1974.
109. NOP Market Research survey conducted between 31 March and 7 April.
110. DT2005/7/628, Visit to Northern Ireland, Donlon, 21/22 March 1974.
111. PREM16/146, Harding to Smith, 26 April 1974.
112. *Dáil Debates*, 13 March 1974.
113. DT2005/7/628, Speech by Bradford, Belfast, 13 March 1974.
114. *Irish Times*, 14 March 1974.
115. *Irish Times*, 13 March 1974.
116. Northern Ireland Assembly, vol. 2, cols 1520–1, 12 March 1974.
117. DT2005/7/628, Statement on Status of Northern Ireland, 12 March 1974.

6

The Other End of the Bridge

Following the general election defeat, Faulkner's task was to renegotiate the Sunningdale Communiqué and ratify a more balanced settlement. To succeed he would need robust support from the British government, for his unionist opponents had begun plotting to remove him from office by bringing down the power-sharing executive. So in April 1974, the executive's chances of survival depended on two things: the propensity of Faulkner's nationalist colleagues in Belfast and Dublin to compromise over the Council of Ireland proposals; and the level of force the British were prepared to use to defend it against both loyalist and republican paramilitaries.

Should the Sunningdale Communiqué be pushed through against the wishes of the majority of the people, then the executive would face an 'uprising' that would constitute a 'rebellion' against the British government in Northern Ireland. This was Paisley's warning to Rees, when he signalled that the UUUC's constitutional opposition to power-sharing was drawing to a close. From 2 April, it would no longer be a part of the assembly; its members did not recognise the executive as the legitimate government of Northern Ireland and therefore they would only participate in matters beyond its scope.[1]

Faulkner's reaction to Cosgrave's declaration on status was more encouraging. Having finally attained one of his prerequisites for agreement, the unionist leader stated that 'for the first time' since partition, an Irish government had publicly recognised Northern Ireland's factual constitutional status and, so long as a majority so wish it, accepted 'our right to remain part of the United Kingdom'.[2] He hoped that the taoiseach's remarks would garner the necessary support in the Republic of Ireland 'to remove the status of Northern Ireland from public controversy'.[3] Partly confirming Hume's pessimistic analysis, Faulkner indicated that he expected developments on the other important aspects of the Sunningdale package to be forthcoming. The British were happy that Cosgrave's statement had achieved its primary objective, but they accepted Faulkner's view that immediately ratifying Sunningdale's agreements would cause further damage to the executive.

Cosgrave pressed for the second conference to be held on 10 April, but the British saw no reason to rush the formation of a Council of Ireland. The question of the communiqué's ratification provided them with a pressure point on which concessions might be squeezed from the Irish on extradition, cross-border security and the Strasbourg case, although Heath had not raised the human rights case at Sunningdale, perhaps having accepted that he would lose it.[4] The Irish government was concerned by the nuanced, yet clearly discernable, shift in British policy towards Northern Ireland since Wilson had taken office. They suspected that he was less willing than his predecessor to rebut backbench pressure to disengage from Northern Ireland altogether. Moreover, Faulkner confided in Fitt his belief that the Labour leader had again been in direct contact with the IRA, prompting Frank Cooper to reassure them both that he would 'not let Wilson, Rees or any of them' get involved in dealings with the IRA.[5]

John Laird tabled a motion for the 'renegotiation of the constitutional arrangements',[6] and an assembly debate on the power-sharing settlement began on 19 March. Acknowledging that he had heard the 'cry of outrage' from a divided community which had seen no let-up in the bloodshed and the terror that was being directed against the state, Faulkner made an impassioned defence of the Sunningdale Communiqué as an agreement designed primarily to address an 'all-Ireland terrorist problem on an all-Ireland basis'. Demanding 'wholehearted action in and by the Republic of Ireland' in the struggle against terrorism, he warned his unionist adversaries that it would be a grave mistake to 'alienate and rebuff' the nationalist community by passing the anti-Sunningdale motion.[7] Official Unionist Austin Ardill declared that his colleagues were 'not against power-sharing'; they were simply opposed to the establishment of a Council of Ireland with executive powers. Faulkner supporter Peter McLachlan suggested that its provisions could be renegotiated with a less complex formula put in place for developing cross-border relations. But he then broke ranks with his leader by agreeing to hold talks with the unionist assembly member for West Belfast, John Laird, thereby handing the UUUC a measure of respectability.[8]

In Dublin, Donlon was dismayed by the attitude of some SDLP backbenchers towards the Council of Ireland proposals. Lacking any solid ideological commitment to the idea, he complained that their attachment appeared to be premised on the argument that it is 'what we negotiated and we are not going to be pushed around by Faulkner'. They did not view the establishment of an all-Ireland body as the jewel in the crown of an Anglo-Irish agreement upon which the door to a united Ireland might be prised open. With the exception of Fitt, however, the SDLP ministerial team were convinced that Faulkner was using his old 'crucial vote' trick to stall the political process. They stressed to the Irish government that pressure was now required to 'bring him gently along the road'.[9] Moreover, they were convinced that a senior civil servant in the information department at Stormont was leaking information to Paisley on a daily basis.

In contrast to his colleagues, Hume did not believe that Faulkner intended to honour his commitments at Sunningdale, and he maintained his gloomy prognosis of the executive's short-term chances of survival. Faulkner's supporters and the Alliance Party assembly members were prepared to maintain the executive provided the Irish government carried out its security commitments to Northern Ireland. The longer this issue lay unaddressed, he argued, the less likely it was that Faulkner would deliver on the Council of Ireland proposals. Despite Cosgrave's statement on status, if Faulkner failed to renegotiate the Council of Ireland proposals then it was doubtful whether he could rely on his entire assembly group to rebuff the UUUC's anti-Sunningdale motion, which was scheduled for debate on 2 April. Moreover, the SDLP ministers signalled that they would withdraw and collapse the executive if the full implementation of this aspect of the package settlement lay unfulfilled.

Anglo-Irish relations had chilled considerably since the Westminster general election. Both governments were now considering how they might disengage from the Sunningdale process and, at the same time, avoid being blamed for the executive's collapse. Having hinted that a British withdrawal from Northern Ireland was a distinct possibility, Wilson had both increased the Irish government's anxieties over the prospect of civil war and encouraged the IRA to maintain its campaign of violence. At the end of March, O'Brien suggested that in order to ensure that the power-sharing executive survived, the Irish government should put some 'water' in the Council of Ireland proposals. FitzGerald agreed that more might have to be given to the unionists than had previously been envisaged, and while overt security cooperation with the British was one possibility, he remained implacably opposed to diluting the Council of Ireland proposals in any way. O'Brien argued passionately that a move to facilitate the implementation of this aspect of the settlement was the opposite of what the political process required. He stressed that measures to reconstruct unionist support for the agreements reached at Sunningdale were imperative, and this meant providing Faulkner with a considerable degree of political leeway.[10] Nevertheless, the government concluded that the least dangerous way for it to proceed would be to press ahead with the ratification process.

In Whitehall, British officials revamped secret contingency plans for the government to maintain control over the province in the event of the Northern Ireland Executive's collapse.[11] On 26 March, Rees shocked the power-sharing administration when he announced that the British government was 'reconsidering its wider Northern Ireland policy'.[12] He advised the executive that mounting pressure from within the Labour Party for the withdrawal of the British Army from Northern Ireland meant that its present military commitment of 15,000 troops was unsustainable. He did not inform the executive of defence minister Roy Mason's plan to reduce the army's strength in Northern Ireland, from sixteen to thirteen battalions, by withdrawing one unit per month over the next three months.[13] The government subsequently agreed to this with the proviso that flexibility might be introduced over timing.[14]

Reminding Rees that the executive was facing an insurgency, Faulkner complained that Northern Ireland would be 'left naked' if the army's military commitment was significantly scaled down. It was more appropriate, he argued, at this critical juncture in the peace process for the security forces to meet the threat posed by paramilitaries with the level of force that was required to prevent them from destroying the constitutional government of Northern Ireland. Bradford told Rees in no uncertain terms that the executive was being held accountable by the public for the Irish government's refusal to meet its security commitments to Northern Ireland. Yet Rees stunned the executive when he asserted that the only radical action he was minded to take was the legalisation of Sinn Féin and the UVF. He believed that this would enable Northern Ireland's paramilitary groups to become involved in politics. Faulkner reminded him that since the executive had lost the political initiative during the Westminster general election, it had in fact experienced a sustained challenge from both loyalist and republican paramilitaries who were hell bent on destroying it. More than that, he warned Rees that the design behind their coordinated campaign of terror was to test the Labour government's commitment to the power-sharing executive, by giving him a 'rough' welcome to Northern Ireland.[15] Nevertheless, Rees left his first encounter with the power-sharing executive under the impression that the three parties to it were completely disunited over how best to reassert governmental authority or improve the security situation.

Although the level of violence was static, and in fact considerably reduced in terms of murder, explosions and shooting incidents when compared to the previous two years, a more synchronised approach to disruption was clearly discernable from the paramilitaries. On 15 March, there were sixty bomb scares and fifteen bombs planted across Northern Ireland, transport links were blocked with over thirty car and train hijackings, and a sharp increase in shooting incidents was recorded. Escalating its campaign of violence, the IRA was focusing its attacks on towns in the east of the province, in an attempt to erode moderate unionist support for the executive. Despite searching over one million people in Belfast during the previous three weeks, and preventing the city centre from being bombed twice, there was no let-up to the violence that the security forces were facing in the capital.[16] And although there had been a marked increase in the number of people being detained, this had not provoked a reciprocal 'howl of rage' from the nationalist community.[17]

SDLP hopes that Rees would initiate a more generous second phase of prisoner releases were dashed, however, when the security forces reported that at least one third of the pre-Christmas releases had been re-interned, and of the sixty-five detainees released at Christmas, only fifteen had not become re-involved in violence to some extent.[18] This exacerbated the dilemma facing the SDLP leaders as executive ministers, for the release of the remaining 582 detainees would represent a major boost to the IRA and considerably hamper efforts to stem the violence that was being directed against a Northern Ireland government of which they were an integral part. Moreover, the Northern Ireland Electricity Board warned that power cuts could be the expected outcome of a pay dispute at the Ballylumford station, and similar strike action had been postponed at Belfast's sewage works. Despite these warnings, the NIO announced plans to replace the twenty-four-hour military guard with visiting patrols at Northern Ireland's power stations. The electricity board responded by expressing its deep concern that this would almost certainly lead to widespread industrial action by power station workers.[19]

Growing in confidence after thirteen months in office, albeit with a majority of only four seats, the Irish government tested bipartisanship on the sensitive issue of cross-border security.[20] It announced that new 'green card' instructions were being given to the army and, more bizarrely, sanctioned the procurement of six fighter jets and a ship to support the police in combating the IRA. Nevertheless, the Irish Army resisted pressure to engage in any overt cross-border cooperation, such as establishing radio contact with the British Army, as this would pose operational and legal difficulties and tarnish its reputation.[21]

* * * *

On 1 April, when Faulkner met Wilson for what was their first encounter as heads of UK administrations, the unionist leader attempted to quash Rees' proposal to politicise the republican movement. Faulkner warned Wilson that the IRA was determined to both destroy the executive and bomb its way to the talks table with a government which it believed was sympathetic towards its ultimate objectives. He argued that the Irish government's refusal to introduce legislative measures to extradite fugitive offenders had made Sunningdale's ratification impossible. To solve this problem, Faulkner offered a 'Fabian approach' to the implementation of the Council of Ireland proposals. The majority community, he said, could see no reason to embolden all-Ireland bodies with executive powers, or a permanent secretariat, when cross-border cooperation was feasible between Belfast and Dublin without 'a formal institution acting as a go between'. Faulkner was particularly disingenuous on this point. He told Wilson that Cosgrave would not allow power-sharing in Northern

Ireland to be lost over the finer technicalities of a 'high flown' Council of Ireland.[22] Bloomfield added that the great emphasis being placed by the Irish government on the Council of Ireland proposals stemmed from the SDLP's view that they were an 'important block in the whole constitutional edifice'.[23] Since ending detention was actually the SDLP's main concern, Faulkner suggested that introducing gradualism into the political process, at this stage, was unlikely to present a significant problem for nationalists outside Londonderry.

Faulkner left London with the impression that Wilson had received and understood his message – power-sharing would be lost if the Irish government was not disabused of the merits of pursuing Hume's myopic nationalist objectives. But on his return to Belfast, Faulkner was denied the assembly's backing in a critical debate on Sunningdale, which the opposition would have lost as it constituted a minority of thirty to the forty-six members who supported the executive. The vote had been scheduled to take place at 6 pm, but Paisley's filibustering resulted in an adjournment until 30 April.[24] Deprived of a major political boost prior to negotiations with the Irish government over ratification, Faulkner stormed from the chamber to jeers and abuse from his unionist detractors. The adjournment was a critical setback for the executive, as public opinion remained in favour of giving the power-sharing administration a chance to work. Almost seven in ten people took this view, and four in ten were strongly supportive of the new government. Support was greater among the Catholic population and the middle classes; 90 per cent of Catholics expressed favourable opinions towards the executive in comparison to 60 per cent of Protestants. Moreover, almost three quarters of the electorate approved of the idea of power-sharing between parties from both communities. Two thirds of Protestants said they approved of the new order, while almost the entire Catholic community was in favour of power-sharing. Just over a quarter of people, however, viewed it as an unacceptable idea, and many were sceptical about the built-in all-Ireland framework. While only a third of Protestants thought that the UUUC should share power in an executive, public opinion favoured it playing a normal role in the assembly. Despite such favourable findings, 58 per cent of Protestants still viewed the idea of a return to one-party rule at Stormont as an acceptable alternative. Unsurprising perhaps, as this form of government had reflected and reinforced the majority community's constitutional aspirations for the past half century. As for the alternative of fully integrating Northern Ireland into the UK, two thirds of the population found this acceptable, of whom 80 per cent were Protestant.[25]

Faulkner then sent Bloomfield to Dublin to deliver 'four proposals' on which progress towards the ratification of Sunningdale might be achieved: the three governments could press ahead with the early ratification and full implementation of the settlement which, in Faulkner's view, was 'no longer within the realm of practical politics'; they could conclude that the Council of Ireland proposals would be more acceptable if there was 'a substantial period of further delay' which, he felt, was a fairly 'unattractive course'; they could accept that the full Council of Ireland package was unacceptable to a majority of the population in Northern Ireland and 'cannot in any conceivable circumstances be made acceptable'; or they could accept that a Council of Ireland was still desirable, but recognise that 'progress can only be by stages, and phased in such a way as to win public confidence and support'.[26] Bloomfield signalled that Faulkner believed the solution to the outstanding problems at the heart of Northern Ireland's political process, lay somewhere between the third and fourth options.

The Irish government recognised that it could make no further progress on the Council of Ireland proposals without Faulkner. It believed, however, that he would have to proceed at some point with Sunningdale's ratification.[27] Faulkner suggested that agreement should be reached on the areas were substantial intergovernmental action could be explored. The all-Ireland ministerial body could be introduced to review the implementation of agreements reached every few months, and fulfil a role in relation to policing and human rights. Such a step would be balanced by a public commitment to progress towards a 'second and deeper state of cooperation', if and when the institutions enjoyed popular support, and this support could be measured by referenda.[28] Arguing that this would create a period of further uncertainty, Hume indicated that the SDLP were unlikely to accept these proposals.[29] He urged the Irish government to take the initiative while Faulkner was recovering his position at Stormont, and press for the Sunningdale settlement to be ratified within six weeks before he suffered another setback. The previous week, however, had been one the unionist leader would wish to forget.

Rees took some of the criticism that followed an upsurge in IRA violence; his announcement that troop reductions rather than reinforcements should be expected did little to dispel the notion that the Labour government could be bombed into setting a date for withdrawal. Devlin was approached by the IRA to engage in talks with the UVF over Desmond Boal's idea of establishing a federal Ireland, but Hume rejected the idea and stressed his total opposition to 'talking even to Sinn Féin'.[30] This proposal found little favour among the general public either, with only 14 per cent showing a positive interest in Boal's idea, and two thirds rejecting it.[31] The IRA's offensive increased pressure on Faulkner to squeeze credible security proposals from Dublin, and, vulgarly abused on the streets of Belfast and in the assembly, he faced the possibility that some of his assembly group would support the UUUC on the anti-Sunningdale motion.[32] Among the potential defectors were executive ministers Bradford and Kirk, and of the assembly group William Morgan, Reginald Magee and Peter McLachlan. This may have been a tactical move on the part of McLachlan to exaggerate the precariousness of Faulkner's position, as they had been close, but it illustrated just how isolated Faulkner was at this point. Nevertheless, with the exception of Hume, who still doubted the sincerity of Faulkner's intentions, the SDLP ministers believed that the unionist 'political survivor par excellence' would deliver, for without the executive he was finished.

With Wilson ruling out the possibility of fresh assembly elections, Faulkner had the remainder of the executive's four-year parliamentary term to convince his community of the settlement's virtues. Although Rees pressed the SDLP to both recognise the RUC and support its anti-terror campaign, they refused to do so until the Northern Ireland Police Authority was reconstituted following the establishment of a Council of Ireland. Illustrating his growing scepticism towards the Whitelaw settlement, Rees publicly announced that Sinn Féin and the UVF were being decriminalised to help them 'find a way back to political activity'.[33]

* * * *

On 5 April, Cosgrave travelled to Downing Street to defend his government's security record and set out its case for the early ratification of the Sunningdale Communiqué. One thousand Irish troops were being sent to support a thousand Irish police officers along the 300-mile Northern Ireland border, a 50 per cent increase in five months; therefore, with his security obligations fulfilled, Cosgrave saw no reason to delay the ratification process any further. Wilson told Cosgrave that Faulkner's crumbling support base within the unionist community was the settlement's Achilles' heel.[34] Conceding that the unionist leader was not 'fireproof', FitzGerald nevertheless expressed his exasperation at Faulkner's latest attempt to dilute the pre-agreed Council of Ireland proposals.

Rees requested a ministerial-level security conference to address the issue of interstate terrorism, stressing that results were essential before a signature could be arranged.[35] When he criticised the Irish government's success rate in targeting the IRA along the border, FitzGerald retorted that this was another example of 'Northern mythology', wherein all security headaches emanated from the South. Cross-border terrorism was not an important issue, he argued, as Northern Ireland was basically experiencing an 'indigenous' campaign of violence. Cosgrave highlighted that of the 108 political murders which had occurred over the previous six months, only eighteen had taken place in border areas and twelve of those in or around Crossmaglen, in south Armagh. But these statistics only reinforced the British view that there was indeed a very significant cross-border problem with which the Irish government should immediately concern itself. Rees highlighted that there had recently been forty-four border incidents in a single week; therefore cross-border cooperation was imperative, not least to ease unionist anxieties before making the Council of Ireland proposals a reality. Accepting that these proposals could not be renegotiated, Wilson indicated that in return for tough security action Faulkner would have to make the necessary 'jumps' that lay ahead in the political process.

Pressed by Cosgrave on British attitudes toward the plight of the Northern Ireland Executive, Wilson said British public opinion could be summed up in a nutshell: 'pull out and let them cut each other's throats'. Should the executive collapse, then the issue of British soldiers serving in Northern Ireland could well bring about an 'agonising reappraisal' of British policy. Wilson stressed that a second period of direct rule would be set against an entirely different psychological reality – the government would have abandoned almost all hope of finding a solution.[36] The two governments agreed that reciprocal legislation was required to provide extraterritorial jurisdiction on both sides of the border, Cosgrave would then conclude his discussions with the executive at a second Hillsborough summit and Sunningdale would be ratified after the independent Law Commission published its delayed report.

Following the meeting, Cosgrave's concerns deepened over what Wilson was prepared to do, in the short-term, to preserve the Northern Ireland peace process. When the delegation returned to Dublin, Dermot Nally urged him to strengthen the Republic of Ireland's security forces, not as a sop to Faulkner but in response to Wilson's comment that if he was forced to re-impose direct rule it would 'not be of the same sort'. Nally feared that the collapse of the executive might coincide with a declaration of intent by the British to withdraw from Northern Ireland altogether.[37]

Back in Belfast, attempting to regain the initiative by appealing for the devolution of security powers,[38] Faulkner claimed that he would not have re-entered government had he imagined that they had been permanently reserved. The SDLP leaders defeated a motion put to their party's central council which demanded their withdrawal from the executive if internment was not ended before 31 July 1974.[39] On 8 April, Faulkner again dispatched Bloomfield to Dublin to do his bidding. He informed Irish officials that Faulkner could not sign up to the full Sunningdale package unless the Council of Ireland proposals were significantly modified. Unionists were in a 'worrying mood', he said, and there appeared to be a real danger of widespread civil disobedience. Having received the message from his constituency – 'we will not be pushed any further' – Faulkner had fallen into line with the median unionist voter. If a 'new point of balance' could not be found on the executive, then Faulkner would resign and 'retire to the farm'. The Irish government could either act in accordance with developing political realities in Northern Ireland or it could attempt to impose its political agenda on Northern Ireland over the heads of the majority community.[40] When Irish officials suggested that Faulkner had not been a 'super salesman' for Sunningdale's agreements, Bloomfield told them that his difficulty now lay in selling those arrangements to his own assembly group. Having failed to provoke a violent rejection towards the idea of power-sharing from within the unionist community, the UUUC was considering launching a campaign of widespread civil disobedience, as a last resort, to destroy the executive before it became established as an acceptable form of government to both communities in Northern Ireland.

While Bloomfield was in Dublin, his political master informed Rees of the *fait accompli* that he had presented the Irish government with. This situation had arisen, he said, due to its intransigence on the key issues that the Sunningdale conference had sought to resolve. Should the British press ahead with ratification at this stage, Faulkner warned, a strong possibility existed that civil war would break out in Northern Ireland. He convinced Rees that provided the executive accepted its basic principles, the Irish government might accept a watered down Council of Ireland.[41] Having discussed the matter with Fitt, Hume and Currie, the unionist leader suggested that the SDLP would not allow the executive to collapse over the reduction of the Council of Ireland proposals. Once the nationalist party accepted his proposal that the all-Ireland structures should be adopted in stages, the details of which he had shown only to Fitt,[42] then the Irish government would fall into line with the SDLP and Sunningdale could be ratified.[43] The SDLP leaders gave the British a less rosy appraisal of how this idea was being received by the party faithful. Faulkner was losing his nerve, they said, but if he agreed to the Council of Ireland proposals, as set out in the Sunningdale Communiqué, then they were willing to accommodate him over the question of timing. This was, in effect, the reversal of Faulkner's proposed solution.

Late on Good Friday 12 April, Fitt told the British that, having held further talks with Faulkner, there was a 'ray of hope' that the SDLP would sign up to his phased implementation proposals, which he believed were in tune with public opinion.[44] Donlon was more explicit: although the nationalists would agree to postpone Sunningdale's full implementation 'for two months or so', they would not acquiesce in a process whereby the all-Ireland bodies became significantly reduced. The Irish government was concerned that a major U-turn on the Council of Ireland proposals would precipitate a backlash of opposition from Fianna Fáil. Lynch's support was conditional on the implementation of this aspect of the settlement, and Fine Gael had not forgotten the three decades that it had spent in the political wilderness, having been rejected at the ballot box as traitors to the republican cause in the 1920s.⁴⁵

From the British government's perspective, the key to moving the political process forward lay in convincing the SDLP that it was their turn to compromise, as the Irish government would then have no option but to follow the northern nationalist line. O'Brien confirmed this view during a visit to London, informing Rees that his government was likely to accept an agreement between the parties to the Northern Ireland Executive over the Council of Ireland proposals.⁴⁶ He stressed, however, that should the British Army be present at the forthcoming security conference, it would be a 'kiss of death' for the political process.⁴⁷ And he rebuked former Northern Ireland prime minister Terrance O'Neill for suggesting that a solution to the present crisis might be found between the province's extremes. Perplexed by this intervention, O'Brien said that the 'substance of the Sunningdale agreements is the best, and perhaps the only, hope in the middle or long term for peace in Northern Ireland'.⁴⁸

* * * *

On 18 April, Wilson made his first visit to Northern Ireland since becoming prime minister for the second time. Dispensing with pleasantries, the Labour leader told the Northern Ireland Executive that its recent experience of direct rule was a temporary expedient; therefore any return to this form of government would be brought about in radically different circumstances, as 'it would not be possible to go through it all again'.⁴⁹ He said that if all the other parties honoured the commitments they had entered into at Sunningdale, then he too was committed to those agreements. Contrary to assertions made by Cosgrave after his recent visit to London,⁵⁰ Wilson insisted that no firm date had been discussed on which ratification might take place. During the meeting, the prime minister gained a sense of how disunited the parties to the Northern Ireland Executive were in their approach to avoiding the re-imposition of direct rule. Fitt and Faulkner presented their respective cases for and against the early ratification of Sunningdale and detailed the different concessions that their parties required to reach agreement on a way forward. Backing Faulkner, Napier warned the prime minister that ratification day would be a 'D-Day' for extremists on both sides of the sectarian divide. Although it was clear from the discussions that the SDLP had no agreed party line towards Faulkner's proposal, Fitt was more with the unionist leader than against him. Attempting to settle the executive's nerves, Rees promised that there would be no early or wholesale withdrawal of British troops. But Wilson warned that should the army be caught in crossfire between the two communities, pressure to go would be hard to resist.[51]

GOC Sir Frank King and RUC chief constable Jamie Flanagan both informed Wilson that the continuing crisis at the heart of the Northern Ireland government had given the IRA a significant boost in morale. Their intelligence suggested that nine active service units, or 250 men, were currently operating from within the Republic of Ireland, and approximately 100 IRA supporters in Londonderry were facilitating their cross-border attacks. They complained that their task along the border was magnified by the fact that the Garda Síochána were unarmed, the Irish Army were unable to arrest IRA suspects and the Irish government were unwilling to propose the legislative changes that would empower them to do so. Although the IRA's capacity to create chaos and destruction was unquestionable, they suggested that its strength may be exaggerated, as its leadership were presently engaged in intensive indirect talks with British officials in Londonderry, which were being facilitated by the SDLP and the bishop of Derry, Edward Daly.[52]

King saw the political argument for placating the SDLP by quickly phasing out detention. From a security perspective, however, he argued that initiating wholesale prisoner releases would only further reinvigorate the IRA. The government could not improve the security situation without detention; therefore King believed that no further releases should be considered until violence had been brought to an end. Having learned of Wilson's plan to reduce the British Army's policing role, Flanagan stressed that his force, currently at 4,400 officers, was approximately 2,000 officers short of its normal peacetime strength.[53] The security situation was not quite as bad as it appeared, however, and King blamed this distortion on media hype, citing the example of a recent incident in which a BBC film crew had paid local children to stone British soldiers in order to obtain footage for a piece they were shooting on Londonderry.[54]

The British had stronger intelligence on the activities of the Protestant paramilitary groups than it had on their IRA counterparts. Although the mood among the UDA and UVF was bitter, King noted that a general acceptance of the power-sharing arrangements within the unionist community was apparent. Keeping their organisations supplied with weapons appeared to pose no significant problems to Northern Ireland's paramilitary leaders. Detonators were readily available in the Republic of Ireland, with guns and explosives arriving predominately from the US and a number of European channels. FitzGerald and Hume had both recently made speeches in the US warning of the consequences of providing financial support to the IRA. Hume had condemned the 'extreme and warped forms of patriotism' that were providing 'moral and financial support' on both sides of the Atlantic for the IRA. He told Irish America: 'I could easily wrap myself in a green flag ... and generate great feelings of "patriotism"' but instead, 'what we have done and are doing is to build new institutions in which conflict is replaced by partnership'.[55]

In a speech described by Rees as having been made with 'neither a script nor clearance', Mason made a *faux pas* which confirmed suspicions that his government was not committed to Northern Ireland in the long term.[56] During a miners' rally in Newcastle on 24 April, Mason said that 'demands are being made to set a date for withdrawal', and he suggested that this would force the 'warring factions to get together and hammer out a solution'.[57] His remarks caused considerable embarrassment to the government and forced Wilson to reiterate that there had been no change to its policy on Northern Ireland. Nevertheless, the incident was indicative of the 'hands off' attitude that had been adopted by Wilson towards Northern Ireland since returning to Downing Street, putting the onus on Belfast and Dublin to settle Irish problems between themselves.

Faulkner's relationship with his support base had continued to deteriorate. In administrative terms, the pro-assembly group was in complete disarray, and his efforts to explain his political strategy to them were, at best, lacklustre. But then his Official Unionist opponents, who his supporters remained in contact with through the assembly, were, as Napier put it, 'out to burn him at the stake'; therefore he had very few colleagues in whom he could confide.[58] By mid-April, unhappy with what he viewed as a demotion to the Department of the Environment,

Bradford was becoming increasingly 'anxious for the top job'.[59] By joining the pledged unionist faction he had hoped to replace Faulkner as chief executive when his leadership became untenable. He appeared to be preparing to lead a 'palace revolution', and many of his ministerial colleagues viewed him as 'with us but not of us'.[60] Bradford was also the main obstacle on the executive to progressing with Sunningdale's ratification and Rees was aware that he was looking for a way out.[61] Faulkner had been reluctant to bring Bradford into his ministerial team, but had he excluded him this would have significantly reduced his number of supporters in the assembly.

Bradford's relationship with the nationalist ministers was also deteriorating, especially so with Devlin, who represented 'the red rag to the Bradford bull'.[62] Devlin warned the Irish government that he was plotting an internal coup against Faulkner, by planning to bring Laird, Taylor and West onto the executive.[63] Outside the palace, Glengall Street was pressuring Faulkner's weakest, or most disloyal, assembly members in efforts to pick them off, one by one. Bradford, Magee and Lord Brookeborough had tied themselves to achieving movement from Dublin on extradition, which was the wedge issue on which Bradford hoped to lead an exodus from the pro-assembly group. Furthermore, assembly speaker Nat Minford doubted whether the Sunningdale debate could be closed on 30 April, after Paisley threw a procedural spanner in the works.[64] And in efforts to inject life into its flagging anti-Sunningdale campaign, at a three-day conference in Portrush,[65] the UUUC called for the 'Ulsterisation' of the fight against the IRA, as the Provisionals claimed the one thousandth casualty of the troubles on 20 April.

By the end of the month, the SDLP were presenting a more united front, with Fitt isolated in his support for Faulkner on the executive. Devlin had shifted away from the SDLP leader, signalling that unless the British moved on policing, internment and the Council of Ireland proposals, he was minded to resign within a month.[66] Currie accused Fitt of being totally out of touch with the assembly party who, he said, felt particularly boxed in over the executive's failure to end internment. Responding to pressure from those backbenchers, Hume called for the British to release all those who had been detained in 1971. Moreover, Currie linked the ratification issue to the problem of running down the rent and rates strike, as fixing a date would assist the party's efforts in bringing the protest to a close.

In Fitt's absence, the SDLP's executive body unanimously accepted the idea of implementing Sunningdale's agreements in phases, provided they were ratified immediately in their original form. Currie indicated that the party could concede to Faulkner's re-phasing proposals, but what it really needed was a 'ratification ceremony, document and banquet' to boost morale and keep the nationalist population with the political process.[67] Out of step with his nationalist colleagues on the executive, Fitt's 'politics came from the seat of his pants'[68] and he did not believe that his constituents shared Hume's view that power-sharing should be sacrificed if the Council of Ireland proposals fell by the wayside. Consequently, he ignored protests from west of the Bann SDLP hardliners such as Séamus Mallon and Hugh Logue, who were making life uncomfortable for Hume and Currie.

Further exposing the deepening fissures between the unionist and nationalist members on the executive, Robert Cooper led an Alliance Party delegation to Dublin in support of Faulkner's proposals to renegotiate aspects of the Sunningdale Communiqué. They lobbied the Irish government to make its implementation more broadly acceptable to both communities by amending Articles 2 and 3 of the Irish constitution. They argued that since the Council of Ireland proposals could not be successfully passed in the Northern Ireland Assembly at this point, Faulkner could not presently agree to a Council of Ireland with executive powers and a consultative assembly. Time was required for the executive to prove to the electorate that the all-Ireland structures were harmless. Meetings could occur every two months, allowing for cooperation to incrementally pave the way for a formal ratification conference in the assembly's mid-term. The all-Ireland bodies could then develop organically, without the blowing of trumpets and waving of flags. Nationalists should view this as 'Sunningdale by stealth', Cooper said, rather than seeing it as a fundamental renegotiation of its basic principles.[69]

* * * *

What the formal ratification of the Sunningdale Communiqué actually entailed remained unclear. The Irish government were expecting to sign an Anglo-Irish treaty, whereas the British were more inclined to sign an agreement as a declaration of government policy rather than as a legally binding accord. That the conference produced a communiqué rather than an agreement was a consequence of the parties agreeing to a number of politically binding measures in principle, which were not legally binding until further agreement was reached.[70] So it was an odd mixture of agreements, statements, unilateral declarations and multilateral undertakings which set out a multifaceted programme of governmental work on many interrelated issues. Tying them all together and making progress on all of them at once was neither politically possible nor administratively practical. Sunningdale had been negotiated as a package settlement, but being seen to ratify it as such was as attractive to certain parties as it was unattractive to others. Consequently, fear that certain parties would seek to renegotiate some of its agreements, or fail to implement policies that the communiqué had committed them to, lay at the heart of the ratification debate.

Fuelling speculation that a second Westminster general election would take place in June, the British signalled that, due to Faulkner's weakened position, ratification was unlikely to take place within the next six months. Press leaks suggested that disagreements between the British and Irish members of the Law Commission had resulted in British judges Robert Lowry and Brian Hutton writing a minority report. The commission was 'evenly divided', and had therefore been unable to make any 'agreed recommendation on extradition'. New extradition legislation was the first choice of the Northern Ireland and British members. The Irish members rejected this on the basis that introducing such measures would likely provoke constitutional legal challenges,[71] which Napier described as 'one of the thinnest legal arguments I have ever heard in my bloody life'.[72] The British members complained that the Irish government's unwillingness to introduce extradition legislation was motivated by political rather than security considerations. Although the British judges agreed with Napier's interpretation, they indicated that they were willing to settle for an extension of territorial jurisdiction.

British and Irish officials agreed that when the Law Commission's report was published, it would be a 'minus' rather than a 'plus' in their efforts to implement the settlement. Anglo-Irish relations soured further when Bradford and Rees both claimed to have information that a copy of the report had been given to the SDLP, which prompted strenuous denials from the Irish government. But the debacle was indicative of the backward-looking phase Anglo-Irish relations had entered. More than that, the Irish government suspected that Wilson had already decided to withdraw from Northern Ireland, but it had no official evidence with which to substantiate this view. And becoming evermore concerned about the threat posed to the executive by the unionist opposition, Frank Cooper urged his political masters to make a major effort to ratify Sunningdale within the next few weeks.[73]

On 7 May, Faulkner met with the full Northern Ireland administration after announcing that his pro-assembly group would form its own unionist party. Before the meeting, he had written to Rees urging him to reverse the government's 'dangerous' decision to withdraw the round-the-clock military guard from two of Belfast's electricity power stations. This was 'a potentially disastrous' move, he said, the announcement of which could lead to 'immediate, widespread industrial action by the power station workers' in Ballylumford and Belfast, where there was 'a militant labour force with a strong core of extreme loyalist supporters'. He asked Rees whether this was the sort of issue 'on which confrontation should be invited' by the government, pointing out that past experiences indicated that power station workers could control Northern Ireland's electricity grid. 'We could not win', Faulkner warned him, if a confrontation of this nature was allowed to develop.[74] The pressure was now on Faulkner and his ministerial colleagues to reassert their authority and avoid such a scenario.

The executive then turned its attention to a memo presented by Faulkner, dated 1 May, which suggested that the implementation of a Council of Ireland should occur in phases.[75] Attempting to drive a wedge between the SDLP negotiators and the Irish government, Faulkner argued that Dublin had pushed too hard for too many executive functions through the joint study groups. He said that there had been a 'firm political directive' from Irish officials to impose a Council of Ireland with extensive executive powers. They had simply refused to consider the negative political impact these measures would have on the executive. Cosgrave had responded to his 'four proposals' on 3 May, indicating that his government's position was that the outstanding issues were for the three parties to the Northern Ireland Executive to resolve; therefore if a consensus could be found then they should follow the timetable laid out by the two governments.[76] Faulkner argued that if the executive agreed a statement on how they intended to proceed, it would then be in a very strong position to persuade the Irish government to accept its collective view. If consensus could be found, then the executive would survive and the Irish government would not be able to challenge the decision it had reached. The unionists, the Alliance members and Fitt were all in agreement that it was no longer feasible to implement the settlement to the extent that had been agreed in December 1973.

The general unwillingness of all ministers to devolve power, or facilitate the kind of structures that the Irish government wanted, considerably strengthened Faulkner's hand in his efforts to renegotiate this aspect of the settlement. Reminding his colleagues that Sunningdale was binding, but 'not necessarily immediately', Napier argued that it was 'totally impractical' to fully implement the accord over the summer. Hume disagreed with this interpretation entirely. 'All parties had committed themselves to a concept', he said, and while he appreciated the problems of support the unionist members were experiencing, this idea should not be 'diluted' for the sake of 'political expediency'. If Sunningdale was ratified, he argued, then violence and opposition to the political process would evaporate and the SDLP would be able to support the police. Hume concluded that the executive should 'show strength and ratify', otherwise the British would pull out and 'the Protestants' would be the 'long-term losers'. Morrell retorted that unionists would think there was something 'very terrible' behind Sunningdale if the SDLP were suddenly able to support policing 'after ratification' but were unwilling to do so now. Moreover, the pro-assembly group had only accepted the second tier of a Council of Ireland on the premise that it would give loyalists a voice in the process. They clearly did not want that voice, so as far as the unionist ministers were concerned, the all-Ireland assembly proposals were excess baggage. Faulkner concluded that a consultative assembly should only come into operation when all, or almost all, of the members of the Irish parliament and the Northern Ireland Assembly were in favour of convening it. The unionists were all prepared to move forward with Sunningdale, Morrell and McIvor particularly constructive, and Bradford was boxed into a corner over his commitment to the executive and to the pro-assembly unionist group.[77] His chances of successfully leading a coup against Faulkner had diminished, as the majority of the unionist ministers and their pro-assembly party now supported Faulkner's strategy.

The unionist leader argued that the executive's strength lay in the fact that all its members supported the Sunningdale Communiqué's agreements. The SDLP had to be able to demonstrate that they were not abandoning the objective of a united Ireland, while the pro-assembly unionist group had to be able to persuade their supporters that they were not bringing about a united Ireland by the back door. A subcommittee was set up on which Bradford, Robert Cooper, Devlin, Hume, Morrell and Napier were tasked with exploring the different options available regarding executive functions, the consultative assembly and the secretariat, before proposing an acceptable package and having Sunningdale 'settled and out of the way' by the end of May. The committee would report back to the executive on 10 May, before it met with Rees the next day to discuss the Law Commission Report.

Faulkner envisaged two steps in this process. The executive would meet with the Irish government to agree the selection of a council of ministers, which would have a consultancy role in relation to appointments to the police authorities and human rights. It would be duty bound to review progress on agreed matters where cooperation between the two governments could take place.[78] In other words, the executive would renegotiate the aspects of the Sunningdale Communiqué that had brought the Irish government to enter into an agreement with the British government over Northern Ireland. The second step would be the signing of a document with the British government which incorporated the declarations on status, before registering this with the UN, which would mean that it was on record there as a legally binding accord.[79] Further stages in Sunningdale's implementation process might then be undertaken, depending on their acceptability to the Northern Ireland Assembly and the Irish parliament.

The executive broke with a renewed spirit of optimism and a determination to overcome the threat posed by sustained paramilitary violence and unionist opposition. Faulkner had convinced the SDLP members that they had to make concessions if the executive was to survive. It was agreed that there should initially be 'executive decision-making' and 'harmonisation' but no 'executive action'; therefore the establishment of the second tier of a Council of Ireland would be delayed, and the unionists would veto the immediate establishment of its headquarters and secretariat.[80] In return, the SDLP would seek the release of detainees as an expedient to offering its full support for the police.

Faulkner's success in unifying the executive around a new policy was a significant setback for FitzGerald, given his determination to at the very least see the nucleus of a secretariat formed and, at best, see some form of executive functions in which it could engage. The Irish government was also concerned that Wilson might attempt to devolve his security problems to either the executive or an all-Ireland council.[81] Nally stressed that if a weak Council of Ireland was established without a secretariat, then security powers would logically be devolved to the Northern Ireland Executive, reducing its ability to act as a stepping stone towards a united Ireland. However, the Irish government decided not to restrict the SDLP's negotiating position in a way that might prove detrimental to the survival of the executive. Donlon informed the nationalist ministers that the government had reluctantly accepted the proposed compromise, but that it favoured the immediate publication of the Law Commission Report.[82] And in what would be his last correspondence with Cosgrave as chief executive, Faulkner requested a meeting between their respective governments, despite having previously stressed his preference for moving directly to a tripartite conference.[83]

* * * *

On 8 May, the executive subcommittee met twice and produced a draft timetable for action: a second Hillsborough summit should be held before the end of the month and agreement must be reached on the phases by which, and under the conditions in which, a Council of Ireland could be implemented.[84] The document strongly represented Faulkner's view and gave the SDLP a good deal to negotiate away from. The nationalists were shocked to hear of Faulkner's request for a meeting between the executive and the Irish government. Faulkner had placed Bradford on the subcommittee both to raise the bar on unionist agreement and reinforce his isolation on the executive. The unionist members insisted that everything that the executive agreed to had to be subject to a 'test of opinion', i.e. implementation would be dependent on public approval by referenda. This made agreement harder to come by and ensured that Bradford's relationship with the SDLP members continued to deteriorate.[85] At long last, Faulkner was gaining the upper hand over his unionist rivals.

The SDLP ministers could not depart from their commitment to a 'full signing of Sunningdale', but they could agree to a gradual implementation of its provisions if the draft Council of Ireland proposals were strengthened and the referendum idea was dropped. For if the electorate rejected the idea of a Council of Ireland, as it likely would, then the SDLP would be stuck in a power-sharing executive, without the all-Ireland bodies that had enticed the Irish government to sign the Sunningdale Communiqué. This might preserve the executive, but if it came to enjoy widespread support in both communities, the agreements reached at Sunningdale would effectively reinforce partition. More than that, it would do more to legitimise partition than half a century of unionist rule from Stormont. Consequently, the SDLP and the Irish government both viewed the document as a significant step backwards from what had been agreed at Sunningdale, as it provided for a Council of Ireland that had the power to refuse to take any executive functions based on the unanimity rule. In other words, it established a unionist veto on all of the functions that the all-Ireland bodies might exercise and a permanent unionist veto on the composition of its secretariat. Meetings between ministers from the North and South would be held on certain 'cooperative agreements', as opposed to executive functions, so that decisions relating to the implementation of these agreements, such as the Foyle fisheries arrangements, 'may be made in the council of ministers, subject to the unanimity rule'.[86]

Faulkner had played his hand at a moment when the British government was broadly supportive of his position. Like his predecessor, Wilson was more concerned with quickly concluding agreement than with getting involved in the minutiae of the debate over the all-Ireland bodies. Although it appeared that Faulkner would follow the British government's position of begrudging acceptance on the Law Commission, he would only agree to ratify the Sunningdale Communiqué if he could renegotiate it with the Irish government and with the SDLP's support. This was a reversal of the position Faulkner had found himself in at Sunningdale. He could now negotiate directly as the chief executive of a functioning government rather than as the leader of a divided Northern Ireland party. By proceeding with ratification on this basis Faulkner had manoeuvred himself into a position that, should the British and Irish governments not support him, they might be blamed for the executive's collapse.

If Faulkner could reach agreement with his SDLP colleagues and take credit for having secured their acceptance of, and support for, the RUC, then this might allow him to consolidate his position and secure broad-based support for the power-sharing administration. He planned to force the Irish government into conceding on the Council of Ireland and, if it refused, blame Dublin for the collapse of the executive. In the space of four months, Faulkner's political fortunes had been revived, as he was now poised to grasp a significant victory for unionism out of the withering defeat that Sunningdale had represented for his community.

Beginning a day of talks with the executive on 10 May, Rees indicated that while troop reductions were still planned, the army would remain in Northern Ireland so long as it had a job to do in preventing violence. Fitt asked Rees whether the British were presently in contact with the IRA, and Hume suggested that while the IRA's Belfast brigade wished to continue its campaign of violence, the remainder of the organisation was willing to call a ceasefire. Rees replied that, on the basis of recent speculation, Hume's assertion was probably correct, but stressed that he was not talking to the IRA and could not talk to the IRA. The precondition for a Provisional IRA ceasefire, he said, would be the withdrawal of all British troops to barracks and an amnesty for political and special-category prisoners. He confirmed that the government was expecting it to mount a major campaign in Britain in order to create a climate in which withdrawal became politically acceptable.

Turning to security issues, Faulkner was reluctant to accept what the British members of the Law Commission viewed as a second-best option. Agreeing that Northern Ireland should not totally reject the extraterritorial formula that had been put forward, he insisted that it should be applied retrospectively, at least from the date of the Sunningdale conference. Rees reported that in future, detainee releases would be timed to coincide with political developments, so as to maximise their impact on the nationalist community and minimise the tensions they caused within the unionist community. With a summer general election looking increasingly likely, the executive agreed a timetable for political progress: the British government and the executive would finalise the details of agreement the week commencing 13 May; the Law Commission report would be published the following week; the second Hillsborough summit would take place the week commencing 27 May; and a formal ceremony confirming Sunningdale, as opposed to a second conference, would be held in the first week of June.[87]

Further signs were evident that elements within the UUUC intended to replace its constitutional opposition campaign against Sunningdale with a more sinister approach. Describing sectarian assassinations in Northern Ireland as 'unfortunate but understandable', Craig warned that unionists 'were not going to sit back and see Ulster jointly governed by the Republic and Britain'. He said that if democracy is to be 'trampled into the ground', then people are 'entitled to take whatever action is needed' to defend it.[88] Against Orme's advice, Wilson delivered an ill-timed statement to the House of Commons, on 13 May,[89] announcing the army's discovery of an IRA 'scorched earth' plot. Documents had been found at a house in Belfast where Brendan Hughes, one of the IRA's most wanted operatives, had been arrested. The papers contained a 'specific and calculated' plan detailing how the IRA would stoke 'inter-sectarian hatred' in Belfast, create 'a degree of chaos' through 'ruthless and indiscriminate violence', before taking over parts of the capital.[90] Wilson's official reason for making the statement was to pre-empt press leaks that might have provoked a hostile response from Protestant paramilitaries. However, the prime minister seemed intent on generating as much publicity from the disclosure as possible, perhaps both to reduce the SDLP's expectations on detention and pressure the IRA in Belfast to fall into line with their colleagues elsewhere in the province.

As Rees met with FitzGerald in Dublin on 13 May, Provisional IRA leader Dáithí Ó Conaill held a press conference showcasing a British Army deserter and brandishing a letter from the secretary of state to a Mrs Adams of Dundalk, dated 19 March 1973. The Labour Party, he said quoting Rees, had 'not the faintest desire to stay in Ireland and the quicker we are out the better'.[91] The secretary of state claimed the letter had been intended to give the impression that British troops were not being sent to Northern Ireland just for 'the hell of it'.[92] He told Fitzgerald that the political vacuum in Belfast, the prospect of a second UK general election, and the possibility that the executive might collapse meant that immediate completion on all aspects of Sunningdale was now imperative. He argued that should Faulkner fail to visibly renegotiate the aspects of the settlement which were most unpalatable to unionists, then his support base could be reduced to less than ten assembly members. Furthermore, Frank Cooper emphasised that the success of the Law Commission report rested on the British government's ability to sell it as a practical solution to the problems presented by fugitive offenders and inter-state terrorism. The Irish, however, were more concerned about Fianna Fáil's reaction to the introduction of any further security measures which assisted the British Army, and the danger of a repeat of the Boland fiasco, given the legal challenges introducing extradition legislation might provoke.

Rees asked FitzGerald why Sunningdale had produced an agreed communiqué rather than a formal agreement. The Irish foreign minister told him that, 'purely as a formal move to help the Unionists', the Irish government had agreed to postpone the signing of a Sunningdale agreement until after the executive was formed. With the benefit of hindsight, FitzGerald told him that this had been a mistake.[93] On the question of 'phasing', the British offered Napier's idea of initially establishing a council of ministers which could pass a number of non-controversial measures, thereby enabling unionists to see it in action prior to ratification. FitzGerald was concerned that if the Council of Ireland was not established with clear executive functions, then it would be rendered useless by the extravagant application of the unionist veto. If it was implemented gradually, he argued, then the use of veto or referenda could be employed as a means of obstructing progress for an indefinite period. He conceded, however, that it might be possible to only establish the council of ministers in the first instance if there was a private agreement to establish the consultative assembly in due course. FitzGerald envisaged no difficulties over 'phasing' in a Council of Ireland should an agreement be reached to set out specific dates for future progress.

The executive's subcommittee produced a draft document detailing the executive functions of a Council of Ireland, which the SDLP described as 'the maximum the unionists are prepared to consider'. Confident of reaching agreement on the executive later that week, Faulkner encouraged the British to press ahead with the announcement of the Law Commission's report and the intergovernmental security conference.[94] He was no longer willing to proceed with a consultative assembly without a test of public opinion. Hume rejected the idea of a referendum, but stopped short of ruling out the possibility of using the next assembly election as a litmus test on the feasibility of a Council of Ireland. The unionist position on the secretariat remained equally firm; a Council of Ireland could only be served by civil servants from North and South, paid by and responsible to their respective departments. The SDLP felt that there was still room for compromise on this issue, as Faulkner was primarily interested in stalling the establishment of a consultative assembly and they were willing to concede that the Council of Ireland should initially have no permanent base. The SDLP ministers informed Donlon that they were pessimistic about the prospects of reaching agreement, but promised not to take any decision that might result in the power-sharing executive's disintegration without prior consultation with the Irish government.

Hume and Devlin both felt that their own political survival now depended on the manner in which the executive collapsed; Faulkner was not the only leader facing backbench pressure from colleagues who had little knowledge or understanding of the ongoing negotiations. Séamus Mallon, who led hardline opposition to the direction the SDLP negotiating team were taking, produced a letter signed by a long list of local branch officers, district councillors and prominent supporters. This called for the party leadership to withdraw from the executive unless Sunningdale was fully implemented. The group also sent a letter of censure to Fitt, on 8 May, 'expressing concern' at the 'lack of leadership' he had shown by making a number of statements which ran 'contrary to party policy'. In a characteristic response, the West Belfast MP told his assembly colleagues to 'stuff it'; he had 'survived in politics' without the SDLP for nineteen elections and could survive without them 'for another nineteen'.[95]

On the basis of Donlon's gloomy prognosis, the Irish government began considering the political, security, military and economic implications of the executive's collapse on the Republic of Ireland. Donlon believed that if the British moved on internment, as a means of soothing the pain of accepting a phased Council of Ireland, then Faulkner might ease up on some of his demands and allow the SDLP to weather the storm. But when the SDLP leader put his party's demands on internment to Rees, and complained about the position that Faulkner was placing them in, the secretary of state told him bluntly that if the executive collapsed, then it would be difficult to resist pressure for the withdrawal of British troops.[96]

In Belfast, the day of reckoning had arrived for the anti-Sunningdale unionists, the Northern Ireland Assembly providing the stage for the last constitutional outpost in their campaign to prevent Faulkner from consolidating power-sharing as an acceptable form of government. The Ulster Army Council, an array of loyalist paramilitary groups formed to synchronise opposition to the executive and support for the UUUC, issued a warning: 'if Westminster is not prepared to restore democracy ... then the only other way it can be restored is by a *coup d'état*.'[97] Claiming to represent the disenfranchised voices of 400,000 unionists, UWC leader Harry Murray issued a final call to 'those Faulknerite Republicans', to 'stop at the brink', or face an 'indefinite' and 'complete cut off' of electricity supply in Northern Ireland.[98]

On 14 May, Minford allowed the democratic process to take its course in the assembly; Faulkner's supporters cast their votes, defeating the anti-Sunningdale motion by forty-four votes to twenty-eight.[99] Immediately after the vote, at 6.08 pm, Harry Murray and Bob Pagels of the UWC announced that unconstitutional opposition to the executive had begun in the form of an industrial stoppage. Northern Ireland's electricity supply would be reduced from 725 to 400 megawatts, the strikers' objective being to pressure the British government into holding fresh assembly elections as a means of testing public opinion towards Sunningdale. Having 'ignored the wishes of 400,000 people in the general election', they said that the executive must now 'take responsibility' for the outcome of its political actions. Faulkner had forced the UWC into adopting unconstitutional means to achieve constitutional ends;[100] therefore if the public had a problem with its electricity supply they should take it up with the minister for commerce, John Hume.

The executive and its supporters had voted against the motion calling for Sunningdale to be renegotiated, despite the fact that Faulkner was on the cusp of doing just that. Therefore, the UWC began its campaign of unconstitutional opposition, in coordination with the UUUC and the Protestant paramilitary groups, regardless of the fact that the Council of Ireland proposals were about to be greatly reduced, with the consent of both the Irish government and the SDLP.

This was the issue on which the UUUC had won the February election, and the nomenclature of 're-phasing' was merely a verbal smokescreen for changes to Sunningdale's agreements that many of its members had been demanding all along.

With hindsight, Bradford argued that opposing the anti-Sunningdale motion caused Faulkner to lose the support of many 'fair-minded' people, who subsequently took the view that the executive was 'hell-bent on bull-dozing Sunningdale through' against the grain of majority opinion.[101] More than that, the unionist leader had failed to dispel the public impression that had been generated by the vote, that Sunningdale was actually being ratified during the divisive assembly debate. Given the SDLP's internal difficulties over re-phasing, the executive could not have survived a split in the assembly between the pro-assembly unionists and the nationalist members who were opposed to the re-negotiation its leadership had agreed to under the fig leaf of 're-phasing'. Bradford lamented that 'having won the vote on 14 May' his colleagues had sunk the executive.[102] His scheming against and disloyalty to the executive aside, Bradford had a point, for Faulkner had not explicitly conveyed, even to his own party, how he had renegotiated Sunningdale's agreements. So much so that the following day, when Morrell informed the pro-assembly group that Faulkner had achieved all his objectives in reducing the Council of Ireland proposals, apart from the provision of executive powers, he was met with renewed criticism.

So the strike began in desperation, but by design, at what was a critical juncture in the Northern Ireland peace process; Faulkner stood on the verge of a political breakthrough that had the potential to transform the agreements reached, in December 1973, from a settlement premised on the establishment of powerful all-Ireland bodies, which might have led to a united Ireland, to one primarily focused on reforming Northern Ireland's political system on the basis of power-sharing between moderate unionists and nationalists. This was to be his defining moment. Having survived the UUUC's constitutional opposition and a sustained onslaught of IRA violence since taking office, Faulkner's executive now faced the much-feared Protestant backlash.

NOTES

1. CJ4/785, Meeting between Rees and UUUC, Stormont, 2 April 1974.
2. *Belfast Telegraph*, 13 March 1974.
3. *Guardian*, 14 March 1974.
4. Interview with Declan Costello, Dublin, 23 July 2007; Interview with Mahon Hayes, Dublin, 24 July 2007.
5. DT2005/7/628, Visit to Northern Ireland, Donlon, 21/22 March 1974.
6. Northern Ireland Assembly, vol. 2, col. 1787, 19 March 1974.
7. Northern Ireland Assembly, vol. 2, cols 1794–1816, 19 March 1974.
8. *Belfast News Letter*, 22 March 1974.
9. DT2005/7/628, Visit to Northern Ireland, Donlon, 21/22 March 1974.
10. DT2007/7/628, Report on Meeting of Ministers, 26 March 1974.
11. CJ4/506, Political contingency plans, 5 April 1974.
12. OE1/24, Executive Meeting with the Secretary of State, Stormont, 26 March 1974.
13. PREM16/146, Hunt to Wilson, 29 March 1974.
14. CAB134/3778, Meeting of the Ministerial Committee on Northern Ireland, Downing Street, 1 April 1974.
15. OE1/24, Executive meeting with the Secretary of State, Stormont, 26 March 1974.
16. CENT1/3/37, Meeting between Faulkner and Wilson, Downing Street, 1 April 1974.
17. DT2005/7/629, Visit to Northern Ireland, Donlon, 2/3 April 1974.
18. CJ4/505, Meeting between Wilson and King, Belfast, 18 April 1974.
19. OE1/10, Mais to Sythes, 11 April 1974.
20. DT2007/7/628, Meeting with O'Sullivan and Rees, London, 28 March 1974.
21. DT2005/7/629, O'Carroll to Donegan, 2 April 1974.
22. PREM16/146, Meeting between Wilson and Faulkner, Downing Street, 1 April 1974.
23. CENT1/3/37, Meeting between Faulkner and Wilson, Downing Street, 1 April 1974.
24. *The Times*, 3 April 1974.
25. NOP Market Research survey conducted between 31 March and 7 April on behalf of the BBC from a random sample of the Northern Ireland electoral register. Only 979 of 2000 interviews were actually completed or 49 per cent. Of those interviewed, 68 per cent were Protestant and 31 per cent Catholic, thus slightly over-representing Protestant adults. These results published in the *Belfast Telegraph* on 18 May 1974.
26. OE1/35, Faulkner to Cosgrave, 3 April 1974.
27. DT2005/7/628, Report on Meeting of Ministers, 26 March 1974.
28. OE1/35, Faulkner to Cosgrave, 3 April 1974.
29. DT2005/7/629, Nally to Cosgrave, 1 April 1974.
30. DT2005/7/629, Visit to Northern Ireland, Donlon, 2/3 April 1974.
31. NOP Market Research survey conducted between 31 March and 7 April 1974.
32. DT2005/7/629, Meeting between Cosgrave and Wilson, London, 5 April 1974.
33. Hansard, vol. 871, cols 1462–5840, 4 April 1974.
34. CJ4/471, Meeting between Wilson and Cosgrave, London, 5 April 1974.
35. DT2005/7/629, Meeting between Cosgrave and Wilson, London, 5 April 1974.
36. Ibid.
37. DT2005/7/629, Nally to Cosgrave, 9 April 1974.
38. *Irish Times*, 8 April 1974.
39. DT2005/7/629, Visit to Northern Ireland, Donlon, 6 April 1974.
40. DT2005/7/629, Donlon to FitzGerald, 9 April 1974.
41. CJ4/471, Reid to Trevelyan, 9 April 1974.
42. DT2005/7/629, Visit to Belfast, Donlon, 24 April 1974.
43. CJ4/473, Reid to Woodfield, 12 April 1974.
44. CJ4/473, Reid to Woodfield, 15 April 1974.
45. CJ4/505, Thom to Trevelyan, 18 April 1974.
46. DT2005/7/629, Meeting between O'Brien and Rees, London, 19 April 1974.
47. CJ4/471, Note for the Record, Woodfield, 22 April 1974.

48. *Observer*, 14 April 1974.
49. PREM16/146, Meeting between the Prime Minister and the Northern Ireland Executive, Stormont, 18 April 1974.
50. *Irish Times*, 8 May 1974.
51. OE1/24, Meeting between the Northern Ireland Administration and the Prime Minister, Stormont, 18 April 1974.
52. DT2005/7/630, Report by Donlon, 8 May 1974.
53. CJ4/505, Meeting between Wilson and Flanagan, Belfast, 18 April 1974.
54. CJ4/505, Meeting between Wilson and King, Belfast, 18 April 1974.
55. PRONI CENT/1/3/12, Commerce Minister hits out at IRA fund-raising in US, 25 April 1974.
56. DT2005/7/629, Visit to Belfast, Donlon, 24 April 1974.
57. *The Times*, 25 April 1974.
58. Interview with Sir Oliver Napier, Holywood, 29 December 2000.
59. Interview with Basil McIvor, Spa, 24 August 2001.
60. Interview with Leslie Morrell, Belfast, 4 January 2001.
61. DT2005/7/629, Meeting between O'Brien and Rees, London, 19 April 1974.
62. Interview with Leslie Morrell, Belfast, 4 January 2001.
63. DT2005/7/629, Meeting between SDLP and the Government, Dublin, 22 April 1974.
64. DT2005/7/629, Visit to Belfast, Donlon, 24 April 1974.
65. Faulkner Papers, PRONI, D3591/6/1, UUUC – Portrush, April, 1974.
66. DT2005/7/629, Meeting between SDLP and the Government, Dublin, 22 April 1974.
67. DT2005/7/629, Visit to Belfast, Donlon, 24 April 1974.
68. Interview with Leslie Morrell, Belfast, 4 January 2001.
69. DT2005/7/630, Report of a meeting with Alliance, 1 May 1974.
70. Interview with Mahon Hayes, Dublin, 24 July 2007.
71. *Report of the Law Enforcement Commission* (London: HMSO, 1974).
72. Interview with Sir Oliver Napier, Holywood, 29 December 2000.
73. CJ4/470, Cooper to Woodfield, 6 May 1974.
74. OE1/10, Faulkner to Rees, 7 May 1974. There appears to be no open record of any official response from Rees to this correspondence.
75. CJ4/472, Executive memo by Chief Executive, 1 May 1974.
76. D3591/6/1, Cosgrave to Faulkner, 3 May 1974.
77. DT2005/7/630, Report by Donlon, 8 May 1974.
78. OE2/19, Minutes of Executive meeting, Stormont, 7 May 1974.
79. Interview with Mahon Hayes, Dublin, 24 July 2007.
80. DT2005/7/630, Report by Donlon, 8 May 1974.
81. DT2005/7/630, Nally to Cosgrave, 9 May 1974.
82. DT2005/7/630, Meeting of Sunningdale Ministers, 8 May 1974.
83. OE1/35, Faulkner to Cosgrave, 7 May 1974.
84. OE2/21, Subcommittee meeting, 8 May 1974.
85. DT2005/7/630, Nally to Cosgrave, 10 May 1974.
86. DT2005/7/630, Meeting between Government Ministers and SDLP, 11/12 May 1974.
87. CJ4/472, Meeting between Rees and the Northern Irish Administration, 10 May 1974.
88. PREM16/146, Summary of political events, 9–14 May 1974.
89. PREM16/146, Note of meeting between Wilson and Orme, 13 May 1974.
90. Hansard, vol. 351, cols 750–2, 13 May 1974.
91. DT2005/7/630, Copy of letter from Rees to Adams, 19 March 1973.
92. *Irish Times*, 14 May 1974.
93. DT2005/7/630, Meeting between FitzGerald and Rees, Dublin, 13 May 1974.
94. CJ4/504, Cooper to Woodfield, 15 May 1974.
95. DT2005/7/630, Visit to Northern Ireland, Donlon, 14/15 May 1974.
96. CJ4/473, Meeting between Rees and SDLP, Stormont, 15 May 1974.
97. R. Fisk, *The Point of No Return: The Strike Which Broke the British in Ulster* (London: André Deutsch, 1975), p.33.
98. OE/1/16, UTV interview with Harry Murray, 13 May 1974.

99. Northern Ireland Assembly, vol. 3, col. 898, 14 May 1974.
100. Fisk, *The Point of No Return*, pp.17–19.
101. D4211/4/1/23, Roy Bradford Papers.
102. D4211/4/1/23, Roy Bradford Papers. The first ten pages of Bradford's journal are missing. It appears to have been written in March 1975.

7

The Widcats Strike

For those who took up the challenge of sharing power in the Northern Ireland Executive, 28 May 1974 was to be their last day in office. With his administration irreparably damaged, Faulkner left his colleagues and made the short walk over to Stormont Castle. There he informed Rees that the majority view on the executive was that some form of communication should be opened with the UWC. If the British government could not accept dialogue with the strikers, then he and the five other unionist ministers would resign. Rees stood firm. The strikers would be given no quarter; under no circumstances would the government enter into talks with the UWC.

Rising above his past, as chief executive, Faulkner had in many ways proved to be a politician capable of leading Northern Ireland out of the troubles. The challenge his executive faced from the moment it took office was to build up new institutions in Northern Ireland faster than its republican and unionist opponents could tear them down and destroy them. The question of whether or not the executive would survive and succeed was one of political authority. Almost entirely dependent on the Westminster parliament, Faulkner and his colleagues had lacked the power to determine their own fate during the first months of 1974. After the February election, Wilson's government did little to support the executive and, in fact, often appeared to be deliberately undermining it. But the executive endured despite its weaknesses and despite Faulkner's failings prior to and at Sunningdale. His threat to collapse the power-sharing administration had forced the Irish government and the SDLP to reconsider their positions, and to make considerable concessions on the Council of Ireland proposals. The consequence of this renegotiation was the emergence of a more evenly balanced agreement and one that Faulkner could have sold to the unionist population had he been given the chance. Time was not on Faulkner's side, however, nor had he been a 'super salesman' of the Sunningdale Communiqué, as all his efforts had been focused on renegotiating it. So banding together, and exposing the executive's lack of external support, Faulkner's enemies seized the moment to silence its collective voice through the imposition of a general strike.

When the UWC announced its industrial stoppage, on 14 May, the British did not take the unconstitutional threat it posed to the Northern Ireland Executive particularly seriously.[1] Rees immediately reported to Wilson that the strike simply represented 'a last fling by the Protestants' in their opposition campaign to power-sharing.[2] Rees believed that the British government would be in a strong position to ratify Sunningdale if it faced down the executive's opponents.

An emergency committee was established tasked with assessing the UWC's capacity to run down electricity production at Northern Ireland's four power stations, and examining the impact that a major reduction of power would have on essential services across the province. Northern Ireland's electricity supply functioned on a geographical basis. This meant that the UWC could not protect essential services by selectively cutting power at industrial sites. Therefore, shutting down the power supply would have a negative impact upon the UWC's opponents and supporters alike. Surprisingly, there was very little other information available to the government at this point, but the committee believed that the outbreak of a general strike was neither imminent nor likely.

Rees had several options open to him when the strike commenced: he could immediately order the security forces to break the strike; he could open negotiations with the UWC and agree to hold fresh assembly elections; he could attempt to produce a compromise that might save the executive and allow the strikers to call off the stoppage without completely losing face; or he could attempt to drive a wedge between the UWC and the UUUC by calling their bluff and allowing the situation to deteriorate. In framing its policy towards the strike, however, the British government's primary concern was to avoid entering into a major military confrontation with the Protestant paramilitaries. This factor led to the executive's collapse; its fate was determined by how far the loyalist opposition was prepared to take their protest and how far the British were prepared to go in meeting the challenge they posed to constitutional government within the UK.

Faulkner was quick to disabuse his opponents for unconstitutionally 'taking on to themselves greater importance than the democratically elected representatives' of Northern Ireland. Comparing the UWC to the republican extremists who had recently plotted to bring death and destruction to the streets of Belfast, he asked the people of Northern Ireland to consider where they got their authority from.[3] For when the strike got underway, one thing was certain: its outcome would be determined, to a great extent, by the public's perception of where political authority and power in Northern Ireland lay; whether it was at Stormont, at Westminster, or at the UWC's headquarters on the Hawthornden Road, in east Belfast.

The strike leaders were well aware that they would have 'to force' the working-class Protestant population to actively support the stoppage.[4] To counter the impression that it might fizzle out after a few days, the UDA ensured that large numbers of industrial workers went on strike in Belfast, Carrick and Larne. For example, in the capital's Harland and Wolff shipyard, 8,000 workers downed tools after learning that their cars would be set alight if they crossed the picket line.[5] Calling for the British to initiate political negotiations, the UWC announced that if its demands were not met, roadblocks would be installed across Northern Ireland's main arteries the following morning. Meanwhile, Rees was considering the introduction of military personnel to run the power stations and sewage plants, but the Ministry of Defence (MOD) advised that its army technicians were presently stationed outside of the UK. Moreover, military intervention might make the situation worse, as the army would require the assistance of power station managers to maintain electricity supplies, for at least seven days, and if troops entered the stations then this might prompt them to join the strike.[6]

Rees resisted pressure to open negotiations with the UWC and announced that the power generators would function at approximately 60 per cent of normal production levels, as the electricity board had persuaded workers to continue fuelling the stations. At Stormont, Orme had an extremely confrontational meeting with Craig, Paisley and Laird, which turned out to be of some significance. Craig was the UWC's key political backer from the outset of the strike, but the three UUUC politicians had yet to publicly endorse the stoppage. Craig informed Orme that the UWC was prepared to generate enough electricity to maintain the grid at 60 per cent, but only on the condition that it maintained control over Northern Ireland's power supplies, which would be used for the protection of essential services if industrial sites were completely shut down. If the government refused to immediately open negotiations with the UWC, then dire consequences would ensue. The UUUC leaders complained bitterly to Orme about the electricity board's decision to deny certain shop stewards entry to the power stations which they had been sent to control, and of its refusal to talk with the UWC. Although the electricity board denied this, Paisley claimed that Hume had ordered the move, and he rejected Orme's accusation that the UDA was intimidating workers and power station managers by making threatening telephone calls to their homes.

UWC leaders Harry Murray, Bob Pagels and Harry Patterson then joined the meeting, along with UDA and UVF representatives Andy Tyrie, Tommy Lyttle and Ken Gibson, who Orme suspected were armed. Tempers flared when the loyalists accused the British of deliberately diverting electricity supplies from essential services to undermine public support for the strike. They conceded that if the government gave an immediate commitment to holding fresh elections, then the UWC would consider cooperating with the electricity board. Orme told his guests, in no uncertain terms, that the British would not be intimidated or blackmailed by paramilitaries. He warned that the government was prepared to use the army to secure the operation of essential services, to which Paisley retorted that such provocation would cause a 'bloodbath' in Northern Ireland.[7] And accusing Orme of attempting to push them into 'a united Ireland', they challenged him to reveal the government's true policy on Northern Ireland.[8]

Orme was shaken by his clash with the men who were openly challenging the government's authority in Northern Ireland. He did not, however, make any commitment to enter into negotiations with the UWC, conceding only that the government would consider finding a formula for maintaining essential services through the level of electricity supply that the strikers were offering to generate.[9] The meeting was an entirely counterproductive exchange, leaving little room for manoeuvre on the battle lines that had been drawn between the government and the UWC. So much so that Bradford described the encounter as a 'golden opportunity to cool the situation' from which the strikers emerged 'infuriated'.[10] More than that, he accused Orme of causing the strike to escalate by displaying a total lack of diplomacy towards the

UWC, calling them 'bigots' and 'sectarian extremists' during a diatribe of verbal abuse.[11]

Having failed to make any progress with Orme, Craig and Paisley immediately offered to facilitate dialogue between the UWC and the government, providing Frank Cooper with numerous telephone numbers on which the strike leaders could be reached. Cooper believed that the UWC's strategy was to force the British into negotiations by maintaining essential services, while running down the electricity supply to the extent that Northern Ireland teetered on the brink of collapse. It was a dangerous game to play, as signs of public irritation at the electricity cuts were already evident. But if Rees immediately entered into negotiations with the UWC, then this might enable them to shift responsibility for the reduction of Northern Ireland's electricity supply onto the Westminster and Stormont governments.[12] Furthermore, if he was drawn into negotiations, then the onus would be on him to swiftly end the disruption to day-to-day life that the province was experiencing.

Once the strike had been called, the UUUC had little choice but to acquiesce in the industrial stoppage; therefore Cooper advised Rees that the best course of action available at this time was to drive a wedge between the politicians and the strikers by refusing to talk to the latter. Craig and Paisley held grave reservations about supporting a political strike that was beyond their control, as the collapse of essential services would have an extremely damaging impact on their standing as political representatives. Thus, they were keen for an agreement to be reached between the power station managers and the UWC whereby the electricity grid would be maintained at 60 per cent. The UUUC and the UWC shared a common objective in their desire to bring down Faulkner's power-sharing executive. The UWC's motivation for seeking fresh assembly elections, however, was to transform their militant power base into working-class political support.

* * * *

In its first two days, the British took no action to break the strike and when the army removed UDA roadblocks across Belfast, the UWC simply re-established them elsewhere. No decisions were taken regarding the possibility of using the army to man the power stations, all four of which were affected by the industrial action, and the military thought that it would be prudent only to take such action as a last resort. Moreover, it would require the assistance of on-site electricity technicians and middle management if it was to successfully take control of the power stations. The supply of oil for essential services was also a major concern, as a large number of petrol stations were closed and the UDA had established control over the access points to many Protestant areas across Northern Ireland. In Belfast, workers on the coal feeders at the Twin Island power stations had resumed their duties and a complete shutdown had been avoided. Hume presented the executive with a revised oil contingency plan for the control and distribution of petrol to thousands of essential workers, which would require two to three days' organisation if Rees instructed the army to carry it out.

Trade Union Congress general secretary Len Murray disowned the UWC, describing it as a non-union organisation designed to 'pursue a sectarian policy'.[13] Accusing the government of giving in to intimidation and threats, the Northern Ireland Transport Association demanded protection for its 5,000-strong workforce, 90 per cent of which had so far resisted pressure to strike. They warned Rees that the lack of security force action to break the strike and the army's 'low profile' approach across Northern Ireland might force them to look to the 'opposition' for protection.[14]

Although the government was under increasing pressure to assert its authority in Northern Ireland, the army was extremely reluctant to enter into any confrontation with the UWC. GOC Frank King insisted that any military response to the escalating security crisis must not be interpreted by the UWC as a 'strike breaker'.[15] Having spent the first days of the stoppage sitting 'in Hawthornden Road waiting to be arrested', the UWC leaders were shocked by the army's 'frozen' reaction.[16] This suited the strike leaders well, for at that point they too were determined to avoid any 'confrontation with the security forces', as a serious clash could have quickly eroded support for the stoppage within the unionist community.[17] Had the RUC been instructed to confront the UWC from the beginning of the strike, this would have made it very difficult for the UUUC to politically endorse the stoppage. If the government had called the UWC's bluff, then many of them would have stood down.[18]

At Stormont, Rees and Frank Cooper maintained responsibility for all security matters, and neither the executive nor its civil servants were fully consulted over how the strike was being handled. Cooper tasked a small steering group to direct the emergency committee in producing detailed reports on electricity, fuel and oil supply, and water and sewage services. The government had to determine exactly how much time it would take the army to return Northern Ireland's essential services to functional levels, while weighing up the impact that the intimidation of power-station middle managers, or simply their refusal to cooperate, would have on its efforts to salvage the grid from complete meltdown. Not taking immediate military action, the government explored the possibility of fuelling the provision of emergency services by nuclear power through the deployment of a Polaris submarine to Belfast. This was quickly ruled out as a potential solution due to problems of capacity, conversion and transmission.[19]

Displaying extreme reluctance to see the army becoming any further involved in the crisis, Mason refused to put the 320 military service technicians in England on less than seven days' redeployment notice. British military commanders believed that in the event of a real crisis, enough technicians could be sent to Northern Ireland to keep open the two main power stations at Ballylumford in Larne and Coolkeeragh in Londonderry, but for no more than one to two days. The electricity board indicated that if it experienced a total withdrawal of its general workforce, then senior and middle management would only be able to operate the two main power stations for one week and this would be reduced to a forty-eight-hour period should middle management refuse to cooperate. Ordering the military to operate the stations was likely to alienate those middle managers, as it would leave them open to paramilitary intimidation. Therefore, the military argued that such action must be reserved as an emergency option, to be used only in the event of a complete breakdown or when it became clear that the managers were no longer willing or able to run the stations. Moreover, there was no practical way of preventing the intimidation of the power station managers that lived in loyalist areas. Should these workers be forced to vacate the stations, no permanent damage would be done to the generating system, provided that military technicians took their place within roughly twelve hours. But if this kind of military action appeared inevitable, then the possibility of loyalists pre-empting such a move by sabotaging the Ballylumford station could not be discounted. Such destruction would ensure that Northern Ireland ceased to function as an administrative political unit. The army would then be faced with anarchy in the UK.

The industrial aspect to the strike was developing in Northern Ireland's capital. When he was refused entry to the power stations, workers at the west Belfast station remained loyal to UWC strike leader Billy Kelly. But although the coal and ash squads in east Belfast supported the strike, they also maintained their allegiance to the trade union. Moreover, local managers did not meet Kelly's demand for a 30-megawatt power reduction in Belfast that morning, and similar reports were emerging from Ballylumford. In fact, the UWC was forced to back off, for imposing such a reduction would have left north Antrim and Londonderry in complete blackout. Furthermore, the strikers lacked the full commitment of the UUUC leadership at this point, and they were reliant on intimidation to both extend the stoppage and enforce the reduction of the electricity supply. During this period of uncertainty, the government had the capacity to act effectively to test the resolve of the UWC – action that might have prevented the strike from going beyond the point of no return.

On the third day of the strike, there was some improvement in the security situation. Fewer roadblocks were set up and the UDA was again forced to employ overt intimidation to maintain the stoppage.[20] Rees advised the Northern Ireland administration that he had taken the necessary measures to ensure the maintenance of adequate power supplies.[21] He informed Wilson that although the situation in the power stations was deteriorating, enough troops were available to run them, at forty-eight hours' notice, with the support of middle management. Rees would wait for middle management to signal that they could no longer cope before making any announcement about introducing the army into the stations. He was deeply troubled by Mason's attitude towards the unfolding crisis, however, so much so that he implored the prime minister to ensure that the defence minister was actually aware there was one.[22]

* * * *

Faulkner faced his administration on 17 May. All the roadblocks appeared to have been removed, and although power generation had been reduced in Belfast it had been reintroduced at Coolkeeragh. Judging by the number of complaints the RUC were receiving, the level of UDA intimidation had been sustained if not increased. Nevertheless, Devlin carried out his threat to resign over the introduction of a 25p levy against those who remained on the 'rent and rates strike', only to 'freeze' it when news of shocking terrorist atrocities in the Republic of Ireland reached Stormont.[23] Cross-border attacks by loyalist extremists had brought carnage and devastation to the streets of Dublin and Monaghan, car bombs claiming thirty-three lives and injuring over one hundred people.[24]

Rees joined the executive that afternoon, rejecting the UUUC's accusation that the government had broken an agreement to protect essential services by maintaining the electricity supply at 60 per cent. Orme had made no such commitment to the UWC, he insisted, for the government could not and would not negotiate with people conducting a political strike. Later that day, Rees did in fact meet with a loyalist deputation that included Craig and UDA figure Glen Barr. Craig warned him that although the UWC was willing and able to reach an arrangement by which the crisis could be swiftly resolved, the government's continued refusal to negotiate would destroy the executive and initiate a return to direct rule.[25]

On Saturday 18 May, Northern Ireland experienced six-hour blackouts and government estimates put electricity output at 30 per cent of 'basic need'. This would be reduced to 25 per cent by Monday if action was not taken immediately. Although the Coolkeeragh station could be restarted by middle management and some of its workforce, an increase in the overall output of electricity could only be raised to 30 per cent. Although oil, gas and water supplies remained satisfactory, Northern Ireland was reliant for its power supply on the Ballylumford station, which continued to operate three generators. While the electricity board was confident that the power supply could be maintained at 30 per cent, Rees informed the executive that this could not be increased even with military intervention. He favoured closing large industrial sites to preserve essential services, but if such an industrial stoppage was to be imposed across the province, he advised the Northern Ireland Executive that they would have to order it.

The Northern Ireland Executive put it to Rees that the government seemed willing to send troops into the power stations only as a last resort. Rejecting his notion that they should order an industrial stoppage, the executive argued that this would be tantamount to finishing off the very job that the UWC had started. Although all Northern Ireland's Protestant paramilitary groups had 'offered unreserved support' for the strike,

Faulkner told Rees that the UUUC leaders remained extremely apprehensive and, with the exception of Craig, were looking for a way to end it. Arriving by helicopter from Londonderry, Hume rejected the army's view that it could not increase electricity output beyond 30 per cent; a power capacity of 50 to 60 per cent could now be achieved, he argued, subject only to levels of exhaustion and intimidation. Rees accepted that if this was in fact correct, then it changed the picture dramatically and he appeared to swing towards the idea of introducing troops into the stations.

The executive believed that although the Northern Ireland workforce was generally against the strike, blatant intimidation was preventing people from speaking out against it. Shop stewards reinforced their optimism, signalling that they had the full backing of the trade union in taking a firm stand against the strike. Although they were not recommending the introduction of troops into the stations, they would not oppose this course of action if the government decided to take it. A return to work campaign would be launched on Monday morning, with a 'right to work' march planned for the following day. Accepting that the executive should not order an industrial shutdown at this point, Rees conceded that his previous estimates had been unduly pessimistic. The stand-off with the UWC, he said, should be allowed to drag on, without the immediate introduction of troops, until the strike was broken.[26]

The UWC responded to these developments by upping the ante. Its leadership called for a province-wide general strike to begin at midnight, with the complete closure of all industrial and commercial businesses, public transport systems and schools. If the government sent troops into the power stations, then workers would be withdrawn from other essential services.[27] Hume concluded that, to conserve all available electricity for the maintenance of essential services, the executive would have to order industry to shutdown after all. Rees had made up his mind. Advance troops should be brought in, as quickly and quietly as possible, and put on standby to move into the power stations. But although Mason's phased troop withdrawals had been frozen due to the strike, he stalled after Rees requested that fresh soldiers be air-lifted into Northern Ireland.

The same day, Wilson received a telegram from the chairman of the UWC requesting his 'direct intervention', as the 'deliberate and calculated refusal by the Secretary of State for Northern Ireland to discuss the serious situation at present prevailing is leading to a confrontation'.[28] At Westminster, unionist MPs implored Wilson not to deploy the army or the UDR onto the streets of Northern Ireland. But the Labour leader had no intention of being bounced by Rees into taking drastic military action. South Antrim MP James Molyneaux recalls him taking 'his pipe out of his mouth', and saying, '"Listen boys, I did not become the prime minister to use the Queen's forces against the verdict of the ballot box".'[29]

Keeping a foot in both camps, Bradford was meeting secretly with UDA and UVF leaders. In a private conversation with Frank Cooper, he pleaded with the NIO chief to bring about a change in British government policy. Bradford warned him that, if troops were introduced to the power stations, then he would be at the barricades 'on the Newtownards Road along with the strikers'.[30] Cooper told him that there could be no negotiation with the UWC because its strike was blatantly political, but Bradford likened the crisis to the recent industrial action taken by British coalminers, arguing that the premise of their strike had been to undermine the Heath government.

Even if enough army personnel were available to ensure that Northern Ireland continued to function in an emergency situation, Rees faced a Hobson's choice over how he might effectively deploy them. If he did not initiate military action, either in an attempt to increase the power supply or to break the picket lines, his authority would be further eroded. If he immediately committed the army to breaking the strike, then there was a distinct possibility that the remaining workers would desert the power stations, prompting widespread disruption on the streets and a military confrontation with the loyalist paramilitaries. Furthermore, if the army was sent into the power stations to increase supply in order to maintain essential services, then there was a considerable risk that the government would be blamed for putting those very services in jeopardy. Nevertheless, Rees rang Wilson again, insisting that he must immediately force Mason to hasten the deployment of troops to Northern Ireland. The prime minister offered him his 'strongest possible support'.[31]

According to one unionist minister, the Northern Ireland civil service was 'probably as divided in opinion' over the strike 'as anybody else'. Although there was no firm evidence to suggest that significant sections of the civil service were actively working against the executive, leaks were emanating from Stormont's information department and many low-level officials appeared content to simply 'let their cars run out of petrol'.[32] 'There were some', as Austin Currie put it, 'who accepted all too easily that the government should give in'.[33] Bradford claimed to have conducted a straw poll within his department, asking staff how they would react if the military took over Northern Ireland's power stations. Half of those polled signalled their willingness to remain at work, as a matter of principle, while the remainder were more doubtful, concerned that continuing to actively support the executive in such circumstances might place them in danger. These were of course government officials in a department where the minister was privately advocating dialogue with the strikers. Nevertheless, it was an indication that the tide was beginning to turn against the executive.[34]

* * * *

On Sunday 19 May, Rees declared a new state of emergency, which superseded the prevailing state of emergency that had been declared in 1971. Protestant church leaders intervened, stressing that the UWC was ready to discuss the maintenance of essential services without addressing the broader issues of the strike, and Bradford pressed Rees to 'reopen communication and prevent a slide into anarchy'.[35] But before he departed for Chequers to meet with the prime minister, Rees dismissed these calls and authorised an army reconnaissance mission on the Ballylumford station. This merely confirmed what the army suggested: specialist navel personnel could not operate the grid without the support of senior technical staff, as they did not understand the workings of its main control system.[36]

The following day the UWC responded, setting fire to hijacked buses and erecting 172 roadblocks across Belfast. Rees refused to speak to Craig when he telephoned requesting a meeting to discuss how a further escalation of the strike could be averted. The electricity shortage had reached a critical level: supply was at less than 30 per cent; consumers were experiencing periods of approximately three hours of electricity and nine hours without; industry had virtually closed; and should the entire grid shut due to lack of maintenance, then Northern Ireland would experience a complete blackout for at least three days.

At Stormont, the executive 'generally agreed' that it would be unwise to enter into a deal with the UWC, while Rees clashed with both Frank King and RUC chief Jamie Flanagan over the tepid response the security forces had taken towards the strike. He demanded that Belfast's main arterial routes must be cleared immediately, but King insisted that it would be best if the army continued to 'maintain its low profile'. They both warned Rees that forcibly removing the blockades posed difficulties for the security forces and 'possible serious consequences'. The risk had to be taken, Rees said, and he ordered them to draw up plans to ensure that the capital remained accessible.[37]

The *Belfast News Letter* reported that the steering committee of the UUUC had decided the previous evening to give its full support to the strike. And so on its sixth day, both the Protestant paramilitaries and the political coalition that represented unionist opposition to the executive had come out in favour of the UWC strike.

With the roads to Stormont blocked, Faulkner arrived by helicopter and told his colleagues that further effort must be made to reach agreement on the Council of Ireland proposals with the 'greatest urgency'.[38] At 2.30 pm, Rees and Cooper burst in to the meeting with the same message. The executive had to 'reach agreement' on the Sunningdale Communiqué as Rees, who promised troops in addition to the 500 that had arrived that day, was determined to see it ratified within a fortnight.[39] When he informed Faulkner that all the roadblocks had now been removed, finally losing his patience with the government's failure to break the strike, the unionist leader 'took him out and showed him one at the main gates' of Stormont.[40] The executive complained that the RUC had not been instructed to dismantle these road blocks. More than that, its presence at many of the protest sites was giving the public the impression that the police were actually acquiescing in it. The army's response was no better, but rejecting criticism from Wilson, its commanders argued that if the government was irritated by the military approach that was being taken towards the strike, then the government 'should have given some orders for the Army to do something else'.[41]

In Dublin, O'Brien linked the recent terror attacks in the Republic to his government's insistence on establishing extensive all-Ireland bodies, which he viewed as a grave mistake. He urged his colleagues to modify their approach by ending their insistence on a Council of Ireland with executive functions and accepting all-Ireland bodies along the lines 'originally envisaged by Faulkner'. Calling for Articles 2 and 3 to be replaced with an expression of 'our aspiration towards eventual unity by free consent', he wanted a new constitution to be put before the electorate by the end of the year, regardless of whether Fianna Fáil supported it or not.[42] Rejecting O'Brien's proposals, FitzGerald told the British that the establishment of an all-Ireland assembly should not be dependent on the whims of public opinion. While his government would be guided by any consensus that the executive arrived at, it expected some executive functions to be assigned to a Council of Ireland 'from the beginning'. Conceding that Sunningdale should not be rushed given the problems the strike had created for the executive, FitzGerald suggested that progress might be hastened if the British were to arrest Craig and prosecute him for fomenting sectarian passions.[43] And by that evening, the executive had finally reached agreement over how a Council of Ireland would be implemented. Faulkner told his colleagues that he had a written assurance from Cosgrave stipulating that 'any consensus arrived at by the Northern Ireland Executive' in relation to Sunningdale's agreements would be acceptable in Dublin.[44]

By 21 May widespread support for the UWC was all but assured and Wilson informed parliament that Northern Ireland's power-sharing government was under threat from 'a sectarian strike which is aimed at destroying decisions taken by this House of Commons'.[45] Finally breaking ranks with the executive, Bradford implored his colleagues to consider opening dialogue with the strikers. The UWC enjoyed 'very wide support' from the unionist community; therefore it was time, he said, for the Northern Ireland Executive to face up to 'the realities of the situation'.[46] In the strike's first days, the UWC had drawn its support primarily from working-class Protestants but, 'as the days passed, and it became clear that Rees and the government were not taking any firm action against the strikers, the climate changed' and middle-class unionists and farmers began to abandon their support for the power-sharing executive.[47] Bradford's suggestion was opposed by the majority of his colleagues, but he publicly repeated it after the meeting, warning the government not to push the UWC to the point of 'unconditional surrender'. No responsible government, he said, could tolerate a deterioration of the situation beyond the point that the crisis had now reached; shops were running out of bread, livestock were starving, poultry were suffocating, and dairy farmers were pouring their milk down Northern Ireland's drains.[48] Annoyed with Bradford's scheming, Hume quipped that he 'held his hand up to the window every day' to see which way the wind was blowing, before deciding which way he would blow.[49] But the timing of Bradford's move was significant. Having met that day with representatives of the oil industry, the strike leaders had drawn up a list of the service stations under their control that could be used to distribute petrol to essential users.[50] The UWC had begun to exercise responsibility for some of the administrative functions of Northern Ireland's government.

Rees ignored Bradford's petition and the UWC announced a complete embargo on oil and petrol supplies, accusing the secretary of state of deliberately cutting power supplies to essential services and homes while industrial factories were allowed to operate around the clock.[51] As electricity supplies ran critically low, Orme warned the strikers that although the government wished to avoid a military confrontation, the army could help maintain essential services if it was required to do so.[52] That evening, Rees sent 1,500 troops to clear the barricades, in what Wilson described as a 'mini-motorman operation',[53] and Mason finally placed 134 technical servicemen on standby. They were capable of running two of the four stations with managerial supervision. But by the end of the strike's first week, although Wilson was acutely aware that he faced a battle of wills with the Protestant community itself, one of the most surprising aspects of this standoff, as Philip Woodfield put it, was 'the nil response from Number 10'.[54]

* * * *

The religious makeup of the power station workers in Londonderry was quite different to that of their counterparts in Belfast: 40 per cent of Coolkeeragh's employees were Catholic. They had indicated a willingness to increase the power supply at that station, and Hume was working hard behind the scenes to exploit this factor to the executive's advantage. The UWC responded to Hume's intervention. If Catholic workers attempted to increase power production at the Coolkeeragh station, it would withdraw middle management from Ballylumford and completely shut down that station. Hume then sought to force the government's hand, proposing a directive to the electricity service which pledged support for those who were prepared to man the power stations.[55] Fearful of quickly precipitating a situation in which troops would have to be sent into the stations, and convinced that if provoked in this manner the UWC would completely shut down the power stations, the British told Hume bluntly that the decision to use force would be taken by the government alone.[56]

At Stormont on 21 May, the executive produced a draft statement detailing how a Council of Ireland could be established in 'two phases'. During the first phase, a council of ministers would be set up with seven members from each administration acting on the basis of 'complete unanimity'. Meeting at alternating venues and drawing staff from both jurisdictions, the Council of Ireland would provide the forum for socioeconomic 'consultation, cooperation and coordination of action'. The second phase would see other aspects of Sunningdale's agreements enacted with the Northern Ireland Assembly's consent, following the next election to it, which was due to be held in 1977–8.[57] The executive had agreed to significantly marginalise and reduce the Council of Ireland, with a double veto acting as a check both on its implementation and its potential to evolve. The executive then pressured Rees to take military action against the UWC, so that when it announced the renegotiated Council of Ireland proposals they were not viewed as a reactionary gesture to the strikers.

Although the SDLP ministers had accepted Faulkner's two-pronged approach, they still needed the backing of their assembly party to proceed on this basis. They saw no point in making a concession to save the power-sharing settlement if the British were not prepared to breathe life into the initiative by breaking the strike, fully restoring Northern Ireland's electricity supplies and, if need be, sending troops into the power stations to secure the grid. The nationalist ministers believed that the inert response to the strike by the security forces was the result of a standoff between Rees and Mason over how the army should react. The defence minister was resolute in his view that British troops must not become embroiled in a military confrontation with the Protestant paramilitaries. In such circumstances, he argued, the army would be caught off guard, as the IRA would view its predicament as the 'best chance since 1969' to drive the British out of Ireland.[58] These tensions were evident at Westminster, as Heath clashed with Wilson over the government's failure to tear down the barricades and take a stand to protect constitutional law and authority in Northern Ireland.[59]

By this point the strikers had established a 'dramatic and obvious' degree of control over Northern Ireland, so much so that Seán Donlon reported to Dublin that 'any part of "normal" life which is continuing is doing so only by licence from the UWC'.[60] Furthermore, Hawthornden Road received a propaganda boost that morning when strike supporters jeered and harassed TUC leader Len Murray as he led a 'back to work march' on the streets of Belfast. His humiliation made it all the more clear that power and authority in Northern Ireland was now largely in the hands of the unelected militant loyalist leaders.

At Stormont, Rees announced that troop reinforcements had enabled him to keep Northern Ireland's main roads open, and he twice made the point that since the security services were already heavily stretched, it would be necessary to send more troops to the province. Although the next few days would be critical, Rees was confident that if the security services were seen to be reasserting the authority of the Northern Ireland Executive, then it would be in a position to announce the agreed rephrasing of the Council of Ireland proposals. He continued to reject any suggestion of opening negotiations with the UWC, while Wilson noted that 'further and possibly heavy' demands for military reinforcement could be expected in the days ahead. Mason argued that any such reinforcements would have serious repercussions for the British Army, squeezing its forces in Germany and severely disrupting important training programmes. His objections were overruled. A battalion of troops was sent to Northern Ireland the following day and a team of signalmen was put on standby to cope with the threat to its telecommunications systems.[61]

When Rees telephoned King that morning requesting an urgent meeting to discuss the 'next step or steps' that were necessary to deal with 'loyalist activities', the GOC stressed his extreme reluctance to involve the army in an open-ended military commitment. Once the army was deployed in this manner, he said, there could be no turning back. Nevertheless, Rees put his request in writing to King, offering a list of possible options for military intervention which ranged from dismantling the road blockades and UWC pass control systems to rounding up and arresting its leaders. Rees also wanted to discuss 'the practicability, if it should be so decided, of the gaining of technical control by service personnel of some of the power stations in such a way as to frustrate sabotage'.[62]

That night, when King tested 'the temperature of the Protestant people' by deploying 3,000 troops to the Village and Sandy Row areas of Belfast,[63] his officers successfully 'talked down' the UDA's barricades in the small hours of the morning. Removing the barricades was one thing; preventing them from being resurrected would require the army to maintain a presence in loyalist areas and, if action was to be taken on that scale, then large troop reinforcements would be required. Increasingly confident of its capacity to continue the strike without confronting the military, the UWC had in fact removed most of its own barricades by 5 pm that day. Public support had grown incrementally as a result of the government's failure to break the strike at the outset, and the UWC's authority was magnified by television images of the TUC's embarrassing collapse that morning.

On Wednesday 22 May, all major roads remained open and oil was being distributed to Northern Ireland's hospitals. The agriculture situation had deteriorated, however, and although the UWC was beginning to allow animal feed to be distributed to farmers, around 100,000 poultry had been slaughtered in a twenty-four-hour period.[64] Not only had the power supply been reduced to 30 per cent, the executive believed that, by the end of the day, responsibility for fuel distribution would be completely under the UWC's control. To obtain petrol supplies, the Ulster Bank and the Confederation of British Industry (CBI) had engaged in negotiations with the UWC at its headquarters. Urging Orme to open talks with the UWC, the CBI accused the government of holding Northern Ireland industry to ransom.[65] Rejecting this notion, the Labour minister told them that loyalist action was not in opposition to the executive but a strike against the 'very fabric of society in Northern Ireland'.[66]

At this point, Paisley finally came out in open support of the strike. Focusing on Wilson's reluctance to 'talk to the UWC', Paisley challenged him over why he had been happy to talk to the IRA in 1972 when they were 'killing members of Her Majesty's forces'. Newsman John Snow suggested to the DUP leader that he was kicking the crown in the teeth by supporting an illegal strike, to which Paisley replied, 'no ... we're kicking the government in the teeth which is a different thing'. More than that, Paisley told him that he had 'no loyalty to any British Government', especially one led by a man who 'wants a united Ireland'.[67] Hinting at the UWC's true intentions, strike leader Jim Smith said it would 'participate in a government of this country or no one will run this country'. Furthermore, his colleague Harry Murray claimed that the UWC's actions had been planned for 'five to six months', and he warned the government that they were prepared to go on 'forever'.[68]

By 22 May the UWC enjoyed widespread support across Northern Ireland. Intelligence reports indicated that its leadership and the Protestant paramilitaries were operating across the province with an 'unusual degree of determination and unity of purpose'.[69] Their tactic of maintaining the crisis at its present level, and avoiding conflict with the military by dismantling the barricades, had been very effective. As Barr put it, the army's dilemma was that 'the whole strike was run on the basis of: "if you do this, then we will do that"'.[70] Although Craig claimed to be in 'effective control of the country', and Barr boasted that they were ready to form a 'provisional government',[71] both Craig and Paisley were now desperate to take ownership of the strike. But the UWC and the loyalist paramilitaries had no faith in the self-serving UUUC politicians to represent their interests after it was all over.[72]

* * * *

Amid the deepening crisis, the executive again divided over how it should proceed with Sunningdale's ratification. Bradford was accused of meeting with the UWC behind the executive's back and chastised for taking a public position that was more in tune with the strikers than with the administration that he was a part of. Barr contends, however, that while Bradford did try to open dialogue with the UWC, his overtures were rejected as they did not trust him either. They took the view, in fact, that 'if anybody cracks it was going to be the Faulknerites'; therefore Bradford's betrayal of his unionist colleagues was merely a sign that the pressure being brought to bear on the executive was having its desired effect.[73] Moreover, Bradford had his offer to resign from the executive rejected on two occasions. Faulkner had no intention of letting his unionist rival off the hook that easily and, had he gone, his colleagues would have blamed him for precipitating the implosion of the power-sharing administration.

The SDLP ministers demanded action from the government prior to the announcement of the executive's U-turn on the Council of Ireland proposals. They argued that if the executive were to immediately announce its agreed statement, then the initiative would be viewed as a knee-jerk reaction to the crisis and simply strengthen the UWC's hand. Faulkner took the opposite view. He told the executive that both Rees and Pym had assured him that they had parliament's full support, but that it needed 'the executive's backing urgently by way of this initiative so they could continue their support'. In other words, Faulkner was asking his nationalist colleagues to jump first, because the British government was asking the executive to jump first, so as to ensure the survival of Northern Ireland's power-sharing arrangements.

With no clear consensus, Faulkner's proposal to release the agreed statement was put to a vote. This was the first time that any executive decision had been decided between the three parties to it in that manner. All other decisions had been agreed unanimously. The executive split. Seven members voted in favour of the proposal, Napier siding with the unionists, while the SDLP four voted in dissent. Fitt informed his colleagues that, 'with the deepest regret', his ministers could no longer regard themselves as being bound by the principle of collective responsibility.[74]

As the SDLP withdrew, Fitt rushed over to Stormont Castle and informed Orme that his assembly party had voted eleven to eight against the leadership's proposal to re-phase Sunningdale. When Orme met with a hostile group of SDLP backbenchers in Stormont buildings, they accused him of 'ducking' the challenge of using troops to break a strike which represented the best opportunity the British had ever had to confront 'Fascist Unionism'. Responding to their demand for rapid military action, Orme argued that while Whitelaw's Operation Motorman had taken meticulous advance preparation, his government had only been able to react to the UWC strike after it had begun. Since support for the strike within the Protestant community had grown over the last week, taking immediate military action, he argued, would simply escalate an ongoing standoff between the government and the UWC.

SDLP assembly members insisted that the strike must be broken prior to any renegotiation of the Sunningdale agreement, and accused the government of forcing the SDLP to make unnecessary concessions while the strike was in full swing. Orme reminded them that the parties to the executive alone had renegotiated the Council of Ireland proposals. And making an emotional appeal, he warned the SDLP men that if their decision resulted in the collapse of the Northern Ireland Executive, then the UWC would be victorious and the potential that the power-sharing settlement contained to regulate the troubles would lie dormant, 'possibly for as long as twenty years'.[75]

Orme's last-minute diplomacy saved the day, and with a new sense of realism the SDLP assembly members voted by fourteen to five in favour of the proposals, before unanimously agreeing to accept re-phasing after a second ballot. Without consulting the Irish government, Fitt announced to a reconvened executive at 4.20 pm that the SDLP had unanimously accepted Faulkner's proposal. In the spirit of this compromise, Hume's oil plan was agreed and submitted to Rees for approval.[76] He told Orme that the situation had become so dire that a decision to use troops had to be taken that day. Orme responded ominously, noting that if the government accepted what the executive was proposing, then it would be entering into 'uncharted waters'.[77]

NOTES

1. ICBH, *British Policy in Northern Ireland, 1970–4*, p.67.
2. PREM16/146, Note of telephone conversation between Wilson and Rees, 16 May 1974.
3. CJ4/503, Statement by Brian Faulkner, 15 May 1974.
4. Interview with Glen Barr, Londonderry, 22 August 2001.
5. Fisk, *The Point of No Return*, p.59.
6. CJ4/504, Meeting of Emergency Committee, Dundonald House, 15 May 1974.
7. CJ4/504, Meeting between Orme and Loyalist deputation, Stormont, 15 May 1974.
8. Fisk, *The Point of No Return*, p.65.
9. CJ4/504, Meeting between Orme and Loyalist deputation, Stormont, 15 May 1974.
10. PRONI, D4211/4/1/23, Roy Bradford Papers.
11. PRONI, T3300/6/2, Meeting with Minister of State, 15 May 1974.
12. CJ4/503, Cooper to Rees, 16 May 1974.
13. CJ4/503, Statement by Len Murray, 17 May 1974.
14. CJ4504, Meeting between British officials and the Road Transport Association, Stormont, 17 May 1974.
15. CJ4/504, King to Cooper, 16 May 1974.
16. Interview with Leslie Morrell, Belfast, 4 January 2001.
17. Interview with Glen Barr, Londonderry, 22 August 2001.
18. ICBH, *British Policy in Northern Ireland, 1970–4*, p.53.
19. CJ4/503, Nicholls to Butler, 17 May 1974.
20. CJ4/504, Meeting between Rees and security officials, Stormont, 17 May 1974.
21. CENT/1/3/38, Meeting between Rees and the Northern Ireland Administration, 17 May 1974.
22. PREM16/146, Record of conversation between Wilson and Rees, 17 May 1974.
23. Fisk, *The Point of No Return*, p.106.
24. See D. Mullan, *Dublin and Monaghan Bombings* (Dublin: Wolfhound Press, 2000), pp.131–45.
25. CJ4/504, Meeting between Rees and loyalist deputation, Stormont, 17 May 1974.
26. CJ4/504, Secretary of State's meetings, Stormont, 18/19 May 1974.
27. CJ4/503, Statement by the UWC, 19 May 1974.
28. CJ4/503, Telegram to Wilson, 18 May 1974.
29. Interview with Lord Molyneaux, Westminster, 30 January 2001.
30. D4211/4/1/23, Roy Bradford Papers.
31. CJ4/504, Secretary of State's meetings, Stormont, 18/19 May 1974.

32. Interview with Leslie Morrell, Belfast, 4 January 2001.
33. Interview with Austin Currie, Dublin, 5 January 2001.
34. D4211/4/1/23, Roy Bradford Papers.
35. D4211/4/1/23, Roy Bradford Papers.
36. Fisk, *The Point of No Return*, pp.88–9.
37. CJ4/1148, Emergency Security Meeting, Stormont, 20 May 1974.
38. OE2/24, Minutes of a meeting of the Northern Ireland Executive, Stormont, 20 May 1974.
39. DT2005/7/630, Meeting between FitzGerald and Galsworthy, 21 May 1974.
40. Interview with Leslie Morrell, Belfast, 4 January 2001.
41. ICBH, *British Policy in Northern Ireland, 1970–4*, p.58.
42. DT2005/7/630, Memo from Minister for Posts and Telegraphs, 20 May 1974.
43. DT2005/7/630, Meeting between FitzGerald and Galsworthy, 20 May 1974.
44. DT2005/7/630, Northern Ireland Situation, 21 May 1974.
45. Hansard, vol. 874, col. 184, 16 May 1974.
46. OE2/25, Minutes of a Meeting of the Northern Ireland Executive, Stormont, 21 May 1974.
47. Interview with Leslie Morrell, Belfast, 4 January 2001.
48. PREM16/146, Roy Bradford on 'World at One', 21 May 1974.
49. Interview with John Hume, Londonderry, 13 September 2001.
50. OE1/16, Situation Report, 21 May 2001.
51. CJ4/503, Statement by the UWC, 21 May 1974.
52. Hansard, vol. 874, cols. 32–4, 20 May 1974.
53. PREM16/146, Record of a conversation between Wilson and Rees, 20 May 1974.
54. ICBH, *British Policy in Northern Ireland, 1970–4*, p.58.
55. CJ4/503, Hume to Rees, 21 May 1974.
56. CJ4/504, Note of security meeting, Stormont, 21 May 1974.
57. DT2005/7/630, Draft Statement, 21 May 1974.
58. PREM16/147, Daily intelligence summary, No. 341, 23 May 1974.
59. Hansard, vol. 874, cols. 184–6, 21 May 1974.
60. DT2005/7/630, Northern Ireland Situation, 21 May 1974.
61. CAB134/3778, Minutes of Ministerial Committee on Northern Ireland, Downing Street, 21 May 1974.
62. CJ4/503, Cooper to King, 21 May 1974.
63. CJ4/504, Note of security meeting, Stormont, 21 May 1974.
64. OE1/16, Situation Report, 22 May 1974.
65. CJ4/504, Meeting between Orme and CBI, Stormont, 22 May 1974.
66. CJ4/504, Meeting between Orme and the Business Employers Association, Stormont, 23 May 1974.
67. CJ4/503, Transcript of a LBC interview with Paisley, 22 May 1974.
68. CJ4/503, Interview with Jim Smith, BBC, 22 May 1974.
69. PREM16/147, Northern Ireland Security Report, 22 May 1974.
70. Interview with Glen Barr, Londonderry, 22 August 2001.
71. CJ4/503, Northern Ireland News Summary, 22 May 1974.
72. Interview with Glen Barr, Londonderry, 22 August 2001.
73. Ibid.
74. OE2/26, Minutes of a meeting of the Northern Ireland Executive, 22 May 1973.
75. CJ4/504, Note of SDLP assembly party meeting, 22 May 1974.
76. OE2/27, Minutes of a Meeting of the Northern Ireland Executive, Stormont, 22 May 1974.
77. CJ4/504, Note of Emergency Meeting, 23 May 1974.

8

The Triumph of the Destructors

Making a statement which he described as 'perhaps the most important that has ever been made' in either the Northern Ireland Assembly or the Stormont parliament that preceded it, Faulkner presented his 'new look' power-sharing settlement, on behalf of 'a united executive', at 4.30 pm, on 22 May 1974.[1] Under 'Phase I', ministers appointed by the Northern Ireland Executive and the Irish government, acting on the basis of unanimity, would provide an all-Ireland forum for 'consultation, cooperation and coordination of action' on socio-economic matters. Further steps in Sunningdale's implementation would be taken under 'Phase II', following a public test of opinion in the form of the next assembly election.[2] Rees described the executive's initiative as both 'realistic and sensible'.[3] Cosgrave accepted that it was the consequence of a necessity 'to face the reality' of the present situation in Northern Ireland. But Lynch viewed the dilution of the Sunningdale Communiqué with 'keen disappointment',[4] as Fianna Fáil had only swallowed its more unpalatable ingredients because it provided for the establishment of a Council of Ireland.

Renegotiating the Council of Ireland proposals was undoubtedly the masterstroke of Faulkner's political career. His adversaries in Dublin, who had succeeded in maximising the council's scope at Sunningdale, certainly viewed it as such, for he had reduced it 'to a meeting of Ministers North and South' that would 'cooperate in certain defined areas'. So much so that Dermot Nally warned Cosgrave that it would be 'a mistake' to have Sunningdale registered at the UN, following a second tripartite meeting, as this would 'give formal international recognition to the power of veto of the majority in Northern Ireland over any further development of the Council of Ireland'.[5]

Amid the mounting chaos that gripped the province, the subtlety of

Faulkner's re-phasing proposals was lost on the Northern Ireland electorate, as Paisley contemptuously dismissed his initiative as Sunningdale 'in two spoonfuls' rather than one.[6] Rees sent another 500 troops to Northern Ireland and Wilson decided to withdraw financial support to Harland and Wolff for the duration of the strike. The British government 'had now reached the crunch'[7] in confronting what Wilson described as both a 'political' and a 'sectarian' strike led by a throwback force from 'the seventeenth century'.[8] Furious with the UWC, he took the view that parliament should be very slow in financially offsetting the damage that they had caused to the Northern Ireland economy. He believed that intimidation had silenced the voices of people who were determined to get back to work, and weakened the morale that financial hardship nurtured in working-class communities in normal instances of industrial strife. His fiscal sanction on the shipyard was intended to remind the UWC that without subsidy from Westminster, Northern Ireland would be forced to half its expenditure or double its taxation to balance its current budget. Wilson's action had the opposite effect, however, aiding the UWC's efforts to consolidate its working-class Protestant support base. The UWC was overseeing a wide number of services, having issued passes to essential workers, as the heads of industry, commerce and the farmers' union recognised its authority due to government inaction. Support for the strike was solidifying across other sections of society, as people who had not supported it from the beginning began acquiescing in the stoppage.

Although Northern Ireland still had ample oil supplies, the government was uncertain whether it could distribute them to key sites without confronting the UWC. Voicing these concerns, Hume told the assembly that the UWC were threatening 'the very life of the Northern Ireland community'.[9] The Oil Industry Security Committee was convinced that the use of troops to dispense oil, even for essential purposes, would cause Northern Ireland's fuel distribution workforce to stand down. Enough managerial staff could still be relied upon to provide the army with the information that was necessary to fulfil this task, but they stressed that the government would have to pay for any oil it requisitioned. Should the UWC respond to this action by withdrawing personnel from the power stations, the government would be caught between a rock and a hard place. In other words, putting oil distribution under the control of the military would be viewed as the beginning of an attempt to break the strike and restore the executive's political authority. If the government precipitated a situation in which it became necessary to use troops against the UWC, this military action was more likely to be negatively received within the Protestant population if the government did not state, at the outset, that it intended to break the strike and restore order. This was the 'catch 22' that Rees found himself in. If he made any such declaration, then the UWC could easily orchestrate a level of chaos that rendered military intervention ineffective.

An official from the Department of the Environment illustrated the extent to which the government had already lost control of Northern Ireland. He said that if personnel from his department were forced to gain petrol from the army in order to get to work, then there might be 'a withdrawal of staff through intimidation and sympathy with the strikers'.[10] Furthermore, the government was in fact facing a serious staffing problem at Stormont, as civil servants were unable to easily gain access to petrol in order to travel to work, as the UWC did not view them as essential workers.

* * * *

On Thursday 23 May, Faulkner's administration had a tense meeting with Northern Ireland's trade union leaders and its heads of industry and commerce. Although he reassured them that the executive's desire was in fact to govern, Faulkner told them that it was far easier to cry 'Govern!' than it was to put that desire into effect when political authority lay elsewhere. He rejected calls from the industrial leaders to immediately open dialogue with the UWC, for they were unconstitutional renegades attempting to mount a coup against the executive.[11] Faulkner immediately informed Rees of their collective disbelief at the general feeling of malaise that was pervasive at Stormont, as the British showed 'no urgency' and took 'no action' against the band of 'street dictators' who were threatening constitutional government in Northern Ireland. Although the union bosses admitted that they had badly underestimated the extent to which intimidation was affecting their workers, the UWC had raised the stakes by calling on the RUC and UDR to refrain from duty. Moreover, the electricity board indicated that the entire grid would break down by the weekend due a shortage of chemical and gas supplies. Faulkner relayed their main concern directly to the secretary of state, asking him: 'Will the

Government not govern?' And he pressed Rees to make an immediate decision over using troops to maintain essential services. If Sunningdale's renegotiation was to have any political impact, then the executive's statement of the previous evening must be reinforced by military action from Westminster to create an environment in which people could go back to work.

In office but no longer in power, the Northern Ireland Executive felt that it was being hung out to dry by the government. It again discussed the wisdom of holding talks with the UWC, which had begun to remove all the barricades in Belfast and allow petrol to be delivered to designated stations. They acknowledged that the strike had 'highly intelligent direction' and that the UWC had enough 'intimate knowledge' of the supply system to both maintain essential services and apply pressure at precise points in that system. Bradford argued that opening dialogue would at least enable the executive to hear what the UWC had to say before the situation became completely unsalvageable. He felt that 'the UWC had not expected such complete success and they were probably becoming apprehensive at the anarchy which could follow' from their actions. The SDLP opposed his suggestion since the UWC intended to overthrow the executive anyway. They believed the strike must be resisted with the full resources of the Stormont and Westminster governments. It was unclear what level of force would be required to either hold the line or break the strike, but there was a strong possibility that Northern Ireland would be completely devastated in the process, even with the intervention of 30,000 troops. Once again, Bradford made 'a strong plea' for his colleagues to open a line of communication with the UWC, but the majority were 'generally' not in favour of following this course of action.[12]

News then reached the executive that Rees was likely to take a decision that day and would most probably act in full support of the executive. At 6.30 pm, Hume informed Orme, on behalf of the executive, that if the oil plan was not supported then they would resign.[13] But the secretary of state for Northern Ireland dashed their hopes. The only reference he made to the crisis, in a statement to the House of Commons, was that he would take 'steps in connection with the strike and the maintenance of essential services'. He added that it made him 'a little sick' that certain MPs should 'attempt to set up a provisional Government in Northern Ireland' and 'then come here and draw pay as democrats'. Paisley responded, chiding Rees that it was the UWC that was maintaining essential services in Northern Ireland, a situation that could have been averted had he not rejected their offer to operate the power stations at 60 per cent output.[14] There is something to Paisley's remark, as the UWC were not expecting to be tasked by the public and industry with running the country, and they were developing an alternative strand of government out of necessity and opportunism, which was a direct consequence of Wilson's inaction.

Rees had indicated to Wilson that the Irish government, the Northern Ireland Executive and the general public now felt that the British government was doing nothing to challenge the strike. In a tersely worded letter to Wilson, Cosgrave accused the British of inertia in its standoff with the UWC and of exacerbating a situation that was 'destroying the prospect of peace and the authority of the Northern Ireland Executive'. Highlighting the sacrifices that his government and the SDLP had made to preserve power-sharing, which had been accepted with great reluctance and disappointment, he beseeched Wilson to 'guarantee yesterday's agreement' at a formal conference in the next couple of days.[15]

The British government had the choice of either forcibly taking responsibility for the maintenance of essential services in Northern Ireland or letting matters go further adrift and allowing the executive to fall. The Irish government were convinced that 'protecting the British Army would take precedence over any other British interest or policy'.[16] The British Army's chief of general staff, Sir Peter Hunt, painted a very gloomy picture to Wilson concerning the deteriorating situation in Northern Ireland. Morale within the UWC was high, he said, and its support base had mushroomed from about 20 to 80 per cent among the Protestant population. Aldergrove airport might be forced to close due to intimidation and Northern Ireland's telecommunication systems were at risk. He feared that should the army confront the UDA, it would be 'sucked into an endless situation' in which running Northern Ireland would require 'greatly increased numbers of soldiers'.[17]

Having thrown his weight behind the strike, Paisley joined Craig in actively planning its course. They each recorded speeches for broadcast on the UWC's pirate radio station, urging the strikers to hold their nerve. Craig warned the government that should the Coolkeeragh station continue to supply power to the Maydown industrial estate in Londonderry, it would have to be shut down. British intelligence suggested that although the UWC leadership had successfully resisted great pressure from the Protestant paramilitaries to take more direct action, they were considering taking over Stormont with the help of some of its security personnel.[18]

The British government remained divided over the way it should act. Wilson was aware that the executive would shortly collapse in the absence of military intervention. Rees advised his colleagues that the RUC was 'at best ineffective' and 'playing a neutral role' towards the strike. There was a delicate balance between the argument for activating the oil plan as a probe to 'test Protestant reaction' and the view that unless the government was prepared to go much further, and provide the extra troop reinforcements in doing so, engaging in limited intervention might do more harm than good. Wilson agreed with Rees that it was 'important' that the executive was seen to be involved in whatever steps the government was taking and that it would be 'advantageous' to invite its three party leaders for talks at Chequers the following day. Arrangements were being made to maintain the military section of Aldergrove airport, and Wilson stressed that measures to ensure petrol supplies to priority users should be at a state of readiness, so as to enable the government to intervene at short notice.[19] Should the army attempt to run the power stations and distribute petrol, then the practical starting point would be between two and a half and three days from the moment a decision was taken.

* * * *

On Friday 24 May, Faulkner, Fitt and Napier met with Wilson for the first time since the strike began. The meeting at Chequers was the second time Faulkner had faced the challenge of convincing a British prime minister to take considerable political risks in order to save a devolved administration which he headed. As Northern Ireland's last prime minister, he had met Heath at Downing Street to state his case for the maintenance of the old Stormont regime. There was a fundamental difference on this occasion, however; Faulkner required Wilson to take massive military action to restore the authority of an administration which represented the outcome of Heath's policy in Northern Ireland after that fateful day in March 1972. En route to England, Napier asked Faulkner what it was that had made him change course and pursue power-sharing with the same vigour and determination with which he had defended one-party rule at Stormont. Faulkner told him bluntly that it was 'the union' that was of paramount importance to him. He had 'no objection to sharing power with Catholics', but it had been made clear to him that 'power-sharing was the price of the union'. Napier was convinced that other unionist leaders such as Craig and West had also been 'leant on' by the British, but unlike Faulkner they had dismissed it as 'all bluff'.[20]

Wilson, who was accompanied by Rees, Mason and attorney general Samuel Silkin, began the meeting by emphasising his government's support for the executive and his determination to make his predecessor's policy stick. The prime minister, 'breathing fire and brimstone' over the UWC's defiance, questioned Faulkner over just how far he thought the loyalists would take their strike.[21] Did they want a confrontation with the British or were they simply hoping that his government would allow power-sharing to collapse without a clash? Faulkner conceded that the administration of Northern Ireland was now virtually in the hands of the strikers, but argued that if the British government asserted its authority, then the UWC's support base would crumble anyway. Faulkner said that if no action was taken, then a state of anarchy would spread which would constitute a threat to government in the UK as a whole.

Northern Ireland's health and social security system was approaching the point of disintegration, with thousands of emergency benefit claims flooding in from workers who had been laid off because of the stoppage. All non-essential work had been suspended and employees had been reallocated to handling claims and issuing giro cheques. Employers in Northern Ireland were so desperate for action that they cared more about someone running the country than they did about who that someone was. Faulkner said that this message had been driven home to the executive the previous day, when representatives of the Ulster Farmers' Union told them to simply 'govern or talk'.[22]

In reply to Wilson's question, Faulkner stated that the UWC would avoid a confrontation with British troops for some time. Napier added that he had information from 'paramilitary sources' indicating that the UWC planned to take over the distribution of food the following week. Fitt complained to the prime minister that by publishing details of the UWC's petrol supply arrangements, BBC Northern Ireland had seriously undermined the executive. The broadcasting service was having a significant impact on the public's perception of where power lay in

Northern Ireland and on the morale of the executive. The service had been broadcasting daily despatches from electricity spokesmen who painted apocalyptic visions of the province's economic meltdown. So much so that FitzGerald described it as a 'rebel radio station' backed by the BBC.[23] When O'Brien rang its London headquarters to complain about the damage its propaganda machine was doing to the executive, he was informed that they knew nothing about this, as the BBC's central authority 'did not monitor what was happening in Northern Ireland'.[24]

On Fitt's suggestion, Wilson agreed that the army could have a role in petrol distribution. The prime minister was unsure about putting troops into the power stations, however, as this might result in the production of even less electricity. Faulkner conceded that any decision on the question of using troops would be a 'gamble'. But the only way to reassert governmental authority in Northern Ireland was to wrest control of power and fuel supplies from the UWC. Together, he said, the two British administrations faced the most serious challenge to constitutional government in the UK since the Second World War.

Wilson told the three Northern Ireland party leaders that no decisions had yet been reached and whatever action he took would require the full backing of his cabinet. He acknowledged that the secretary of state and the Northern Ireland Executive were being treated like a 'government in exile'. He said that should the British government decide to assert its authority, then this should be done in such a way as to show that this authority lay within the executive. He asked them whether the executive wanted the army to enter the power stations, even if this were to precipitate an exodus of middle management – an assertion of political authority that might well lead to a further reduction of electricity output.

At this point, the three Northern Ireland party leaders clashed openly. It was obvious to Wilson that, only days after they had agreed a new Sunningdale formula, the UWC had succeeded in driving a wedge between the executive parties over the question of deploying British troops to break the strike. Fitt suggested that the army should focus its efforts on the Ballylumford station, as the Catholic workforce at Coolkeeragh could be relied upon, even in the face of intimidation from the UWC.[25] He claimed that the Coolkeeragh power station could work 'full blast' to compensate for reductions elsewhere. Napier argued that this could precipitate an act of sabotage at the Ballylumford station, which would sound the death knell for the executive. Faulkner was more concerned than Fitt about maintaining middle management at Ballylumford. He believed that it was the least bad option to have control of slightly less power than to be reliant on concessions from the strikers. Wilson observed the division within the executive between the SDLP, who strongly favoured rapid military action, of varying degrees, and those who took a more cautious approach, the unionists and Napier, from favouring the oil plan to opening government-led talks with the strikers.

Rees then offered the possibility of using troops to protect the Belfast harbour area, before distributing oil and fuel supplies from there. The executive planned to issue permits to all essential users and Faulkner felt that while this system was 'not perfect', it could work provided oil depots were not sabotaged at key installation points and there were enough troops on the ground to protect them. Rees then asked Mason whether the necessary protection would be forthcoming. Moreover, he said that a contingency plan already existed for the army to requisition the twenty-one service stations that would be required for it to fully assume oil distribution duties.

Likening the situation to a game of cards, Wilson wondered if his government 'played five of trumps, could they be sure the strikers would not play the seven'; thereby opening a dangerous bidding process. Fitt was confident that the UWC would back down. While not disagreeing, Faulkner argued that they would adopt other disruptive tactics to avoid an overt confrontation. And when Rees asked Faulkner whether the RUC would remain loyal if the oil plan was initiated, he said that he believed they would, conceding only that they might have to be 'jacked up' by the politicians to take 'vigorous action'. Napier agreed with Faulkner's assessment, but questioned the commitment of the RUC Reserve, adding that it would be 'unwise' to rely too heavily on that part of the force west of the River Bann.[26]

The difference of opinion between the three Northern Ireland leaders over the impact that introducing troops into the power stations would have on the strike intensified as the talks unfolded. Rees stated that prior to taking any decision the government had to know precisely what the reaction of power station managers would be. At this point, Mason began to argue that should the army be sent in, then it 'seemed likely' that the Power Engineers Association would extract its men and, without 'some senior advisory management', army personnel could not operate the stations. Wilson added that if these employees came out in favour of the strike, then threatening their pension rights 'might make them see reason'. He had that day received a letter at Chequers from their general secretary which indicated that, having sounded out the opinion of its members, a clear majority would withdraw and have the backing of the association.[27] Moreover, the heads of Northern Ireland's fifteen largest companies had met with the CBI and were of the unanimous view that the government should begin talks with the UWC.[28]

At 3.10 pm, Wilson again pressed Faulkner for his political assessment. Faulkner replied, that 'with every hour that passed', the governments in Stormont and Westminster 'enjoyed less support and credibility'. Their inaction, he said, was making it increasingly evident that the administration of Northern Ireland was under the control of the UWC. This could be quickly rectified by an assertion of confidence and authority on the streets of Northern Ireland. He argued that those who advocated opening a 'lifeline' to the strikers were missing the point. Paisley and Craig were no longer in control of the opposition in Northern Ireland – it was now in far more dangerous hands. Playing his last card, Faulkner warned Wilson that this strike was not about power-sharing or a Council of Ireland; it was about the desire of Protestant extremists to set up an 'independent, neo-fascist Northern Ireland'. The executive had a political initiative on which to win back public opinion, he said, but it needed the British government's power and authority to deliver it from the hands of the destructors.[29]

Wilson then announced that a cabinet meeting would be held at 6 pm that evening, at which proposals would be put before his colleagues. While recognising the need to act swiftly, he trusted the executive members would not disclose the details of their discussions. He indicated that he would shortly announce his intention to deliver a broadcast to the nation on Saturday night. Although this did not mean that he was 'guaranteeing' that action would be taken on Saturday, Wilson was aware of the need to 'keep the ball spinning'. Attempting to gain an indication as to what course of action he would take, Faulkner asked for the oil plan to be implemented as soon as possible. He contended that Wilson should not make his broadcast unless the government was in a position to take action on the ground. Wilson replied that although he had understood and received this request, it was important that they all recognised the possibility of an 'escalation of the crisis to still more dangerous proportions'.

The Northern Ireland party leaders had travelled to Chequers in the hope of returning to the executive with both a promise of political support to breathe life into its initiative and a military commitment to preserve it. Yet they had not displayed a unity of purpose over how the initiative might be preserved. Wilson's motivation for holding the meeting had partly been to establish, at first hand, a view of how strong the executive was and how unified the parties to it were regarding the action they were proposing. Downing Street press chief Joe Haines recalls that both Faulkner and Fitt appeared to have 'lost their nerve', as the 'whole thing was lost at that point'.[30] As they departed, Wilson left the question of what he was prepared to do to rescue the Northern Ireland Executive hanging. He said that if the view was that the UWC were likely to withdraw, then coolness would 'be the more productive course'. But 'if the assessment of Mr Faulkner and his colleagues about the attitude of the UWC was correct – and the government's own assessments coincided with it – it could well prove that boldness could pay'.[31]

Wilson took the view that the executive was going to collapse anyway. Haines reflects that 'it wasn't in our interests to carry on … we had our own problems. The British – the English, Scots and Welsh – had been ravaged by the miner's strike … and the original blackout was a nasty reminder of what things could be.'[32] Having observed the divisions between the parties to the executive widen during the strike, Rees had come to view the Northern Ireland power-sharing coalition as 'unbelievably poor'.[33] Furthermore, he harboured grave reservations about the reliability of Northern Ireland's security forces, the emergency committee at Stormont and the Northern Ireland civil service in general. The security situation was quiet, yet Rees believed that the 'reliability of the RUC was in some doubt' – west of the Bann 'very uncertain' and east of the Bann 'somewhat more reliable' – with the loyalty of the UDR varying a good deal from place to place.[34] And although republican areas were quiet, British intelligence suggested that the Provisional and the Official IRA were jointly preparing to defend Catholic areas against a Protestant backlash.

When the British cabinet met at 6 pm for its first discussion of the Northern Ireland crisis since the stoppage began, Rees signalled his opposition to the idea of sending the army into the power stations at this stage. He argued that if the executive should collapse, then it was important that the government should not be open to the charge that this had occurred due to its refusal to meet the executive's request for political and military support. Wilson stressed that due to the uncertainty clouding the debate over the army's ability to run the power stations, he did not favour military intervention in advance of action to preserve fuel and oil supplies. Given the dangerous situation that such action might provoke, Wilson said that the executive was extremely concerned with 'improving our public relations activities', and that the Northern Ireland party leaders 'had suggested that he should make a broadcast' to the nation.[35] This assertion directly contradicts the minutes of his meeting with the executive leaders at Chequers, as recorded separately by both Northern Ireland and British government officials.[36] These documents both confirm that Wilson informed his guests that he was minded to make a broadcast to the nation, before Faulkner urged him not to do so until he was in a position to take action in Northern Ireland.

Mason again raised concerns over the heavy demands that taking military action to supply and protect oil and fuel resources would place on the British Army, whose numbers had been increased by 1,500 during the course of the strike. He did not believe that the army could match the UWC's ability to distribute fuel; therefore military intervention of this nature could potentially demonstrate that the British government's 'will and capacity to govern was less than convincing'. Mason reiterated his view that the army 'did not expect' to be able to run the electricity power stations if middle management were to withdraw. Moreover, the government could not 'expect to obtain' managers from Great Britain to replace those who had been withdrawn in Northern Ireland. He concluded by questioning whether it would be appropriate to use troops in a role 'where life and limb were not directly threatened'.[37]

The British government's responsibility for maintaining constitutional authority in Northern Ireland had been negated by its overwhelming desire to avoid a military confrontation with the majority community and, in effect, both communities. GOC Frank King wrote to Rees that day, accepting that under the present circumstances the secretary of state might 'feel obliged' to order him 'to take over the running of the essential utility services'. He warned Rees that 'in security and eventually political terms', taking such a decision 'would almost certainly prove to be disastrous at the present time'. Should the government attempt to take over any one of the three main services – electricity, oil or gas – he felt that it could quickly find itself in the position of having to run all three. The situation in Northern Ireland might then pass from 'relative calm' to 'near chaos' in a very short period of time. King only envisaged the army intervening to run any of the major utilities in a 'humane and rescuing role', after they had been seen to break down as a result of the UWC's actions.[38]

The weight of opinion in cabinet was against using robust military action to reassert governmental authority in Northern Ireland. The government feared that securing fuel distribution might not be enough to demonstrate its authority, as a situation might then arise where the executive made successive demands for further intervention. It now seemed unlikely that the government could meet such demands and the executive would collapse anyway. There was an 'argument for allowing matters to take their course and facing the possible collapse of the Executive in the expectation that the Protestant community would ultimately weary of the hardships they were suffering and would reject the UWC'. If this occurred, the British government could stand firm on the constitutional issues and resist pressure to withdraw.

There was another view which was most probably that of Rees. The government should first meet the executive's request for action, which was agreed, prior to allowing events to run their natural course. The army would undertake the distribution of oil, petrol and chemical supplies to the gas works in Londonderry and consider supplying food to nationalist areas. Wilson concluded that this action should not be taken to imply 'any commitment to intervene further in running the means of production and distribution'. He said that it should be regarded as 'consistent with the policy of maintaining the Executive in office so long as that might be possible, while allowing the population to experience the hard consequences of supporting the UWC'.[39]

So the fate of Northern Ireland's first power-sharing administration was sealed. It no longer had the political support of the British government. Rees and Mason were authorised to take action against the strike, but their intervention would amount to little more than a face-saving gesture. Wilson hoped this tactic would drive a wedge between the UWC and the Protestant community from which it drew its support, thereby exposing the strikers as the sectarian extremists he believed them to be. Rather than becoming fed up with the UWC, an altogether different sea change in Protestant opinion had occurred, incrementally, over the previous ten days. As agriculture minister Leslie Morrell put it, those middle of the road unionists who had been phoning Stormont pledging their support for the executive in the early days of the strike 'were on the phone again saying you've got to resign'.[40]

Back in Northern Ireland, the UWC had adopted a more liberal approach to the distribution of petrol and food. The paramilitary representatives on the UWC coordinating committee were experiencing increasing difficulties in restraining extreme elements within their organisations from clashing with the army. They were also having difficulty in reducing the influence of Paisley and Craig, who they suspected of simply using the strike to eliminate Faulkner and destroy the concept of power-sharing. The government had no concrete evidence that the strike coordinating committee planned to use violence if the army intervened. It believed that there was 'reliable evidence', however, to suggest that the 'paramilitary bodies acting in concert and probably coordinated by Mr William Craig MP' would quickly gain the initiative in such circumstances.[41] Although Paisley told a gathering in Larne that there would be chaos if troops took over the power stations, he cautioned loyalists against confronting the army. And when Faulkner, Fitt and Napier returned to an apprehensive executive at 7 pm, they said that they had gained a 'clear impression' that Wilson was firm in his desire to do 'whatever was necessary' and 'within his capability' to save their government.[42] However, they did not convey the prime minister's vague commitments to the executive nor his non-committal approach towards military intervention.

It is difficult to judge exactly what conclusions the three leaders led their colleagues towards regarding Wilson's intentions, as the minutes to the executive are not explicit or detailed on this point. But all parties to the executive attest that Wilson misled them in this regard. Unionist ministers recall that when Faulkner returned he was 'quite optimistic that Wilson was going to do something effective',[43] telling colleagues 'don't listen to what the papers are saying, we know that help is on its way'.[44] Napier accurately reflects that he, Faulkner and Fitt gained the impression that the prime minister would act but that he gave no specific timeframe.[45] Faulkner contends that the prime minister gave him a private assurance that he would be recommending support for the executive's proposal. If the government informed them that it was 'OK', then this could be taken to mean that the plan would go ahead, and at midnight Rees called Faulkner to say 'everything is OK'. Consequently, the executive expected military intervention to follow without delay.[46]

The Triumph of the Destructors 237

Faulkner would begin reselling the revamped power-sharing settlement through a public broadcast immediately after Wilson's national address. The process of clawing back the Northern Ireland Executive's political authority from Hawthornden Road would then commence. That day Bradford had again broken ranks with his colleagues. Before the executive broke, the idea of opening communication with the UWC through intermediaries was broached. He argued that not only was it 'unnecessarily provocative' to describe the UWC as 'fascist thugs', it showed 'a frightening ignorance of the true situation'.[47] Although Wilson had bought Faulkner's argument that the strike represented a 'neo-Fascist' putsch, this only stiffened the prime minister's resolve not to be drawn any further into a dispute that was not of his making. In a note circulated by Wilson to his cabinet colleagues, he argued that all paths ahead entailed political risk and should the government refrain from taking risks the executive would collapse over the weekend. He believed that if the army attempted to take over Northern Ireland it would 'probably fail', but added that the executive had not sought such action.[48]

* * * *

On Saturday 25 May, after a day of widespread intimidation and violence by Protestant paramilitaries in Antrim which culminated in the murder of two Catholic brothers, Northern Ireland fell silent in anticipation of Wilson's address. The UWC pre-empted his statement, denying that the strike was a 'rebellion' against 'legal authority'. Their action, it said, represented the 'democratically expressed' voice of majority opinion against a British government that 'had imposed on the people a form of government which would not be imposed on any other part of the United Kingdom'.[49] More than that, the UWC further eased food and fuel distribution, restored telecommunications, and allowed essential chemicals to be transported to the gasworks in Londonderry.

Pressure on Rees was increasing from a wide variety of Protestant business and church leaders to at least open indirect communication with the strike leaders. There were rumours that the UWC had already sought a commitment of cooperation and support from Northern Ireland civil servants in the event that they should set up a provisional loyalist government.[50] The previous evening, Faulkner informed Hume that the British would put the oil plan into effect on 26 May and take action against the

UWC, at Hawthornden Road, in the early hours of the morning. Rees was not subsequently forthcoming on either of these points. Hume feared that the secretary of state now lacked the will to provide enough troops to successfully conduct the plan. He informed Dublin that the loyalty of Northern Ireland's public servants, including those within his own ministry, had become questionable and that Bradford had leaked the details of the oil plan to the UWC.[51] Should Rees refrain from ordering military intervention that very night, he said, then the SDLP would have to resign from the executive.

Wilson then dramatically consolidated unionist support for the strike, sinking the executive with an inflammatory and divisive televised address that jarred all political sensibilities in Northern Ireland. Through this medium, the prime minister gave vent to his distaste for Ulster unionism and for what he viewed as an arrogant and unconstitutional attempt by 'political wildcats' to set up a 'sectarian and undemocratic state'. He warned the militants that the patience of the British had been strained by their behaviour. British parents had seen their sons vilified and murdered, while British taxpayers' money, over £300m that year, had poured into Northern Ireland. And he complained that British citizens had been repeatedly forced to pick up the bill for the 'evil violence' that was a daily occurrence across Northern Ireland.

Those in Northern Ireland who benefit from all this, Wilson concluded, 'now viciously defy Westminster, purporting to act as though they were an elected government; people who spend their lives sponging on Westminster and British democracy and then systematically assault democratic methods'.[52] The impact of these words was predicable. Strike supporters across Northern Ireland sported lumps of sponge on their lapels, adding to the bravado that instilled a 'wartime feeling of undaunted solidarity' among those who were destroying their own country.[53] So much so that Barr suggested sarcastically that the prime minister should be made an 'honorary member' of the UWC, for his remarks had snuffed out any lingering illusions that the British might rescue the executive.[54] They illustrated the Labour leader's rather crass approach to the problem of Northern Ireland and his complete lack of empathy with people living in a divided society within the UK.

There is much debate over what Wilson's intentions were in making his infamous 'spongers' speech, and over who drafted, altered or had access to it before it was delivered. Having received an advance copy that afternoon, Faulkner attempted, through Rees, to alter the provocative tone of the speech.[55] The unionist leader must have realised at that very moment that his political career was effectively over. Bernard Donoughue, who headed Downing Street's Policy Unit, records that neither himself nor Joe Haines had any involvement in the drafting of the speech,[56] although both shared its sentiments and discussed its contents with him. Haines blamed the NIO for giving Wilson the idea of calling the UWC 'spongers'. Although he advised against using such provocative language, he conceded that 'it had a political purpose. Harold was not talking to the people of Northern Ireland; he was talking to the voters in England, Scotland and Wales.' Winning the next election was his first priority.[57] The speech certainly does appear to have been written for domestic British consumption rather than as an appeal for moderation in Northern Ireland. This was how it was perceived at Westminster, as Wilson was 'getting hell' from his own backbenchers on economic cuts and subsidies.[58] Although Donoughue claims that it was drafted by Wilson and the NIO,[59] the prime minister's principle private secretary, Robert Armstrong, sent him notes for the broadcast that he had compiled with two very senior Cabinet Office colleagues, John Hunt and Howard Smith.[60] These notes closely resemble some parts of Wilson's speech, while its tone and flavour, which Donoughue blamed on 'irritation and frustration',[61] appear to have been added by the prime minister himself, reflecting his own personal views.

In the event, no action was taken on Sunday morning, but having learned of the government's plans, the strike leaders had gone into hiding for the night.[62] Without informing the RUC, the army conducted an operation in north Belfast, arresting the people they believed were behind the Dublin and Monaghan bombings, which escalated tensions within the UDA. On Sunday evening, Devlin and Cooper met Cosgrave at FitzGerald's house in Dublin. The Irish government was deeply concerned that violence might again spill over the border following the car bomb attacks. The SDLP men informed the taoiseach that, in the absence of British action, the UWC had almost complete control over the Northern Ireland economy. The UWC had copied and extended the government's oil plan, opening about fifty outlets from which petrol could be distributed to essential users in possession of UWC passes. The strikers now appeared to enjoy the support of the 'vast majority of the Protestant community' and, on the executive, 'none of Faulkner's

Unionist colleagues fully backed him' any longer. They all advocated that the British government should open some form of dialogue with the UWC.

The SDLP proposed to resign from the executive, but not the assembly, at 6 am the following morning. By accepting the 're-phasing' proposals, the nationalists felt that they had lost considerable support within their community. Only an 'immediate pullout' from the executive, they argued, would enable them to salvage the party's political position. Devlin and Cooper realised that this meant 'walking into complete sectarian confrontation', but the alternative was to hand Northern Ireland over to the IRA and the UWC. In their view, only immediate military action on a massive scale would enable the British government to alter the situation. They now feared a British withdrawal and pogroms in Belfast and rural areas where there were nationalist minorities. The SDLP men warned Cosgrave that both his government and the opposition must support and identify with the SDLP, as they were now facing a situation in which everyone would effectively 'go back to their own tribe'.[63]

Late Sunday afternoon, Rees travelled to the Royal Navy air station at Culdrose, in Cornwall, to seek the prime minister's approval for his decision to take control of oil and petrol supplies that evening. He told Wilson that he had 'held his hand' so far due to leaks from the Northern Ireland civil service, which had disclosed details of the operation and prompted the UWC to stockpile petrol supplies. Up-to-date intelligence reports indicated that the strike leaders intended to knock out the power stations if the army moved into the oil depots. Rees informed him of further splits within the executive: Fitt had drifted away from his SDLP colleagues; Devlin had called for the imposition of martial law in the North; and Faulkner was 'beginning to think of giving up'.[64] Faulkner's colleagues blamed Hume, believing that Fitt, Devlin, Currie and Napier would have 'ditched the Council of Ireland' had it not been for his obduracy.[65] Nevertheless, Rees warned Wilson that in terms of international criticism and the political fallout in Northern Ireland, to continue to sit out the strike without taking any 'decisive action' would bring the government the 'worst of all worlds'.[66]

Wilson's attention was focused on the question of a return to direct rule, and on the different policy options the government would have open to it after the strike. Rees raised the possibility of using the assembly as a forum for devising a new constitution for Northern Ireland, but the prime minister was thinking more in terms of how financial sanctions might be imposed, so as to ensure that Northern Ireland paid for the damage that had been caused by the strike. If Britain decided to 'pull out' in more or less peaceful circumstances, then some troops could remain in Northern Ireland with the continuation of a diminished subsidy, but should the government be 'forced out', Wilson told Rees, 'we would owe them nothing'.[67] Ironically, fearful of the long-term economic damage the strike would have on foreign investment, Northern Ireland's leaders of industry were, at that very moment, pleading with officials at Stormont to urgently open talks to avert an economic meltdown.

Frank Cooper intervened at this point, sending Rees an urgent message to the helicopter base advising him to announce that while law and order measures were being stepped up, the government would not interfere with the strike 'other than to save life and limb'. Basing his judgement on 'G.B. interest' and potential 'international repercussions', Cooper argued that this course was defensible and would command public support should the executive resign. Believing that it was fraught with danger, he cautioned Rees strongly against going ahead with the oil plan. The likely outcome of this measure, he said, would be 'a degree of chaos, large-scale and unsuccessful intervention and public humiliation' for the British government.[68] Wilson accepted Cooper's view, which was also the view of the army, that there appeared to be no practicable 'middle way', as the executive was liable to collapse regardless of whether or not the government 'grasped the nettle' of intervention and took over oil distribution. He concluded, however, that if the executive was destined to fall, then 'it was better that it should go as a result of firm action on our part rather than of indecision'.[69] On that note, the prime mister gave Rees the authority, and the oil plan was launched at 5 am on Monday morning.

* * * *

Barricading themselves into a garage in Corporation Street, near the Belfast harbour, British troops put up a sign which read 'under new management'.[70] The SDLP did not resign and Hume announced that petrol coupons would be issued to an estimated 6,500 essential users. However, his officials failed to arrive at eight of the twenty-one government-controlled filling stations and by that afternoon only seven fuel points were functional. The problem was that electricity was required to operate the fuel pumps and the delivery of generators had been delayed.

When their car approached a road blockade on the return journey from Dublin, an attempt was made to ambush Devlin and Cooper. The SDLP negotiators, who were being escorted by the RUC, narrowly evaded capture as a crowd attempted to block their subsequent retreat towards the border. An RUC Land Rover was present at the blockade, but the police took no action to help the ministers. When RTÉ made enquiries to the local police station they were informed that no such blockade existed.[71] When Rees himself made enquiries the RUC chief constable said that the allegations of Devlin and Cooper 'differed greatly' from the police account of the affair,[72] and a police statement said that at no stage were they in 'immediate danger'.[73]

Tension on Northern Ireland's streets rose when Craig declared that the British Army had arrived 'to break the strike'. Governing the province was now the sole responsibility of the army, he said; the UWC was 'withdrawing from the scene'. The strikers responded with measured pressure, and Barr quipped that they would sit back and 'eat grass' until all their demands had been met.[74] New blockades were erected across all the major towns surrounding Belfast and the UWC announced that from midnight, sewerage station workers and security personnel at all factories would be withdrawn. This left the army with ultimate responsibility for these facilities and, if the pumps were left unattended, then raw sewage would soon flood low-lying parts of Belfast. The UWC's tactic was to stretch the army by involving it in as many non-military tasks as possible, thereby testing its capacity to conduct any of them efficiently. At the same time, the strikers planned to carry out their threat to reduce electricity supply.

The UWC ordered managers at Ballylumford to shut down one 120-megawatt unit and, when this demand was initially refused, it called upon the entire workforce to withdraw. In Coolkeeragh, the 60-megawatt generator remained operational despite the departure of Protestant industrial workers. British intelligence suggested that bombs may have been placed at the Ballylumford station, which would be detonated if the troops moved in. Compounding the government's dilemma, the UWC coordinating committee received a message which indicated that so long as the army manned essential services, the IRA would support the total withdrawal of labour.[75] Gas workers walked out in Belfast, rubbish piled up in the streets and Northern Ireland's industry stood on the brink of collapse. The Ulster Farmers' Union warned that, in a matter of days, farmers would have to decide whether to slaughter livestock or simply allow their animals to starve. Petrol-tank drivers complained that they were putting their lives at risk by delivering essential fuel supplies and, in a sardonic twist, the UWC instructed gravediggers to put down their shovels today and 'let the army bury the dead tomorrow'.[76]

Facing defeat, Faulkner told the executive that there was a 'need to open talks' with the UWC leadership 'before the Northern Ireland economy collapses'. With a shutdown of electricity supply at Ballylumford now expected, Northern Ireland was on the verge of total economic, political and social disintegration. The army reluctantly held the line, in what was an increasingly malevolent atmosphere. The electricity board told Hume that almost all of its technicians were prepared to walk out and join the strike. The permanent secretaries of the Northern Ireland civil service and a majority of his ministerial colleagues urged Faulkner to find a way of communicating with the strikers before it was too late.[77] Split down the middle, the executive fudged the issue, declaring that it was 'prepared to discuss any particular matter within their competence with other elected leaders'.[78]

With the prospect of anarchy outside Stormont's gates, Rees made a final appeal to the people of Northern Ireland to resume work and relinquish their support for 'the wreckers'.[79] Adding insult to injury, Ugandan president Idi Amin put his 'good offices' at Wilson's disposal should he wish to hold a peace conference in Kampala, and offered to mediate between the government and the UWC.[80] Of more pressing concern to the prime minister was the question of whether the collapse of the executive would end the strike or whether it could be maintained until fresh elections were conceded. One way of avoiding an election would be to hold a constitutional conference. While there was 'virtually no hope of any agreement emerging' from such a convention, Rees felt that it would delay an election, resurrect bipartisanship at Westminster, minimise criticism from Dublin and demonstrate that the government had 'not given up the search for a non-sectarian and rational solution'.[81]

Much to the annoyance of British intelligence, Barr attempted to arrange a meeting with Rees that day through American Quaker intermediaries. The strike leaders were particularly concerned that Paisley, Craig and West would be representing the working class in talks, as rumours of a proposed meeting with the secretary of state spread. They feared that working-class loyalists would be excluded from any future deal with the British.[82] The UWC coordinating committee felt that it should be the one to call off the strike and be the judge of whether or not its demands had been met. By 28 May it seemed that the argument against allowing the politicians alone to negotiate had won the day. Barr's attitude had suddenly changed, and he indicated to the Quakers that he would not meet Rees unless he could be accompanied by his colleagues from the UWC coordinating committee.[83]

Reports then confirmed that electricity production was being run down at Ballylumford and a total shutdown was expected by early that evening. The water taps ran dry in north Belfast and Antrim after Dunore Point pumping station lost its electricity supply. Bradford announced his willingness to act as a go-between in order to help end the crisis. And farmers, rallied by speeches from Paisley, began arriving at Stormont on foot and in their tractors.

At the top of the hill, Northern Ireland's power-sharing administration gathered for what would be its last meeting. At 11.15 am, in the absence of Devlin, McGrady and Ivan Cooper, Faulkner argued that the executive must ask Rees to 'open discussions', through intermediaries, with the strikers. Napier favoured talking directly to the UWC, regardless of whether Rees supported it or not, fearing that if the executive collapsed it might mark the last day ever of devolved government in Northern Ireland. Fitt was in two minds. He was not against this course, in principle, but he simply saw no possibility of the UWC allowing the executive to survive through a negotiated compromise. This was a conclusion, Bradford argued, which had led Northern Ireland to the brink of anarchy. Hume expressed his 'total disagreement' with the conclusion that the unionists had come to. He would not resign. He believed that the executive must 'stand firm', in the face of what Bradford described as a 'pan-Protestant strike', for what were 'fundamental political principles not only for the authority of the Executive, but for British authority in Northern Ireland'.[84] Bradford argued that by pressing Rees to take such a strong line, the executive had already made a 'disastrous misjudgement'.[85]

Faulkner then informed Rees that he no longer spoke for the Alliance and SDLP members of the executive. Moved by the courage that Faulkner had displayed, Rees accepted his resignation as chief executive.

The British government's position remained unaltered; there would be no negotiations with the UWC, an unelected body, over the constitutional future of Northern Ireland. In parting, Rees told Faulkner that they had reached the 'end of the road'; Craig and his colleagues would have the satisfaction of knowing that they had 'robbed the province of power-sharing'.[86] To his credit, Faulkner made no complaint of any sort to Rees about the way in which his government had handled the crisis. Others were not so diplomatic: Heath believed that 'Wilson's approach' had 'brought about the collapse' of the executive through complete inaction,[87] which the SDLP viewed as one of the greatest tragedies in modern Irish history.[88] But it was Heath's unwillingness to devolve security powers to the executive that had left it powerless, and Hume lamented that had the executive enjoyed control over Northern Ireland's security forces, it would have had 'no problem' in breaking the strike in its first days.[89] Even Hume, who had thrived in his role as a Northern Ireland government minister, had come to value the power-sharing executive for what it was, and his determination to remain in office epitomised the tragedy that Northern Ireland was experiencing.

Faulkner relayed the secretary of state's decision to the executive at 1.35 pm, before announcing publicly that he believed 'some sort of dialogue between government and those confronting it should now take place'.[90] Rees informed the SDLP and Alliance Party members, who had not resigned, that there was no statutory basis for the continuation of the executive under the Constitution Act. The executive broke, with ministers expressing sorrow and regret that their power-sharing settlement had been destroyed by an organisation which had usurped the authority of a British government that had been unwilling to uphold the democratically constituted administration of Northern Ireland. The executive ministers regretted that they had been unable to act in complete unanimity, as they had invariably done since taking office, but in their final act as a representative government they agreed 'to do everything possible to avoid all personal or political recrimination and that they would not deviate one jot or tittle from the principles on which the Executive was founded'.[91]

The following day Northern Ireland began to return to normal. Electricity output exceeded 30 per cent, water and sewage services returned and gas workers built up levels of supply during the day. At midday the UWC announced a *de facto* end to the strike, recommending a phased return to work, with heavy industry waiting until the following Monday for the power supply to return. While suffering a humiliating blow in its capitulation to the rebellion, the British government's 'sit it out' approach to the strike had in one sense been successful, for as the executive collapsed, Protestants were keen to return to work. Momentum for the UWC to hold out and achieve all its political objectives evaporated. The UDA had been most reluctant to call off the strike without first gaining the promise of fresh elections. The UUUC, however, were keen to recapture their influence from the militant forces that Rees viewed as the working-class exponents of a new Ulster nationalism. There was a great deal of resentment on the UWC's coordinating committee towards the UUUC politicians for attempting to take control of the strike. The UVF leaders were determined to hold them to their word that they were in favour of power-sharing.[92]

After he resigned, Faulkner praised the 'spirit' in which the power-sharing executive had conducted its business since the beginning of 1974. He reiterated his belief that Northern Ireland could only remain a part of the UK on the basis of 'cooperation between Protestants and Roman Catholics'.[93] Ken Bloomfield reflected that, in operation, the executive had been 'by and large harmonious', for with the exception of the debate over the Council of Ireland proposals, 'the strains which developed in its final phase were due to conflicts of personality as much as of ideology'.[94]

On the other side of the Atlantic, Edward Kennedy said that while the functions of government may be temporarily in the hands of extremists, the British 'cannot yield to their outrageous acts' and allow power-sharing to fail.[95] In Dublin, Cosgrave praised the 'courage and dedication' of those who had engaged in the 'great experiment in community cooperation', and blamed the IRA for provoking the 'massive sectarian backlash' which had destroyed it.[96] The *Irish Times* described the executive as the first men to have ploughed 'a decent straight line for decent straight Ulster people'.[97] But when the news came over that Faulkner had resigned, the teeming mob of protesters outside Stormont, and strike supporters on the streets across Protestant Ulster, celebrated the destruction of the power-sharing executive as if it was VE Day.

The Triumph of the Destructors 247

NOTES

1. Northern Ireland Assembly, vol. 3, cols. 1153–8, 22 May 1973.
2. D3591/6/1, Executive Statement.
3. *Financial Times*, 23 May 1974.
4. *Dáil Debates*, cols. 2038–41, 22 May 1974.
5. DT2005/7/631, Nally to Cosgrave, 23 May 1974.
6. Fisk, *The Point of No Return*, p.159.
7. PREM16/147, Meeting between Wilson and O'Sullivan, Downing Street, 23 May 1974.
8. Hansard, vol. 874, cols. 184–5, 21 May 1974.
9. D3591/6/2, Statement by John Hume, Northern Ireland Assembly debate, 23 May 1974.
10. CJ4/504, Note of Emergency Meeting, 23 May 1974.
11. D3591/6/2, Northern Ireland Administration meeting, Stormont, 23 May 1974.
12. OE2/29, Minutes of a meeting of the Northern Ireland Executive, Stormont, 23 May 1974.
13. Faulkner, *Memoirs*, p.274.
14. Hansard, vol. 874, cols. 611–19, 23 May 1974.
15. PREM16/147, Cosgrave to Wilson, 23 May 1974.
16. Interview with Garret FitzGerald, Dublin, 12 September 2001.
17. PREM16/147, Hunt to Wilson, 23 May 1974.
18. PREM16/147, Daily intelligence summary, No. 341, 23 May 1974.
19. CAB134/3778, Minutes of Ministerial Committee on Northern Ireland, Downing Street, 23 May 1974.
20. Interview with Sir Oliver Napier, Holywood, 29 December 2000.
21. Ibid.
22. CENT1/3/24, Note of a Meeting at Chequers, 24 May 1974.
23. ICBH, *British Policy in Northern Ireland, 1970–4*, p.55.
24. Interview with Garret FitzGerald, Dublin, 12 September 2001.
25. PREM16/147, Meeting between Wilson and Executive Leaders, Chequers, 24 May 1974.
26. CENT1/3/24, Note of a Meeting at Chequers, 24 May 1974.
27. PREM16/147, Lyons to Wilson, 24 May 1974.
28. PREM16/147, Adamson to Armstrong, 24 May 1974.
29. PREM16/147, Meeting between Wilson and Executive Leaders, Chequers, 24 May 1974.
30. Interview with Joe Haines, Tunbridge Wells, 19 February 2008.
31. PREM16/147, Meeting between Wilson and Executive Leaders, Chequers, 24 May 1974.
32. Interview with Joe Haines, Tunbridge Wells, 19 February 2008.
33. Rees1/4, *Northern Ireland*, p.11.
34. CAB128/54, Cabinet Conclusions, Downing Street, 24 May 1974.
35. Ibid.
36. PREM16/147, Meeting between Wilson and Executive Leaders, Chequers, 24 May 1974; CENT1/3/24, Note of a Meeting at Chequers, 24 May 1974.
37. CAB128/54, Cabinet Conclusions, Downing Street, 24 May 1974.
38. CJ4/1148, King to Rees, 24 May 1974.
39. CAB128/54, Cabinet Conclusions, Downing Street, 24 May 1974.
40. Interview with Leslie Morrell, Belfast, 4 January 2001.
41. PREM16/147, Northern Ireland Strike Report to Prime Minister, 24 May 1974.
42. OE2/30, Minutes of the Northern Ireland Executive, Stormont, 24 May 1974.
43. Interview with Leslie Morrell, Belfast, 4 January 2001.
44. Interview with Basil McIvor, Spa, 24 August 2001.
45. Interview with Sir Oliver Napier, Holywood, 29 December 2000.
46. Faulkner, *Memoirs of a Statesman*, p.275.
47. Fisk, *Point of No Return*, p.198.
48. CAB129/177, Note by the Secretary of the Cabinet, 24 May 1974.
49. CJ4/503, UWC statement, 25 May 1974.
50. PREM16/147, Northern Ireland Strike Report to Prime Minster, 25 May 1974.
51. DT2005/7/631, Developments relating to Northern Ireland Situation, Donlon, 25/26 May 1974.

52. There is a full transcript of Wilson's speech in Fisk, *Point of No Return*, pp.252–4.
53. D4211/4/1/23, Roy Bradford Papers.
54. Fisk, *Point of No Return*, p.201–2.
55. Faulkner, *Memoirs of a Statesman*, p.275.
56. B. Donoughue, *Downing Street Diary: With Harold Wilson* (London: Jonathan Cape, 2005), p.128.
57. Interview with Joe Haines, Tunbridge Wells, 19 February 2008; J. Haines, *The Politics of Power* (London: Jonathan Cape, 1977), p.133.
58. Interview with Lord Molyneaux, Westminster, 30 January 2001.
59. Bernard Donoughue, *Prime Minister: The Conduct of Policy under Harold Wilson and James Callaghan* (London: Jonathan Cape, 1987), p.130.
60. PREM16/147, Downing Street to Chequers, 24 May 1974.
61. ICBH, *British Policy in Northern Ireland, 1970–4*, p.60.
62. DT2005/7/631, Meeting between O'Sullivan and Wilson, London, 23 May 1973.
63. DT2005/7/631, Developments relating to Northern Ireland Situation, Donlon, 25/26 May 1974.
64. PREM16/148, Conversation between Wilson and Rees, Culdrose, 26 May 1974.
65. Interview with Basil McIvor, Spa, 24 August 2001.
66. PREM16/148, Conversation between Wilson and Rees, Culdrose, 26 May 1974.
67. Ibid.
68. PREM16/148, Cooper to Rees, 26 May 1974.
69. PREM16/148, Conversation between Wilson and Rees, Culdrose, 26 May 1974.
70. *Daily Telegraph*, 28 May 1974.
71. CJ4/1147, Dublin to Belfast, Tel. No. 21, 27 May 1974.
72. CJ4/1147, Note of a Security Meeting, Stormont, 28 May 1974.
73. CJ4/1147, RUC statement, 27 May 1974.
74. *Daily Telegraph*, 28 May 1974.
75. PREM16/148, NIO strike report to Prime Minister, 27 May 1974.
76. *Daily Telegraph*, 28 May 1974.
77. OE2/31, Minutes of the Northern Ireland Executive, Stormont, 27 May 1974.
78. *Financial Times*, 28 May 1974.
79. *Daily Telegraph*, 28 May 1974.
80. PREM16/148, Kampala to London, Tel. No. 537, 28 May 1974.
81. PREM16/148, Rees to Wilson, 27 May 1974.
82. CJ4/1147, Meeting with UVF at Laneside, 27 May 1974.
83. CJ4/1147, Allan to Cooper, 28 May 1974.
84. OE2/32, Minutes of the Northern Ireland Executive, Stormont, 28 May 1974.
85. D4211/4/1/23, Roy Bradford Papers.
86. CJ4/1147, Meeting between Rees and Faulkner, Stormont, 18 May 1974.
87. Interview with Lord Heath, London, 4 April 2001.
88. Interview with John Hume, Londonderry, 13 September 2001.
89. Ibid.
90. CJ4/1147, Statement by Faulkner, 28 May 1974.
91. OE1/16, Extract from Executive Minutes, 28 May 1974.
92. CJ4/1147, UVF meeting at Laneside, 29 May 1974.
93. CJ4/1147, Statement by Faulkner, 28 May 1974.
94. CENT/1/3/24, Constitutional Convention Discussion Paper 1974, The Northern Ireland Executive: Some Retrospective Conclusions, 19 July 1974.
95. CJ4/1147, Washington to Dublin, Tel. No. 1902, 28 May 1974.
96. DT2005/7/631, Statement by Cosgrave, 28 May 1974.
97. *Irish Times*, 28 May 1974.

PART III
MAJORITY REPORT

Fourteen days into the UWC strike, the collapse of the Northern Ireland Executive was a severe setback for those who sought to quickly resolve the troubles through a power-sharing settlement. Its collapse marked a significant shift in British policy. Wilson did not share Heath's interpretation of where the British government's responsibilities in Northern Ireland lay. Wilson began to search for a more radical policy by which to end direct rule. Abandoning the moderate parties which had formed the executive, and the Irish dimension that was integral to the Whitelaw settlement, Rees attempted to force reasonableness upon those who had destroyed it. Brokering a lengthy Provisional IRA ceasefire and leaving the Northern Ireland parties to determine their own future through a constitutional convention, Wilson and Rees intimated that some form of British withdrawal was the government's preferred policy option. The threat of civil war hung over the Northern Ireland political process. Rees hoped that the prospect of war in Ireland, and the marginalisation of Northern Ireland's elected representatives, might entice those who had destroyed the executive into accepting a form of compromise that restored devolved government, paved the way for dominion status, or provoked an independence movement that resulted in Northern Ireland leaving the UK.

Responsibility Without Power

In the wake of the UWC strike Northern Ireland stood at a crossroads. Unionists had momentarily unified to destroy its power-sharing institutions, in what was the strongest display of domestic defiance experienced by any British government since the home rule crisis that led to partition. Having exercised the 'unionist veto', the UWC handed administrative responsibility for Northern Ireland back to Rees, leaving him in control of the province but without a policy on which a political settlement might be established to end direct rule. The strike had severely damaged the idea of using power-sharing to manage the Northern Ireland conflict. However, the collapse of Whitelaw's power-sharing executive was not the last opportunity that unionists and nationalists would have to peaceably coexist in government. The strike leaders, and their political backers, were seeking a return to majority rule rather than one-party rule. Thus the concept of governing Northern Ireland through some form of coalition was not, in principle, objectionable to any of those who had been excluded from the executive which they had destroyed.

In Dublin, Cosgrave lamented that violence was 'accentuating the mental partition' that divided Ireland. 'Irish history,' he said, 'is nothing but a long series of repetitions', and those who failed to learn lessons from old struggles concerning 'abstract legalistic or constitutional definitions' would simply be 'condemned' to repeat them.[1] The UUUC leaders did not share his sorrow nor were they in the mood for compromise. During a mock funeral oration in Ballymena, Faulkner's detractors rejoiced at the demise of the Northern Ireland Executive, Paisley describing it as 'a sickly infant that died from lack of orange juice'.[2] Craig declared that the political stalemate in Northern Ireland must come to an end. The only question that mattered, he said, was how that end would come about: 'If we don't talk' then 'we'll have to fight'. Paisley threw down the gauntlet to the Provisional IRA, warning republicans, 'if you don't quit', then 'we will destroy you'.[3]

The British government's capitulation to brutal sectarian force would frame its thinking on Northern Ireland for the remainder of the decade. Rees prorogued the assembly for four months, announcing that he would attempt to preserve the fabric of the Constitution Act by forming a 'caretaker' executive following inter-party talks. If no agreement could be reached, he would nominate an executive made up of British ministers and civil servants.

Tarnished by the widely held perception that his government had been, at best, very slow to react to the strike, Wilson criticised the MOD for suggesting that the British Army had been against the decision to intervene and distribute oil supplies.[4] The strike had exposed its 'grave reservations' about opening a 'war on two fronts' in Northern Ireland.[5] Following the executive's collapse, Rees adopted the army's view that once the strike tactic had been played it was impossible to defeat the UWC militarily. In entering into any such confrontation with the Protestant community, he concluded, 'you don't control the situation and you can't hope to control it'.[6]

Lacking an alternative policy, the Conservative Party maintained bipartisanship over Northern Ireland[7] in much the same way as the Labour Party had in its support for the Constitution Act; not because they believed it contained the right policies but 'because there was nowhere else to go'.[8] Heath believed that the strike could and should have been broken in its first days,[9] and reflecting on the demise of Whitelaw's executive, Carrington charged the government with 'throwing it away'.[10] Donoughue admitted that once the strike began, 'nobody in Whitehall' did much to support the executive and 'Wilson was just reflecting that'.[11] If the government's early attempts to remove the barricades had not been so 'wishy-washy', Frank Cooper argued, the strike would have collapsed.[12] Although Wilson was almost 'allergic to doing anything positive about Northern Ireland' after the strike,[13] and there was a great 'repulsion' in the government towards the province,[14] he shared the prime minister's view that the executive's fate had been sealed by the February general election result.

In the aftermath of the strike, the British government's priority was to prevent Northern Ireland returning to the same form of direct rule that it had experienced prior to 1974, but the strike had greatly reduced its capacity to shape the political process. It left Rees, who was 'almost in despair',[15] with the prerogative of a eunuch – in a position of 'responsibility without power'. Not sharing his despondent mood, Wilson immediately began to consider a 'Doomsday scenario' – a situation in which British authority was rebuffed by the threat of a second political strike and the government was forced to make a complete military and political withdrawal from Northern Ireland. The most desirable solution to such a crisis, in his view, was to make preparations to grant dominion status to Northern Ireland the 'moment when we decided Doomsday was in sight'.[16]

Suspecting that there was a real danger that Britain would withdraw from Northern Ireland, the Irish government concluded that, in a doomsday scenario, the introduction of military conscription would become a necessity, the country would be flooded with refugees, internment might be required, and there would be a considerable threat to constitutional government in the Republic.[17] Wilson's doomsday plan was meant to be 'the most top secret operation' in Whitehall; therefore Donoughue was stunned to hear from the taoiseach's office that Cosgrave was concerned that 'Number 10 were planning something radical' for Northern Ireland.[18] '"What are you talking about?"' Donoughue snapped back to the person on the other end of the phone, who simply replied, '"Don't".' Unsurprisingly, Anglo-Irish relations had entered 'a very negative period', with the Irish taking the view that they could no longer 'trust the British at all'.[19]

As workers across the province began returning to their places of employment, Rees negotiated a withdrawal of British forces from the requisitioned fuel sites and withdrew the extra troops that had been deployed to address the emergency. On 30 May, he met with the Northern Ireland party leaders, at Stormont, to ascertain whether an executive could be established. The SDLP indicated its willingness to participate in this process, but Harry West, having been completely subdued by Paisley, informed Rees that the Official Unionists would have difficulty sitting in government with ministers who were opposed to Northern Ireland's constitutional status. When Rees attempted to determine Paisley's precise attitude towards the idea of power-sharing, the DUP leader did not say that he was against it in principle, nor that he was against the formation of a voluntary coalition, but he certainly was against power-sharing as set out under the terms of the Constitution Act.

Paisley had kept his distance from Craig, especially regarding his preparedness to consider a unilateral declaration of independence. While Craig visibly directed the strike, Paisley had been more guarded in his manipulation of the UWC, visiting Canada during its first week and only publicly endorsing the stoppage when the executive's collapse was inevitable. So despite the UWC victory, unionism remained fundamentally divided and former prime ministers Terrance O'Neill and James Chichester-Clark were busy trying to prise West from Paisley's camp and reunite Faulkner's supporters with the Official Unionist Party. Rees concluded that the best course of action open to the government was to 'let Ulstermen try and work it out by themselves' in a consultative forum. Following elections, the Northern Ireland parties would discuss the available constitutional options and report back to parliament.[20] Paisley sought a commitment from Rees to hold elections prior to any further talks. Faulkner, and the Protestant paramilitaries who had broken his government, both warned Rees that they would be swept aside by the UUUC if he followed this course. The Irish government and the Conservative Party both felt that early elections would enable the more extreme elements of the UUUC to consolidate their electoral positions and gain a mandate for constitutional positions which were unacceptable to both governments.[21]

Rees hoped that holding elections would temporarily pacify the UUUC and create a political process through which direct rule might be ended. Convinced that any power-sharing government directed by Westminster would fail, he hoped that in abandoning Whitelaw's policy an opportunity to politically withdraw from Northern Ireland might rise up 'out of the ashes' of its failure.[22] His main problem in adopting a disengagement policy was that the government lacked the political authority to enforce it. Moreover, the Conservatives would likely end bipartisanship on Northern Ireland if he pursued this course.

Rees believed that he could either continue under a Constitution Act that he lacked the power to enforce, return to the direct rule system that Northern Ireland had experienced during 1972–3, or consider various forms of withdrawal. The government was reluctant to accept the level of political responsibility that maintaining direct rule entailed, but the domestic and international implications of a complete withdrawal remained unpalatable, and all the more so if Edward Kennedy were to enter the White House in 1976. Consequently, Rees sought to form a policy that would distance Britain from the resolution of Northern Ireland's constitutional problems to the extent that a political, military and economic disengagement became not only possible but broadly acceptable. Should Britain endeavour to withdraw in phases, however, negative repercussions would only be lessened if an acceptable form of government was established to which power or sovereignty could be granted.

Rees intended to adopt the position that the government was both unable and unwilling to impose power-sharing as a method of regulating Northern Ireland's political conflicts, while indicating that it would be content and supportive if the parties came to such an arrangement on their own. To achieve this end, Rees needed to convince Craig and Paisley that a return to one-party rule under some form of independence, dominion status or devolved government would have drastic economic consequences for Northern Ireland's public sector. Having taken a non-confrontational approach to the strike and indicated that the British military presence would be scaled down from fifteen to thirteen units, the government was determined to ensure that the Northern Ireland parties received the correct message from its security policies. Violence had reached an 'unacceptable level';[23] therefore it was now 'unrealistic' to expect anything more from the army than to 'underpin whatever political framework' the government established by ensuring that violence was 'contained'.[24]

The financial cost of Britain's union with Northern Ireland reinforced Wilson's determination to 'get out'.[25] The government's trump card in this process would be to threaten to turn Northern Ireland into an 'economic desert' if the UUUC attempted to force a return to majority rule.[26] Economic sanctions would come in the form of a reduction in the total yearly supplement to the Northern Ireland economy, which at £376m in 1973–4 amounted to approximately £250 per head, and this was predicted to rise by £54m in 1974–5. Over the following five years, the treasury estimated that Harland and Wolff alone would require £30–40m simply to prevent it from going into liquidation.[27] Angry with the shipbuilding firm for seeking grant aid while its workforce participated in the UWC strike, Wilson considered withdrawing government support altogether. However, the social upheaval that would ensue from its economic collapse, with up to 10,000 Protestant workers joining growing unemployment queues in Belfast and the possibility that the government would have to meet the company's financial liabilities anyway, ruled this out as a serious option.[28]

Bipartisanship on Northern Ireland policy was also severely strained in Dublin. Abandoning all hope of implementing the Council of Ireland proposals, Cosgrave moved closer to O'Brien's position, as his thoughts turned to the potential impact that a British withdrawal would have on both his government and the minority community in Northern Ireland. Reflecting on the strike's long-term repercussions, O'Brien remarked that there was no chance of persuading unionists to join a united Ireland in his lifetime.[29] FitzGerald reopened the debate over Articles 2 and 3 of the Irish constitution, suggesting that if aspects of it were 'an obstacle' to closer North–South relations then this presented a very strong reason for removing them.[30]

Frank Cooper informed the Irish government that, following assembly elections in the autumn, Ulstermen could reach a power-sharing settlement between themselves. But there was very little reason to believe that adopting a policy of distancing Northern Ireland from Westminster would produce this outcome. For on the one hand, the loyalist coalition rejected the idea of power-sharing with parties who, as Glen Barr put it, refused to accept that the next Northern Ireland government would serve 'Ulster and the Queen'.[31] And on the other hand, the SDLP rejected the idea of power-sharing as an end in and of itself; a power-sharing system that lacked an Irish dimension would not satisfy its aspiration to see Ireland eventually unified by consent.

When Irish officials quizzed Cooper over Wilson's long-term intentions in Northern Ireland, he dismissed the suggestion that the British were preparing for, or even considering, withdrawal as in 'way out territory'. This was the opposite of what the Irish were hearing from the North: Devlin warned that the 'smell of it' was in the air; and Currie insisted that the only way to avoid withdrawal was to split the UUUC and resist its attempts to establish a Protestant state.[32] Acting on these concerns, FitzGerald advised US secretary of state Henry Kissinger that if there was even a possibility of a British withdrawal, then the Irish government would 'ask the Americans to intervene to stop them'.[33]

On 4 June, Wilson told parliament that unless it was 'prepared to risk a holocaust', then the withdrawal of British troops would provide no solution to the Northern Ireland crisis.[34] Considering how violence could be reduced to an 'acceptable level', Cooper advised FitzGerald that it would be a mistake to view necessary troop reductions in Northern Ireland as an indication that the government was prepared to withdraw. FitzGerald suggested that this misconception may have arisen from its mishandling of the UWC strike, the success of which, he said, seemed to indicate that more rather than fewer troops were required to maintain control over Northern Ireland. More than that, 'hundreds of thousands' of troops would be required if the British sought to impose their will on the unionist community.[35]

At the beginning of July, a government white paper was published setting out proposals for the establishment of a fixed-term seventy-eight-member consultative assembly, elected by proportional representation, with constitutional advisors and an appointed chairman. The concept of holding an elected constitutional conference was neither new nor without precedent in Labour Party history. Having established a national convention following the Second World War, under the chairmanship of a senior judge, British prime minister Clement Attlee allowed Newfoundlanders to decide whether their future lay in union with Canada, the US, or dominion status. The convention's outcome was tested by successive referenda, before Newfoundland became Canada's tenth province in 1949. Until 1934, it had enjoyed dominion status with its own parliament, but economic problems had resulted in power being passed to a governor, with the promise that its parliament could be restored if it learned to balance its books.

Rees advised his colleagues that, if left to their own devices, the people of Northern Ireland could resolve their own constitutional differences, including their relationship with the Republic of Ireland. To Rees, the strike represented an upsurge in Ulster nationalism, leading him to conclude that unionists were never 'going to accept a meal cooked up by outside influences'.[36] By establishing a constitutional convention, he hoped to send a message to the parties which said: 'we are not going to intervene, we've had a go at various things and they haven't worked ... now you get on with it.' Thus, he was adopting a policy of having no policy, which, according to a senior NIO official, was a 'quite deliberate' reversal of Whitelaw's approach.[37] Although Rees believed that Whitelaw had placed too much stock in Northern Ireland's moderates, he hoped a constitutional convention would produce a settlement along the lines that his predecessor had sought to impose.

Northern Ireland's constitutional convention would be required to make a report, or reports, at its conclusion and these findings would then be presented to parliament. Any constitutional settlement that the convention agreed upon had to entail a form of multiparty government if it was to be acceptable to parliament, but Rees was not going to make this an explicit requirement. So it was not an open constitutional convention; the constitutional options available to it were restricted by the fact that they had to be approved. More than that, the government's willingness to continue to shoulder the financial burden currently placed by Northern Ireland on the British exchequer would 'inevitably be affected by the progress of events there'.[38] The government would not interfere in the convention's proceedings, but it would act to legislate for and facilitate its conclusions should they find a wide basis of support. If the convention failed, then the government would consider whether to continue with direct rule on an indefinite basis or reach some form of negotiated constitutional status which left behind a fair, equitable and stable polity. The white paper stated: 'There must be some form of power-sharing and partnership because no political system will survive, or be supported, unless there is widespread acceptance of it within the community. There must be participation by the whole community.'[39]

* * * *

When Fitt had suggested to Faulkner during the castle talks that he was the weakest man in the room, his response was that had Whitelaw not imposed a requirement for power-sharing with the SDLP, he would have had no problem in forming an executive from the ranks of the fifty-nine unionist members in the assembly.[40] Despite Faulkner's majority on the Northern Ireland Executive, not only was it unrepresentative in electoral terms, it was a government dominated by SDLP 'big hitters', from Fitt and Devlin at one end of the spectrum to Hume and Currie at the other, for with the exception of Bradford, none of Faulkner's appointments were influential political figures. Although Rees lacked the power to impose a more balanced administration, he nevertheless hoped that this would be the outcome of the convention, wherein the Northern Ireland parties, all of them this time, would conclude that power-sharing was the best means of ending the troubles and settling their constitutional differences.

Taking the opposite approach to Heath, who had removed Stormont's powers and taken full responsibility for Northern Ireland prior to imposing what Whitelaw viewed as the most desirable and realistic settlement which reflected British interests, Wilson agreed to delegate the task of determining its future to those who had broken his authority and weakened his resolve to exercise the government's constitutional responsibilities there. Unsurprisingly then, Craig concluded from this that the UUUC 'might not get everything we want, but we're in a position to stop anything we don't want'. More than that, he believed that 'any democratic system will produce a Protestant parliament as long as Catholics refuse to respect the separate identity of Ulster [from the Irish Republic] and give their loyalty to it'.[41] Nevertheless, the British government now took the view that its responsibility lay in ensuring that the minority community had sufficient guarantees in any future administration, whether that was a 'reconstituted power-sharing executive' or an 'independent Northern Ireland'.[42] Although what Wilson was prepared to do to implement such guarantees remained unclear, having concluded that his government's objective was 'not to get too deeply involved in the Irish problem',[43] the uncertainty over government policy continued to fuel the excesses of Vanguard and the political pretensions of the IRA.

In response to the government's proposals, Heath informed Wilson that bipartisanship could possibly be maintained, and Cosgrave gave a cautious welcome to the idea of a constitutional forum that sought power-sharing with a broader base. Lynch charged the Irish government with suffering from a surfeit of spokesmen 'speaking with varying nuances' on its relationship with the North, which prompted Cosgrave to reiterate his commitment to an 'Irish dimension'.[44] Cosgrave was troubled by the approach taken by Rees in his efforts to force the IRA to end its campaign of violence, as some of the men appointed to a resettlement committee for ex-detainees had a 'strong Provo orientation'.[45] Furthermore, his government's credibility was dented when, on political grounds, the high court in Dublin ruled that it could not extradite a man wanted in connection with a bomb attack on an RUC station, in which two people had died. Anglo-Irish relations continued to deteriorate when British forces made a string of incursions into the Republic of Ireland, and Devlin and Fitt appeared as witnesses at the Strasbourg hearings into human rights abuses. Nevertheless,

Northern Ireland was experiencing a lull in politically motivated violence and, in order to ease the 'planned, orderly and progressive reduction' of troops, Rees signalled that he would accept discussion, on a wide basis throughout the community, as a means of achieving support for the RUC. He hoped to encourage both communities to take responsibility for policing, by making it 'starkly clear' that the government's aim was to 'get the army out'.[46]

During 12 July Orange Order celebrations, unionists accused the government of relinquishing its security obligations in Northern Ireland. Taylor called for the establishment of an armed 'Home Guard' of 20,000 men to 'defeat the IRA', and Paisley told unionists it is 'our right to arm ourselves and to protect our homes and property'.[47] Rees accepted that an unarmed 'low-level' volunteer police force, formed in close association with community leaders and under the control of the RUC, would be an addition to the planned extension of both the RUC Reserve and the UDR.

The veneer of unity within the loyalist alliance was beginning to crack: the UVF formed the Volunteer Political Party and applied for UUUC membership; Craig scolded strike leader Harry Murray for signalling his willingness to enter into dialogue with the Provisional IRA in the event of a ceasefire; and the UDA ended its association with the UWC following speculation that it was already talking to the Provisionals. Having concluded that working-class Protestants 'suspected and detested' the old unionist elite more than ever, the British were actively promoting these divisions in the hope that they would be prepared to support alternative leadership should it emerge. In his efforts to prevent the UUUC from forming a monolithic bloc in the convention, Rees was prepared to sideline the SDLP and Faulkner in preference of working-class representatives who might breach the sectarian divide. However, he was somewhat discouraged in these endeavours during a meeting with a UWC delegation, who he noted were 'not all workers by any means'.[48]

Denying that the British had any official or unofficial contacts with the IRA, Orme told FitzGerald that should the Provisionals agree to a ceasefire, then the whole situation in Northern Ireland could be radically transformed in a period of three or four months.[49] Wilson reiterated this view, telling Lynch that the 'ideal' of Irish unity was most likely to be achieved through 'agreement between the IRA and Protestant extremists' as the latter now viewed the traditional unionist leadership as outdated and discredited.[50] Bishop Daly called for the IRA to 'order the cessation of violence' and embrace democratic politics,[51] and responding to questions in parliament regarding the possibility of 'former terrorists' being allowed to stand in the convention elections, Rees signalled that he had not ruled out this possibility.[52]

Rees wanted to announce the government's intention to withdraw from Northern Ireland before it announced a general election, but he had not found a suitable political context in which to do so. His belief in the existence of latent working-class Ulster nationalism,[53] and the antipathy towards Northern Ireland that Wilson openly displayed, fostered the idea that a British disengagement from Northern Ireland would logically follow an agreement between its extremes. Responding to a question over whether the government's proposals were a sign that an incremental 'British political disengagement' from Northern Ireland was under way, Rees replied that he envisaged the future role of the government as that of a 'watchdog'. More than that, he suggested that although the government did have 'ultimate responsibility', the proposition was correct in that the proposals represented 'a beginning' in a process of 'facing up to the reality that was shown in May of this year'.[54]

Before the summer recess, the Conservative Party responded to Wilson's policy shift, holding talks with the Official Unionists, abandoning the Irish dimension, and declaring that it favoured the connection between Northern Ireland and the rest of the UK.[55] This prompted a bitter public spat with the government, Wilson accusing the Tories of attempting to 'wriggle out' of bipartisanship at Westminster. It was 'utterly squalid', he said, for the opposition to attempt to gain a few extra votes for some future Conservative government from 'extremists they would not have been seen dead with when Mr Whitelaw was there'.[56] The Irish government backed the Conservative line, criticising Wilson's Northern Ireland policy as 'completely weak and dangerous', and the SDLP effectively withdrew its support for the government.[57] In a scathing reproach, Hume described the Rees proposals as 'non-policy' designed to tide the government over until the next general election and pave the way for an announcement that it intended to withdraw from Northern Ireland.[58] Voicing the SDLP's increasing discomfort, newsman Robert Fisk disclosed details of how Faulkner, Fitt and Napier had returned from their fateful meeting at Chequers, in May, with the distinct impression that Wilson was 'more interested in how his policies were presented than in actually working them out'.[59] And Faulkner warned that the white paper was certain to produce a 'confrontation with the British government', for it encouraged people to elect representatives on the assumption that whatever the majority decided would be accepted and would become the law of the land.[60]

The SDLP called on Wilson to end the constitutional uncertainty over Northern Ireland's future by making an unequivocal commitment to ensure that 'some form of power-sharing' meant guaranteed ministerial places for nationalists in any future executive. The SDLP argued that if he refused, then the UUUC would simply bide their time before presenting the government with a democratically reinforced *fait accompli* which, in political terms, would amount to a return to majority rule. Moreover, Devlin alarmed the Irish government when he suggested that northern nationalists could only counter the British disinclination to protect them by forcing the Irish Army to intervene in Northern Ireland.[61]

Reacting to what he described as 'self-generating uncertainty' over the government's proposals, Rees stated that there would be no resurrection of the B Specials through the creation of a 'third force' in Northern Ireland. However, he planned to expand the RUC from 4,400 to 6,500 officers, triple the size of the RUC Reserve, increase UDR numbers and introduce local police posts and community wardens. As the army was reduced by a further 1,000 men, this would extend normal policing services across the province, with local communities taking responsibility for local policing. Publicly reiterating that there would be no British withdrawal, he said that while Northern Ireland must 'work out its own salvation', to 'throw in one's hand would be the worst policy possible'. Justifying his refusal to specify in advance the form of power-sharing that would be acceptable to the government, Rees announced that there had to be 'genuine participation by both communities in the direction of affairs' in a system that recognises a 'special relationship' with the South.[62]

Isolated in the North, the SDLP stated that having accepted the white paper the Irish government had left the minority community 'in the lurch' and surrendered its right to participate in negotiations over Northern Ireland's future. Devlin accused Dublin of fuelling the

UUUC's determination to establish a Protestant state by abandoning its role as a guarantor of the northern nationalist position.[63] Fitt warned FitzGerald that the Catholic community had fallen into a state of depression and hysteria; loyalists were reinforcing their political strength with military might, while the British were busy engineering a situation in which withdrawal would be viewed as an acceptable option. The SDLP's relations with Rees had deteriorated to the extent that Fitt lamented that the worst thing that had happened to Northern Ireland in recent years was the 'defeat of the Tory Government'. Heath, who was horrified at the 'neurosis' he detected in the Labour Party's thinking on Northern Ireland, reassured the SDLP that the Constitution Act remained the anchor-sheet of Conservative Party policy.[64]

Attempting to soothe relations with the SDLP leaders, FitzGerald insisted that the coalition government's policy remained unchanged: there must be power-sharing in a Northern Ireland Executive and there must be an Irish dimension to any settlement that brought it about. Unconvinced, they demanded a statement from the Irish government repudiating O'Brien's comment that the Irish dimension must be sacrificed to save the ideal of power-sharing. More than that, the SDLP leaders wanted Cosgrave to state publicly that if a doomsday situation were to arise, on which both parties agreed might result in a 'holocaust' for the Catholic community in Northern Ireland, not only would his government stand by that community, it would stand up to the unionist community by intervening to save it should such action be required. As there was little they could do to secure power-sharing in Northern Ireland, the SDLP leaders were minded to boycott the convention elections as a means of rendering the process a farce.[65] They stressed that it was the Irish government's responsibility to use all its resources to force Rees, who they feared was on the verge of a nervous breakdown, to fulfil his government's responsibilities in Northern Ireland. They complained bitterly about the roving brief that the Irish government had given DFA officials, who were busy making contacts with unionist representatives across the province, and of leaks in the press of the SDLP's 'ad limina' visits to Dublin, which made the party look every bit as desperate for support as it actually was. But it was over the Irish dimension that the split within the nationalist alliance was most evident. Hume insisted that some form of all-Ireland governmental institution must be established, as a 'bridgehead towards unity', whereas

Cosgrave's key political strategist on Northern Ireland, Dermot Nally, advised that this could be 'the rock on which we would all perish'.[66]

At a conference in Donegal, which took place during 24–5 August, the SDLP adopted a new hardline policy. The party would attempt to achieve a united Ireland after providing the British with a face-saving rationale for withdrawal. There was no hope of cooperation between the SDLP and the UUUC; therefore the nationalists would seek to force the British to confront the loyalist threat and produce a settlement that would in all likelihood require joint military action by the two governments. By taking such a radical approach, the SDLP were attempting to coerce the Irish government from the political and psychological retreat it had made from Northern Ireland following the Dublin and Monaghan bombings and the executive's collapse.[67] In considering the political, economic and social consequences of civil war in Ireland, the government split between the FitzGerald and O'Brien factions. The majority view, however, was that a British withdrawal would not lead to a united Ireland. FitzGerald argued that, to secure the SDLP's participation in the convention, the government must press the British to spell out that power-sharing with an Irish dimension was a prerequisite for any agreement. O'Brien implored him not to repeat the key mistake of Sunningdale, by again putting Hume's demand for an institutionalised Irish dimension at the heart of a settlement. He argued that the underlying logic of the SDLP's proposals, which were edging close to the demands of the Provisional IRA, would pave the way for 'repartition'. In the face of unionist intransigence, he said, some of its leaders, west of the Bann, had succumbed to the dangerous argument that 'half a loaf is better than no bread'.[68]

A British withdrawal was likely to be followed by an attempt on the part of the unionist community to establish an independent Northern Ireland in the six counties or, failing that, a repartitioned rump Protestant state. Although the Labour government was on record stating that this was an unacceptable constitutional option, the inertia in Northern Ireland's political process led others to an entirely different conclusion. The Irish government estimated that to secure the Republic of Ireland in the event of a doomsday situation in the North through military containment which fell short of intervention, an increase in its security personnel by 20,000 at a cost of £39m would be necessary. Regardless of the SDLP's assertions, the government was generally of the view that if it made an overt threat to become militarily involved, then this would directly counter its objective of 'splitting the unionist monolith' in the North.[69] The only realistic way in which it could constructively further this goal was to press Wilson to spell out to the unionists just how costly attempting to 'go it alone' would be, i.e. the loss of subsidies that amounted to nearly half of Northern Ireland's gross domestic product, the loss of the British security umbrella and the international isolation that an independent Ulster would face.

On the rebound from Dublin, the SDLP clashed with Rees during a hostile and abusive encounter at Stormont; they laid the blame for the collapse of the executive on his government's 'total and abject surrender' to the forces of unconstitutional loyalism. They accused Rees of directing a new policy of army harassment, the aim of which was to 'put the boot in' to the Catholic community and set it so against the army that support for the RUC and for his local policing proposals would materialise.[70] There was speculation, however, that it was the army that was actually directing this line. Frustrated by detainee releases of roughly ten to fifteen per week, and with Sunningdale's failure having stiffened their resolve to withdraw, senior officers likened their role in Northern Ireland to the 'unwilling doing the unpleasant for the ungrateful'.[71]

Hume accused Rees of providing a 'cloak of respectability' for a 'loyalist takeover' through his convention proposals. Fitt warned that if a doomsday scenario was allowed to unfold, then the Irish Army might march across the border to 'defend their Catholic brothers'.[72] Rees dismissed their threats contemptuously, taking the view that the SDLP and their mentors in Dublin were prepared to 'fight to the last British soldier'.[73] Under pressure from all sides, he conceded that should Protestant paramilitary groups come out in force, then at present levels the armed forces in Northern Ireland lacked the power to challenge them. And at the end of a meeting which saw the SDLP completely break with the government, Fitt told Rees to 'stop the drift' to violence in Northern Ireland before it spread to the rest of the UK.[74]

On 4 September, Faulkner launched the Unionist Party of Northern Ireland, which advocated power-sharing between unionists and nationalists and opposed the establishment of all-Ireland bodies prior to the amendment of Articles 2 and 3 of the Irish constitution. Deriding the new liberal unionist organisation, Bradford described it as 'a pallid facsimile of the Alliance Party', but Morrell cautioned his former colleague against playing into Wilson's hands and enhancing the prospect of Northern Ireland being forced from the UK.[75] On the same day, the SDLP called for the two governments to issue a joint declaration stating that power-sharing with an Irish dimension was a non-negotiable starting point for any discussions over Northern Ireland's constitutional future. They argued that loyalists, who constituted just over 1 per cent of the total UK population, should not be allowed to 'frustrate the agreed will of all the rest of the British and Irish people by their intransigence'.[76] Tory maverick Enoch Powell became the Official Unionist candidate for South Down, renewing calls for Northern Ireland to be completely integrated within the UK, a policy which Rees pledged to oppose 'tooth and nail'. And John Laird, who had rejoined the Official Unionist Party, signalled to the Irish government that in the absence of an Irish dimension, his party were prepared to share power with the SDLP, on a proportional basis, with them representing around one quarter of the electorate.[77]

Disillusioned with the loyalist triumvirate and with Craig in particular, the UWC leaders split from the UUUC and committed themselves to building a non-political cross-community working-class movement.[78] British officials had been facilitating dialogue between loyalist and republican paramilitaries, most notably between UDA leader Andy Tyrie and republican leaders. Of the IRA factions, the Officials were more enthusiastic about the idea of holding cross-community talks than the Provisionals. Of the loyalist paramilitaries, the UDA were willing to experiment, while the UVF was unable to participate due to the extreme attitude of the majority of its members. Sinn Féin was considering running in the forthcoming elections and the UVF intended to. With the exception of Tyrie and Barr, who signalled a willingness to end violence prior to talks with the SDLP in August, the UDA were as bereft of political talent as their republican counterparts. And although divisions had intensified within the Provisional IRA over the summer, the British held back from engaging in talks that might lead to another ceasefire.[79]

On 10 September, when Wilson held talks with the SDLP leadership at Downing Street, Fitt told him how personally let down he felt by the Labour Party, which he had supported throughout his entire political life. The Protestant community now sought 'total ascendancy' in Northern Ireland, he said, on the basis of a white paper which was an 'open cheque drawn in their favour'. Wilson stressed that he could not accept a unilateral declaration of independence from the unionist community. Peace and stability could only be achieved through power-sharing, he said, as Protestant extremists could not run Northern Ireland for three weeks without British support.[80] Signalling to Cosgrave that a return to majority rule and a unilateral declaration of independence were both unacceptable options to his government, Wilson stopped short of insisting that the acceptance of power-sharing at government level would be required of the convention. In turn, Barr threatened Wilson with 'another strike' should he persist in 'bowing to the wills of Mr Cosgrave and the SDLP' by insisted on 'enforced power-sharing with republicans'.[81] Moreover, deepening fissures within the Irish coalition were exposed when a Labour Party document was leaked to *The Irish Times* in which O'Brien argued that the government could only reduce the possibility of a majority report in the convention by keeping a 'low profile'. But Paisley labelled him an 'enemy of the Ulster Loyalist people' for suggesting that should a loyalist majority emerge in the convention then the British should immediately dissolve it.[82]

* * * *

On 10 October, Wilson's victory in the second Westminster general election of 1974 ended all hope in nationalist Ireland that Heath might return and enforce the Constitution Act. During the election, unionists abandoned Faulkner for the Official Unionist Party and Vanguard. The UUUC increased its share of the vote by 7 per cent, winning a clear majority with 58 per cent of the poll. West lost his seat in Fermanagh and South Tyrone to anti-unionist candidate Frank Maguire, and his leadership of the UUUC parliamentary party to James Molyneaux. While the SDLP held its share of the vote at 22 per cent and Fitt was comfortably returned in West Belfast, the party lost narrowly to Powell in South Down. Powell was an asset for the UUUC at Westminster, but his arrival intensified divisions within its leadership, for while his strong integrationist leanings influenced Molyneaux, they contrasted sharply with Craig's calls for unionist self-determination and Paisley's ambition to lead a devolved Northern Ireland government.

The results offered no comfort for the beleaguered secretary of state on the perilous road that lay before him in Northern Ireland. He expected nothing constructive to come from either the Irish government or the SDLP. He had come to view the latter as a rudderless party of protest, inflated by Whitelaw, which had not yet adjusted to political life without its 'English nanny'.[83] Irish justice minister Paddy Cooney confirmed his suspicion of the former when he disowned his own statement, at the first sign of criticism from Lynch, that the time had come to invite the people to delete their constitutional claim to Northern Ireland. The election result left Rees in no doubt, however, that the UUUC would gain a substantial majority in the convention. He had the option to cancel the convention elections, which both the Irish government and the SDLP favoured as a forerunner to a return to direct rule, or he could hold out and reject a majority report which supported a return to majority rule. Either course ran the risk of provoking a second strike. And when Bradford was blacklisted as a future UUUC electoral candidate, after publicly lending his support to Craig and West, the stiffening of unionist opinion towards any form of power-sharing seemed complete.

At Westminster, there was disunity in the British government over how to proceed in Northern Ireland. Attorney general Samuel Silken spoke in favour of integration, while home secretary Roy Jenkins felt that in the event of the convention's failure the government would probably have to withdraw.[84] Unable to forge agreement among his colleagues, Wilson resolved to reconsider further the spectrum of 'diverse options' that remained open to the government.[85] Mindful of the difficulties that lay ahead in maintaining bipartisanship at Westminster, he suggested holding a Lancaster House conference of all Westminster parties, before holding a second conference with the Northern Ireland parties.[86] Eager to press ahead with the convention elections in early March, Rees rejected any form of integration. Furthermore, he opposed Wilson's suggestion on the grounds that this would further strain bipartisanship, provoke a confrontation with the UUUC, and deflect attention from the convention's proceedings. Should the convention fail, he insisted, then the government must be able to develop a policy that allowed Great Britain to move away from its present relationship with Northern Ireland, perhaps towards some form of independence or dominion status with cantonal arrangements like Switzerland. Moreover, he had sent Northern Ireland and British civil servants to Switzerland,

Holland and Belgium to investigate the different forms of power-sharing they were using.

In contrast, Donoughue argued that if the government accepted that creating a power-sharing system by consent was unfeasible, and took into account that Heath's efforts to impose this option had failed, then abandoning it as a policy may be the only way out of the 'responsibility without power' situation that it presently found itself in. He suggested to Wilson that the government only had alternatives to power-sharing open to it; therefore it could threaten the Northern Ireland parties with repartition should the convention fail to produce a more voluntary and inclusive version of multiparty government. Considering withdrawal or a surgical 'once-for-all' repartition that would involve population transfers, he reluctantly favoured the later.[87]

At a meeting between Cosgrave and Wilson, on 1 November, the prime minister insisted that the British parliament would reject any constitutional report that did not suggest power-sharing as a basic foundation for a settlement. If unionists decided to 'strike out on their own', he said, then they would have to realise that their status would be that of 'a foreign country'. Should a second strike occur after parliament rejected a majority report favouring a return to majority rule, Wilson felt that 'we should have a very different situation and a very serious problem on our hands'. Therefore, the only short-term option open was to press ahead with the elections and force the UUUC to either provoke a 'doomsday' situation or negotiate with the SDLP.[88] Wilson reasoned that this would make it very difficult for the UUUC to drum up support for a political strike which would not be against something that the government was seeking to impose. The UWC strike had been designed to destroy the Northern Ireland Executive, but a strike which primarily aimed to force parliament into agreeing to a return to majority rule would be a very different creature.

* * * *

The British returned to the idea of securing an IRA ceasefire before holding elections to the convention. On 13 November, Wilson approved the opening of 'secret' and 'non-attributable' contacts with the IRA through MI6 officer Michael Oatley and Foreign Office official James Allan, so that they might 'wean' certain willing IRA leaders from violence by steering them towards political participation.[89] Wilson doubted whether IRA army council members who favoured calling a ceasefire, such as Séamus Loughran from west Belfast, had the 'gold backing' to justify any further reduction on internment. He took the view that moving on internment at this point might strengthen the more intransigent IRA leaders and tie the hands of the moderates.[90]

Aware that the UWC strike had severely weakened the British government's resolve to remain in Northern Ireland, the Provisional IRA were fearful of the impact that an immediate withdrawal might have on the Protestant community. Should the British government 'open the jails' and make clear its desire to 'disengage', Dáithí Ó Conaill signalled that this would lead to an entirely 'different situation'. In the absence of such measures, however, the IRA's campaign of violence would be extended and intensified. Having engaged in dialogue 'across the board', the IRA now sought all-party negotiations. Moreover, Ó Conaill suggested that it might participate in elections to an all-Ireland constitutional convention. It would be unfortunate if people opted out of an all-Ireland settlement, he said, but the Algerian experience of 1962 illustrated how this could be overcome. Approximately 90 per cent of the one million-strong European settler community had fled the country in the months following Charles de Gaulle's declaration that over 130 years of French colonial rule was at an end.[91]

Convinced that the ending of detention remained the key to reducing the Provisional IRA's support base, the SDLP asked Rees to release all the remaining prisoners in return for a ceasefire, with the stipulation that those on special category status, who should also be released in due course, would serve their full sentences if violence was resumed. Frank Cooper was in favour of slowly releasing the detainees, reducing sentences, and ending the special category system, but only if a 'genuine and sustained cessation of violence' enabled the government to transform the army's role in Northern Ireland.[92] The army was concerned that if a ceasefire were to collapse, the wholesale release of prisoners would magnify the challenge it faced in containing political violence. The Irish government opposed the idea of opening the jails, arguing that this would send a clear signal that the SDLP had been abandoned by the British and mark the beginning of a *de facto* IRA takeover in certain parts of Northern Ireland, especially west of the Bann.

Pouring scorn on some of the unrealistic and fanciful policy proposals that were emanating from Downing Street, Whitelaw stated that it would be a 'considerable moral disgrace' to withdraw British troops from Northern Ireland and that anyone thinking that the loss of life that would ensue would not spread to British cities such as Glasgow or Liverpool was 'living in a fool's paradise'.[93] FitzGerald remarked that if the Provisionals were successful in bringing civil war to Ireland, then it was hard to imagine 'any situation in which there would not emerge a *de facto* Protestant state in part of Northern Ireland'. Moving closer to Craig, Paisley told his supporters that in the present climate it was imperative that the convention produced a 'blueprint' for a 'united Ulster'.[94]

Acknowledging that an immediate British withdrawal would lead to civil war, Rees conceded that British troops would remain in Northern Ireland for the foreseeable future, but he continued to resist pressure to spell out exactly what different forms of government would be an acceptable alternative to direct rule. He stated that any new arrangements must 'command the most widespread acceptance throughout the country' before parliament took 'the balance of opinion' into account. This did little to clear up the confusion over the government's ambiguous stance on power-sharing in Northern Ireland.[95] Of the realists at the heart of the policy debate, Frank Cooper and cabinet secretary John Hunt were now practically convinced that the only viable option open to the government was an 'indefinite continuation of direct rule', under which incremental constitutional changes might bring about further minority participation in government and society.[96] They shared Wilson's view that a second strike could only be mounted by the UUUC if the British provided something unpalatable for it to strike against. They concluded that the maximum the government could expect to achieve in such circumstances was the provision of minimum services. Summing up the government's frustrations, Callaghan quipped that if a second strike was launched, then the population of Northern Ireland would 'simply have to sweat it out'.[97]

On 21 November, anti-Irish sentiment in Britain intensified when the Provisional IRA bombed two crowded pubs in Birmingham, from which twenty-one people eventually died. Depressed, and disabused of some of the more naïve notions he had held towards the IRA while in opposition, Rees concluded that they were a 'wicked lot' who must 'be beaten'. Outlawing the Provisionals and extending detention without charge to the mainland for seven days, he mused that if they are 'not beaten by us' then they 'would be beaten by the Protestants'.[98] Although himself describing the introduction of these powers as 'draconian', home secretary Roy Jenkins stated that given the 'clear and present danger' Britain faced from Irish terrorists, they were 'fully justified'.[99] The attacks heightened the desire in Whitehall to insulate Great Britain from the tragedy of Northern Ireland and all the ailments that continued to afflict it. The government believed that the divergence of political attitudes and conditions in Great Britain and Northern Ireland had become so great that the phrase 'United Kingdom' no longer had any meaning.[100]

In policy terms, this meant exercising governmental responsibility in a 'low key' manner and discarding the Irish dimension altogether. Should the convention fail or be cancelled, Hunt advised Wilson that abandoning the 'search for a solution', and keeping a lid on the Northern Ireland problem by containing the Provisional IRA, would be the most realistic course to follow.[101] The government remained divided, however, between ministers who were willing to contemplate the possibility of repartition – independence being granted to the part of Northern Ireland that did not go to the South – and those who favoured integration with some devolutionary aspect.

In Dublin, further cracks appeared in the coalition's approach to the crisis when FitzGerald suggested that pressure might be applied to the British to have Northern Ireland placed under UN trusteeship. Nally warned Cosgrave that not only would the British firmly resist this option, the UN itself, at the very least until a time when civil war in the North had run its course, would be reluctant to become embroiled in Northern Ireland's troubles.[102] O'Brien retorted that the notion that either a UN trusteeship or a UN force would avert civil war in the North was quite 'illusory'. There was 'absolutely no chance' of selling such an idea to a Protestant community, he said, that was 'notably inaccessible to new ideas'. Not only would it be unworkable, he argued, it would be 'particularly dangerous' for the Irish government to be seen to be entertaining the idea, as it would surely aid Wilson in his search for a policy that provided him with an 'honourable' withdrawal from Northern Ireland. Rather than letting the British off the hook of their constitutional responsibilities in Northern Ireland, and implicitly courting responsibility by inviting a UN force to intervene, O'Brien insisted that the government's policy should be to make it as 'difficult as possible for the British to extricate themselves' from the Ulster imbroglio. The government should make it clear to the SDLP, he said, that military intervention, from either the Irish Army or the UN, was completely out of the question, as the consequences of such action could only be 'self-defeating'. He reminded his colleagues that in the event of a British retreat the IRA's next target would be the Irish government itself.[103]

Having received the message from the British that an institutionalised Irish dimension was 'out', FitzGerald chastised Rees during an aggressive encounter in London for 'watering down' the concept of 'power-sharing' in both his discussion papers and recent statements. FitzGerald said that his references to power-sharing in other countries were particularly unhelpful, as it was not a constitutional requirement under any of the examples that he had cited.[104] Donlon impressed on the British that in the absence of an Irish dimension which reflected the aspiration of nationalists to unite Ireland by consent it was 'probably not possible' to bring the minority community into a power-sharing arrangement. The principles of power-sharing and the Irish dimension were inseparable; therefore it was only the form of expression of each of these principles that the SDLP and the Irish government could negotiate over. Encouraging Donlon to convince the SDLP of the merits of dropping the Irish dimension altogether, the British suggested that the 'interrelationship between the two principles was emotional rather than logical'.[105] Re-emphasising the point, Orme said that they should not assume that a 'prolonged period of direct rule' would automatically follow a convention if it failed to bring about an acceptable constitutional outcome.[106]

Applying logic rather than emotion to the debate, O'Brien advised his colleagues that the British government's attitude towards the Irish dimension contained two dangerous pitfalls. If the Irish government paid anything less than public lip service to an institutionalised Irish dimension, then it would come under considerable flack from Fianna Fáil and the SDLP for having abandoned the Council of Ireland proposals. But if the government insisted on 'an institutionalised Irish dimension', which was a Council of Ireland under a different name, it would ensure that the convention failed by overloading it with a negotiating position that again provided unionists with something to unify in opposition to. He concluded, therefore, that the government should inform the British that it could not abandon the Irish dimension, and signal that the institutional form that it might take should not be predefined or discussed between Irishmen until a Northern Ireland power-sharing administration was fully functional. O'Brien stressed that FitzGerald's counter-argument, which was to maintain the 'high water mark' of an Irish dimension in any Anglo-Irish negotiations, had already proved to be a disastrous policy. The government had stacked 'bargaining counters' to the ceiling in the pre-Sunningdale negotiations over the Council of Ireland proposals, when the British and Faulkner had been all too willing to concede to virtually all of the Irish government's demands, only for the whole agreement to come crashing down in a matter of months, 'partly under the weight', he said, 'of our own too-successful bargaining'. With Faulkner replaced at the negotiating table by the parties who had destroyed that power-sharing settlement, O'Brien insisted that a change of approach was the only course of action available to the Irish government that would 'avoid giving any hostages to the SDLP's version of confrontation politics'.[107]

O'Brien's view won out on this occasion. The Irish cabinet rejected British overtures to abandon the Irish dimension and agreed that any 'enduring' political arrangements must account for the 'special relationship' that exists between North and South, which should be the subject of further discussions with whatever administration emerged in the North.[108] This new policy was underscored when Cosgrave sought a personal assurance from Wilson that there had been no change to his government's position that a form of institutionalised power-sharing was required at government level. Alarmed that the British had begun to speak in terms of 'participation' as opposed to power-sharing, the Irish sought a guarantee that it remained a prerequisite to agreement on any form of government proposed through the convention. And Cosgrave urged Wilson to make this explicitly clear in the forthcoming discussion paper on the subject.

* * * *

The British government's tactic of politically distancing Northern Ireland from Westminster was having the desired effect on its political parties. Shifting from the UUUC's anti-power-sharing stance, Official Unionist Martin Smyth stated that although any party that formed a majority in the convention should have an absolute right to choose a ministerial team, he saw no reason why his party would object to there being a number of Catholics in government. He suggested that if the SDLP became 'good Ulstermen', supporting the police and not 'running to Dublin' every time there was a political crisis in the North, then they could be included. Stepping back from the hardline approach his party had adopted in Donegal, Hume stressed that only the SDLP could 'deliver a Catholic bloc vote willing to compromise'. Other prominent unionists, such as deputy leader of Vanguard Ernest Baird, were also 'drawing in their horns' over the UUUC's absolute refusal to share power with the SDLP.[109] Moreover, Faulkner was showing signs of recovery from his poor showing in the general election, and former DUP man Desmond Boal offered to mediate for the British between the different paramilitary factions.

Stiffening the DUP's position towards power-sharing, so as to attract the intransigent rump of Vanguard supporters should Craig feel tempted to hold out an olive branch to the SDLP, Paisley pressed Rees to call an early election. In a bizarre twist to Craig's endeavour to lead an independent Northern Ireland, Barr was asked to resign from Vanguard following the disclosure that he had led a UDA delegation to visit Colonel Gaddafi's Libya. The timing of his trip coincided with that of a visit by a group of IRA members, as both sets of paramilitaries sought to discover the degree of financial or military support, if any, the anti-British Arab nationalist leader was prepared to offer an independent Northern Ireland.[110]

As secret talks between the British and the Provisional IRA progressed, Devlin suggested publicly that an IRA ceasefire could be brought about by prisoner releases and the withdrawal of troops to certain designated areas. In fact, the moment for a ceasefire was ripe. Splits between its Belfast, Dublin and Londonderry factions led British military chiefs to conclude that having 'put the screws on' the Provisional IRA for six months,[111] and with the exception of the south Armagh and Fermanagh brigades, they were 'on their knees'.[112] Recent military successes in Belfast and Londonderry, adverse reaction to the Birmingham atrocities, and internal divisions had all significantly contributed to the erosion of the republican movement's capacity to sustain a campaign of violence. So much so that Frank Cooper believed that these contributing factors might well create a majority view in the

Provisional army council in favour of an extended ceasefire. He argued that releasing some of its brigade staff would allow pro-ceasefire IRA leaders to regain credibility by securing an incremental end to detention. Moreover, if they rejected the British government's overtures then they would be further marginalised by the SDLP.

In return for a ceasefire, Rees would offer the phased release of detainees and reduce the army's presence in republican areas. This would present him with his first real opportunity to seize the initiative in Northern Ireland, end republican violence from a position of military strength, and inject urgency into his flagging political process. Releases would commence after at least one month's ceasefire. If a ceasefire held, then detention and special category status would be ended before the middle of 1976, the RUC would replace the army as it withdrew in phases, and Provisional Sinn Féin would be free to participate in the convention. Cooper viewed this as a golden opportunity to restore 'a clean sheet for the legal system on the law and order ticket' and begin to restore the credibility of civil policing; therefore, if talking to the IRA enabled the government to get rid of internment, then it was worth the risk.[113]

Following an initiative by a group of seven Protestant clergymen who were acting as intermediaries between the British government and the Provisional IRA, a Christmas ceasefire was declared in 'Britain and Ireland' and this commenced on 22 December. The cessation of IRA violence was made on the 'clear understanding' that the British government would subsequently make a 'positive response' to proposals for a 'permanent ceasefire', and in the hope that it would take the 'opportunity to bring an end to the evil of internment'.[114] On 18 December, Rees had received a proposal from the clergymen, at Westminster, which they hoped would lead to the first Provisional IRA ceasefire since Whitelaw's failed engagement of 1972. Following their meeting, he signalled that if a 'genuine cessation of violence' was established, then a new situation would arise wherein the government would 'naturally respond'. The document indicated that the IRA might consider that its requirements for a permanent ceasefire had been met if the British declared that they had no 'political or territorial' interest in Northern Ireland and the army were relieved of their internal security duties.[115]

These proposals, along with an outline of current thinking within the Protestant community, had been put to Séamus Loughran, Ruairí Ó Brádaigh and Belfast IRA commander Billy McKee on 12 December by the clergymen at Feakle, in County Clare. While these proposals were accepted following consultation with the IRA army council, the initiative provided a useful smokescreen for the ongoing secret discussions that British officials were holding with the Provisionals. Unknown to the church leaders, Michael Oatley had reopened a back channel with the Provisional IRA through Londonderry businessman Brendan Duddy.[116] They had agreed to use the churchmen's initiative as a cover story for reaching a ceasefire. Rees had told the clergymen that if the ceasefire was not extended to Great Britain, then this would constrain any positive response his government might be prepared to make. The IRA's response was that if the British made a 'face-saving' announcement, by 30 December, that internment could be phased out if the ceasefire was maintained, and hinted that reduced sentences for those who had been convicted might be introduced, then this might be enough to secure its continuation.[117]

With the IRA deadline closing, Reverend William Arlow informed Cooper, on 30 December, of Dáithí Ó Conaill's suggestion that, as a gesture of goodwill, should the British release all those who had been interned by Faulkner on 9 August 1971, then the Provisional IRA ceasefire would be extended 'indefinitely'. The message to Ó Conaill from Cooper was that although direct negotiations were presently out of the question, if the truce held then the British could take some 'definite steps'.[118] Rees then made a measured gesture, on 31 December, releasing twenty republican and loyalist detainees, offering parole until 3 January to fifty others and remission for over 100 prisoners whose sentences were due to expire on or before 31 March 1975.

The British had not rushed to meet the IRA's request, Rees wishing to avoid being drawn into a process in which he appeared to be meeting their deadlines after having engaged in negotiations. He held out for an indefinite extension to the ceasefire by promising that if this was established then other developments would follow. Wilson was delighted by the ceasefire, but insisted on attaining 'the word permanent' from the Provisional IRA. Repeating a phrase he had used previously in reference to Rhodesian prime minister Ian Smith, when he declared a unilateral declaration of independence from the UK in 1965, Wilson said, 'the test is not calendar but achievement'.[119] The government was also seeking to bring about an extension of the truce in circumstances that did not provoke a violent loyalist backlash. As part of these efforts,

Wilson urged Ireland's main church leaders to appeal to politicians in Northern Ireland to 'cool the situation' and garner public support for a peace process that included the IRA.[120] Meanwhile, at Laneside, British officials were busy trying to convince loyalist paramilitary leaders that they had nothing to fear from an IRA ceasefire.

Fearing that they were being drawn into a political cul-de-sac by the British, the IRA signalled that the steps taken thus far by the government did not warrant a 'permanent' ceasefire. Moreover, the Provisionals threatened to resume hostilities with the British if 'substantial progress' was not made by 16 January. The UUUC's reaction to these political developments was predictable. By conducting 'hole-in-the-wall negotiations between IRA mass murderers and top civil servants acting for the secretary of state', Laird charged the government with betraying the people of Northern Ireland.[121] Disturbed by rumours of the secret back channel, the Irish government stated its implacable opposition to holding any direct contacts or negotiations with the IRA. Furious with Rees for his refusal to meet with him, FitzGerald felt that he had been 'lied to' by the British regarding their talks with the IRA.[122] Warning Rees of the double danger that lay in any form of negotiation with the IRA, Bloomfield argued that it would 'undermine the position of the Irish Government and tend to cut the feet from under the SDLP'. The Provisional IRA had indicated clearly that they had no intention of surrendering or dumping their arms. Therefore, allowing the British Army to be replaced in nationalist areas by a republican 'vigilante police force', Bloomfield warned, could prompt a drift 'back into a type of "no-go" situation' that Operation Motorman had ended.[123]

Hoping that they too would gain prisoner releases and better jail conditions from an IRA truce, Protestant paramilitaries did not react violently to these political developments. The SDLP held to the view that the longer a ceasefire lasted the more difficult it would be for the IRA to resume its campaign of terror. Hume suggested to Rees that a republican hunger strike in the prisons could be avoided if he released the remaining detainees.[124] But the Provisionals were hoping that a prolonged cessation of violence would lead to direct negotiations with the British and provide them with a significant degree of political legitimacy in the nationalist community. Having guaranteed that their contacts with the British would remain secret and be conducted through third parties, for the time being at least, the Provisionals waited for the British to respond. They were under severe pressure from the Irish security forces, however, and Ó Conaill accused the coalition government of trying to 'smash the peace initiative' and warned Wilson that time was 'running out'.[125]

Just before the IRA deadline was set to expire, Rees made an unannounced statement to the House of Commons, on 14 January, which he viewed as the most important speech of his political career.[126] Stressing that there would be no direct negotiations with the IRA, he invited Provisional Sinn Féin to join the political process by opening discussions with British officials. He signalled that in the 'later stages' of his response to a 'genuine and sustained cessation of violence', 'the Army could be reduced to a peace-time level ... no longer undertake foot or vehicle patrols in towns' and gradually be withdrawn to barracks.[127] More than that, he pledged to continue the government's positive and measured response to the IRA ceasefire by progressively releasing detainees, with a view to releasing them all and ending internment. Mindful not to pre-empt the report of the Gardiner Committee which was examining measures to deal with the 550 remaining detainees and the 700 republican and 400 loyalist special category prisoners, Rees made no reference to these issues. Although he gave no undertaking as to the rate or timescale of planned army reductions or prisoner releases, the following morning he released twenty-five detainees and offered three days' parole to a further fifty.

The Provisionals were disappointed by these measures. Loughran had publicly stated that there was little hope of the present ceasefire being extended, or becoming permanent, unless the government entered into direct negotiations. Publishing tycoon Cecil King suggested ominously that the only way to move any British government is by 'violence or the imminent threat of violence', before the Provisionals broke their twenty-five-day truce.[128] Attempting to mask internal divisions, the Provisionals stated a continued desire for dialogue, having only resumed hostilities due to the British Army's failure to observe the truce and the government's inadequate response to the Feakle 'peace proposals'. The IRA army council's decision to engage in talks with the British had not been unanimous. Neither was its decision to end the ceasefire but, at this point, the 'hawks' had been vindicated in their assertion that the British were not prepared to publicly articulate an intent to disengage from Northern Ireland. These divisions were further exacerbated by the arrest of pro-truce army council member Kevin Mallon in Dublin and the death of an IRA man in a clash with the British Army along the border. The British were peeved that the Irish were trying to wreck the talks by arresting high-profile IRA leaders, whereas the Irish were peeved that they had been kept in the dark and misled by the British over a secret talks process which they viewed with deep apprehension.[129] But as the Irish arrested a second IRA army council member in Dublin, Joe O'Hagan, the Feakle churchmen stepped up their efforts to restore the ceasefire.

The British were in no hurry to enter into negotiations with the Provisional IRA; they could neither meet its request for elections to an all-Ireland constitutional convention nor commit to a total withdrawal of the army a year after an assembly concluded its proceedings. Rees denied that either he or any of his officials had discussed or considered 'proposals' put to the government by the Provisional IRA, stressing that he had only decided to enter into talks with Sinn Féin. Rees was intending to 'string them along' to the point where their military capacity 'went soggy' and their support base within the Catholic community evaporated. As one British intelligence officer put it, the 'game for the ceasefire was helping the doves to con the hawks'.[130] However, Rees was not fully informed of the secret talks process that was taking place with the Provisionals, as Cooper and his officials relayed much of this information directly to Wilson.[131]

The secret discussions between British officials and the Provisionals, and his statement on 14 January, had both been designed to ease the pressure on those IRA leaders on the army council who were arguing for an extended ceasefire. These republicans exaggerated what they were achieving in their discussions with the British in order to secure their objective, which was to engage in politics and probably take a place in some power-sharing arrangement. But when the crunch came and the ceasefire collapsed, the British were surprised both by the weakness of Ó Conaill and Ó Brádaigh within the republican movement and at just how badly they wanted peace.[132] Cooper was encouraged, however, by the fact that the Provisionals had kept the secret talks secret and that the 'hawks', led by Belfast commander Séamus Twomey, had left open the possibility of another cessation of violence.

On 17 January, Ó Conaill informed the British that the *de facto* IRA ceasefire would actually hold until midnight the following day, in lieu of a response to the IRA's conditions for declaring a permanent cessation of violence. Irish politician John O'Connell, who had facilitated a meeting between Wilson, Rees and the Provisionals when they were in opposition, passed a message from Ó Conaill to Wilson stating that the IRA wanted him to send over 'two people to negotiate, in total secretary, a further truce'. For a 'permanent peace' to be established, the IRA demanded an end to internment, a private commitment to announce an amnesty for political prisoners, the dismantling of security installations in nationalist areas, and the immediate establishment of a three-man commission to mediate and produce recommendations between all the parties to the conflict. The Provisionals would accept former IRA leader Seán MacBride as a nationalist representative on this commission, Desmond Boal was willing to participate for the unionists, and the British could make one nominee. Marking a significant shift from Seán Mac Stíofáin's demands to Whitelaw in 1972, Ó Conaill said that although the IRA held to its requirement for a British 'declaration' of intent to withdraw, while the other points were not negotiable, this one was.[133]

On Sunday afternoon, 19 January, as thousands gathered in Belfast and Dublin to pray for peace, a seven-year-old Catholic boy from Armagh became the Provisional IRA's first victim of 1975. He was killed instantly when a booby trap bomb detonated as he and a friend were herding cattle into a field. The IRA army council then met to consider extending its ceasefire. Rees reiterated his commitment to the peace process, before announcing that two British officials had that day entered into discussions with Provisional Sinn Féin in Belfast. Should the ceasefire hold, he wished to put in place 'effective arrangements' to ensure that it did not break down again.[134] A further meeting between British officials and Ó Brádaigh remained secret. At Laneside, senior Belfast IRA man Jimmy Drumm said that the Provisionals hoped to resume their ceasefire, possibly indefinitely. He suggested that the two sides should enter into a private 'gentleman's agreement' on a bilateral truce, whereby the army would end all searches on premises in nationalist areas, with points of contact established between the government and Sinn Féin leaders to help maintain the truce.[135] Loyalist paramilitaries, Vanguard and the Official Unionists joined Paisley in condemning Rees for dishonouring his commitment not to negotiate with the Provisional IRA. The loyalist paramilitaries accepted assurances from

Cooper that government policy had not changed. They warned him, however, that if the Provisionals did not ceasefire, then they would resume hostilities.

The two sides met again, officially, on 22 January, only this time the British informed the Provisionals that Rees would allow no more formal contact with them until the recent upsurge in violence had come to an end. The Provisionals responded violently, setting off bombs in London and Manchester over the next few days. Wilson informed Rees that his contacts in the Republic of Ireland suggested that, from Monday night, under certain conditions, the Provisionals were prepared to cease their operations in Great Britain. John O'Connell delivered a letter to Wilson containing a message from Dáithí Ó Conaill. But Rees was upset both by O'Connell's intervention and by the pressure the church leaders were bringing to bear on the government through the media. The delay in the resumption of the IRA's ceasefire appeared also to be influenced by the Irish government's unwillingness to meet demands for political status to be granted to republican prisoners on hunger strike in Portlaoise jail.

The unionist community had lost all faith in Rees' handling of the political process. Speculation was rife that the loyalist paramilitaries were drawing up plans for war, and Paisley made an impassioned call 'to Protestants of Ulster' to preserve their country against the enemy within and the double dealings of 'perfidious British Governments'.[136] Seeking to temper disquiet among the Westminster unionist MPs, Rees denied that there was any truth to Paisley's claim that GOC Frank King had tendered his resignation over differences in security policy only to have retracted it under pressure from Wilson. Molyneaux informed Rees that the Irish government were in fact urging his party 'not to rock the boat' at this decisive moment. He suggested that it might be better if NIO officials talked directly to the IRA, as relying on third parties appeared to be quite an unreliable course to follow.[137]

The British then held a third official meeting with Provisional Sinn Féin, providing cover for their ongoing unofficial discussions with Ó Brádaigh and McKee. These talks successfully established the mechanisms by which the ceasefire would be resumed and monitored. This time the British informed Cosgrave of the developments that were taking place in Northern Ireland. Although he continued to support the IRA leaders who were arguing in favour of a permanent ceasefire, Rees moved to defeat the Provisionals in the 'broken-backed warfare' that was taking place in south Armagh and Fermanagh by sending a 'mailed fist' in the form of fresh army units to those areas.[138]

At the end of January, Lord Gardiner recommended that special category status should be terminated. Furthermore, responsibility for releasing detainees should be transferred from the judiciary to the secretary of state, with a single judge acting in an advisory capacity. Heath was replaced by Margaret Thatcher as Conservative Party leader on 11 February, after she defeated Whitelaw on a second ballot in the Tory leadership contest by almost two votes to one, and Airey Neave became opposition spokesman for Northern Ireland. In Dublin, adopting Charles Haughey's position, Fianna Fáil called for a declaration of British intent to withdraw from Northern Ireland. And in Belfast, the UUUC leaders attempted to heal their rift with the loyalist paramilitaries, while the SDLP threatened to boycott the convention if the British sacrificed the concept of power-sharing.[139]

The IRA declared that an 'indefinite truce' would begin at 6.00 pm on 10 February.[140] Intensive negotiations over the issue of on-the-run IRA men and policing in republican areas had occurred, before Cooper approved a document which had emerged from the talks between his officials and the Provisionals. Rees informed parliament that arrangements had been agreed with Provisional Sinn Féin for the establishment of more than half a dozen 'incident centres' in nationalist areas. These would act as a point of contact between the government and the IRA, both to monitor the ceasefire and to solve any problems that should arise. He strenuously denied claims made by Loughran that the IRA would be policing Catholic areas and representing nationalists to the British government. Loughran had even suggested that, in serious cases, the IRA would hand criminals over to the RUC. This intensified fears in Dublin that the Provisionals had succeeded in negotiating an agreement with the British that provided them with the means to politicise the republican movement.

Rees denied that this document, or any of the other written agreements that might emerge from the negotiations, had been signed by British officials.[141] Comments attributed to IRA army council members suggested that the British had, in fact, agreed to engage in further negotiations to prepare for the end of British rule in Northern Ireland.[142] Nevertheless, the split within the Provisional IRA deepened over the resumption of its ceasefire. The leadership in the South had strongly backed this move, while sceptics in Belfast opposed it on the grounds that they did not believe that Rees would concede anything of any substance. One serious disincentive for the IRA to abandon violence was obvious to these hardliners. If the Provisional IRA entered the convention elections under the guise of Sinn Féin, then winning two or three seats was the maximum that they could expect to achieve; therefore, constitutional politics offered precious little in return for giving up the ghost of armed struggle.

Rather than enabling the Provisional IRA to regroup, recruit and recover its strength, the resumption of its ceasefire merely exacerbated existing fissures within its leadership. A fortnight into the new cessation, Rees came to the aid of the IRA 'doves', announcing that he would be releasing a further eighty detainees in the coming weeks. Although Rees was aware that many of the IRA detainees who were set to be released in March would immediately resume their activities, he viewed this as a price worth paying for maintaining the ceasefire before the convention opened in May. The army was extremely unhappy about implementing a security policy which was principally designed to breathe life into Rees' ailing political process. Rees remained convinced that a settlement could only be reached with the consent and cooperation of extremists on both sides. In stark contrast, army officers were convinced that Rees was passing up a golden opportunity to militarily defeat the IRA at a moment when it was weak, isolated and completely divided.

Realising the potential impact that his security policies might have on their political standing, the SDLP were horrified that Rees was preparing to release all the Provisional IRA detainees. They warned the British that the creation of rival political 'centres' in republican areas was a 'colossal mistake', which could only lead to the deliberate re-establishment of 'no-go areas'.[143] Going back on his party's policies on detention and policing, Fitt insisted that the government must only discuss these matters with Northern Ireland's elected representatives, and his colleagues implored Orme not to grant an amnesty to the Provisional IRA. Nevertheless, the Provisionals immediately established over a dozen incident centres, which were independent of the official government centres agreed to by Cooper. The ceasefire held despite various incidents, such as the shooting of two Provisional IRA men by the British Army in Belfast and an attempt by the IRA in Newry to end the truce.

Rees made further troop reductions and, against the advice of King, brought the number of detainee releases to 215 for the period 23 December 1974 to 14 April 1975. These did not, however, represent a great increase on the rate of releases during the pre-ceasefire period of 9 July 1974 to 22 December 1974, when 174 detainees were set free.[144] Rees believed that prisoner releases would not cause a significant security problem until they reached the 100 hardcore Provisional IRA detainees. His logic for releasing them was that if they were not released, then the Provisional IRA would resume its campaign of violence. King argued that they would resume violence either way; therefore it was obviously better not to release them at all. The split between the two had become so bad that King publicly criticised the secretary of state's security policies. He said that the ceasefire had 'come at a bad time for the army', as it had reached the point where it would be able to force the Provisional IRA to abandon its campaign of violence in another 'two or three months'.[145] More than that, King argued that if the current release rate was sustained, then the Provisional IRA would shortly be in a position to start over again militarily, while having gained a degree of political legitimacy.

After ten people died during a weekend of violence in Belfast,[146] physically and mentally exhausted, unsure as to how much longer he would remain in charge of Northern Ireland, Rees concluded that nothing constructive would emerge from the convention. Although he had no clear idea as to what might follow, he remained hopeful that the convention might eventually lead to a situation where the British could withdraw the army and leave Northern Ireland with some form of independent government that enjoyed harmonious relations with the South.[147] A cabinet reshuffle was expected to follow a referendum, on 6 June, concerning Britain's continued membership of the EEC. Not expecting to be at Stormont Castle after that date, Rees pondered Louis XV's grim prophecy, *'Après moi, le déluge'*.

NOTES

1. DT2005/7/631, Speech by Cosgrave at Royal Marine Hotel, Dun Laoghaire, 13 June 1974.
2. *The Listener*, 10 June 1974.
3. *Time Magazine*, 10 June 1974.
4. CAB134/3778, Meeting of the Ministerial Committee on Northern Ireland, Downing Street, 29 May 1974.
5. Interview with Sir Robert Andrew, London, 14 November 2007.
6. DT2005/151/696, Meeting between FitzGerald and Rees, Dublin, 19 April 1975.
7. Interview with Lord McNally, Westminster, 9 June 2008.
8. Haines, *The Politics of Power*, pp.131–2.
9. Interview with Lord Heath, London, 4 April 2001.
10. Interview with Lord Carrington, Knightsbridge, 21 November 2007.
11. Interview with Lord Donoughue, Westminster, 27 February 2007.
12. ICBH, *British Policy in Northern Ireland, 1975–82*, pp.67–8.
13. Ibid., p.14.
14. Ibid., p.20.
15. Interview with Lord McNally, Westminster, 9 June 2008.
16. PREM16/148, Wilson to Armstrong, 30 May 1974.
17. Interview with Seán Donlon, Limerick, 25 September 2007.
18. Institute of Contemporary British History, Witness Seminar held at King's College London, 11 February 1993.
19. Interview with Garret FitzGerald, Dublin, 12 September 2001.
20. PREM16/148, Rees to Wilson, 31 May 1974.
21. DT2005/7/631, Meeting between FitzGerald and Cooper, 5 June 1974.
22. Rees1/4, *Northern Ireland*, p.12.
23. CJ4/531, Cooper to Hunt, 29 May 1974.
24. CJ4/531, Bryars to Smith, 31 May 1974.
25. Interview with Lord Donoughue, Westminster, 27 February 2007.
26. CJ4/531, Cooper to Hunt, 29 May 1974.
27. CJ4/531, Henley to Hunt, 31 May 1974.
28. CAB134/3778, Ministerial Committee on Northern Ireland, 12 June 1974.
29. *Irish News*, 24 June 1974.
30. *Irish Press*, 8 July 1974.
31. *The Times*, 7 June 1974.
32. DT2005/7/631, Meeting with SDLP delegation, Dublin, 10 June 1974.
33. ICBH, *British Policy on Northern Ireland, 1975–82*, p.17.
34. Hansard, vol. 874, cols. 1038–183, 4 June 1974.
35. DT2005/7/631, Meeting between FitzGerald and Cooper, 5 June 1974.
36. Interview with Sir Ken Bloomfield, Craigavad, 19 December 2007.
37. Interview with senior NIO official.
38. White Paper, *The Northern Ireland Constitution* (London: HMSO, 1974).
39. Ibid., Part 7, Paragraph 45 (a).
40. Austin Currie, *All Hell Will Break Loose* (Dublin: O'Brien Press, 2004), p.219.
41. *Time Magazine*, 10 June 1974.
42. CAB128/54, Cabinet Conclusions, Downing Street, 13 June 1974.
43. Bernard Donoughue, *Prime Minister: The Conduct of Policy under Harold Wilson and James Callaghan* (London: Jonathan Cape, 1987), p.132.
44. *Dáil Debates*, 25 July 1974.
45. DT2005/7/633, Meeting between FitzGerald and Orme, Dublin, 18 July 1974.
46. Rees1/4, *Northern Ireland*, p.24.
47. *The Times*, 13 July 1974.
48. Rees1/4, *Northern Ireland*, p.30.
49. DT2005/7/633, Meeting between FitzGerald and Orme, Dublin, 18 July 1974.
50. PREM16/149, Meeting between Wilson and Lynch, Downing Street, 15 July 1974.

51. *Irish Times*, 8 August 1974.
52. Hansard, vol. 877, col. 180, 25 July 1974.
53. Rees, *Northern Ireland: A Personal Perspective*, p.91.
54. PREM16/150, Summary of Political Events, 8–15 August 1974.
55. Rees1/4, *Northern Ireland*, p.30.
56. *The Times*, 5 August 1974.
57. DT2005/7/633, Keating to Nally, 15 August 1974.
58. *Guardian*, 9 August 1974.
59. *The Times*, 9 August 1974.
60. *Irish Times*, 14 August 1974.
61. *Irish Times*, 15 August 1974.
62. PREM16/150, Summary of Political Events, 15–22 August 1974.
63. *Irish Times*, 28 August 1974.
64. DT2005/7/633, Meeting between Irish Government and SDLP, Dublin, 20 August 1974.
65. Ibid.
66. DT2005/7/633, Nally to Cosgrave, 22 August 1974.
67. DT2005/7/633, SDLP Conference, Bunbeg, 24–25 August 1974.
68. DT2005/7/633, O'Brien to FitzGerald, 5 September 1974.
69. DT2005/7/633, Government Memo, 3 September 1974.
70. PREM16/150, Meeting between Rees and the SDLP, Stormont, 29 August 1974.
71. *Monday World*, September 1974.
72. PREM16/150, Meeting between Rees and the SDLP, Stormont, 29 August 1974.
73. Rees1/4, *Northern Ireland*, p.37.
74. PREM16/150, Meeting between Rees and the SDLP, Stormont, 29 August 1974.
75. *Irish Times*, 29 August 1974.
76. *The Times*, 5 September 1974.
77. DT2005/7/633, Visit to Northern Ireland, McColgan, 2–3 September 1974.
78. *The Times*, 9 September 1974.
79. PREM16/151, Extremist Groups, 26 September 1974.
80. PREM16/151, Meeting between Wilson and the SDLP, Downing Street, 10 September 1974.
81. *The Times*, 16 September 1974.
82. *The Times*, 26 September 1974.
83. PREM16/151, Rees to Wilson, 28 October 1974.
84. PREM16/153, Hunt to Wilson, 22 November 1974.
85. CAB134/3778, Minutes of the Ministerial Committee on Northern Ireland, Downing Street, 24 October 1974.
86. PREM16/151, Wilson to Rees, 22 October 1974.
87. PREM16/151, Donoughue to Wilson, 23 October 1974.
88. PREM16/153, Meeting between Wilson and Cosgrave, Downing Street, 1 November 1974.
89. Interview with senior NIO Official.
90. PREM16/153, Bridges to Jordan, 13 November 1974.
91. DT2005/7/663, London Weekend interview with David O'Connell, 17 November 1974.
92. Interview with NIO official, 30 January 2008.
93. *The Times*, 8 November 1974.
94. *Irish Times*, 25 November 1974.
95. *Northern Ireland: Constitutional Convention – Procedure* (London: HMSO, 1974).
96. CAB134/3780, Official Committee on Northern Ireland, London, 1 November 1974.
97. PREM16/153, Hunt to Wilson, 22 November 1974.
98. Rees1/5, *Northern Ireland*, p.17.
99. Hansard, vol. 882, col. 35, 25 November 1974.
100. CAB134/3778, Ministerial Committee on Northern Ireland, 4 December 1974.
101. PREM16/153, Hunt to Wilson, 22 November 1974.
102. DT2005/7/663, Kirwan to Nally, 20 November 1974.

103. DT2005/7/664, Northern Ireland Situation, Comments on a memo by FitzGerald from O'Brien, December 1974.
104. PREM16/153, Meeting between Rees and FitzGerald, London, 19 December 1974.
105. DT2005/7/664, Meeting of British and Irish officials, Dublin, 12 December 1974.
106. DT2005/7/664, Northern Ireland Situation, 16 December 1974.
107. DT2005/7/664, The Irish Dimension: Memo by O'Brien on recent British suggestions, 18 December 1974.
108. DT2005/7/664, Cabinet Minutes, 17 December 1974.
109. CJ4/530, Ramsey to Bloomfield, 5 December 1974.
110. *The Times*, 30 November 1974.
111. PREM16/515, Telephone Conversation between Wilson and Rees, 31 December 1974.
112. CJ4/860, Meeting between Rees and Flanagan, Stormont, 6 January 1974.
113. ICBH, *British Policy in Northern Ireland, 1975–82*, p.40.
114. CJ4/860, IRA ceasefire announcement, 20 December 1974.
115. CJ4/860, Meeting between Rees and Protestant Clergy, Westminster, 18 December 1974.
116. Interview with Michael Oatley, London, 13 November 2007.
117. PREM16/515, Morrall to Rees, 27 December 1974.
118. PREM16/515, Cooper to Rees, 30 December 1974.
119. PREM16/515, Telephone Conversation between Wilson and Rees, 31 December 1974.
120. CJ4/860, meeting between Wilson and Northern Ireland Church Leaders, 1 January 1975.
121. *The Times*, 2 January 1975.
122. Interview with Garret FitzGerald, Dublin, 12 September 2001; ICBH, *British Policy on Northern Ireland, 1975–82*, p.13.
123. CENT/1/3/12, Bloomfield to Rees, 3 January 1975.
124. CENT/1/3/40, Meeting between Rees and the SDLP, Stormont, 10 January 1975.
125. *Sunday Independent*, 12 January 1975.
126. Rees1/6, *Northern Ireland*, p.4.
127. Hansard, vol. 884, cols. 201–10, 14 January 1975.
128. *Irish Times*, 15 January 1975.
129. ICBH, *British Policy on Northern Ireland, 1975–82*, pp.42–3.
130. Confidential source.
131. Confidential source.
132. PREM16/515, The end of the IRA ceasefire, Cooper, January 1974.
133. PREM16/515, 'J' to Wilson, 17 January 1974.
134. PREM16/515, Statement by Rees, 19 January 1975.
135. PREM16/515, Meeting between Allan and Provisional Sinn Féin, Laneside, 19 January 1975.
136. *The Times*, 28 January 1975.
137. CENT/1/3/40, Meeting between Rees and Molyneaux, London, 21 January 1975.
138. Rees1/6, *Northern Ireland*, p.13.
139. CJ4/792, SDLP warns on danger of 'failed convention', 11 February 1975.
140. *The Times*, 10 February 1975.
141. Rees1/6, *Northern Ireland*, p.23.
142. *Der Spiegel*, 17 February 1975.
143. CJ4/792, Meeting between Allan and Devlin, Belfast, 11 February 1975.
144. DT2005/151/696, NIO Press Release, 15 April 1975.
145. *Sunday Independent*, 13 April 1975.
146. *The Times*, 7 April 1975.
147. Rees1/7, *Northern Ireland*, p.8.

No Direction Home

In the run-up to the constitutional convention elections that were held on 1 May 1975, Enoch Powell described power-sharing as an 'empty catch-phrase', which must be abandoned by 'constitution peddlers', so that the same democratic standards could be applied to Northern Ireland, in its devolutionary and administrative provisions, as would be applied to Scotland and Wales.[1] Triumphing at the poll, having sought a mandate to return 'British parliamentary standards' to Northern Ireland, the UUUC secured over 53 per cent of the vote, winning forty-six of the seventy-eight seats, an increase of seventeen on the 1973 assembly election. The election of a UVF candidate in West Belfast brought the anti-power-sharing bloc to forty-seven, with over 360,000 first-preference votes. This was not quite the 400,000 unionist voices which Paisley had accused Heath and Whitelaw of ignoring, in December 1973, but it was a resounding endorsement for the UUUC's policy to reject involuntary power-sharing in Northern Ireland. With nineteen seats, the Official Unionist Party remained Northern Ireland's largest party, but it lost ground to both the DUP and Vanguard who returned twelve and fourteen members respectively. Furthermore, the DUP's increased vote share meant that even if the Official Unionists aligned with Vanguard, Paisley would be strong enough in the convention to act as a spoiler to any agreement that they might seek to reach with the SDLP.

Prior to the elections, the British had dropped all reference to the Irish dimension that was the centrepiece of the Sunningdale Communiqué. Furthermore, Fianna Fáil actually aided Cosgrave's efforts to distance his government from the SDLP when he stated that the Irish constitution could not be applied to Northern Ireland 'without prior agreement and consent'.[2] Nevertheless, winning a mandate for 'power-sharing in government and the institutionalised recognition of the Irish dimension', the SDLP increased its vote share to 23.7 per cent.[3] With only seventeen seats in the convention, and with the support of neither the British nor the Irish government, the nationalists would have to concede on the latter point if the UUUC were to accept them as partners in government. Although the Alliance Party held its ground, taking eight seats, Faulkner's party won just five and the former chief executive scraped through on the ninth count with Alliance transfers.

Before the election, Craig appeared more willing to consider alternative constitutional ideas than Paisley, holding private talks with both the Irish government and the SDLP, and hinting at the idea of forming an emergency coalition with northern nationalists. But Paisley had convincingly surpassed Craig in terms of vote share and the Official Unionists had still not recovered from their split with Faulkner. The media's description of West as the Lepidus of the loyalist triumvirate was apt; he posed no leadership threat to his rivals and would follow the line of whichever one emerged victorious from the ongoing power struggle within the UUUC. The British remained hopeful that rivalry between the Craig and Paisley factions might act as a catalyst for compromise in the convention; if Craig became isolated then Paisley might finally be convinced that compromise was in his party's interests.

Magnanimous in victory and all too aware that public opinion might turn against them should they resort to the hooligan tactics that they employed to disrupt the assembly's proceedings, Craig and Paisley adopted a positive approach to the convention. In participating in its proceedings, the UUUC's objective was to reject the idea of executive power-sharing with the SDLP, reject the concept of an Irish dimension, offer a powerful all-party committee system as a compromise to the nationalists, and establish something akin to the old Stormont parliament. To achieve this end they planned to isolate the SDLP in the convention, before pressuring it towards a compromise by courting the support of the Alliance Party and Faulkner's unionists. Although they were prepared to fully engage in constitutional discussions, the UUUC had signalled to the British that they were prepared to establish a different form of government in Northern Ireland if they were forced to do so. Should it reject their compromise, the UUUC believed that the British government would be forced to run the risk of civil war in Northern Ireland by accepting some form of negotiated independence, continue with direct rule, or adopt a variant of Powell's integrationist proposals.

The coalition could accept direct rule with Powell's integrative design for increased Northern Ireland representation at Westminster and the restoration of democratic local government.

Following the elections, tensions between Rees and the British military worsened as internecine violence and sectarian assassinations continuing unabated. Despite having released roughly half the detainees over the previous six months, he expected the army to act in support of a police force that had not been accepted by any nationalist representatives. By abandoning the army's position of military strength, Rees intensified the pervasive sense of fear and instability that was evident within the Catholic community. While his security policies had brought about a Provisional IRA ceasefire, he had not developed a coherent strategy for delivering the parties who had opposed the Northern Ireland Executive in a settlement with some of its supporters. Nevertheless, Rees hoped that the politicians he viewed as the real enemies of the British government in Northern Ireland – Paisley, Craig and West – might be coaxed into accepting a heavily watered down version of the Whitelaw settlement, with no Irish dimension, or be foolish enough to force Britain to accept some form of negotiated independence. Moreover, by cutting the SDLP loose, he hoped that FitzGerald would finally abandon the idea that the British could impose power-sharing with an Irish dimension if this could not be achieved by consent.

Rees planned to step up his efforts to force reasonableness on the UUUC, the SDLP and the Provisionals by allowing political instability and constitutional uncertainty in Northern Ireland to continue. This was a high-risk tactic and, given the election results to the convention, it was one that had already backfired. Despite the working-class pretensions of the UWC and the Provisionals, the electoral bloc that stood in opposition to power-sharing in the convention was a rough manifestation of the elected opposition which had set out to destroy Faulkner and the Northern Ireland Executive. Yet Rees had less power at his disposal in May 1975 with which to impose his will upon them than he had had in May 1974. More than that, the parties to the former executive believed that Wilson and Rees had set the British government on a collision course, of their own design, which they were both politically and militarily incapable of seeing through.

FitzGerald pressed Rees to spell out firmly to the UUUC that the only way that unionists could regain power was by sharing it with the SDLP, as integration and majority rule were unacceptable options to his government. Dejected, Rees replied to his nemesis in the Irish ministry of foreign affairs, 'you can tell them, but not convince them'.[4] Orme muddied the waters further, signalling to Dublin that the British would not 'sanction' any settlement that the minority did not acquiesce in, but, nevertheless, it could not refuse to permit any such settlement, as it could not impose anything.[5]

O'Brien was concerned that the UUUC would use the momentum created by the election to make a unilateral declaration of independence and then sit back while the loyalist paramilitaries eliminated the IRA. The election result meant that there was 'no possibility of agreement on a power-sharing executive' or on an 'institutionalised Irish dimension'. It was simply 'not in the power of Dublin or London to bring it into being', he said, and 'that is a fact'. O'Brien argued that the establishment of the convention 'was a mistake', and since 'you can't make people share power' the only realistic alternative is to prevent the 'emergence of a non-power-sharing executive', or an independent Northern Ireland, through the continuation of direct rule from Westminster.[6] Devlin retorted that O'Brien's remarks were 'cold sabotage', describing his contradiction of Irish government policy as a 'stab in the back' to the SDLP.[7] Conveying its 'supreme dismay' to Cosgrave, the SDLP threatened to withdraw from the convention if O'Brien's statement was, in fact, the first official signal that the Irish government had abandoned the principle of power-sharing with an Irish dimension.[8] And at Westminster, the Conservatives took a step back from Whitelaw's Constitution Act, when Neave announced that it was 'no longer possible to talk in terms of enforcing power-sharing with people who do not want to share power'.[9]

* * * *

Rees expected a collective report in the autumn, written by Northern Ireland's lord chief justice Robert Lowry, who had agreed to chair the convention's proceedings, setting out its views. Maurice Hayes and Dr John Oliver, the two senior civil servants who would assist Lowry in his neutral role, believed that the convention's main function would be to 'fudge over' the constitutional failures of the last two years and iron out areas of disagreement. Rees would remain aloof from these proceedings so as not to be seen to be influencing their outcome in any way. He stressed that 'there will be no majority report' from the convention, for its function was to collectively determine 'what provision for the government of Northern Ireland is likely to command the most widespread acceptance throughout the community there'.[10] Lowry expected the convention to work in committees, with negotiations taking place out of the media spotlight. This would avoid long-drawn-out plenary sessions and prevent the UUUC from turning the convention into a parliament in all but power. Rees intended to play on the fact that, having elected them, the public would expect its members to act as local representatives, addressing their interests, despite the fact that the convention had no legislative powers.

When Lowry met with the Northern Ireland party leaders on 5 May, he stressed that Rees had provided him with no steering brief or instruction and, three days later, the convention held its opening plenary session. It began in acrimony, the SDLP reacting hysterically as Paisley pushed through a proposal that 'the convention shall be master of its own business' and precluded the presentation of a minority report to parliament. The Alliance and SDLP members complained bitterly that by concentrating power in the business committee and stripping Lowry of any effective procedural control the UUUC had negated the 'whole spirit' of the convention.[11] Responding to pressure from FitzGerald, who was in Lebanon, to keep the convention 'on the rails',[12] Rees retorted that he 'could not care less what rules of procedure they adopted'.[13] He snapped that if the convention could not even reach agreement on its own rules of procedure, then this simply proved how flawed the Heath and Cosgrave governments were in their determination to impose power-sharing.[14] He was standing aside. Responsibility rests, he said, with the Northern Ireland parties to adjust to reality and find a compromise between their seemingly intractable positions. He then exposed further the powerlessness of Northern Ireland's elected representatives to their constituents by restricting their access to the British ministers who were running the province. Since the convention was 'not involved in any way' with the government of Northern Ireland, Rees said that it would be 'wrong' for him or his ministers to receive delegations from it 'to deal with issues affecting their electors'.[15]

Having turned down a move to the Department of Education, Rees was comforted by a private assurance from Wilson that he could remain in Northern Ireland until later in 1975. In the short term, Rees planned to intervene in the proceedings of the convention only if collapse was imminent. In preparing for the event of a second loyalist strike, he intended to avoid a confrontation with the UUUC on any issue that might cause it to band together. Cooper told the Irish government that majority rule in Northern Ireland would not be accepted by parliament. As far as the present government were concerned, integrating it within the UK was completely out of the question. He saw four possible outcomes from the convention: it might reach a degree of disagreement after which a recalled convention might attempt to finalise a settlement; it might reach a degree of agreement on an internal settlement and a referendum would then be used to settle points of dispute; it might reach a state of unbridgeable disagreement that led to a second strike or a unilateral declaration of independence; or it might attempt to conclude an agreement that left Northern Ireland outside the UK by consensus.[16]

British intelligence suggested that the Provisional IRA was training in the South and 'creeping back to violence' in the North,[17] yet Rees expected the ceasefire to hold for the duration of the convention's deliberations. If action was taken to assuage loyalist discontent over the continuing flow of IRA releases, Rees believed that the beginning of the end to special category status for prisoners might be in sight. Although sectarian murder and paramilitary feuding across Northern Ireland was largely going unchecked, given the reduced British Army presence, with the exception of the murder of an RUC man by the Provisionals in Londonderry, violence against the state was minimal. With loyalists accounting for approximately one third of the 1,400 special category prisoners, Rees felt that introducing a parole system, as a means of reducing sentences from the two thirds minimum convicted prisoners currently had to serve, was 'politically necessary'. But his proposal to release prisoners who had served one third of their sentences or twelve months, whichever was longer, was met with hostility in cabinet from both Jenkins and Mason.[18] Watering down his approach, Rees suggested releasing prisoners who had served half their sentences, from which point onwards they would be on conditional release until their full term expired. This was not quite an amnesty, but nonetheless it was a means by which to end any new admissions to special category status. Mason again stood in opposition, arguing that these measures would be seen as an amnesty for convicted terrorists. They would undermine Northern Ireland's security forces and prison staff, he argued, and bring strong pressure for Irish prisoners convicted of terrorist offences in Britain to be transferred to Northern Ireland. On a security basis, there was simply no case to be made for releasing any of these prisoners, or the hardcore of the IRA detainees, as both sides were preparing for widespread inter-communal violence. Nevertheless, this proposal was approved and was to be put before parliament in October.[19]

As Rees scaled down the British Army's presence in Northern Ireland, the Irish government reconsidered its contingency plans for the event of a British withdrawal. The Irish Army estimated that if it was to provide humanitarian aid to the Catholic community in Northern Ireland, then it would have to increase troop levels to 20,000, while its present full capacity of 12,000 would be required to secure the state from spillover violence and the threat of a *coup d'état* from the Provisional IRA, which was the Irish government's main concern.[20] The government believed that it was highly unlikely that such reinforcements could be made without creating the impression that it was preparing to intervene in Northern Ireland. The Irish public would only expect military intervention to provide humanitarian relief to the minority community. The government doubted, however, whether such intervention could be limited in this capacity, as it would inevitably provoke retaliation from loyalists. Deep ground penetration into the Catholic enclaves of Belfast, to permit refugees to evacuate the city or to provide military assistance, was deemed to be far beyond the army's capability. Moreover, military assistance might prove counterproductive; arms distribution would be hard to control and it would inevitably strengthen the IRA in both parts of Ireland.[21]

Rees' continued refusal to clarify which form or forms of government he was prepared to accept from the convention heightened fears in Dublin that the ground was being paved for a 'pull out'. This ambiguity was designed in part to convince the Provisional IRA to maintain its ceasefire, by creating the impression that the private commitments they had received from the British were, in fact, policy. FitzGerald and O'Brien clashed over this issue. FitzGerald was willing, in the event of a British withdrawal, to contemplate a 'fall-out' position of a form of negotiated independence as the 'least undesirable' potential development. O'Brien was totally opposed to the government even considering taking such a step, as this would 'diminish the prospects of continued direct rule' and let Wilson 'off the hook' by allowing him to 'withdraw in a favourable international climate'.[22]

Rees asked his cabinet colleagues to consider a strategy for distancing Northern Ireland from Westminster, in the convention's aftermath, by extending direct rule through a minister resident or commissioner to whom a wide range of transferred items would be devolved. Wilson stressed that any such consideration 'must not however preclude further consideration of other policy options', such as integration or withdrawal, should the outcome of the convention 'make such consideration necessary'.[23] The majority view in government was that making direct rule more remote from Westminster was the direction British policy on Northern Ireland should take, prior to an eventual break with the UK.

* * * *

Further questions were raised over the British government's willingness to meet its constitutional responsibilities in Northern Ireland when Reverend Arlow made public the details of discussions that had taken place the previous February between government officials and the Provisional IRA. He stated that the government had given a 'firm commitment to the Provisional IRA that they will withdraw the army from Northern Ireland'. When questioned about the timing of a British withdrawal Arlow stressed that, in his own interpretation, this would be in the wake of the convention's failure 'to produce a solution to our problem'.[24] In response, Paisley called on Ulstermen to 'establish and defend' an 'independent state'[25] and Barr suggested that a 'Loyalist cabinet in waiting' was ready to govern the province.[26] Paisley's reaction was particularly significant, for up until this point he had resisted joining the ranks of those who had publicly endorsed the idea of a unilateral declaration of independence – Craig, Barr and Vanguard's paramilitary backers – or those who viewed negotiated independence as a viable fallback option – Official Unionists Taylor, Smyth and West.

Arlow had made similar comments in the US on 9 May.[27] By Friday 23 May, Rees was aware that Arlow intended to repeat the allegations on RTÉ that weekend. Nevertheless, Rees refused to comment or firmly rebut his remarks until late on Sunday evening, fuelling speculation that the churchman's interpretation was in fact correct. Moreover, his denial focused on the assertion that the British would withdraw if the convention broke down, which was simply Arlow's interpretation and not what British officials had reportedly said to the IRA. Arlow even informed the US State Department that the Provisionals wanted the convention to collapse, as they were convinced that this would lead to a British withdrawal and provoke a conflict in which the Catholic community would look to them for protection, and in which the Irish government would be forced to participate.[28] This was a view shared by Hume and the majority of his SDLP colleagues. If a confrontation between loyalists and the government erupted after the convention had run its course, they believed that the two governments would have to devise governmental institutions for Northern Ireland and, if necessary, enforce these structures militarily. Some SDLP members favoured independence, provided that an entrenched position in government for nationalists was established prior to a British withdrawal. Others took an entirely different view, their minds focused on the dangers the Catholic community in east Ulster would face in such circumstances. Currie and Fitt argued that it was highly unlikely that either government would take any such military action.[29]

Rees was worried that the documents that were exchanged at early meetings between his officials and the Provisionals might enter the public domain. In his statement, Arlow had stressed that his information had originated from both sides. This fuelled speculation that he had, in fact, been encouraged by British officials to speak out in the hope that his remarks might sober the SDLP and the UUUC to the consequences of failing to reach accord.[30] Moreover, the disclosure of John O'Connell's unsolicited attempts to engage the Provisional IRA directly with Wilson, or the idea that British minister Shirley Williams had encouraged Arlow to speak out, would certainly cause further embarrassment to the government.[31]

Fitt left a meeting with Wilson and Rees on 14 May under the distinct impression that the Labour leaders were preparing to withdraw from Northern Ireland.[32] Wilson had remarked that 'if there is another UWC strike we will not be there to deal with it'.[33] The tactics that Rees was using to nudge the province towards some form of negotiated independence – taking a back seat in the political process, reducing the British Army's role, and indicating that the government would consider an immediate pullout if the convention failed – were at last beginning to have their desired effect. Rees was delighted to learn that his 'clear eyed view' of the direction the Northern Ireland political process was taking had been digested by the British press: the government has 'no policy' on Northern Ireland because it had 'no power to enforce one';

the 'Gladstonian' desire in the Labour Party for 'British withdrawal is becoming a fact'; and its intention to withdraw should be read simply as its 'renunciation' of any 'attempt to wield power' there.[34]

As a consequence of recent political developments, Rees believed that the Provisional IRA had reached the point of 'realised eschatology' – the end of time in a theological struggle to rid Ireland of British influence – but they 'had not realised that they were there and they didn't know quite what to do'.[35] In his willingness to accept independence as a central component of a British exit strategy, Rees had greatly exaggerated the level of support that existed in Northern Ireland for this option. The Official Unionists complained to him that Arlow's intervention had actually stiffened the resolve of those who favoured independence at the very time when the UUUC had been ploughing an accommodating line.[36] Shortly after the convention had begun, Lowry warned Rees that he was making a grave mistake by encouraging the extremists who viewed independence as a viable option. Although three years of direct rule had emphasised the attractiveness of local autonomy from Westminster, Lowry stressed that none of the parties to the convention would willingly choose independence in preference to some form of devolved government within the UK.

Rees was pleased with the approach that the Northern Ireland parties were taking to the convention. He saw in it the potential for the seeds of Ulster nationalism to germinate, as Irish minds focused on where their real loyalties lay. MI6 officer Robert Browning had been acting as an *agent provocateur* for Rees, impressing upon the loyalist paramilitaries that the prevalent attitude in Britain was 'a plague on all your houses'. Powell accused Rees of fostering the idea of independence by encouraging loyalists to engage in dialogue with republicans and pressing home the notion that Britain had lost any desire to maintain the union.[37] The gulf between Powell and his UUUC colleagues widened over his integrationist stance and their desire to lead an autonomous Northern Ireland. Attacking the convention as a 'trap' set with the 'bait of self determination' to prise Northern Ireland from its union with Great Britain, he publicly questioned the 'loyalism' of the advocates of independence.[38] His colleagues responded in kind, proposing that the convention should be transformed into an Ulster government, without the SDLP in cabinet, for a trial period of four years. Not only had they taken the bait, it was clear that their loyalty was to Ulster before the British crown or parliament.

Nevertheless, erstwhile opponents in the convention began to focus on the task that lay ahead. UUUC members Craig, Austin Ardill and William Beattie arranged to meet with the SDLP during the six-week summer recess to establish possible 'meeting points' on the road to an agreed solution.[39] The atmosphere was cordial during the nineteen plenary sessions that were held between 8 May and 3 July. The parties avoided addressing controversial issues and concentrated their collective hostility towards the British government. Hume softened the SDLP position, hinting that power could be shared in 'different ways', through 'partnership' and 'responsibility sharing'. Craig declared that he was against a form of independence that would not engender 'allegiance right across the board'.[40]

On 17 July, the ceasefire was broken when the Provisional IRA killed four soldiers in a bomb attack at Forkhill, County Armagh. Two weeks later, in what was a botched attempt to create the impression that Irish musicians were transporting explosives across the border, three members of the Miami Showband were shot dead, following a gig in Banbridge, at a fake UDR roadblock in County Down. Two of their assailants were also killed when the bomb they had planted in the band's van exploded prematurely.[41] Rees informed parliament that 'an arm with the letters "UVF" tattooed on it' had been discovered at the scene.[42]

Since the start of the cessation, ninety civilians had lost their lives in violence across Northern Ireland, which was more than the civilian death toll for the same periods in 1973 and 1974. The Provisional IRA was psychologically and militarily prepared for a resumption of violence, but they lacked a pretext for bringing their ceasefire to a close. Rees sought to exploit both the desire for an immediate resumption of violence within the Provisional IRA and the Catholic community's yearning for peace by continuing to drip-feed detainees back into society and fomenting public revulsion towards those who were perpetrating sectarian violence across the province. He was under pressure to halt the wave of sectarian murders and Independent Fianna Fáil TD Neil Blaney demanded the release of the remaining republican prisoners so that they 'can defend the community in the north'.[43] However, Rees was delighted that the ceasefire had resulted in a reactionary crackdown on the IRA in the Republic of Ireland. After Irish special branch arrested Dáithí Ó Conaill, he chastised his captors from the dock, describing them as 'cowardly and bankrupt politicians' who had done their 'utmost to sabotage' the twenty-two week-old truce.[44] Another consequence of the cessation was the growth of the Irish National Liberation Army (INLA), an extreme republican splinter group who were busy recruiting disenfranchised members from both IRA factions.

* * * *

In the convention, Lowry's team structured the talks by putting together proposals that might provide the widest possible 'involvement' of all parties in the legislative process. This would build on Faulkner's old committee system but fall short of the executive power-sharing system that the UUUC had undermined. When official talks between the UUUC and SDLP resumed in early August, Paisley hinted privately that if the issue of power-sharing can be settled, then 'all else will fall into place'.[45] The SDLP publicly stuck to its insistence on power-sharing with an institutionalised Irish dimension, but Hume surprised Craig by suggesting to him that a parliamentary system needed an opposition. In turn, Craig remarked that if agreement could be reached on institutions of government for Northern Ireland, then there would be 'no difficulty' in freely negotiating the setting up of a body to address areas of common concern between North and South.

Outside the talks, Hume initiated a committee, chaired by SDLP security spokesman Michael Canavan, to draw up contingency plans for the failure of the convention. These would provide for the relief of Catholic communities in the North and detail the degree of assistance the SDLP would seek from the Irish government in such circumstances.[46] Rees did enough to keep the ceasefire going and further expose the ineffectual status of Northern Ireland's political representatives, announcing that he hoped to release the remaining 246 republican detainees by Christmas. There was speculation that both Rees and Cooper would shortly be departing Northern Ireland, prompting the former to tell Wilson that the Provisionals would treat this as their cue to end the ceasefire. Under growing pressure to address the continuing security crisis outside the talks, Paisley set to initiate a motion of censure in the convention, in efforts to shift pressure back onto the secretary of state for his implementation of security policies that were exacerbating that very crisis.

The convention in plenary was postponed until September, as

substantive negotiations between the SDLP and the UUUC began on 19 August. The aim was to reach agreement within a fortnight and the SDLP set out immediately to unearth the UUUC's technical objections to sharing power with them at government level. The nationalists suggested that referendums could be held, in both parts of Ireland, on any power-sharing formula that was agreed to in the convention. Such agreement, they argued, could provide for an Irish dimension that was acceptable to both communities, and enable the SDLP to support the RUC as the British and Irish armed forces went 'after the Provisionals' in both jurisdictions. In the knowledge that the UUUC would prefer to present a sixty-one to seventeen, rather than a forty-seven to thirty-one majority report to parliament, Napier set out to play the role of kingmaker in an agreement that set aside the SDLP.

With no Whitelaw figure harrying the delegates to imposed deadlines, the negotiations initially took place between the parties in private, with Lowry meeting with them on an individual basis and playing a quietly constructive but purely non-proscriptive role. Progress was slow and it seemed that the convention's outcome would be determined by which party blinked first. The loyalist triumvirate faced a dilemma. If it was to avoid being blamed for the convention's failure to reach agreement, or suffer the same fate as Faulkner by becoming tied to one, then it had to produce credible objections to the SDLP's power-sharing proposals. With Paisley inside the tent and at the negotiating table for the first time in his political career, the lack of trust between the coalition partners was palpable. The UUUC objected to the SDLP's demand that there had to be power-sharing at every level of government in Northern Ireland. They argued that all governments needed an opposition, all members of a government should be supporters of the institutions of the state, and in a democracy the majority party had a right to form a government. Craig and DUP deputy leader William Beattie reported to Lowry that the SDLP were refusing to even discuss the possibility of a UUUC–SDLP voluntary coalition for a trial period of five to ten years.[47] But Fitt agreed with Lowry that this might indeed provide a way out of the current impasse. Moreover, the SDLP leader pledged to make efforts to convince Hume, Currie and Devlin that something short of full executive power-sharing could potentially satisfy his party's objectives. In return, the nationalists would fully support the institutions of the state.

One week into the talks, an air of despair gripped the convention and it looked like they would break down before any serious negotiations had occurred. Both sides believed that it was impossible to reach agreement and neither was inclined to prolong the discussions to satisfy Lowry or anyone else. The majority of UUUC backbenchers wanted to reopen the plenary sessions, wind up the talks and present their report. Hayes pressed Lowry to assume a more interventionist role and coerce the parties to put their manifestos 'on ice', take a 'foothills and pinnacles' approach to the discussions, and return to the question of power-sharing after issues of less significance had been resolved.[48] Lowry attempted to galvanise the negotiators by publicly advocating emergency coalition government as an interim solution to the crisis. This was not entirely dissimilar to how the Whitelaw settlement had taken shape. It made it more difficult for the parties to walk away from a compromise that might allow them to manage the crisis, pending further negotiations.

During a private discussion with Callaghan, FitzGerald sought assurances that the British government would meet its responsibilities in Northern Ireland and assist Irish security forces in the event of a doomsday situation. He stressed that the forces which had been created to replace the B Specials – the UDR and RUC Reserve – already outnumbered the Irish Army at its present strength of 12,500. Callaghan suggested that, in such circumstances, his government would perhaps reintroduce internment to combat republican and loyalist violence. Both FitzGerald and Lynch concurred that their parties 'could support such action' if it was clearly directed against both sets of paramilitary groups.[49] In Callaghan's view, had Whitelaw succeeded him as home secretary and the eighteen-month interlude under Maudling been avoided, power-sharing might well have succeeded in regulating the conflict. Moreover, he indicated that his government would only consider repartition as a last resort, stressing that any declaration of intent to withdraw from Northern Ireland would do more harm than good.

The SDLP sent Canavan to Dublin to spell out their policy and ask the Irish government to open a 'channel of communication' with the party to discuss the circumstances in which a complete breakdown of law and order in Northern Ireland might occur. Should the convention fail due to the UUUC's refusal to share power, the SDLP would call for the British government to withdraw the guarantee of union to Northern

Ireland and initiate joint Anglo-Irish control, as a prelude to a complete British withdrawal. Should the UUUC unilaterally declare independence, the SDLP would assume political and military leadership of the Catholic community in the name of, and as agents of, the Irish government in the South. If a situation arose whereby unelected leaders were seen to be in the ascendancy, as had been the case in May 1974, the SDLP believed that it was essential for them to act, in the event of a breakdown of constitutional government, to prevent the Provisionals from filling the political vacuum. While they had not given up all hope of achieving progress through political dialogue, the SDLP required 'physical resources and expertise' from the Irish government in order for it to take and maintain the initiative on behalf of the Catholic community. Furthermore, Canavan indicated that having taken the initiative in the event of a British withdrawal the SDLP would have to accept a degree of support from the Provisionals.[50] He confirmed that by 'resources' he was referring to 'guns and ammunition', and by 'channels of communication' he meant the 'appointment of army officers with whom the SDLP would immediately begin planning the effective use of the resources'.[51]

Rees' security policies had provoked such a degree of hostility from the Northern Ireland parties that his intervention in the negotiations at this stage would have been counterproductive. But then these policies were designed to bring realism and reasonableness to the convention's proceedings. He again warned Wilson that removing him from Northern Ireland would be read by the UUUC as a capitulation to its demands and interpreted by the Provisionals as a change in government policy on Northern Ireland. He advised the prime minister not to allow either the UUUC or the SDLP to bypass him, by accepting their requests for an audience at Downing Street, before the convention reconvened on 9 September.

The UUUC leaders complained bitterly to Lowry that they had the 'deepest possible' suspicion that Rees intended to undermine their position by making it as difficult as possible for them to remain active in politics if the convention failed. Both the UUUC and the SDLP were convinced that Rees was preparing for negotiations with the paramilitaries, as they were being talked up in the media by government officials as 'the politicians of tomorrow'.[52]

Hayes had reached the conclusion that the maximum the convention could hope to achieve would be to convince the parties that it was presently impossible to apply a long-term solution to Northern Ireland's conflict. Therefore, it might be possible to develop the idea of forming a voluntary coalition for the duration of the emergency as the basis of a future constitutional settlement.[53] When Lowry suggested this interim solution to the unionist troika, Craig described it as 'a sprat to catch a mackerel', and Paisley rejected it on the grounds that once it had been accepted for a time, and had been seen to work, the UUUC would come under pressure to accept it as a long-term solution.[54] The SDLP leaders were pessimistic about coming to any form of compromise with the UUUC. Hayes believed that they had got themselves into a 'straight-jacket' over the issue of participation at cabinet level, as they were presently unable to entertain the suggestion of other forms of sharing power.[55] Isolated by the British government and under pressure from their constituents, the UUUC and the SDLP exchanged policy papers and began backtracking on their rigid manifesto commitments: the UUUC's pledge to reject power-sharing and the SDLP's insistence on institutionalised power-sharing with an Irish dimension.

On 29 August, Lowry reported this change of course to Rees and urged him to consider devolving some security powers to a Northern Ireland government. He argued that this would be a 'unifying' factor in the event of a power-sharing deal, as it would provide the parties with a 'clear brief to put down terrorism'. The SDLP were encouraged by the section of the UUUC's policy document which suggested that an endorsed coalition government might be acceptable when 'an emergency or crisis situation exists and parties by agreement come together in the national interest for the duration of the crisis', subject to approval by the electorate.[56] Since the UUUC could not be seen to be accepting any form of enforced power-sharing, Craig explained that the logic behind this thinking was to create a 'gentleman's agreement', based on mutual trust, which did not entrench the power of any party within the constitution or the right of any party to hold office.[57]

The SDLP indicated that should a trial period of coalition government be agreed for a fixed term – Hume suggested ten years – then they would be prepared to take on the IRA and 'put them down by quite rugged means'. The SDLP appeared willing to forgo their requirement to have power-sharing enshrined in statute, provided that prior agreement on a social and economic programme was reached. They argued that concrete guarantees must be put in place to ensure that, having made a 'gentleman's agreement' to enter a voluntary coalition they could not then be arbitrarily ejected from government.[58] It is telling that, during the negotiations between the SDLP and the UUUC which Lowry chaired, Beattie stood in for Paisley while Craig took the lead.

Tempted by the allure of high office, Craig advised his colleagues that having a small number of SDLP members in government would be 'a small price to pay' for having new institutions that were broadly acceptable to both communities. If this could be seen to work, then the British would be unlikely to intervene, at some future point, to institutionalise power-sharing at the SDLP's request. Voluntary power-sharing presented the UUUC with an opportunity to gain control of Northern Ireland's institutions, with the acceptance and support of the SDLP, having conceded very little at all; the Whitelaw settlement, only in reverse. Craig faced a problem in devising a form of guarantee that would, on the one hand, entice the SDLP to enter into a voluntary coalition and, on the other, not appear to be institutionalised power-sharing in all but name.[59] Hume informed Lowry that fixing a trial period, at the end of which the voluntary coalition would be fully reviewed, was a prerequisite for the SDLP's agreement.

When Lowry attempted to sell this idea to Paisley, the DUP leader asked him what he thought would happen if a voluntary coalition was established and, after a number of years, a majority in parliament decided to revert to a Westminster-style cabinet government. Lowry's response was that such a move would be far more favourable to delivering a majority report that was 'openly going back' on the stated policy of the government and the opposition. Paisley argued that many people would consider the voluntary coalition idea to be a 'betrayal of principle'. He voiced his concern that should it be seen to work well over time, then 'great pressure' would be placed on unionists to continue with this form of government. The DUP was completely opposed to anyone serving in a Northern Ireland cabinet who aspired to bring about a united Ireland.[60] However, all six of the UUUC's main negotiators – Craig, Paisley, West, Beattie, Ardill and Baird – presented no practical or ideological points of opposition to the idea of forming a coalition government, and all saw the advantage of getting governmental institutions up and running. Nevertheless, they were worried that it would set a dangerous precedent if all the major Northern Ireland parties had accepted one form of power-sharing or another, and they remained suspicious over the SDLP's motivations for entertaining the idea of voluntary coalition. The UUUC was divided over the issue. Craig's supporters had come to view voluntary coalition as the best means of attaining power, securing the Catholic community's support for the RUC and reducing the IRA threat, whereas Paisley's supporters favoured calling the government's bluff by presenting a majority report, as this might herald a quicker return to majority rule than entering into a voluntary coalition. Under pressure from both church and party, as violence worsened outside the talks, Paisley informed Lowry, on 3 September, that while he had no objection to entering government with Catholics who supported the state, the question of sharing power with the SDLP was one of both 'conscience' and 'principle'.[61]

In a terrorist attack which the Provisionals blamed on dissident republicans, five Protestant men were fatally injured when two of its members entered an Orange Order meeting in Tullyvallen, County Armagh, and sprayed the gathering with machinegun fire.[62] Both Faulkner and Fitt implored Rees to take firm action to dispel the belief that the government was acting half-heartedly in its efforts to impose law and order, stressing that the fear of civil war was poisoning any hope of compromise in the convention. Citing the example of Joseph Rigby, Fitt complained bitterly that as the status of constitutional politicians diminished, the stature of paramilitary leaders rose. Although Rigby had gained just thirteen votes when he stood against Fitt in the 1973 local government elections, he was manning the Provisional IRA's incident centre in New Lodge and masquerading as someone who held political sway with the government.[63]

Trying to narrow Paisley's room for manoeuvre, Lowry asked him what it was, exactly, that an SDLP Catholic had to do to 'square himself' with the DUP leader's conscience and serve in a British-style coalition government. Paisley responded that he would have to abandon his Irish passport, unconditionally support the security forces, and swear an oath of allegiance to the state. With a hint of sarcasm, Lowry enquired whether the SDLP Catholic would be accepted if he publicly asked the Irish government to repeal Articles 2 and 3, to which Paisley exclaimed, 'Marvellous! Better than anything achieved under Sunningdale.'[64]

Many UUUC backbenchers simply could not identify with the SDLP leaders. To them, they were nationalist rebels who had started Northern

Ireland's troubles under the guise of the civil rights movement, and several UUUC negotiators singled out particular SDLP leaders who they would not sit in government with. In contrast, Craig now viewed security as the key issue on which an agreement might be reached. He indicated that he would not even join a UUUC coalition government as this would 'collapse in no time' without the SDLP's support.[65] Emphasising the danger that entering into a coalition with the UUUC posed, Hume warned his colleagues that the SDLP could be 'discarded' when the emergency period expired after violence had been reduced and the system which caused that violence in the first place could be reinstated. Nevertheless, the SDLP indicated that it would not have a great problem supporting the RUC, and Hume suggested that a renewable ten-year period of government would provide a 'copper fastened' guarantee, which would satisfy the nationalist community in any such agreement.

Just as Lowry and Hayes were narrowing the divisions between the SDLP and the UUUC by carefully drawing them towards the narrow common ground where an agreement might be forged, Paisley threw down the gauntlet to Rees. On 4 September, the DUP leader publicly declared that 'either Rees must go or the Convention has to go', giving the secretary of state 'hours rather than days' to close all incident centres, end all talks with the Provisionals, and seal the border with the Republic.[66] The UUUC's tough talk in the media had been designed to give the impression that they were negotiating hard in the convention and disguise the fact that they were preparing for a deal, but Paisley's statement intensified divisions within the loyalist coalition, as neither Craig nor West had agreed to or seen his statement. They were particularly aggrieved, as Paisley had suggested the idea of making such a statement at a meeting the previous evening, and although the three unionist leaders had agreed to meet again to discuss the idea further, the DUP leader had chosen to go after Rees on his own. Responding to this pressure as Provisional IRA dissidents bombed London, Rees took a gamble. Pledging troop reinforcements, he announced that there was no possibility of the British 'abdicating our responsibilities' by withdrawing from Northern Ireland and allowing a 'Congo-type situation' to ensue.[67]

Craig informed Lowry that while the divergence of views in Vanguard over the voluntary coalition scheme remained small, although Paisley had previously favoured the idea subject to referenda, the DUP had given the proposals a much cooler reception. The following day, a number of Official Unionist and Vanguard members shifted towards Paisley's position and the DUP claimed that it was only the SDLP negotiators, and not the SDLP convention party as a whole, who were interested in the voluntary coalition idea. They suggested that the latter wished to achieve a detailed understanding of the safeguards for nationalists in the proposals before proceeding any further. As Craig searched for a device to lever Paisley off the hook of his hardline statement, this notion was rebutted by Hume. Paisley was correct, however, in his assertion that the SDLP convention party was divided. Its members had refused to grant their negotiating team permission to present a policy document in the negotiations on the grounds that it was too weak on the Irish dimension. Moreover, when the SDLP party executive met, on 6 September, a hardline group were 'not at all happy with the line being taken by the negotiators'. It was evident that any agreement reached on a voluntary power-sharing basis would be difficult to sell to the party as a whole.[68]

Napier called Paisley a 'wrecker' when he threatened to boycott the convention in protest against British security policies and, anxious not to be blamed should the talks collapse, the DUP leader proposed a one-week adjournment as an alternative form of remonstration. Bizarrely, Paisley then sent his deputies to inform Lowry that they had learned, on 'the greatest of authority', that reaching agreement would provoke an onslaught of violence from the IRA that would leave the unionist community exposed, as they had 'only eight guns between them!'[69]

Although Craig remained confident that he could hold Vanguard together, despite opposition to a deal with the SDLP from Ernest Baird and Reg Empey and Taylor's efforts to steer the Official Unionists towards Paisley's position, he was convinced that the DUP would withdraw from the UUUC within a week. Principally through private talks held with Hume over the previous few weeks, Craig agreed with the SDLP that he would float the idea of voluntary coalition the following Monday night, 8 September. The SDLP understood this to be a bid for power by Craig. He would attempt to carry Vanguard and the majority of the Official Unionists with an accord by breaking the UUUC and isolating Paisley.

On 6 September, Craig's position was strengthened at a meeting of the Ulster Loyalist Central Co-ordinating Committee, which comprised UUUC representatives and loyalist paramilitaries. The same day, prominent loyalist paramilitaries held talks with one of the SDLP negotiators, both to gain clarification on what had occurred in the private talks and to reassure the nationalists that they backed Craig's efforts to find a solution.[70] The UDA's support for Craig was pragmatic. It took the view that while Northern Ireland's politicians might find it acceptable to 'start the civil war', it was Northern Ireland's paramilitaries that would 'have to fight it'.[71] But having split with Craig, the UWC threatened to initiate a second strike in response to the government's security policies, and the UVF added their voice to his detractors inside the convention.

Violence outside the convention continued to disrupt the negotiations. The SDLP said that it had 'firm knowledge' that the Provisionals had murdered the two off-duty UDR men, who were shot dead the previous weekend, after learning that the gap between the two sides in the convention had narrowed.[72] When British security forces failed to lift the IRA's new chief of staff Séamus Twomey when he appeared in Belfast, Rees was accused of granting immunity from arrest to the Provisionals.[73] There was speculation that Rees would be forced to resign after Paisley came into possession of a document which revealed that the army unit in question had actually spoken with Twomey.[74]

Paisley advised Lowry that both Craig and West were being 'unrealistic' if they thought that there was any hope of carrying the UUUC and the unionist electorate with the voluntary coalition proposals. There was 'insuperable opposition' within the UUUC, he said, to the idea of having the SDLP in a Northern Ireland cabinet. Lowry said that, naturally, some people hoped that there would be no agreement at all, but suggested to the DUP leader that he, in fact, had both the 'influence and ability' to carry a settlement within the unionist coalition and beyond.[75]

On Monday 8 September, with Paisley dominating the talks in the absence of West and Ardill, Craig advised Lowry that the UUUC negotiators had reached such 'a very grave position' that he felt compelled to review his position.[76] Not only was there a proposal to reject voluntary coalition, but to do so in such terms that it would be crystal clear that there could never be any question of the SDLP taking seats in a Northern Ireland government.[77] Fearing the worst, Lowry began intensive efforts to stop the UUUC from rejecting the emergency coalition proposals in such a way that prevented future negotiations over power-sharing. With the convention teetering on the brink, the UUUC issued a watered down statement reaffirming its manifesto commitment to exclude 'republicans' from any future cabinet. It would seek an adjournment of the convention, on Thursday 11 September, on a motion of censure against Rees, to reconvene a week later for a debate over its report.[78]

Baird then began to backtrack, indicating that the UUUC did not want the convention to 'go up in smoke'. Having kept Craig's thumbs in the dam for the time being, and prevented Paisley from explicitly killing off the concept of power-sharing between unionists and the SDLP through the use of the ambiguous word 'republicans' in the UUUC statement and the omission of any reference to voluntary coalition, Lowry kept the talks going.[79] But having succeeded in splitting Vanguard through Baird's opposition to Craig over the voluntary coalition proposal, and in the absence of the Official Unionist leadership, Paisley made his move that night. The DUP leader pressed a vote on the UUUC to accept a motion ruling out 'power-sharing in cabinet' between the unionist coalition and the SDLP. This was passed by thirty-seven votes to one, with two abstentions, and, resigning his leadership of the Vanguard Convention Party, Craig accused Paisley of wrecking the talks.

Having carried the support of only six of the fourteen Vanguard convention members on a motion to delay the decision over whether to reject the concept of an emergency coalition with the SDLP regardless of policy or circumstances, Craig had no option but to resign. Baird's leadership pretensions had enabled Paisley to split Vanguard and Powell's argument that no British government would accept a 'gentleman's agreement' was instrumental in swaying wavering Official Unionist backbenchers towards Paisley. Powell had argued that the British would certainly not give legislative effect to the convention's report unless the terms of any participatory agreement, reached between the parties, was 'precisely enacted and safeguarded in the statute', which they would presumably insist on being 'permanent'.[80] Paisley, who had faced isolation in the talks the previous week, claimed a victory for the unionist community during Craig's moment of weakness, and he finally replaced the Vanguard leader as the leading political figure within the UUUC. When Craig was asked whether he believed the SDLP were prepared to concede substantial political ground in the search for a settlement, he replied, 'the tragedy is that I will never know because we have slammed the door on exploration, slammed it I think in a most unfair way.'[81]

Craig claimed that the UUUC had devalued the convention by abandoning its electoral commitment to 'work unremittingly and whole heartedly' for the re-establishment of a Northern Ireland government.[82] He stated publicly that, given the grave crisis that Northern Ireland faced, he was prepared to consider entering into a widely based coalition which brought the SDLP into government on the basis of a gentleman's agreement. In describing him as the 'only voice in favour of power-sharing', the media had given Craig the kiss of death. Politically isolated, there would be no way back for unionism's vanguard man.[83] Although the DUP had accepted the idea of a voluntary coalition, through William Beattie, having been warned off by his Presbyterian flock, Paisley had played safe and taken the opportunity to eliminate Craig from the game of musical chairs that had been unionist politics since Whitelaw broke the mould of one-party rule in 1972.[84]

* * * *

In Dublin, the government distanced itself further from the SDLP, fearing the northern nationalists were prepared to call for the withdrawal of British support for the union and ultimately a political and military withdrawal from Northern Ireland. The Irish government's fallback position on the convention was simply to pressure the British government to discharge its responsibilities in Northern Ireland and steer the SDLP back into line with this policy. Nally urged Cosgrave to continue building up the state's defence forces, approve secret contingency plans for the relief of between 20,000 and 50,000 refugees from Northern Ireland, and avoid broaching the subject of withdrawal with the British, as it remained uncertain how Wilson would act if the convention failed. Nally warned Cosgrave that there were 'strong arguments against open and active participation' in present initiatives, and the more the Irish government participated, the more this aided the British 'in any plans they may be developing for shuffling off the Northern coil'. If Cosgrave followed the SDLP's lead, he argued, not only would this provide a pretext for a British withdrawal, it would lead to a situation in which the Irish Army would be forced to intervene, north of the border, under its direction. This would create a 'civil war' situation in which the British, who would have little interest in maintaining their 'guarantees', would likely 'get out as fast as their ships and planes would carry them'. Nally concluded that should the SDLP begin to espouse exactly the same position that the Provisional IRA had taken since the imposition of direct rule, then their 'identification with the men of violence could not be more complete', which could lead to 'anarchy in this island'.[85]

Away from the media gaze and away from Rees, Callaghan met with FitzGerald during an EEC session in Venice, again insisting that there had been no change to the British government's policy on Northern Ireland. FitzGerald was desperate to restore his influence in Northern Ireland, but the British kept him at arm's length. They were concerned, however, that continuing to keep the Irish government in the dark over British policy might result in it losing ground to Fianna Fáil as the SDLP moved closer to the Provisional IRA's position. Rees was under considerable strain in London, snapping back at those accusing him of directing a strategy to push Northern Ireland towards independence: 'you say I'm doing it, I say its happening.'[86] Senior RUC and British Army officers again clashed with Rees over security policy, and there was a general feeling in British government circles that he had no control whatsoever over what was taking place in Northern Ireland. Frank Cooper was so concerned by his demeanour that he urged Wilson to ensure that the beleaguered secretary of state took a holiday, outside the UK, to break his fixation with the minutiae of the deteriorating situation in the convention, which was evidently getting under his skin.[87]

By implementing security policies that were designed neither to address the security crisis nor to practically facilitate the political process, Rees had made it publicly obvious that the Labour government had no policy on Northern Ireland 'other than to survive for another week or fortnight', as Cooper put it.[88] The result of this inertia was a degree of chaos: Neave was pressing the government to halt the release of detainees; army intelligence had been significantly reduced; the UDR had been heavily infiltrated by loyalist paramilitaries; elements within the RUC were leaking information to paramilitary groups and to the UUUC; the Provisionals were disenchanted with their ceasefire; and forty-nine Protestants and fifty-nine Catholics had been victims of sectarian assassination, thus far, in 1975.[89] These were not conditions in which the British could easily or honourably withdraw. But when Rees spoke on the crisis on 20 September, stating that the government would 'not abdicate its responsibilities', he did not make it clear whether he meant its responsibilities to Great Britain or to Northern Ireland.[90]

The British were expecting a majority report from the convention which rejected power-sharing and favoured a return to direct rule, a gradual or immediate end to the IRA ceasefire, and the possibility of a second political strike. With the convention due to end on 7 November, stalling for time, Rees suggested a three-month extension in the hope that divisions within the UUUC might lead to some form of agreement. Molyneaux suggested to him that, should Craig press on, then the Vanguard leader might be able to form an administration with Faulkner, the SDLP and Alliance. He concluded, cryptically, that this might leave the government with a 'worse mess' in Northern Ireland than it had inherited from its predecessors.[91]

On 24 September, Rees suggested in cabinet that if the convention failed then the implications of a 'gradual withdrawal from major responsibility for security in Northern Ireland might have to be considered, and variants of the option of withdrawal, such as the granting of dominion status to Northern Ireland, should not be ruled out in the long term'. British officials disagreed. They argued that an early abdication of responsibility over Northern Ireland or repartition would both be 'extremely damaging' to the UK's international reputation and almost certainly result in widespread violence. There was a major re-think taking place on Northern Ireland policy, which went against the grain of both Powell's integrationist campaign and Wilson's leaning towards dominion status. Despite concerns over how genuine safeguards might be guaranteed for the minority community, and despite the fact that it might drive the Catholic community further into the arms of the IRA, the idea of accepting the 'majority' option, within a democratic framework, while difficult to 'dress up' as 'power-sharing', could not be 'lightly dismissed'. British officials thought that the UUUC might accept minority safeguards, jointly guaranteed by the two governments, if this was the price they had to pay for majority rule, and provided that this was not institutionalised as an Irish dimension. This of course raised the considerable problem of how joint intervention, to uphold such guarantees, might be carried out in practice.[92]

The prospect of a second UWC strike was central to these considerations. Under such circumstances, the British would maintain law and order without seeking to provide essential services. The concept of 'distancing' Northern Ireland from the rest of the UK was prevalent in this thinking; therefore the government would introduce a direct rule system that was based in Belfast rather than London, with a minister resident, as an interim phase prior to further devolution. Direct rule would then bring about a reduction in the government's involvement in Northern Ireland, relegating its problems to a place of lesser importance in British politics. Although Wilson agreed that these ideas should be explored further, he concluded that 'no option or scenario' should, at this stage, be 'finally excluded from examination', including dominion status, 'very early withdrawal, integration, and, except possibly as part of a wider approach, repartition'.[93] Donoughue, who was not party to these discussions, reacted furiously to this new thinking on Northern Ireland. He told Wilson that it was 'a bloody certainty' that the Catholic population would be actively driven to sympathise with the IRA if the government opted for a halfway house between 'distancing' and accepting majority rule. He told Wilson that something 'more radical' was required, for there was 'not an ounce of vision' in the theoretical notion of 'distancing' Northern Ireland from Westminster. Donoughue urged him to reconsider the dominion status option with an Anglo-Irish guarantee, and unwind 'the British imperial legacy' in Ireland, to allow for the future possibility of the 'six counties ultimately resuming their proper place as part of Ireland'.[94]

* * * *

The IRA ceasefire looked as if it was about to collapse: violence flared across the province; the Provisional IRA army council was losing control over its rank and file; the Irish government maintained its crackdown against the IRA in the Republic; and the Provisionals in Belfast were asserting their dominance over the republican movement. Nevertheless, Rees sought to advance his security policies before the ceasefire broke down: by releasing the remaining 183 detainees; introducing a policy of criminalisation against all politically motivated offenders; reintroducing the screening of potential offenders on a selective basis; proscribing the UVF; and shutting down the six republican incident centres.[95] Since the beginning of the year, 934 people had been charged with terrorist-type offences, including 144 with murder. Of those sentenced during that period, 441 had been granted special category status, bringing the total number in custody to almost 1,400, of which 866 were republican and 517 loyalist.[96] Although some of the detainees who had been released, re-offended and were back in custody had gone through the legal system, the flaw in the criminalisation policy was that although Rees had ended detention, the problem of special category prisoners left him no better off than Whitelaw when he inherited internment from Faulkner in 1972.

Bipartisanship in Dublin was threatened when Fianna Fáil foreign affairs spokesman Michael O'Kennedy urged Britain to make a statement of intent to withdraw and quit Northern Ireland altogether.[97] Hume and Currie travelled to meet with Lynch, who assured them that O'Kennedy's remarks amounted to nothing more than a difference of expression rather than policy. Nevertheless, Fianna Fáil subsequently changed its policy, calling on the British to 'encourage the unity of Ireland by agreement' and, to this end, declare its 'commitment to implement an ordered withdrawal' from its involvement in Northern Ireland.[98] Lynch had lost the debate within his party and Fitt accused him of moving into the 'Provisional IRA camp'.[99] Lynch argued that his party was merely calling for the British to encourage unity and, when this had occurred, implement it through an orderly withdrawal, which Rees found reminiscent of the prayer of St Augustine: 'make us good, make us perfect, but not yet'.[100]

The Conservative Party had developed no clear policy on Northern Ireland under Thatcher, but she stressed her commitment to supporting the unity of the UK. Although Whitelaw still favoured power-sharing, he hinted that integrationist demands would be difficult to refuse if the convention failed.[101] More than that, bipartisanship would end if the British Army was withdrawn and senior Tories were now openly questioning whether the convention was a 'manoeuvre towards justifying a pull-out',[102] a device which Powell described as an 'elephant trap' for unionism.[103]

The SDLP were dismayed by statements from Dublin that the Irish Army would in no circumstances intervene in Northern Ireland. Hume and Currie told FitzGerald that if the British government's rebuttal of a majority report was not made in strong and unambiguous terms then 'all was lost'.[104] The Irish government were flabbergasted by the minority report the SDLP were intending to submit to the British, viewing it as a dangerous jolt towards the position of the IRA. The document suggested that 'the problem is the problem of legitimacy of all institutions in Ireland, North and South', which could be resolved by a referendum on these institutions in the Republic of Ireland.[105] Sinn Féin also issued a pamphlet calling on the British to announce that they intended to initiate 'a phased and orderly withdrawal'.[106] In early October, the IRA sent the British government a remarkably detailed document which indicated that should it complete a total military and political withdrawal, then Sinn Féin would be willing to advance a political strategy, North and South, and 'struggle by political means for the achievement of its policies and its own vision of Éire Nua ... a New Ireland'. The statement was some indication of what the IRA leadership had learned from its engagement with the British and a far cry from the list of demands read out by Séan Mac Stíofáin to Whitelaw in July 1972.[107]

Delighted that the IRA intended to 'take the place of the SDLP' after gaining a declaration of intent to withdraw from the British, Rees took Cooper to Chequers on 24 October to discuss the matter personally with the prime minister. Rees was now more convinced than ever that the IRA would not be able to resuscitate its campaign of violence to pre-ceasefire levels, as 'people had to face up' to new political realities in Northern Ireland 'in a situation where the violence is different'.[108] Upon his return to Northern Ireland, he instructed officials to keep talking to the IRA but to 'give nothing at all'.[109] Although the ceasefire held, the political aspirations of the Provisionals had been badly damaged by widespread sectarian violence, their ongoing feud with the Official IRA, and high-profile incidents such as the kidnapping of Dutch businessman Tiede Herrema, which resulted in an eighteen-day siege and a gun battle with the Garda Síochána in Monasterevin, County Kildare. Taking a much colder view of the security crisis in the North, Cosgrave condemned the IRA as criminals whose violence had to be 'eradicated from our lives and our island'. They are not a romantic element of some 'distant quarrel' in Northern Ireland, he said, they are 'a very real threat to the Irish people'.[110] During their first meeting since May, Rees admitted to FitzGerald that, despite good cooperation between the RUC and Garda Síochána, the security situation in south Armagh was 'almost uncontrollable' and therefore a Special Boat Service detachment was being deployed there.[111]

Launching a scathing attack on Rees, Powell claimed that all 'bloodshed in Ulster' could be ended if he desisted from perpetuating the constitutional uncertainty that existed over Northern Ireland and from providing the IRA with 'reason to imagine that one more dose of terror' would be enough to achieve its aims.[112] Powell privately urged Wilson to forget about power-sharing, allow the convention to collapse, and use the leverage that devolution proposals for Scotland and Wales provided to allow local government to develop in Northern Ireland under direct rule.[113]

Rees announced that the RUC would be expanded to 6,900 and the RUC Reserve to 6,500, from present levels of 4,760 and 4,894 respectively, and a new prison at Maze would end the organisation of paramilitary groups in its Long Kesh detention compounds. From 1 March 1976, those convicted of terrorist offences would not be able to claim special category status; therefore all those charged with lawlessness, sectarian murder and paramilitary gang crime would be brought to justice through the courts.[114]

* * * *

In the convention, Napier attempted to rescue the political talks at the eleventh hour, putting forward an amendment to extend its proceedings. He suggested to Lowry that sections of its report might gain the Alliance Party's support, and possibly that of other parties, if it was delayed.[115] Meanwhile, Devlin told Hayes that there was still a possibility of reaching an agreement on the voluntary coalition proposals if the convention was recalled.[116] Some UUUC members remained interested in this idea, as it presented an opportunity to shift the blame for the convention's failure onto the SDLP, who wanted the majority report to be firmly confuted by parliament. But on 7 November the convention approved the UUUC's majority report by forty-two votes to thirty-one. The majority report strongly favoured a return to majority rule, the devolution of all security matters, and an increase in the number of Northern Ireland MPs to between twenty and twenty-four. The temporary expedient of emergency coalition should be avoided, the UUUC said, as this would prolong the 'corrosive uncertainty' and 'aggravate the instability' on the constitutional issues that the convention was tasked with resolving.[117] The convention was then prorogued and Rees ended his policy of non-intervention by holding talks with the Northern Ireland parties over Christmas. The convention would be recalled for further deliberation before it expired on 7 May 1976,[118] and Rees resisted pressure to either comment on or reject the report.[119]

The government's 'distancing' tactic had contributed considerably to the 'overall sense of malaise' in Northern Ireland and created a degree of chaos at local government level.[120] The convention had run its six-month course without walkout, breakdown or the public altercations that had afflicted the Northern Ireland Assembly. But it had failed to reach any cross-community agreement on the composition and nature of any future government, or its relationship with either Britain or the Republic of Ireland. There was little deviation in the reports submitted to parliament by the UUUC and the SDLP from their manifesto commitments. West lamented that it was a 'tremendous embarrassment' to people of his 'vintage', that they had let slip through their fingers what it had taken their 'fathers fifty years to build up'. The British took an altogether less sentimental view of recent events, content to allow the 'realities of the past five years to unfold for themselves'.[121]

Without having first set out broad areas of agreement on subsidiary issues and executive formation, Hayes felt that the convention parties had 'disdained the foothills and aspired to the pinnacles' and made a 'rapid dash to the north face of the Eiger' where they quickly became stuck. Having decided from the outset that the convention would fail to find widespread agreement, the parties had focused on 'tactical ploys' to ensure that the blame for its ultimate collapse would be attributed to their opponents.[122] Nevertheless, the convention had served Rees as a means of keeping them at arm's length while the government undertook a major policy review.

By refusing to reject the majority report, Rees hoped that support for Craig's voluntary coalition proposals might evolve over the coming months, but the absence of a firm rebuttal from parliament gave credence to Paisley's assertion that the British could be forced into accepting a form of majority rule. Cosgrave too held back from completely rejecting the report, for had he done so the SDLP would not have been able to participate in a reconvened convention. Like Paisley, he suspected that the British government's soft response to the report marked the beginning of a major shift in British policy, and one which would see it abandon the idea of power-sharing as a means of regulating Northern Ireland's political divisions.[123] With decision time fast approaching for Wilson, he showed an interest in the idea of 'cantonisation', impracticable as it might seem, and criticised officials for both their lack of 'radical' thinking and their readiness to dismiss the dominion status option; 'indirect distancing', he said, was a phrase rather than a policy.[124]

Wilson's central policy review concluded that while it would be in 'Great Britain's political and economic interest if Northern Ireland were to cease to be part of the UK', there was 'no radical policy option' which presently offered the government 'an easy way out of the Northern Ireland quagmire', and separation would be neither 'an honourable nor a profitable objective' to pursue. It recommended ending the uncertainty over Northern Ireland's future by clearly declaring its policy objectives; continued direct rule or progressive distancing under some form of devolved regional government being the most realistic options.[125] On 11 November, the ministerial committee on Northern Ireland examined all the available options that were open to the government, including the practicalities and unpalatable implications of repartition. It decided that since the moment was not ripe for any major policy change, the only immediate option was to continue with direct rule. Moreover, the Cabinet Office did not think that accepting majority rule was an 'immediately practicable option'.[126] John Hunt advised Wilson that although Rees would not want to reach a decision immediately, the most logical means of initiating the disengagement process would be through a limited process of 'gradual devolution or distancing for a stated period', which would lead to 'majority rule in the form of something akin to Dominion status with entrenched safeguards for the minority'.[127]

Rees supported Hunt's distancing approach, as he planned to delay making his response to the majority report until the new year and recall the convention in late January, following a series of talks with the Northern Ireland parties beginning at the end of November. If these talks were successful, he would then form an executive, as an emergency form of devolved government with a committee system and a new assembly, for a three- or four-year period under Whitelaw's 1973 Constitution Act.[128] Although the SDLP and the UUUC both strongly opposed reconvening the convention, Rees aimed to coax them back into negotiations by neither accepting nor rejecting the majority report, and by giving neither a declaration of intent, or non-intent, on the question of British withdrawal.[129] He hoped that the SDLP would be tempted by the offer of a role in a partnership government, albeit with no Irish dimension, and that the possibility of major policing and justice powers being progressively devolved to an executive, with an increase in Northern Ireland's representation at Westminster, would be enough to entice the UUUC to enter into government with the nationalists.[130]

* * * *

Desperate to salvage something from its ceasefire, the Provisional IRA again pressured the British to make a declaration of intent to withdraw. Launching an attack from the Republic of Ireland on 22 November, the Provisionals shot dead three British soldiers in south Armagh. A week later, they murdered Conservative Party activist Ross McWhirter in London before taking a number of hostages in a Balcombe Street flat, which resulted in a six-day siege. On 27 October, Rees responded to the IRA, through Michael Oatley following his meeting with Wilson at Chequers, stating an interest in their proposals, but stopped short of giving a declaration of intent. Oatley's link to the IRA, Brendan Duddy, who he believed continued to speak on behalf of the Provisionals, signalled that they were prepared to contemplate a loyalist government, on a six-county basis, having engaged in inconclusive contacts with the UDA. But if a private declaration was not made by the British, then a campaign of extreme violence would be waged in Britain. The IRA remained under the influence of Ó Conaill, but the British were aware that a new leadership was emerging in Belfast and Londonderry, one that would happily sanction a fresh campaign of violence across Northern Ireland.

Having strung the Provisional IRA along the political path and created an environment in which a dramatic return to violence would compound its alienation within the nationalist community, Rees finally gained support for his security policies from both the RUC and the British Army. Pre-empting an onslaught of IRA violence by imposing stringent security measures would increase support for a resumption of hostilities. But if Rees gave the IRA the private assurance it sought, and republican violence was completely brought to an end, then it would be obvious that he had done a deal with the Provisionals. This, in turn, would provoke a major confrontation with the UUUC and a complete break with the Irish government. Rees chose to pursue neither of these two options. Resisting pressure for knee-jerk security measures from the Conservatives – Neave was suggesting that the army should be given leeway to shoot and kill IRA terrorists with a view to clearing up the south Armagh area[131] – and pressure from Roy Jenkins to hold back, he brought internment to an end on 5 December by releasing the last forty-six detainees.[132]

Accepting that distancing Northern Ireland from British politics was an unrealistic means of ending direct rule, Rees concluded that ending detention and shifting the policy debate away from the idea that Britain could provide a 'solution' to the troubles were the two main contributions he had made during his time as Northern Ireland secretary of state.[133] He had not completely abandoned the idea of salvaging something from the convention, and was particularly encouraged when Craig tabled proposals for safeguarding minority interests through a Belgian-style coalition agreement.[134] Having drastically altered his opinion of the Vanguard leader, Rees was also impressed by some of his young supporters, such as Queen's University lecturer David Trimble.[135] The UUUC remained divided; ten of its convention members hinted that they would be more open to persuasion over the voluntary coalition proposals if Paisley were to become isolated. The SDLP also remained split over these proposals. Half a dozen or more of its convention members favoured calling for a declaration of Britain's intent to withdraw,[136] while the remainder appeared to be 'waiting for the government to shake the plum of power-sharing into their laps'.[137] Hume told Rees that the phrase 'power-sharing' was 'not sacrosanct', suggesting that the use of the word 'participation' might help consolidate support around Craig and neutralise Paisley.[138]

Paisley was convinced that Wilson and Rees had become so fed up with Northern Ireland that they would eventually accept a devolved government on 'loyalist terms'.[139] Mentally and physically shattered by the obduracy of its politicians after almost two years in office, Rees concluded that Northern Ireland was simply 'a natural fascist little state'.[140] He viewed Paisley as a 'security risk', as 'nothing would be sacred' should he ever be allowed to enter government.[141] Paisley advised his colleagues that Wilson's strategy was to make Northern Ireland's union with Great Britain so politically and economically uncomfortable that unionists would acquiesce in a deal with the Republic of Ireland. He informed Lowry that although the UUUC wanted to retain 'the links' with the UK, if having the SDLP in government was the price to be paid for maintaining those links then independence, which was not presently an issue, could become one. If a confrontation with the British was inevitable, Paisley argued that it might as well come 'sooner than later'.[142] However, loyalist paramilitary leaders had warned both Paisley and Baird not to commit them to further industrial action.[143] Speaking in terms that suggested that the UUUC was preparing for government, Baird said they may have to 'shoot down people' who had supported them in the past. And Paisley remarked that the British were deluded if they thought that UDA 'gangsters,'[144] whom the UUUC leaders naturally deplored and despised, would not back the loyalist coalition when the 'chips were down'.[145]

* * * *

The new year began badly for Northern Ireland. There was no let-up to the sectarian hatred and violence that was consuming the province. The security crisis was so bad that Wilson sent the SAS and the Spearhead Battalion into south Armagh, raising the number of troops in Northern Ireland to 15,500.[146] The INLA had killed three and injured twenty-eight in a bomb attack on a Protestant bar in Gilford, County Armagh, on New Year's Eve. Four days later the UVF hit back, gunning dead six civilians in coordinated attacks on two Catholic families in nearby villages. The following day, at Kingsmill, the IRA stopped a minibus carrying textile workers. After identifying and releasing its sole Catholic passenger, who some of the passengers feared was about to become the victim of a loyalist killing, they machine-gunned the eleven remaining Protestants and only one survived.[147] When the RUC arrived a passer-by was praying for the dead and wounded in the driving rain on the road, which one officer said was an 'indescribable scene of carnage'.[148] And on the back streets of Belfast, a sinister gang of assassins known as the Shankill Butchers terrorised the Catholic community by night through a series of random macabre murders.

Refusing to reject the majority report or be drawn on the question of power-sharing, Rees announced that the convention would be reconvened for a four-week period from 3 February. The parties to it could choose a devolved participatory form of government, with an evolving constitution, on terms acceptable to Westminster. Failing that, there would be no devolved government in Northern Ireland, with no new initiatives planned, and the convention would be terminated on 7 May

1976, along with the mandates and the salaries of its members. The government no longer expected an institutionalised Irish dimension to be central to any agreement reached. The 'prime requirement', Rees said, was to find 'more widespread acceptance of any proposed system of government, providing for some form of partnership and participation'.[149] But he reduced the likelihood of the Northern Ireland parties reaching such an agreement when he suggested that a referendum on Craig's voluntary coalition idea would be held should the convention fail.[150] Although Rees suggested that there should be 'partnership' at executive level, he indicated that if the SDLP were prepared to accept something less, then parliament might also be willing to accept something less.[151]

In the convention, Paisley set out to frustrate Rees by sidelining Craig, ignoring the SDLP and reaching 'wider agreement' with Faulkner, Napier and the NILP.[152] Napier hoped that in an attempt to force the SDLP out of politics the UUUC might be willing to make the Alliance members 'an offer they could not refuse'. Although a voluntary coalition between Alliance and the UUUC would lack widespread support within the Catholic community, it might just have enough credibility to be acceptable to parliament.[153] The Official Unionists were deeply embarrassed by Paisley's dominance in the convention and there remained a possibility that they might accept a voluntary coalition with the SDLP, Alliance and Faulkner, having regrouped around Craig who was pressing the SDLP to publish its proposals in order to help him facilitate this process. Should they reach agreement, Paisley would be excluded from a second power-sharing executive, only this time one that had Craig and the loyalist paramilitaries inside the tent.

When Lowry tested Paisley's inflexibility towards the idea of SDLP members participating in a government, the DUP leader told him that the UUUC would not even discuss the matter when the convention was recalled, as a guaranteed place in cabinet for the SDLP was out of the question. Interrupting him, Baird provided a corrective stating that 'a place in cabinet' was out 'period', and if that led the talks to a collapse then 'so be it'.[154] However, the parties all agreed that Lowry should chair the talks in an attempt to find common ground. When the convention reconvened on 3 February, Hume and Faulkner took the position that both communities must be represented in a Northern Ireland government as of right. The SDLP were prepared to consider three options: a settlement similar to that brokered by Whitelaw in November 1973; a cabinet elected by proportional representation from the assembly using the d'Hondt electoral formula; and the establishment of a voluntary coalition. Taking the same position as Hume, Faulkner warned him that they could not depend upon the Alliance Party as it was refusing to argue for a guaranteed place in cabinet for any party. And when Paisley asked Napier whether his party's opposition to the majority report meant that no agreement could be reached without the SDLP, he suggested that this might not be the case. It might be possible to devise a system, Napier said, preferably with cabinet participation, which enjoyed substantial support in both communities despite opposition from some elected representatives from one community.[155]

When the unionist parties met, West described the SDLP as a party of untrustworthy republicans who were out to destroy Northern Ireland. Faulkner's experience of power-sharing had fundamentally altered his view of the SDLP. He told his former colleagues that although they had their own aspirations, the nationalists had pledged to work for the long-term well being of Northern Ireland and he trusted them to do so.[156] West doubted whether the SDLP could ever prove their trustworthiness, and Paisley argued that any oath of allegiance to Northern Ireland its members took would be 'valueless', as it would be taken with 'mental reservations'.[157] John Taylor, who had recently been sitting on the fence over the voluntary coalition idea, came out against Craig. Dismissing an open letter the SDLP had published in the *Belfast News Letter* following its meetings with Craig, which sought to reassure unionists on the issues of law and order and Northern Ireland's future constitutional status, Taylor said, 'the new Ireland desired by the SDLP is a united Ireland and the only difference between the SDLP and the IRA is on tactics.'[158]

After a week of acrimonious talks, Rees urged the parties to consider whether a committee system might provide an outlet for minority participation. When the two sides finally agreed to meet on 12 February, the UUUC leaders told Lowry that their intention in the talks was merely to outline 'their unshakeable adherence to irreconcilable positions'.[159] In the absence of Paisley, West told the SDLP that while the UUUC was prepared to engage in negotiations, it would not discuss either the issue of an Irish dimension or the proposition that any party should have a place in government as of right. He stressed that the UUUC was entering talks under the firm understanding that they would not serve in government with the SDLP. Fitt then asked West whether the UUUC was ruling out ever serving in a cabinet with the SDLP. West responded that he could not say never, but for today and for as far as he could see, the answer was yes. Hume asked if this meant that there were no circumstances under which the UUUC would presently consider forming a cabinet with the SDLP and West concurred. The talks adjourned and, desperate to keep the SDLP at the negotiating table, Lowry implored the nationalists to call Paisley's bluff and force the UUUC to publicly justify the position taken by West. Isolated in the talks, Fitt blamed Rees for refusing to state unambiguously that anything other than power-sharing, at the highest level, would be unacceptable to parliament. Having taken West's bait, the SDLP leaders stormed out of the negotiations.[160]

Napier then made his play, handing Lowry proposals to form a two-tier cabinet, a privy council with extensive powers, and a committee system with executive chairmen. This might split Faulkner's party, Napier said, but if the UUUC were to accept these three points, then the Alliance Party would be prepared to disregard the SDLP, negotiate an agreement and put it to the electorate in a referendum.[161] Having successfully harassed the SDLP into a position where its negotiators were outside the talks and at odds with Lowry, Paisley planned to spin out the talks with Alliance and tease out exactly what Rees, who was ready to intervene if the talks collapsed, was prepared to accept. Fitt described Napier's formula as 'irrelevant and unrealistic nonsense',[162] and Faulkner warned Lowry that any deal which excluded the SDLP would be unworkable. More than that, it would make Northern Ireland ungovernable and push the nationalist party closer to the Provisional IRA, who had ended their ceasefire on 23 January.

Attempting to focus the parties on the serious consequences of failing to reach agreement, Lowry suggested that since the negotiations between the UUUC and Alliance had reached a 'dead end', the convention should be closed. The UUUC were not collectively opposed to Napier's proposals, but Paisley doubted whether he could carry the DUP with an agreement that saw him entering government with Irish nationalists of any colour. Having been warned off the idea by senior members of his Free Presbyterian Church,[163] he rejected the proposals on the grounds that Rees would not be satisfied unless the SDLP were included.

On 23 February, the last flicker of hope that a power-sharing agreement would be reached was snuffed out when Napier informed Lowry that it was pointless to continue talking; Paisley and West were determined to press for an end to direct rule on their terms.[164] Although rejecting a deal deprived Paisley of the highest office, it left him well placed to lead unionism after all notions of power-sharing had finally been quashed.

* * * *

On 2 March, the convention's final proceedings were reminiscent of the scenes of sectarian bitterness that had been a regular feature of the Northern Ireland Assembly. Lowry struggled to maintain order when Mrs Eileen Paisley, the DUP leader's wife, called Hume a 'twister, a political Jesuit twister'. More statesmanlike, Hume responded in kind, describing her husband as the greatest friend the Provisional IRA had ever made: 'He feeds them with his extremism and in turn they feed him with their extremism.'[165] Surrounded by his three remaining Vanguard supporters, Craig made an emotional appeal for the people of Northern Ireland to be given the chance to vote for or against an agreed temporary coalition government in a referendum. This was rejected by forty-two votes to eighteen.[166]

The convention ended in bedlam the following day after the UUUC passed all the original proposals from its majority report and Paisley used its winding up speech to bury Craig and bury the idea of power-sharing with Irish nationalists. Rees dissolved the convention at midnight on 5 March. Rejecting the majority report and marking the beginning of total and indefinite direct rule from Westminster, he informed parliament that the government would not be contemplating any major new initiative in Northern Ireland for the foreseeable future.[167]

In the fallout of Craig's resignation at Stormont, Paisley mentioned to Hayes that the thinly disguised power-sharing proposals should never have been pushed in the convention, as they held no hope of being successfully implemented between unionists and nationalists. When Lowry's deputy asked him why he believed this to be true, the DUP leader told him that the 'political history of Ulster was littered with the discarded leaders of unionism who had tried to do the same'.[168] And that was the end of the affair.

NOTES

1. DT2005/151/696, Speech by Enoch Powell, Killyleagh, 19 April 1975.
2. *Belfast News Letter*, 25 April 1975.
3. SDLP Constitutional Convention Election Manifesto, May 1975.
4. DT2005/151/697, Meeting between FitzGerald and Rees, London, 15 May 1975.
5. DT2005/151/697, Keating to FitzGerald, 27 May 1975.
6. DT2005/151/697, RTÉ Radio interview with O'Brien, 4 May 1975.
7. *Irish Independent*, 5 May 1975.
8. DT2005/151/697, Nally to Cosgrave, 5 May 1975.
9. *Daily Telegraph*, 6 May 1975.
10. Hansard, vol. 892, cols. 631–3, 15 May 1975.
11. CONV1/1, Chairman's meeting with the SDLP, 20 May 1975.
12. CJ4/768, Meeting between Rees and O'Sullivan, London, 21 May 1975.
13. DT2005/151/697, O'Sullivan to Donlon, 21 May 1975.
14. Rees1/7, *Northern Ireland*, p.27.
15. CJ4/768, Rees to Napier, 10 April 1975.
16. DT2005/151/705, Visit by Sir Frank Cooper, Dublin, 5 June 1974.
17. Ibid.
18. CAB134/3921, Ministerial Committee on Northern Ireland, Downing Street, 19 May 1975.
19. CAB134/3921, Ministerial Committee on Northern Ireland, Downing Street, 9 July 1975.
20. Interview with Wally Kirwan, Dublin, 7 March 2008.
21. DT2005/151/705, Interdepartmental Unit on Northern Ireland: Discussion Paper No. 5, June 1975.
22. DT2005/151/705, Comment by O'Brien, 11 June 1975.
23. CAB134/3921, Ministerial Committee on Northern Ireland, Downing Street, 19 May 1975.
24. CJ4/860, BBC interview with Arlow, 25 May 1975.
25. *The Times*, 26 May 1975.
26. *The Times*, 28 May 1975.
27. *Washington Post*, 10 May 1975.
28. CJ4/792, Walker to Allan, 12 May 1975.
29. DT2005/151/705, Northern Ireland – Assessment of Current Situation, 1 June 1975.
30. *Daily Telegraph*, 6 June 1975.
31. Rees1/7, *Northern Ireland*, pp.33–5; CJ4/860, Rees to Wilson, 4 June 1975.
32. CJ4/792, Meeting between Allan and Hume, 21 May 1975.
33. DT2005/151/705, Northern Ireland: Assessment of Current Situation, 1 June 1975.
34. *Sunday Times*, 23 June 1975.
35. Rees1/7, *Northern Ireland*, p.39.
36. CJ4/785, Meeting between Rees and the Official Unionist Party, Stormont, 28 May 1975.
37. Rees1/8, *Northern Ireland*, p.14.
38. *The Times*, 28 July 1975.
39. CONV1/1, Chairman's lunch with West, 7 July 1975.
40. CJ4/767, 'Newsday', BBC2, 3 July 1975.
41. *The Times*, 1 August 1975.
42. Hansard, vol. 896, cols. 2048–51, 31 July 1975.
43. Rees1/8, *Northern Ireland*, p.14.
44. *The Times*, 11 July 1975.
45. CONV1/1, Blackburn to Lowry, 21 July 1975.
46. DT2005/151/705, Meeting between the Irish Government and the SDLP, Dublin, 14 August 1975.
47. CONV1/1, Chairman's meeting with Craig and Beattie, 20 August 1975.
48. CONV1/1, Hayes report to Lowry, 26 August 1975.
49. DT2005/151/698, Note by FitzGerald of a discussion between himself, Callaghan, Lynch and Peter Jay, Glandore, 23 August 1975.
50. DT2005/151/698, Meeting between Mr T. Fitzpatrick and Canavan, Dublin, 25 August 1975.

51. DT2005/151/698, Donlon to Fitzpatrick, 26 August 1975.
52. *The Times*, 26 August 1975.
53. DT2005/151/698, UUUC Policy Position, 26 August, 1975.
54. CONV1/1, Chairman's meeting with Paisley, West and Craig, 27 August 1975.
55. CONV1/1, Chairman's meeting with Hume and Devlin, 27 August 1975.
56. DT2005/151/698, UUUC Policy Position, 26 August 1975.
57. CONV1/1, Meeting with UUUC negotiators, Stormont, 29 August 1975.
58. CONV1/1, Meeting with SDLP negotiators, Stormont, 29 August 1975.
59. CONV1/2, Chairman's meeting with UUUC, Stormont, 1 September 1975.
60. CONV1/2, Chairman's meeting with UUUC, Stormont, 2 September 1975.
61. CONV1/2, Chairman's meeting with Paisley, Stormont, 3 September 1975.
62. *The Times*, 4 September 1975.
63. CJ4/792, Meeting between Rees and Faulkner, Fitt and Napier, Stormont, 3 September 1975.
64. CONV1/2, Chairman's meeting with Paisley, Stormont, 3 September 1975.
65. CONV1/2, Chairman's meeting with Craig, Beattie and Ardill, Stormont, 3 September 1975.
66. CONV1/2, Statement by Ian Paisley, 4 September 1975.
67. *The Times*, 1 September 1975.
68. DT2005/151/698, Visit to Northern Ireland, Donlon, 6/7 September 1975.
69. CONV1/2, Chairman's meeting with William Beattie and Peter Robinson, Stormont, 5 September 1975.
70. DT2005/151/698, Visit to Northern Ireland, Donlon, 6/7 September 1975.
71. *Irish Times*, 11 September 1975.
72. CONV1/2, Chairman's meeting with Devlin, Hume and Currie, Stormont, 5 September 1975.
73. *The Times*, 5 August 1975.
74. Rees1/8, *Northern Ireland*, p.27.
75. CONV1/2, Chairman's meeting with Paisley, Stormont, 6 September 1975.
76. CONV1/2, Letter from Lowry to Baird, 8 September 1975.
77. CONV1/2, Chairman's meeting with Craig, Stormont, 8 September 1975.
78. CONV1/2, Letter from Lowry to Baird, 8 September 1975.
79. CONV1/2, Chairman's meeting with Baird, Stormont, 8 September 1975.
80. PREM16/520, Speech by Molyneaux to the Newtownabbey Unionist Association, 17 September 1975.
81. *Irish Times*, 10 September 1975.
82. CJ4/768, Craig to Harvey, 9 September 1975.
83. *Irish Times*, 10 September 1975.
84. Interview with Glen Barr, Londonderry, 22 August 2001.
85. DT2005/151/698, Nally to Cosgrave, 15 September 1975.
86. DT2005/151/719, Report on the Tory Conference by Dermot Gallagher, Blackpool, 7–10 October 1975.
87. PREM16/520, Note of telephone conversation with Frank Cooper, 19 September 1975.
88. ICBH oral history archive, *British Policy on Northern Ireland, 1975–82*, p.14.
89. PREM16/520, Note on a meeting between Thatcher and Wilson, Downing Street, 10 September 1975.
90. PREM16/520, Speech by Rees to the Association of Ulster Societies, Cardiff, 20 September 1975.
91. PREM16/520, Meeting between Wilson, Rees and Molyneaux, Downing Street, 24 September 1975.
92. CAB134/3921, Ministerial Committee on Northern Ireland, Downing Street, 24 September 1975.
93. CAB134/3921, Ministerial Committee on Northern Ireland, Downing Street, 24 September 1975.
94. PREM16/520, Donoughue to Wilson, 23 September 1975.
95. PREM16/521, Rees to Wilson, 3 October 1975.
96. Hansard, vol. 898, cols. 192–3, 22 October 1975.
97. *Irish Times*, 14 October 1975.

98. *Irish Times*, 30 October 1975.
99. *Irish Times*, 3 November 1975.
100. Rees1/9, *Northern Ireland*, p.14; *Sunday Telegraph*, 2 November 1975.
101. DT2005/151/719, Report on the Tory Conference by Dermot Gallagher, Blackpool, 7–10 October 1975.
102. CJ4/768, Donaldson to Rees, 6 October 1975.
103. *Irish Times*, 28 July 1975.
104. DT2005/151/719, Meeting between FitzGerald, Hume and Currie, 17 October 1975.
105. DT2005/151/719, Nally to Donlon, 23 October 1975; SDLP Proposals for Government in Northern Ireland: Report to Parliament.
106. PREM16/521, Sinn Féin, *The Moment of Truth*, Dublin, September 1975.
107. PREM16/521, Copy of 'Document 2' from Provisional Sinn Féin to the NIO; Janes to Hunt, 6 October 1975.
108. Rees1/9, *Northern Ireland*, p.14.
109. Ibid., p.10–11.
110. PREM16/521, Speech by Cosgrave, County Mayo, 1 November 1975.
111. PREM16/521, Rees to Brown, 7 November 1975.
112. *Daily Express*, 27 October 1975.
113. PREM16/521, Meeting between Wilson, Rees and Powell, House of Commons, 30 October 1975.
114. Hansard, vol. 899, cols. 233–42, 4 November 1975.
115. CONV1/2, Chairman's meeting with Napier, 6 November 1975.
116. CONV1/2, Meeting between Hayes and Devlin, 19 November 1975.
117. CJ4/785, Report of the Northern Ireland Constitutional Convention (submitted by the UUUC).
118. PREM16/521, Rees to Wilson, 30 October 1975.
119. Hansard, vol. 899, cols. 926–30, 10 November 1975.
120. DT2005/151/719, Note of meeting between Nally and Hayes, 19 November 1975.
121. *The Times*, 13 December 1975.
122. CONV1/10, Reflections on a Convention, Maurice Hayes, 14 November 1975.
123. DT2005/151/719, Discussion with the Secretary of State for Northern Ireland, 5 November 1975.
124. PREM16/958, Wright to Hunt, 10 November 1975.
125. CAB134/3921, Northern Ireland Policy IRN (75) 26, 7 November 1975.
126. CAB134/3921, Northern Ireland: Future Policy Options IRN (75) 25, 7 November 1975.
127. PREM16/958, Hunt to Wilson, 11 November 1975.
128. Rees1/9, *Northern Ireland*, p.17.
129. CONV1/2, Meeting between Hayes and Frank Cooper, 9 December 1975.
130. PREM16/958, Draft letter to Lowry from Rees, 31 December 1975.
131. DT2006/133/691, O'Sullivan to Donlon, 9 January 1976.
132. PREM16/958, Rees to Wilson, 27 November 1975.
133. Rees1/10, *Northern Ireland*, p.8.
134. CENT1/4/33, Meeting between Rees, Craig and Trimble, Stormont, 18 November 1975.
135. Rees1/10, *Northern Ireland*, pp.2–3.
136. DT2006/133/691, Note of meeting between Donlon, Nally and Fitt, 8 January 1976.
137. CONV1/2, Meeting of Convention and NIO officials, Stormont, 31 December 1975.
138. CENT1/4/33, Rees meeting with SDLP, Stormont, 18 November 1975.
139. CONV1/2, Meeting between Lowry, Paisley, West and Baird, Stormont, 29 December 1975.
140. Rees1/10, *Northern Ireland*, p.8.
141. Ibid., pp.2–3.
142. CONV1/2, Meeting between Lowry, Paisley, West and Baird, Stormont, 29 December 1975.
143. Rees5/12, Meeting between Rees and Vanguard, Stormont, 9 January 1976.
144. CONV1/2, Meeting between Lowry, Paisley, West and Baird, Stormont, 29 December 1975.
145. CONV1/2, Dr. Oliver's meeting with UUUC leaders, Stormont, 31 December 1975.
146. *The Times*, 8 January 1976.
147. *The Times*, 6 January 1976.

148. McKittrick et al., *Lost Lives*, pp.611–14.
149. Hansard, vol. 903, cols. 50–162, 12 January 1976.
150. CONV1/3, Meeting between Rees and Convention Secretariat, Stormont, 14 January 1976; *The Times*, 17 January 1976.
151. CONV1/3, Meeting between Lowry and Rees, Stormont, 22 January 1976.
152. CONV1/3, Meeting with UUUC leaders, Stormont, 19 January 1976.
153. CONV1/3, Meeting between Lowry, Napier and Glass, Stormont, 20 January 1976.
154. CONV1/3, Meeting with UUUC leaders, Stormont, 22 January 1976.
155. CONV1/3, Meeting between the UUUC and Alliance, Stormont, 4 February 1976.
156. CONV1/3, Meeting between the UUUC and UPNI, Stormont, 5 February 1976.
157. CONV1/3, Meeting between the UUUC and NILP, Stormont, 11 February 1976.
158. *The Times*, 5 February 1976.
159. CONV1/3, Meeting between the UUUC and NILP, Stormont, 11 February 1976.
160. CONV1/3, Meeting between the UUUC and SDLP, Stormont, 12 February 1976.
161. CONV1/3, Meeting between Lowry and Napier, Stormont, 16 February 1976.
162. *The Times*, 19 February 1976.
163. ICBH, *British Policy on Northern Ireland, 1975–82*, p.8.
164. The Northern Ireland Convention, Inter-Party Talks, 2–23 February 1976; *The Times*, 24 February 1976.
165. *The Times*, 3 March 1976.
166. *The Times*, 4 March 1976.
167. Hansard, vol. 906, cols. 1715–27, 5 March 1976.
168. CONV1/2, Conversation between Hayes and Paisley, Stormont, 11 September 1975.

Select Bibliography

PRIMARY SOURCES

<u>UK National Archives</u>
CAB	Cabinet Office
CJ	The Northern Ireland Office
FCO	Foreign and Commonwealth Office
PREM	Prime Minister's Office

<u>Public Record Office of Northern Ireland (PRONI)</u>
CAB	Cabinet Secretariat
CENT	Central Secretariat
CONV	Constitutional Convention
OE	Minutes of the Northern Ireland Executive
D3591	Brian Faulkner Papers
D4211	Roy Bradford Papers

<u>National Archives of Ireland</u>
DT	Department of the Taoiseach

<u>London School of Economics</u>
Rees	Merlyn Rees Papers

INTERVIEWS

Interview with Sir Robert Andrew, London, 14 November 2007
Interview with Lord Armstrong, Westminster, 24 October 2007
Interview with Sir Ken Bloomfield, Craigavad, 19 December 2007
Interview with Glen Barr, Londonderry, 22 August 2001
Interview with Lord Carrington, Knightsbridge, 21 November 2007

Interview with Sir Robin Chichester-Clark, London, 25 June 2008
Interview with Declan Costello, Dublin, 23 July 2007
Interview with Austin Currie, Dublin, 5 January 2001
Interview with Scán Donlon, Limerick, 25 September 2007
Interview with Lord Donoughue, Westminster, 27 February 2007
Interview with Noel Dorr, Dublin, 12 July 2007
Interview with Garret FitzGerald, Dublin, 12 September 2001
Interview with Joe Haines, Tunbridge Wells, 19 February 2008
Interview with Mahon Hayes, Dublin, 24 July 2007
Interview with Lord Heath, London, 4 April 2001
Interview with Lord Howell, Westminster, 17 October 2007
Interview with John Hume, Londonderry, 13 September 2001
Interview with Lord Kilclooney, Westminster, 15 February 2001
Interview with Wally Kirwan, Dublin, 7 March 2008
Interview with Muiris Mac Conghail, Dublin, 24 July 2007
Interview with John McColgan, Dublin, 9 August 2007
Interview with Keith McDowall, London, 8 January 2008
Interview with Basil McIvor, Spa, 24 August 2001
Interview with Lord McNally, Westminster, 9 June 2008
Interview with Stratton Mills, Belfast, 21 December 2007
Interview with Lord Molyneaux, Westminster, 30 January 2001
Interview with Leslie Morrell, Belfast, 4 January 2001
Interview with Dermot Nally, Dublin, 7 March 2001 and 10 May 2008
Interview with Michael Oatley, London, 13 November 2007
Interview with Sir Oliver Napier, Holywood, 29 December 2000
Interview with Robert Ramsey, Cultra, 6 March 2008
Interview with David Smyth, London, 18 February 2008
Interview with Kelvin White, Didcot, 13 August 2008

SECONDARY SOURCES

Arthur, Paul, *Special Relationships: Britain, Ireland and the Northern Ireland Problem* (Belfast: Blackstaff Press, 2000)
Bew, Paul, *Ireland: The Politics of Enmity 1789–2006* (Oxford: Oxford University Press, 2007)
Bew, Paul and Patterson, Henry, *The British State and the Ulster Crisis: From Wilson to Thatcher* (London: Verso Books, 1985)
Bloomfield, Kenneth, *A Tragedy of Errors: The Government and*

Misgovernment of Northern Ireland (Liverpool: Liverpool University Press, 2007)

Buckland, Patrick, *A History of Northern Ireland* (Dublin: Gill & Macmillan, 1981)

English, Richard, *Armed Struggle: The History of the IRA* (London, Macmillan, 2003)

Fisk, Robert, *The Point of No Return: The Strike that Broke the British in Ulster* (London: Andre Deutsch, 1975)

Hennessey, Thomas, *The Evolution of the Troubles, 1970–72* (Dublin: Irish Academic Press, 2007)

Kerr, Michael, *Imposing Power-Sharing: Conflict and Coexistence in Northern Ireland and Lebanon* (Dublin: Irish Academic Press, 2006)

McGarry, John and O'Leary, Brendan, *Explaining Northern Ireland: Broken Images* (Oxford: Blackwell, 1995)

McGarry, John and O'Leary, Brendan, *The Politics of Antagonism: Understanding Northern Ireland* (London: Athlone Press, 1996)

Murphy, Dervla, *A Place Apart* (Reading: Penguin, 1978)

Patterson, Henry, *Ireland since 1939: The Persistence of Conflict* (Dublin: Penguin, 2006)

Patterson, Henry and Kaufmann, Eric, *Unionism and Orangeism in Northern Ireland since 1945: The Decline of the Loyal Family* (Manchester: Manchester University Press, 2007)

Prince, Simon, *Northern Ireland's '68: Civil Rights, Global Revolt and the Origins of the Troubles* (Dublin: Irish Academic Press, 2007)

Rose, Richard, *Governing Without Consensus* (London: Faber & Faber, 1971)

Ruane, Joseph and Todd, Jennifer, *The Dynamics of Conflict in Northern Ireland: Power, Conflict and Emancipation* (Cambridge: Cambridge University Press, 1996)

Walker, Graham, *A History of the Ulster Unionist Party: Protest, Pragmatism and Pessimism* (Manchester: Manchester University Press, 2004)

Whyte, John, *Interpreting Northern Ireland* (Oxford: Clarendon, 1990)

Index

Adams, Gerry, 36, 37, 38
Aldergrove airport, 227, 228
Algeria, 270
Allan, James, 270
Alliance Party, xv, 14, 36, 64, 66, 68, 70, 73, 185, 188
Assembly members, 75, 76, 83
   Convention and, 290, 293, 301, 317, 323, 324, 325, 326
   Darlington talks (September 1972), 48, 51
   electoral performance, 74, 75, 156, 290
   serves on Northern Ireland Executive, 96, 97, 98, 99, 100, 102, 105, 171, 185
   Stormont Castle negotiations (October-November 1973), 86, 92, 93, 102, 103, 107, 108, 109
   at Sunningdale, 117, 127, 133, 134
Amin, Idi, 243
Andrews, Jack, 29
Anglo-Irish Council proposal, 56–7, 70
Anglo-Irish Free Trade Agreement (1965), 34
Ardill, Captain Austin, 12, 299, 305, 309
Arlow, Rev. William, 277, 296–7, 298
Armstrong, Robert, 157, 239
Attlee, Clement, 257

Bailie, Robin, 64, 73
Baird, Ernest, 12, 275, 305, 308, 310, 322, 323
Balcombe Street siege (December 1975), 320
Ballylumford power station, 174, 187, 207, 208, 209, 212, 215, 230–1, 242, 243, 244
Barr, Glen, xiv, 209, 219, 242, 243–4, 256, 266, 267, 275, 296
Baxter, John, 116, 127
BBC Northern Ireland, 182, 229–30
Beattie, William, 299, 301, 305, 311
Belgium, 54, 269, 321
Bell, Ivor, 38
Birmingham pub bombings (November 1974), 271–2, 275
Blaney, Neil, 145, 155, 299
Bloody Friday (21 July 1972), 41
Bloody Sunday (30 January 1972), 20, 23, 25, 28, 30, 31, 32
Bloomfield, Ken, 51, 113–14, 126, 134, 278
   as permanent secretary to executive, 6, 117, 143–4, 146, 150, 165, 175, 176, 179–80, 246
Boal, Desmond, 27, 177, 275, 281
Boland, Kevin, 147–8, 149–50, 151, 153, 158, 159
Bradford, Roy, 29, 152, 159, 160, 186, 188, 258, 266
   ambition to lead moderate unionism, 32, 86, 183–4, 188
   anti-Sunningdale motion and, 177, 197
   blacklisted as UUUC candidate, 268
   calls for Executive with broader base, 145–6, 158, 164–5
   cross border security issues and, 148, 153, 172–3, 184
   loses seat in February 1974 election, 158
   nationalist ministers and, 184, 190
   offers to resign from Executive, 219
   Stormont Castle negotiations, 89, 91, 94, 102–3, 107
   at Sunningdale, 115, 116, 122, 127, 133–4, 136
   UWC strike and, 204–5, 211, 212, 214–15, 219, 226, 237, 238, 244
   welcomes direct rule, 24, 32
British Army
   arrival in Northern Ireland (August 1969), 1
   direct rule and, 4, 31, 34
   incursions into Republic, 260
   internment and, 21, 29, 182, 270
   IRA ceasefire (June 1972) and, 37, 38
   Operation Motorman (July 1972), 41–2, 45, 47
   post-Executive role of, 255, 265
   Protestant paramilitaries and, 38, 53–4, 227
   reinforcements, 39, 41, 217, 224, 234, 283, 322
   strike (7 February 1973) and, 65–6
   tension with Rees, 284, 285, 291, 312
   troop reductions under Wilson, 172, 177, 192, 210, 253, 255, 257, 260, 262, 294, 295
   UWC strike
      avoidance of confrontation, xiv, 206, 213, 216, 217, 227
      clearing of barricades, 205, 215, 217–18, 252
      oil supply/distribution, 224–5, 230, 231, 241–3, 252, 253
      power stations issue, 203, 205–7, 208, 209–11, 212, 215, 217, 224–5, 228, 230–5, 236, 240
      response to criticism over, 213
   Whitelaw's security policies and, 34–5, 36
British government, xiv, xv, xvii, xviii, xix
   Government of Ireland Act (1920), 2, 3, 23, 51
   internment and, 1, 20–1, 22, 29–30, 32, 34, 35, 161, 195–6
   Ireland Act (1949), 30, 155
   Irish government's dependence on, 9–10, 265
   late 1960s views on partition, 2–3

see also Conservative government (1970-4); Labour government (1974-9)
Brookeborough, Lord, 184
Browning, Robert (MI6 officer), 298

Cabinet Office, 239, 319
Cahill, Joe, 27, 35
Callaghan, Jim, 76, 271, 302, 312
Canada, 54, 257
Canavan, Ivor, 127
Canavan, Michael, 127, 300, 302–3
Carr, Robert, 56
Carrington, Peter, 20, 22, 27–8, 131, 252
Catholic community in Ireland, 2, 28
Catholic community in Northern Ireland
  attitude to RUC, 92, 306
  Belfast anti-violence petition (May 1972), 35
  Constitutional Convention and, 6, 14, 259, 275, 291, 306, 323
  Coolkeeragh power station and, 215, 230
  direct rule and, 3, 4
  doomsday scenario and, 263, 265, 295, 297, 300, 303
  Executive and, 68, 98–9, 175
  Heath and, 4, 28, 30
  internment and, 21, 30
  IRA's standing in, 35, 36, 278, 280, 313, 314, 320
  Northern Ireland civil service and, 90
  Paisley and, 6, 306
  political leadership of, 68
  Protestant paramilitary violence against, 40, 53, 54, 237, 312, 322
  Rees and, 14, 265, 280, 283, 291, 299
  UWC strike and, 215, 230, 233, 237
  Whitelaw's political strategy, 32, 34–5, 36, 39, 59, 68
  see also nationalist community; Social Democratic and Labour Party (SDLP)
Channon, Paul, 38
Chichester-Clark, James, 1, 254
Chichester-Clark, Robin, 64, 74
Claudy car bombings (July 1972), 45
Confederation of British Industry (CBI), 218, 232
Conservative government (1970-4)
  bilateral treaties with Ireland issue, 129–31
  change in security policy (July 1972), 39
  dispute with British trade unions (1973-4), 85, 100, 114
  divisions over direct rule, 26, 27–8
  emergency contingency plans, 22, 46
  The Future of Northern Ireland (October 1972), 54
  mainland domestic politics and, 7, 8, 85, 89, 100, 114
  Operation Folklore and, 45, 61
  reaction to Lynch's electoral defeat, 69
  secret talks with IRA and, 36–7, 38–9
  secret troop reduction plans (late 1973), 106
  united Ireland issue and, 87, 129–30
  White Paper (March 1973), 51, 54–5, 59, 60, 63–4, 67, 70–1, 110
  see also Heath, Edward; Whitelaw, William
Conservative Party in Opposition (1974-9), 261, 283, 292, 315, 320–1
  bipartisanship and, 252, 254, 259, 261, 315
Constitution Act (1973), 101, 121, 245, 252, 253, 254, 263, 292, 319

Northern Ireland executive proposals and, 72, 83, 86, 96, 97, 99, 100, 108, 109
Official Unionist Party and, 86, 89
passage through parliament, 73–4, 76–7
SDLP and, 76, 81, 86, 89, 135
Wilson's abandonment of, 14, 267
Constitutional Convention (8 May 1975–5 March 1976), 257–8, 290–4, 300–11, 315, 317–20, 322–6
  Arlow allegations and, 297, 298
  British expectations of, 313–14
  collapse of, xvi, 6, 325–6
  elections (1 May 1975), 289–90
  'institutionalised Irish dimension' and, 273–4, 304, 308
  majority report, 317, 318, 319, 322, 326
  minority report, 293, 315–16, 318
  Paisley and, 6, 271, 290, 293, 300, 301, 304–11, 318, 321–2, 323, 324, 325–6
  power-sharing issue at, 6, 290, 291–2, 300, 301–2, 304–6, 307–8, 309–10, 317, 325–6
  sectarian violence during, 294, 299, 306, 309, 316, 318
  UUUC/SDLP meetings at, 299, 300–1
  voluntary coalition proposal, 304–6, 307–8, 309–10, 317, 321, 323, 324, 326
  see also Rees, Merlyn; Social Democratic and Labour Party (SDLP)
Coolkeeragh power station, 207, 208, 209, 215, 227, 230, 242
Cooney, Paddy, 116, 127, 133, 145, 149, 268
Cooper, Frank, 114, 156, 160–1, 170, 187, 194, 270, 271, 276, 312
  Irish government and, 256, 257, 294
  negotiations with IRA and, 277, 280, 282, 283, 285
  Rees and, 156, 205, 206, 213, 241, 280, 300, 312, 316
  at Sunningdale, 116, 127, 130, 134, 136, 138
  UWC strike and, 205, 206–7, 211, 213, 241, 252
Cooper, Ivan, 100, 103, 116, 131, 239–40, 242
Cooper, Robert, 102, 108, 117, 127, 133, 185, 189
Corish, Brendan, 116
Cosgrave, Liam
  becomes taoiseach (March 1973), 68–9
  collapse of Executive and, 246, 251
  Constitutional Convention and, 274, 289, 311, 318
  constitutional status issue and, 88, 122, 128, 130, 149–50, 151, 153, 154, 155, 158, 164–5, 169–70
  Council of Ireland proposals and, 9, 70, 81, 83–4, 148, 155, 187–8, 223
  Faulkner and, 147–8, 149–50, 151, 154, 159–60, 165, 187, 190, 214
  Heath and, 70–1, 83–5, 88, 148
  IRA and, 147, 282–3, 316
  Irish constitution and, 88, 128, 147–8, 150, 289
  Lynch and, 154–5
  meeting with Devlin and Cooper (26 May 1974), 239–40
  potential impact of British withdrawal, 256
  at Sunningdale, 115, 116, 118, 122, 137, 144, 145
  on UWC strike, 227
  welcomes power-sharing agreement, 110
  Wilson government and, 177–9, 282–3, 318
Costello, Declan, 116, 131–2

Council of Europe, 95, 98
Council of Ireland proposals
 all-Ireland assembly issue, 87–8, 91, 93, 98, 100, 120, 121
 Anglo-Irish talks (1973), 62–3, 86–9
 civil service view of, 152–3
 common law enforcement area issue, 24, 97, 103, 106, 119, 123–4, 126, 127, 131, 144
 extradition issues *see* extradition issues
 general election (28 February 1974) and, 165
 Labour government and, 170
 Lynch and, 9, 55–6, 57, 67
 ministerial executive body, 87, 119–20, 126, 176, 194
 Northern Ireland Executive and, 151–4, 158, 159, 187–92, 213, 214, 216, 217, 219–21, 246
 Northern Ireland executive proposals and, 83–4, 85–6, 88, 120
 permanent secretariat issue, 93, 102, 120, 121, 174, 189, 190, 191, 195
 planned tripartite conference and, 70, 83, 84, 88–9, 93–4, 97, 102, 103–4, 105–7
 see also Sunningdale Communiqué; Sunningdale conference
 'pledged' unionists and, 90–1
 policing issues and, 81, 82–3, 90–1, 119, 124, 127, 132, 134, 135, 138, 177
 potential functions of, 60, 87–8, 92–3, 126–7, 151–2, 153, 194
 preliminary consultations in England, 98, 103–4, 105–6, 107, 109
 public opinion on (April 1974), 163
 recognition issue, 58, 62, 88–9, 94, 118–19, 122, 127–31, 150, 153–4, 158, 162
 referendum approval and, 190–1
 scope to evolve with unionist confidence, 62, 67, 87–8, 109, 176, 185
 Stormont Castle negotiations and, 92–3
 Sunningdale and, 8, 118–21, 122–4, 125, 126–31, 132–5, 136–7, 149, 176
 unionist opposition to in Assembly, 170–1
 UWC strike and, 213
 as wedge issue for opponents of Whitelaw's reforms, 91, 93–4
Craig, William
 Belgian style coalition suggestion, 321
 Constitutional Convention and, 290, 291, 299, 300, 301, 304–6, 307–11, 313, 318, 323, 324, 326
 Council of Ireland proposals and, 98, 103–4, 105, 107, 109
 exclusion from Sunningdale, 113, 114, 116
 Executive and, 146–7, 251–2
 Faulkner and, 35, 52–3, 60, 66, 69, 72, 323
 FitzGerald calls for arrest of, 214
 independent Ulster and, 32, 52–3, 59, 66, 73, 76–7, 85, 254, 275, 296
 militancy of, 31, 52–3, 66, 71, 76–7, 85
 Paisley and, 73, 94, 156, 254, 271, 290, 310–11
 Rees' views on, 157, 321
 resigns Vanguard leadership, 310
 strike (7 February 1973) and, 65, 69
 support for self-determination, 268
 talks with SDLP, 69, 290, 299, 300, 324
 two-day strike (27 March 1972) and, 31, 33
 UDA and, 66, 309

Ulster Vanguard group, 12, 24, 32
 unconstitutional methods and, 100, 101, 193, 236
 UWC splits with, 266, 309
 UWC strike and, 203–5, 209, 210, 212, 219, 227, 232, 236, 242, 243, 254, 260
 Vanguard Unionist Progressive Party, 72, 73, 156
 voluntary coalition proposal, 14, 290, 304–6, 307–10, 318, 321, 323, 324, 326
 Whitelaw and, 64, 65, 76–7, 85, 108, 109
 Whitelaw's proposals and, 71, 73, 76–7, 83, 85, 98, 102, 103–4, 107, 110
 Wilson government and, 203–5, 209, 212, 255, 259
Currie, Austin, 10, 49, 76, 86, 91, 92, 94, 256, 315
 Constitutional Convention and, 297, 301
 serves on Northern Ireland Executive, 148, 184, 185, 212, 258
 at Sunningdale, 115, 116, 124, 127, 132, 133, 134–5, 136–7
Czechoslovakia, xix

Daly, Bishop Edward, 182, 261
Darlington talks (September 1972), 48, 50, 51–2
Democratic Unionist Party (DUP), 14, 66, 72, 73, 75, 94, 121, 156, 275
 Constitutional Convention and, 6, 289, 290, 307–8, 311
 see also Paisley, Rev. Ian
Detention of Terrorists Order (1972), 57
Devlin, Paddy, 10, 36, 240, 256, 260, 262, 263, 275
 attempted ambush of, 242
 Constitutional Convention and, 292, 301, 317
 meeting with Cosgrave (26 May 1974), 239–40
 serves on Northern Ireland Executive, 148, 152, 153, 161, 162, 177, 184, 189, 195, 208–9, 258
 Stormont Castle negotiations, 89, 90, 94–5, 98–9
 at Sunningdale, 116, 125, 126–7, 133, 136, 137
Dickson, Anne, 100
Diplock Commission report (December 1972), 57
direct rule (March 1973-December 1973), xiv, xv, xvi, xvii, xviii
 administrative transition to, 33–4
 continuation of (1973), 61–2
 first phase of, 32–42, 45–50
 as Heath's decision, 4, 6–7, 8, 12, 19, 20, 21, 27, 30–1
 lead up to, 3–4, 5, 19, 21–2, 23–5, 26–9
 resignation of Northern Ireland government (23 March 1972), 30, 31
 unionist reaction to imposition of, 11–12, 31–2, 33, 35–6
 upsurge of IRA violence during first phase, 32, 34, 35, 41, 45
 Whitehall machine's view of, 3–4, 20, 61–2
Donaldson, Lord Jack, 156
Donlon, Seán, 81–2, 154, 162, 163, 165, 171, 180, 190, 195, 273
 Stormont Castle talks and, 86, 90, 91, 105
 at Sunningdale, 127
 on UWC strike, 216–17
Donoughue, Bernard, 157, 239, 252, 253, 269, 314
Douglas-Home, Alec, 20, 22, 27–8, 116
Drumm, Jimmy, 281
Dublin and Monaghan car bombings, 209, 239, 264
Dublin bombings by UVF (December 1972), 56
Duddy, Brendan, 277, 320

electoral politics
   district council elections (May 1973), 74
   Assembly elections (28 June 1973), 74–5
   Irish general election (February 1973), 66, 68, 69
   proportional representation and, 21, 35, 67, 74, 132
   UK general election (28 February 1974), 13, 155, 156, 157, 158, 159, 160, 164, 165, 201, 252
   UK general election (10 October 1974), 267–8
electricity supply
   one-day strike (7 February 1973), 65
   security issues, 60, 174, 187
   two-day strike (27 March 1972), 31
   UWC strike and, xiv, 196, 202–10, 212, 215, 216, 225, 230–2, 234, 242, 243, 244
Empey, Reg, 308
European Court of Human Rights (Strasbourg), 33, 70, 83, 170, 260
European Economic Community (EEC), 8, 25, 28, 33, 34, 88, 103, 285
extradition issues, 26, 57, 73, 103, 153, 159, 162, 165, 170, 174, 184, 259
   Law Commission, 132, 151, 153, 154, 159, 160, 179, 186, 189, 190, 191, 192–3, 194
   Sunningdale and, 118, 119, 122, 123–4, 131–2, 147, 148

farming and agriculture, 214, 218, 224, 229, 243, 244
Faulkner, Brian
   Constitutional Convention and, 14, 290, 306, 323–4, 325
   constitutional status issue and, 122, 128–9, 130–1, 149–51, 153–4, 158, 160, 161, 165, 169–70
   Cosgrave and, 147–8, 149–50, 151, 154, 159–60, 165, 187, 190, 214
   Council of Ireland proposals, 85–6, 87, 93, 98, 100, 104, 125, 126, 182, 194–5, 213
      all-Ireland consultative assembly issue, 87, 98, 100
      Anglo-Irish context, 95
      attempts to dilute, 174–5, 176, 178, 179, 180, 185
      evolving powers issue, 109
      need for renegotiation, 169, 171
      phased implementation proposals, 180–1, 182, 185, 187–92, 194, 196, 197, 201, 216, 217, 219–21, 223–4
      policing issues, 90–1, 124, 134, 138
      recognition issue, 58, 94, 118–19, 122, 128–9, 131, 144, 150, 153–4, 158, 162
      secretariat issue, 102, 121, 174
      at Sunningdale, 118–19, 120, 121
   Craig and, 35, 52–3, 60, 66, 69, 72, 323
   Darlington talks (September 1972), 51
   Fitt and, 148–9, 180, 182, 184, 258
   general election (28 February 1974) and, 156
   Heath and, 1, 8, 11, 23–4, 26, 27, 53, 55, 64
      Downing Street meetings (February-March 1972), 19, 22, 25, 28–31
      at Sunningdale, 8, 11, 129, 134, 135, 136, 137, 138
   internment and, 1–2, 20–1, 29–30, 48, 162
   Irish government and, 24, 25–6, 91, 119, 121–2, 158–9, 160–1, 176, 179–80, 214
   lead up to direct rule and, 19, 22, 23–5, 26, 27, 28–9
   Lebanon model and, 5
   moves to moderate ground, 69, 72
   Northern Ireland Executive
      becomes head of, 143
      composition of, 96–7, 98–100, 102–3
      first meeting, 145–6
      lack of majority in Assembly, 96–7, 98–100, 258
      praises 'spirit' of, 246
      resignation as chief executive (28 May 1974), 201, 244–5, 246
   October 1974 election and, 267, 275
   on Paddy Wilson's murder, 75
   presents 'new look' power-sharing agreement, 223–4
   ratification issues and, 148, 149, 153, 160–2, 165, 170, 174–6, 180, 181–2, 187–94, 213, 219–21
   referendum proposals and, 24, 25–6, 60, 194–5
   reform proposals (pre-direct rule), 25–6, 28, 29
   resignation as prime minister (23 March 1972), 30, 31
   SDLP and, 76, 85–6, 89–90, 104, 185, 324
   secret discussions at Laneside, 36
   Stormont Castle negotiations (October-November 1973), 89–90, 92, 93, 94, 95, 96–7, 98–100, 102–3, 104–5, 107–9
   Sunningdale, 8, 11, 115, 116, 118–22, 124–6, 128, 130–1, 133–8, 146
      defence of Communiqué, 170
      renegotiation of Communiqué, 13, 148, 169, 185, 187–92, 193–4, 197, 201–2, 219–21, 223–4
   unionism
      address to UUC (20 November 1973), 98, 104
      defeat on UCC over Sunningdale, 146, 147, 149
      forms party from pro-assembly group, 187
      launches Unionist Party of Northern Ireland (September 1974), 265–6
      maintains leadership of Unionist Party (March 1973), 71–2
      opponents of in Unionist Party, 11–12, 73, 75, 90, 94, 183
      as outsider in Unionist Party, 143
      poor relationship with Unionist MPs, 74
      relationship with pro-assembly unionists, 158, 183–4, 197
      resignation as Unionist Party leader (January 1974), 146
      security pact with unionist leaders (February 1973), 66
      Vanguard rally (28 March 1972), 32
   unpopularity of (1973), 64, 76
   UWC strike and, xv, 183–4, 203, 208–9, 210, 213, 219–20, 225, 237–40
      admits need for talks with UWC, 201, 243, 244 245
   Whitelaw and, 8, 11, 51, 58, 59, 62, 64, 68, 69, 71–4, 76, 105
   Wilson government and, 160, 170, 172, 173, 174–5, 180, 220, 225–6, 244–5
      Chequers meeting (24 May 1974), 228–9, 230–1, 232, 233, 234, 236, 262
      Rees, 14, 180, 187, 220, 225–6, 236, 244–5, 262
   Wilson's televised address (25 May 1974) and, 239
Fianna Fáil (1973-7 period), 82, 125, 164, 180–1, 194, 289

calls for British intent to withdraw, 283, 315
reaction to Sunningdale, 144–5, 149, 151, 154–5, 223
see also Lynch, Jack
Fianna Fáil government (1969-73), 2–3, 8–9, 22–3, 25, 33, 34, 56–7, 62–3
   Faulkner and, 24, 25–6
   SDLP and, 23, 26–7, 63
   see also Lynch, Jack
Fine Gael, 56, 180–1
Fine Gael-Labour coalition (1973-7)
   bilateral treaties with UK issue, 129–31
   Boland court case and, 147–8, 149–50, 151, 153, 158, 159
   comes to power (March 1973), 68
   Constitutional Convention and, 268, 291–2, 311
   contingency plans for intervention in North, 295, 311
   Council of Ireland proposals and, 86–9, 94, 120, 123–9, 135–8, 144, 152–3, 171, 175, 176, 179–81, 191, 196
      Cosgrave and, 9, 70, 81, 83–4, 148, 155, 187–8, 223
      FitzGerald and, 9, 91, 92, 97, 103–4, 105–6, 172, 178, 190, 194, 214
      O'Brien and, 9, 136, 138, 172, 181, 213–14, 256, 263, 264, 273–4, 292
   cross border security and, 147, 148, 151, 153, 159 160, 161, 163, 170–4, 177–9, 182, 194
   crackdown on IRA, 280, 299–300, 314
   intergovernmental security conference (1974), 178, 181, 194
   DFA's roving brief post-Executive, 263
   doomsday scenario and, 253, 263, 264–5, 302–3
   Faulkner and, 91, 119, 121–2, 158–9, 160–1, 176, 179–80, 214
   fissures within (from September 1974), 267, 272–3
   Irish dimension post-Executive and, 263–4, 273–4, 292
   Northern Ireland Executive and, 83–4, 153, 158–9, 163, 214, 264
   opposes ending of internment (November 1974), 270–1
   reaction to IRA 'indefinite truce' (February 1975), 284
   republican hunger strikes in Portlaoise jail, 282
   SDLP and, 76, 88, 94–5, 104, 239, 262–4
      Constitutional Convention, 291–2, 302–3, 311–12, 315–16
      Donlon's role, 81–2, 105
      Dublin's distancing, 15, 289, 292, 311–12, 315–16
      Hume's influence, 81–3, 85, 162–3, 164, 238, 264
      military support issues, 15, 262, 263, 265, 273, 303, 311, 315
      Northern Ireland Executive, 149, 153, 161, 190, 195
      O'Brien on, 82, 264, 273, 292
      at Sunningdale, 119, 124, 126–7, 134–5, 137
   Sunningdale, 11, 118, 119, 121–2, 123–5, 126, 127 128–32, 133, 134–5, 136–7, 138, 144–5
      disclosures to press at, 124–5, 126
      Faulkner's phased implementation and, 187–8, 190, 191, 192, 194, 196, 201, 223

ratification issues and, 145, 148, 154, 160–1, 165, 170, 172, 174–6, 177–80, 185–7, 194, 213–14
talks with Craig, 290
UWC strike and, 213–14, 227
views on partition/Irish unity, 9, 82
Whitelaw's White Paper and, 71
Wilson government and, 170, 171–2, 186–7, 190, 193–4, 253, 256, 257, 259–60, 261, 267
   reaction to British government-IRA talks, 278, 280
   Rees, 14, 268
   Rees' White Paper, 259, 263
   views on potential British withdrawal, 10, 171–2, 187, 253, 256–7, 264–5, 271, 272, 295, 311–12, 315
Fisk, Robert, 262
Fitt, Gerry, xv, 10, 47, 76, 90, 94, 195, 260, 265
   Chequers meeting with Wilson (24 May 1974), 228, 229–31, 233, 236, 262
   Constitutional Convention and, 297, 301, 306, 325
   Council of Ireland proposals and, 102, 153, 180
   Executive proposals and, 84, 85, 98, 100, 101, 102, 103, 104, 107, 108
   Faulkner and, 148–9, 180, 182, 184, 258
   ratification issues and, 181, 182, 188, 220–1
   retains Westminster seat in 1974 elections, 156, 267
   RUC issue and, 81, 85
   serves on Executive, 146, 148–9, 162, 171, 184–5, 220–1, 240, 244, 258
   at Sunningdale, 116, 119, 132, 136, 137
   Wilson government and, 263, 266–7, 284, 297
FitzGerald, Garret
   common law enforcement area issue and, 97, 106, 144
   Constitutional Convention and, 291–2, 293, 302
   Council of Ireland proposals and, 9, 91, 92, 97, 103–4, 105–6, 172, 178, 190, 194, 214
   criticises BBC Northern Ireland, 230
   cross border security and, 178
   doomsday scenario and, 302
   extradition issues and, 159
   Irish constitution and, 88, 122, 123, 128, 144, 155, 161, 256
   Irish dimension post-Executive and, 263, 264, 274, 291
   Northern Ireland's constitutional status issue, 128–9, 130–1, 150, 155, 161
   O'Brien and, 68, 82, 172, 214, 263, 272–3, 274, 295
   potential British withdrawal and, 271, 295, 312
   Rees and, 160, 162, 193–4, 273, 278, 291–2, 293, 316
   at Sunningdale, 115, 116, 117, 120, 121, 123, 126–7, 133, 134, 137, 138, 144, 194
   Sunningdale chairman issue, 89, 105, 117
   Sunningdale ratification and, 154
   UN trusteeship suggestion, 272–3
   USA and, 183, 256
   visit to Northern Ireland (October 1973), 91, 92, 94–5
   Whitelaw's draft agreement and, 103, 104
   on Wilson's troop reductions, 257
Flanagan, Jamie, 182, 213
Forkhill bomb attacks, 299
Fox, Senator Billy, 165
Free Presbyterian Church, 6, 325

Galsworthy, Arthur, 84, 85
Gardiner Committee report, 279, 283
Gibson, Ken, 204
Glass, Basil, 102, 126
Government of Ireland Act (1920), 2, 3, 23, 51
Greene, Graham, xiii–xiv

Haines, Joe, 82, 157, 233, 239
Hall-Thompson, Lloyd, 117
Harland and Wolff shipyard, Belfast, 203, 224, 255–6
Haughey, Charles, 149, 283
Hayes, Maurice, 143–4, 152–3, 292, 302, 303–4, 307, 317, 318, 326
Heath, Edward, xv, xvii, xviii
  Assembly election results and, 75
  blames Wilson for collapse of Executive, 245, 252
  Bloody Sunday and, 20, 28, 30
  cabinet reshuffle (November 1973), 113–14
  Constitutional Convention and, 259
  Cosgrave and, 70–1, 83–5, 88, 148
  Council of Ireland proposals and, 60, 67, 70, 83–4 107, 120–1, 124, 129
  devolution policy, 3–4, 7–8
  direct rule decision, 4, 6–7, 8, 12, 19, 20, 21, 27, 30–1
  failure to devolve security powers, 12–13, 59, 84, 87, 127, 133–4, 179, 245
  Faulkner and *see* Faulkner, Brian: Heath and
  general election (February 1974), 13, 155, 156, 160
  integration option, 50, 59, 70, 83, 85, 96
  internment and, 20–1, 22, 29–30
  lead up to direct rule and, 5, 19, 21–2, 23–4, 25, 26, 27–9
  loses Conservative leadership (February 1975), 283
  Lynch and, 33, 45–6, 48, 55–6, 67
  mainland domestic politics and, 7, 8, 100, 101, 113–14, 114
  meeting with Paisley/Kilfedder (November 1973), 95–6
  meetings with Faulkner (February-March 1972), 19, 22, 25, 28–30
  political style of, 4, 6–7, 50
  SDLP and, 48, 132–3, 263
  secret talks with IRA and, 36
  Sunningdale conference and, 8, 114–15, 117–21, 124, 125, 129, 131–7
  technocratic view of the troubles, 7
  united Ireland issue and, 129, 130
  UWC strike and, 216
  Whitelaw's proposals and, 63–4, 67
Herrema, Tiede, 316
Holden, David, 117
Holland, 269
Howell, David, 116
human rights issues, 131–2, 133, 176, 189
  Strasbourg legal case, 33, 70, 83, 170, 260
Hume, John
  analysis of Faulkner's position/motives, 162–3, 169–70, 171, 177
  on Bradford, 214–15
  collapse of Executive and, xv, 245
  Constitutional Convention and, 265, 275, 297, 299 –301, 304, 305, 307, 308, 321, 323–4, 325, 326
  Council of Ireland proposals and, 9, 85–6, 91, 94, 124, 153, 159, 162, 176, 185, 194–5, 240

criticises Wilson's disengagement policies, 261–2
internment and, 92, 184, 278
IRA and, 36, 177
Irish government and, 45, 81–3, 162–3, 164, 238, 264
Irish unity and, 10, 45–6, 52
Lynch and, 45, 315
Northern Ireland executive proposals and, 84, 85–6, 94–5, 99, 101, 103, 106–7, 110
oil supply/distribution and, 206, 221, 224, 237, 238, 241–2
power stations and, 210, 215–16
RUC issue and, 81, 85, 132, 133, 135
serves on Northern Ireland Executive, 152, 153, 158–9, 195, 196, 221, 224, 258
refusal to resign (28 May 1974), 244, 245
at Sunningdale, 116, 125, 126, 128, 132, 133, 134–5, 136, 137
Sunningdale ratification and, 153, 154, 188
unpopularity of with unionists, 76
warning to Irish America, 183
Hunt, John, 239, 271, 272, 319
Hunt, Sir Peter, 227
Hutton, Brian, 186

intelligence services, 32, 49, 182–3, 294, 298, 312
  contact with IRA, 269–70, 277, 281
  Laneside cottage (Cultra), 5, 36, 46–7, 50, 62, 278, 281
  Protestant paramilitaries and, 40, 183, 278
  UWC strike and, 227–8, 233, 240, 242, 243
internment
  British government and, 1, 20–1, 22, 29–30, 32, 34, 35, 161, 195–6
  ending of, 321
  Faulkner and, 1–2, 20–1, 29–30, 48, 162
  Heath and, 20–1, 22, 29–30
  introduction of, 1–2, 20–1
  IRA ceasefire (from Christmas 1974) and, 276, 277, 279, 281, 284, 285
  Rees and, 284, 285, 291, 294, 299, 312, 314, 321
  re-interning of released prisoners, 173–4
  SDLP and *see* Social Democratic and Labour Party (SDLP): interment
  Sunningdale conference and, 133
  Whitelaw and, 32, 34, 35, 47, 106
  Whitelaw's special tribunals, 41, 47–8, 49
  Wilson and, 27
  Wilson government and, 192, 270–1, 276, 277, 279, 284, 285, 291, 294–5
Ireland Act (1949), 30, 155
Irish constitution, Articles 2 and 3 of, 10, 89, 94, 151, 185, 266, 306
  Boland court case and, 147–8, 149–50, 151, 153, 158, 159
  Cosgrave and, 88, 128, 147–8, 150, 289
  FitzGerald and, 88, 122, 123, 128, 144, 155, 161, 256
  Lynch and, 33, 145, 155
  as obligation to pursue unity, 3, 8–9, 82
  O'Brien and, 122, 213–14
  referendum possibility, 69, 88, 122, 150
  Sunningdale and, 118, 119, 121–2, 123, 128, 129–30, 144, 145
Irish Free State, 2

Irish government
  constitutional commitment to reunification *see* Irish constitution, Articles 2 and 3 of
  Department of Foreign Affairs (DFA), 34, 63, 82, 128, 149, 163, 263
  dependence on British government, 9–10, 265
  distrust of Wilson, 157
  doomsday scenario and, 15, 253, 263, 264–5, 302–3
  Strasbourg human rights legal case, 33, 70, 83, 170, 260
  see also Fianna Fáil government (1969-73); Fine Gael-Labour coalition (1973-7)
Irish National Liberation Army (INLA), 300, 322
Irish Republican Army (IRA)
  Official IRA, 24, 34, 35, 47, 233, 266, 316
  Provisional IRA *see* Provisional IRA (IRA)

Jenkins, Roy, 268, 272, 294

Kelly, Billy, 208
Kennedy, Edward, 48, 144, 246, 254
Kilfedder, James, 74, 95–6, 158
King, Sir Frank, 182–3, 206, 213, 217–18, 234–5, 282, 285
Kirk, Herbert, 102–3, 116, 177
Kissinger, Henry, 256
Kundera, Milan, xix

Labour government (1974-9)
  Anglo-Irish relations, 170, 171–2, 186–7, 190, 253, 259–60, 261, 267
  comes to power (4 March 1974), 156–7
  contingency plans (March 1974), 172
  Council of Ireland proposals and, 170, 191
  cross border security and, 178, 179
  direct rule and, 240–1, 251, 252–3
  discarding of Irish dimension, 14, 272, 273, 289, 323
  disengagement policy, 254–9, 260–2, 274–5, 296, 297–8, 312, 313–14, 317–18, 319
  disunity on Northern Ireland policy in late 1974 period, 268, 272
  dominion status idea and, 253, 269, 313, 314, 318–19
  doomsday scenario, 253, 263, 264–5, 269, 302
  financial cost of union and, 255–6, 258, 265
  independent Ulster option, 269, 290, 291, 298
  integration option and, 266, 268, 272, 290, 292, 294, 313, 314
  intergovernmental security conference (1974), 178, 181, 194
  internment and, 192, 270–1, 276, 277, 279, 284, 285, 291, 294–5
  IRA and *see* Provisional IRA (IRA): Labour government and major policy review (1975-6), 318, 319
  official 'incident centres' in nationalist areas, 283, 284–5
  policy after collapse of Executive, xvii, 252–3, 254–9, 274–5, 312
  power-sharing concept and, xiv, 13–15, 160, 262, 269, 271, 273
  see also Constitutional Convention
  prospect of second UWC strike and, 313–14
  repartition option, 264, 269, 272, 302, 313, 314, 319
  SDLP and, 181, 195–6, 245, 261–2, 263, 265, 266–7
  Sunningdale ratification and, 170, 177–80, 181–2, 185–7, 192, 193–4, 213, 221
  UWC strike, 202, 203, 204–5, 210–11
    cabinet meeting on (24 May 1974), 232, 233–4, 235
    inaction over, 13, 205–6, 208, 211, 215, 216, 227, 228, 232–3, 235, 236, 245, 246, 252
    Orme meeting with UWC, 204–5, 209
    plans for financial sanctions, 241
    refuses dialogue with UWC, 201, 204, 205, 217, 237, 245
    Stormont emergency committee on, 202, 206–7, 233
  White Paper (July 1974), 257–9, 262, 263, 267
  withdrawal option and, 15, 20, 164, 178–9, 183, 187, 255–7, 268–9, 296–8, 314
    Irish government's view of, 10, 171–2, 187, 253, 256–7, 264–5, 271, 272, 295, 311–12, 315
    Rees and, 13, 182, 192, 193, 261, 262, 271, 280, 307, 313, 319
    SDLP's view of, 240, 262, 263, 303, 311–12, 315–16
  see also Rees, Merlyn; Wilson, Harold
Labour Party, British, in Opposition (1970-4), 19–20, 27, 39–40, 52, 76, 82, 85, 89
Labour Party, Irish, 9, 57
Laird, John, 170, 171, 184, 203, 266, 278
Laneside cottage (Cultra), 5, 36, 46–7, 50, 62, 278, 281
Lebanon, 5, 54
Libya, 275
local government, 35, 291, 317, 318
Logue, Hugh, 149, 185
Londonderry, 'no-go areas' in, 32, 37, 41, 42
Loughran, Séamus, 270, 277, 279, 283
Lowry, Robert, 186, 292–3, 298, 303, 304, 317, 325, 326
  Paisley and, 305, 306, 308, 309, 321, 323
  SDLP-UUUC negotiations and, 305, 307, 323, 324, 325
  structure of Convention talks, 293, 300, 301
  voluntary coalition proposal and, 301, 302, 304, 305, 307, 309, 310
Loyalist Association of Workers, 27, 40, 53, 61, 65, 69
Lynch, Jack
  anti-terrorism legislation, 56, 57
  attitude to violence in North, 22–3
  border referendum and, 60
  Cosgrave government and, 144, 145, 151, 154–5, 259, 268
  Council of Ireland proposals and, 9, 55–6, 57, 67, 223
  cross border security and, 22, 24, 33, 35, 38, 55, 56, 57, 67
  doomsday scenario and, 302
  general election defeat (February 1973), 66, 68, 69
  Heath and, 33, 45–6, 48, 55–6, 67
  Irish constitution and, 33, 145, 155
  Irish unity and, 22, 33, 45–6, 54, 82
  SDLP and, 23, 26–7, 45, 46, 49, 315
  Sunningdale and, 144, 145, 151, 154–5, 223

supports power-sharing, 23, 54
welcomes direct rule, 31
Whitelaw and, 33, 36–7, 38
Lyttle, Tommy, 204

Mac Stíofáin, Seán, 36, 38–9, 45, 55, 58, 281, 316
   meeting with Labour leadership (July 1972), 39–40
MacBride, Seán, 281
Magee, Reginald, 177, 184
Maguire, Frank, 267
Mallon, Kevin, 280
Mallon, Séamus, 185, 195
Mason, Roy, 172, 183, 207, 208, 210, 211, 215, 216, 217, 234, 235, 294–5
   Chequers meeting with Executive leaders (24 May 1974), 229, 231–2
Maudling, Reginald, 20, 21, 22, 25, 129, 302
Maze prison, 317
McCarthy, David, 90
McGrady, Eddie, 76, 100, 116–17, 244
McGuinness, Martin, 38, 57, 147
McIvor, Basil, 75, 91, 116, 122, 131, 132, 188
McKee, Billy, 277, 282
McLachlan, Peter, 170–1, 177
McWhirter, Ross, 320
MI6, 5, 270, 298
Miami Showband killings, 299
Mills, Stratton, 64, 73
Minford, Nat, 81, 90, 184, 196
Molyneaux, James, 12, 211, 267–8, 282, 313
Monaghan and Dublin car bombings, 209, 239, 264
Morgan, William, 177
Morrell, Leslie, 75, 109, 152, 159, 188, 189, 197, 235–6, 266
   at Sunningdale, 116, 126, 135
Murray, Harry, 196, 204, 218–19, 260
Murray, Len, 206, 217

Nally, Dermot, 91, 165, 179, 190, 223, 264, 272, 311–12
Napier, Oliver, 64, 76, 147, 149, 181–2, 183, 186, 188, 194, 220, 244
   Chequers meeting with Wilson (24 May 1974), 228–9, 230, 231, 236, 262
   Constitutional Convention and, 301, 308, 317, 323, 324, 325, 326
   Stormont Castle negotiations, 92, 100, 102, 107, 108
   at Sunningdale, 116, 119, 128, 131, 132, 133, 134, 136, 137
nationalist community
   alienation from British state, 25
   army's low profile in nationalist areas, 34–5, 36, 41
   boycott of border poll (March 1973), 69
   direct rule and, 26, 32
   enters government in North for first time, 143–4
   Fianna Fáil as 'keepers of the holy grail', 82
   'incident centres' in nationalist areas, 283, 284–5, 306, 307, 314
   integration option and, 50
   internment and, 1–2, 27, 32, 192
   power-sharing proposals and, 9, 11, 12, 21
   splits in post-Executive period, 262–4
   UWC strike and, 235, 240
   Whitelaw's White Paper and, 71

   see also Catholic community in Northern Ireland; Social Democratic and Labour Party (SDLP)
Neave, Airey, 283, 292, 312, 320–1
Newfoundland, 257
1922 Committee of Conservative Party, 114
Northern Ireland
   arrival of British Army (August 1969), 1
   border referendum (8 March 1973), 69, 99
   civil service, 33–4, 50–1, 90, 117, 152–3, 171, 211–12, 225, 233, 237, 238, 240, 243
   constitutional status issue, 128–31, 153–5, 158, 160–2, 164–5, 189
      Faulkner and, 122, 128–9, 130–1, 149–51, 153–4, 158, 160, 161, 165, 169–70
      see also Irish constitution, Articles 2 and 3
   dominion status idea, 253, 269, 313, 314, 318–19
   financial cost of union, 255–6, 258, 265
   independent Ulster option, 76–7, 85, 269, 275, 290, 291, 296, 298, 321–2
      Craig and, 32, 52–3, 59, 66, 73, 76–7, 85, 254, 275, 296
   integration option, 50–1, 85, 86, 176, 266, 267–8, 290–1, 294, 298, 315, 317
      Heath and, 50, 59, 70, 83, 85, 96
      Labour government and, 266, 268, 272, 290, 292, 294, 313, 314
   local government, 35, 291, 317, 318
   number of MPs from, 59, 64, 317
   repartition option, 22, 264, 269, 272, 302, 313, 314, 319
   republican 'no-go areas' in, 32, 36, 37, 40, 41, 42, 45
   role of British army after collapse of Executive, 255, 262
   sectarian violence in first phase of direct rule, 32, 34, 45
   South Armagh security crisis (1975-6), 316, 322
   two-day strike (27 March 1972), 31, 33
   withdrawal option *see* Labour government (1974–9): withdrawal option
Northern Ireland Assembly
   anti-Sunningdale motion in, 170, 171, 177, 196–7
   anti-white paper members, 75, 92, 94, 100, 108, 109–10, 146
   Council of Ireland proposals and, 70
   debates on Sunningdale, 170–1, 175, 184
   elections to (28 June 1973), 74–5
   expiry of UUUC membership, 169
   Faulkner's lack of majority in, 96–7, 98–100, 258
   Faulkner's 'pledged' candidates/members, 73, 74, 75–6, 81, 83, 86, 90–1, 96, 146, 148, 183–4, 189
   first sitting (31 July 1973), 81
   legislative procedures, 143
   Paisley's disruptions of, 81, 110, 151, 175, 184
   proposed role post-Executive, 240–1
   Rees' prorogation of, 252
   SDLP and Sunningdale ratification, 220–1
   STV for elections, 67, 74
Northern Ireland Constitutional Proposals (White Paper, 20 March 1973), 51, 54–5, 59, 60, 63–4, 67, 70–1
Northern Ireland Electricity Board, 174, 203, 204, 207, 209, 225, 243
Northern Ireland Executive (from 1 January 1974)

Bloomfield as permanent secretary, 143–4
role of Bradford in, 184, 188, 190
Chequers meeting with Wilson (24 May 1974), 228–33, 234, 236, 262
collapse of (28 May 1974), xv, xvi, 13, 201, 244–5, 246, 251–2
Council of Ireland proposals and, 151–4, 187–92, 213, 214, 216, 217, 219–21, 246
Faulkner-Fitt relationship, 148–9
Faulkner's resignation (28 May 1974), 244–5
first meeting of, 145–6
general election (28 February 1974) and, 156, 158, 159, 164, 165, 201, 252
Heath's failure to devolve security powers, 12–13, 59, 84, 87, 127, 133–4, 179, 245
instability of (March 1974), 159–60
IRA violence during, 173–4
Irish government and, 153, 158–9, 163, 214, 264
last meeting (28 May 1974), 244–5
meeting with Wilson (April 1974), 181–2
meetings with Irish government, 153
Paisley/Craig campaign to destroy, 146–7
public opinion and, 175
SDLP serves on, 148–9, 151, 152–3, 161–3, 171, 177, 184–5, 189, 190–1, 216
plan to resign from (27 May 1974), 240, 241
SDLP 'big hitters', 258
split over Sunningdale re-phasing, 185, 195, 220–1
sub-committee, 189, 190, 194
takes power (1 January 1974), 143–4
timetable for progress (May 1974), 192–3
UWC strike, 206, 208–10, 212–13, 214–15, 216, 217, 219–21, 223–4, 225–6, 237–40
Faulkner admits need for talks with UWC, 201, 243, 244, 245
refusal to enter talks with UWC, 225, 226
split over using troops to break, 230–2
Whitelaw's proposals, 58–60, 62, 63–5, 67, 71–2
Wilson government and, xiv, 13–15, 172, 192–3, 201, 217, 228–35, 244–5
Northern Ireland Labour Party (NILP), 48, 51, 66, 68, 74, 75, 323
Northern Ireland Office (NIO), 33–4, 51, 114, 116, 239, 282
Northern Ireland Transport Association, 206

Ó Brádaigh, Ruairí, 35, 37, 277, 280, 281, 282
Ó Conaill, Dáithí, 71, 161, 193, 320
arrest of by Irish special branch, 299–300
contacts with Whitelaw, 36, 37, 38
Wilson government and, 270, 277, 279, 280, 281, 282
Oatley, Michael, 270, 277, 320
O'Brien, Conor Cruise, 57, 154, 213–14, 230, 267
Council of Ireland proposals and, 9, 136, 138, 172, 181, 213–14, 256, 263, 264, 273–4, 292
FitzGerald and, 68, 82, 172, 214, 263, 272–3, 274, 295
at Sunningdale, 116, 122, 124–5, 128, 130, 136, 138
views on Irish unity, 9, 82, 256
O'Connell, John, 27, 281, 282, 297
Offences against the Person Act (1861), 132
Offences against the State (Amendment) Bill (December 1972), 56
Official IRA, 24, 34, 35, 47, 233, 266, 316

Official Unionist Party
British government's break with, 9, 11, 82
Constitution Act and, 86, 89
Constitutional Convention and, 289, 298, 308, 310
Darlington talks (September 1972), 48, 51
divisions after UWC strike, 254
divisions over direct rule, 11, 12, 31
electoral performance (May/June 1973), 74
Faulkner maintains leadership (March 1973), 71–2
Faulkner resigns as leader of (January 1974), 146
meeting with Rees (30 May 1974) and, 253
MPs' motion to defeat Whitelaw's bill, 73–4
negotiations after February 1974 election, 160
October 1974 election and, 267–8
opponents of Faulkner within, 11–12, 73, 75, 90, 94, 183
political supremacy, 1–2
Enoch Powell and, 266, 267–8, 298, 310
reaction to government-IRA talks, 281–2
softening of anti-power-sharing stance, 275
Stormont Castle negotiations (October-November 1973), 86, 89–90, 91, 92, 93, 94, 95, 96–7, 98–100, 102–3, 104–5
at Sunningdale, 115, 117, 122, 127, 130–1, 133–5
talks with Conservative Opposition, 261
Ulster Vanguard group, 12, 14, 24, 32, 52–3, 64
'unpledged' members of, 75, 94, 97, 100, 108, 109–10
UUC ruling body, 90, 98, 104, 136, 146, 147, 149
in UUUC, 14, 156
voluntary coalition proposal and, 323, 324
West elected leader, 151
Whitelaw's proposals and, 72, 73
O'Hagan, Joe, 280
O'Kennedy, Michael, 315
Oliver, Dr John, 292
O'Neill, Phelim, 66
O'Neill, Terrance, 181, 254
Orange Order, 90, 260, 306
Orme, Stan, 156, 157, 193, 215, 218, 220–1, 273, 284, 292
denies government contacts with IRA, 260–1
meeting with UUUC and UWC leaders, 203–5, 209
Orr, Captain, 160
O'Sullivan, Donal, 154

Pagels, Bob, 196, 204
Paisley, Mrs Eileen, 326
Paisley, Rev. Ian
alleged civil service leaks to, 171
Constitutional Convention and, 6, 271, 290, 293, 300, 301, 304–11, 318, 321–2, 323, 324, 325–6
Frank Cooper on, 156
Council of Ireland proposals and, 98, 103–4, 105, 107, 109
Craig and, 73, 94, 156, 254, 271, 290, 310–11
direct rule and, 24–5, 31–2
disruptions of Assembly by, 81, 110, 151, 175, 184
Faulkner and, 69, 94, 224
independent Ulster and, 296, 321–2
meeting with Heath (November 1973), 95–6
Northern Ireland Executive and, 108, 110, 113, 146–7, 165, 251
on O'Brien, 267
John O'Connell and, 27

Enoch Powell and, 268
  Pym and, 113, 151
  reaction to government-IRA talks, 281–2
  security pact with unionist leaders (February 1973), 66
  Stormont Castle negotiations and, 92, 95
  Sunningdale and, 114, 116
  on unionists' 'right to arm', 260
  UWC strike and, 203, 204, 205, 218, 219, 226–7, 232, 236, 243, 244, 254
  warning to Provisional IRA (June 1974), 252
  Whitelaw and, 72, 101, 102, 107, 108, 109
  Wilson government and, 6, 14, 169, 218, 253, 254, 255, 275, 282, 321
  on Paddy Wilson's murder, 75
paramilitary groups, dissident republican, 306, 307
paramilitary groups, Protestant, xiv, xv, 12, 40, 65–7, 266, 281–2, 308–9, 312
  British intelligence and, 40, 183, 278
  Dublin and Monaghan car bombings, 209, 239, 264
  sectarian violence by, 40, 53, 54, 57–8, 75, 173, 209, 239, 264, 299
  Shankill Butchers, 322
  UWC and, 196, 209, 227–8, 236, 237
  Whitelaw and, 35–6, 39, 45, 65, 98
  see also Ulster Defence Association (UDA); Ulster Volunteer Force (UVF)
Patterson, Harry, 204
policing issues
  Hume and, 81, 85, 132, 133, 135
  Rees and, 260, 262, 265, 312, 317
  SDLP and, 85, 86, 100, 104, 133, 188, 189, 192, 301, 307
  Council of Ireland proposals, 81, 82–3, 119, 124, 127, 132, 134, 135, 177
  name change issue, 81, 90, 97, 124
  at Sunningdale, 131–5, 138
  see also Royal Ulster Constabulary (RUC)
Pounder, Rafton, 134
Powell, Enoch, 89, 266, 267–8, 290–1, 298, 310, 313, 315, 316–17
power stations, 27, 31, 47, 53, 60–1, 65
  British Army and, 203, 205–7, 208, 209–11, 212, 215, 217, 224–5, 228, 230–5, 236, 240
  security at, 174, 187
  UWC and, xiv, 196, 202–12, 215–17, 224–5, 227, 228, 230–6, 240, 242, 243, 244
power-sharing proposals, xvi, xix, 5–14, 39, 67, 157, 269, 289
  agreement reached on (22 November 1973), 108–10
  allocation of portfolios, 100, 101, 102–3, 108
  Constitution Act and, 83, 96, 97, 99, 100, 108, 109
  Council of Ireland proposals and, 83, 84, 85–6, 88, 120
  The Future of Northern Ireland (October 1972), 54
  Irish dimension and, 11–12, 263–4, 266, 272, 273–4, 289, 291, 292, 301, 304, 308, 323
  see also Council of Ireland proposals
  Irish government's view of, 83–4
  Northern Ireland's constitutional status issue *see* Northern Ireland: constitutional status issue
  other countries and, xvii–xviii, 5, 54, 269, 273, 321
  planned tripartite conference, 70, 75, 83, 84, 88–9, 93–4, 96, 97, 102, 103–4, 105–7
  see also Sunningdale Communiqué; Sunningdale conference proposed composition of executive, 67–8, 72–3, 96–7, 98–100, 101–3, 107–8
  public opinion on, 72, 175–6, 183
  reserved matters and, 87, 95–6, 109, 115
  Stormont Castle negotiations (October-November 1973), 86, 89–95, 96–7, 98–100, 101–5, 106–9
  see also Constitutional Convention; Northern Ireland Executive (from 1 January 1974); Whitelaw, William: power-sharing proposals
prisoners
  political status issue, 36, 37
  special category, 36, 192, 270, 276, 279, 283, 294–5, 314–15, 317
  special tribunals and, 49
proportional representation, 21, 35, 67, 74, 132
Protestant community *see under* unionist organisations
Provisional IRA (IRA)
  attitude to elections, 270, 284
  ceasefire (June-July 1972), 37, 38, 39, 58
  ceasefires (late 1974-1976 period), 14, 276, 277–81, 291, 294, 295, 299, 300, 312, 314, 316, 320
    ending of (23 January 1976), 325
  Conservative government and, 7, 34–5, 36–7, 38–9, 40, 45, 71
  emergence of new leadership (1975), 320
  estimated strength of, 34, 182
  Executive and, 6, 10, 110
  Feakle churchmen and, 276–7, 279, 280
  feud with Official IRA, 316
  'indefinite truce' (from 10 February 1975), 283–5
  internment and, 1, 21, 29–30
  Irish government and, 3, 147, 148, 151, 153, 161, 163, 182, 284
    Cosgrave government crackdown, 280, 299–300, 314
    Lynch government, 23, 33, 35, 55, 56, 67
  Labour government and, 14, 182, 192, 259, 260–1, 281, 297, 316
    secret contacts with (from late 1974 period), 14, 269–70, 275–9, 280, 281–3, 296–7
    Wilson's Commons statement (13 May 1974), 193
  leadership struggle (1972), 37
  meetings with Labour leadership (1972), 27, 39–40, 157
  Operation Motorman against (July 1972), 41–2, 45, 47
  SDLP and, 36, 177
  special tribunals and, 41, 48, 49
  splits within (1974-5 period), 275, 284, 314
  supply of weapons to, 183
  unofficial incident centres set up by, 284–5, 306, 307, 314
  UWC strike and, 233, 242
  violence
    Birmingham pub bombings (November 1974), 271–2, 275
    Bloody Friday (21 July 1972), 41
    bombings in early 1974 period, 161
    erosion of capacity for (late 1974 period), 275–6
    during Executive period, 173–4, 177, 182, 197
    late 1975 period, 320
    London bombings (8 March 1973), 69
    Monasterevin siege (October 1975), 316
    murder of Senator Billy Fox, 165

upsurge of in first phase of direct rule, 32, 34, 35, 41, 45
Pym, Francis, 113, 122–3, 127, 133, 143, 151, 220

Rawlinson, Sir Peter, 116, 131
Red Hand Commando, 98
Rees, Merlyn
  Arlow allegations and, 296–7, 298
  attitude to Sunningdale, 160, 177
  becomes secretary of state, 156
  Constitutional Convention, 13–14, 291–2, 303, 312, 317, 318, 319–20, 321, 322–3, 324
    dissolves (5 March 1976), 326
    majority report of, 318, 319, 322, 326
    proceedings of, 292–3
    proposals for, 243, 254, 257–9, 265, 268–9, 285
    reconvening of, 319–20, 322–6
    refuses to receive delegations, 293
    suggests three-month extension (September 1975), 313
    tactics at, 293–4, 297–8
    voluntary coalition idea, 323
  contempt for unionism, 157, 321
  Craig and, 157, 321
  criminalisation policy, 314–15, 317
  cross border security and, 178
  decriminalisation of Sinn Féin and UVF, 173, 177
  detainee releases by, 284, 285, 291, 294, 299, 312, 314, 321
  disengagement policy, 254–5, 260–2, 296, 297–8, 312, 319
  Faulkner and, 180, 187, 220, 225–6, 236, 244–5
  FitzGerald and, 160, 162, 193–4, 273, 278, 291–2, 293, 316
  IRA
    ceasefires (from Christmas 1974) and, 276, 277, 279, 280, 291, 294, 295, 299, 300
    efforts to end violence by, 259, 261
    'indefinite truce', 283–4
    meeting with (July 1972), 39–40
    secret contacts with, 281–2, 296–7, 316, 320
  Irish government and, 14, 268
  meeting with party leaders (30 May 1974), 253–4
  meets loyalist deputation (17 May 1974), 209
  mental/physical toll on, 157, 253, 263, 285, 321
  Northern Ireland Executive, 172–3, 182, 192–3, 195–6, 213, 223, 233
    Chequers meeting with leaders (24 May 1974), 229, 231
    collapse of, 201, 244, 245
  opposes integration option, 266, 268
  Paisley and, 307, 308, 321
  policing issues and, 260, 262, 265, 312, 317
  Enoch Powell on, 316–17
  Provisional Sinn Féin and, 276, 279, 280, 281, 283
  refusal to specify acceptable forms of power-sharing, 262, 271, 295
  reinforces army in south Armagh and Fermanagh, 283
  response to Birmingham bombings, 271–2
  resumption of direct rule (May 1974), 251, 252–3
  SDLP and, 14, 265, 268
  security policies, 14, 255, 284, 285, 291, 300, 303, 306, 312, 314–15, 320–1
  South Armagh security crisis (1975), 316
  special category prisoners and, 270, 276, 279, 294–5, 314–15, 317
  statement to Commons (14 January 1975), 279
  strike (7 February 1973) and, 65
  talks with Northern Ireland parties (Christmas 1975), 317, 319
  tension with British Army, 284, 285, 291, 312
  troop reductions and, 172, 177, 192, 210, 255, 257, 260, 262, 294, 295
  UWC strike, 202, 203, 206–7, 208–13, 215, 216, 221, 225–6, 228, 237–8, 240–1
    cabinet meeting on (24 May 1974), 233–4, 235
    end of, 253
    final appeal for return to work, 243
    launch of oil plan (27 May 1974), 241–2
    proclaims state of emergency (19 May 1974), 212
    refusal to enter talks with UWC, 201, 205, 217, 237, 245
    troop reinforcements during, 217, 224, 253
    views on failure to defeat, 252
  White Paper (July 1974), 257–9, 262, 263
  withdrawal option and, 13, 182, 192, 193, 261, 262, 271, 280, 307, 313, 319
  working-class Ulster nationalism and, 246, 257, 260, 261, 298
referendum, border (8 March 1973), 60, 69, 99
'rent and rates strike' against internment, 76, 86, 104, 152, 184, 209
Rigby, Joseph, 306
Royal Ulster Constabulary (RUC), xiv, 33, 58
  attempted ambush of Devlin/Cooper and, 242
  brutality allegations against, 33, 154
  Council of Ireland proposals and, 81, 82–3, 87, 119, 124, 127, 132, 134, 135, 177
  extradition warrants and, 57
  leaks to loyalist community from, 312
  numerical strength of, 182
  Rees and, 260, 262, 312, 317
  Reserve, 260, 262, 302, 317
  SDLP and see policing issues: SDLP and
  special interrogation centres, 35
  in state of 'total collapse', 40
  strike (7 February 1973) and, 65
  UWC strike and, 206, 213, 225, 228, 231, 233
  Whitelaw and, 49
Ryan, Richie, 116

sewage system, 174, 203, 207, 242, 245
Silkin, Samuel, 229, 268
Simpson, Vivian, 66
single transferable vote (STV), 67, 74, 121
Sinn Féin, 266, 276, 279, 280, 281, 282, 284, 316
  decriminalisation of, 173, 177
  'incident centres' in nationalist areas, 283, 284–5
Smith, Howard, 5, 239
Smith, Ian, 277
Smith, Jim, 218
Smyth, Rev. Martin, 12, 275, 296
Snow, John, 218
Social Democratic and Labour Party (SDLP)
  Assembly members, 75, 76, 83
  civil service recruitment and, 90
  Constitution Act and, 76, 81, 86, 89, 135
  Constitutional Convention, 6, 283, 289–90, 292,

293, 297, 299–309, 315–21, 323–4, 325
  elections to, 263, 268, 289–90
  minority report, 293, 315–16, 318
Council of Ireland proposals and, 85–6, 93–4, 98, 151–3, 162–3, 176, 194–5, 196
Irish government and, 84, 85, 94, 97, 124, 127, 134, 149, 162–3, 171, 190–2
  phased implementation proposals and, 180–1, 182, 185, 188, 189, 191, 216, 219
  policing issues, 81, 82–3, 119, 124, 127, 132, 134, 135, 177
  secretariat issue, 93, 102, 195
  at Sunningdale, 119, 121, 124, 127, 132, 134, 135
doomsday scenario and, 302–3
'east of the Bann' pragmatists, 10, 49
electoral performance (May/June 1973), 74
Faulkner's renegotiation of Sunningdale and, 197, 201, 216, 219–21
general election (28 February 1974) and, 156
inflexibility and inexperience, 68
intelligence services and, 5
internment, 85, 86, 95, 182, 184, 189, 195–6, 270, 278
  dilemma over IRA releases, 173–4, 284
  as key issue, 22, 34, 46–8, 58, 153, 163, 175, 179
  'rent and rates strike' against, 76, 86, 104, 152, 184, 209
  Stormont Castle talks, 92, 93, 100, 102, 103, 104
IRA ceasefire (Christmas 1974) and, 278
Irish dimension post-Executive and, 264, 266, 289, 292, 301, 304, 308
Irish government and, 23, 26–7, 46, 49, 63
  see also Fine Gael-Labour coalition (1973-7): SDLP and Lynch and, 26–7, 45, 46, 49, 315
  meetings with UUUC, 299, 300–1
  new hard-line policy (August 1974), 264, 275
October 1974 election and, 267
opposes talks with UWC, 226
post-Executive attitude to power-sharing, 256, 262–4, 266
power-sharing proposals and, 84, 85–6, 96, 97, 98, 99–100, 101–2, 103, 104, 105, 110
reaction to Whitelaw's White Paper, 71
RUC issue and see policing issues: SDLP and
secret discussions at Laneside, 36
secret talks with IRA, 36
serves on Northern Ireland Executive, 148–9, 151, 152–3, 158–9, 161–3, 171, 177, 184–5, 189, 190–2, 216, 238
  backlash against Executive and, 195
  collapse of Executive and, 245
  plan to resign (27 May 1974), 240, 241
Stormont Castle negotiations (October-November 1973), 86, 89–90, 92, 93–4, 96, 98–100, 101–2, 103, 104–5, 106–9
at Sunningdale, 117, 119, 121, 126–7, 131, 132–4
Sunningdale ratification and, 153, 154, 162, 181–2, 184–5, 188, 189, 190–2, 220–1
support for military action over UWC strike, 220, 231, 238
talks with Craig, 69, 290, 299, 300, 324
talks with UDA (August 1974), 266
Towards a New Ireland, 48–9
views on potential British withdrawal, 240, 262,

263, 303, 311–12, 315–16
voluntary coalition proposal and, 321, 324
welcomes direct rule, 31
'west of the Bann' ideologues, 10, 49, 185, 195
Whitelaw's mission to include, 10, 32, 34, 35, 46–8
willing to serve in new executive (30 May 1974), 253
Wilson government, xv, 157, 181, 195–6, 245, 261–2, 265, 266–7
  Rees and, 14, 265, 268
  talks with Wilson (10 September 1974), 266–7
  withdraws support for, 261–2
Soviet Union, xix
special category prisoners, 36, 192, 270, 276, 279, 283, 294–5, 314–15, 317
Special Powers Act (1922), 49
Steele, Frank, 5, 36–7, 42
Stormont parliament, 1–2, 8–9, 21, 24, 27, 30–2
strike, one-day (7 February 1973), 65–6, 69
strike, two-day (27 March 1972), 31, 33
strike, UWC, xiv–xv, 12
  announcement of, 196–7, 202
  BBC Northern Ireland and, 229–30
  electricity supply and, xiv, 196, 202–10, 212, 215, 216, 225, 230–2, 234, 242, 243, 244
  end of, 245–6, 253
  Executive during see Northern Ireland Executive (from 1 January 1974): UWC strike
  Faulkner and, 201, 208–9, 210, 213, 219–20, 237–40, 243, 244, 245
  health and social security system during, 229
  Irish government and, 213–14, 227
  Northern Ireland civil service and, 211–12, 225, 233, 237, 238, 240, 243
  oil supply/distribution during, 206, 221, 224–6, 228–31, 232, 234, 237–42, 252
  Orme's meeting with UUUC and UWC leaders, 203–5, 209
  Paisley declares open support for, 218, 254
  Protestant church leaders and, 212
  road blocks/barricades, 205, 206, 208, 217–18, 226, 242, 252
  sea change in Protestant opinion over, 235–6
  sewage system and, 203, 207, 242, 245
  threats and intimidation during, 203, 204, 208, 225
  UUUC gives full support to (19 May 1974), 213
  UWC request Wilson's intervention, 210–11
  UWC roadblocks, 212, 213, 215, 217–18
  violence during, 212, 225
  widespread support for (by 22 May 1974), 214–15, 218, 219, 227, 239–40
  Wilson government and see Labour government (1974-9): UWC strike; Rees, Merlyn: UWC strike
  Wilson's televised address (25 May 1974), 212, 238–9
  see also British Army: UWC strike; Ulster Workers' Council (UWC)
Stronge, James, 148, 158
Sunningdale Communiqué, 135, 136–8
  Faulkner's defence of, 170
  Faulkner's renegotiation of, 13, 148, 169, 185, 187–92, 193–4, 197, 201–2, 216, 219–21, 223–4
  general election (28 February 1974) and, 156, 164, 165

Irish constitution and, 149
nature of, 186
Paisley threatens 'uprising' over, 169
as political defeat for unionism, 11
ratification issues, 187–94, 219–21
    Faulkner and, 148, 149, 153, 160–2, 165, 170, 174–6, 180, 181–2, 187–94, 213, 219–21
    Irish government and, 145, 148, 154, 160–1, 165, 170, 172, 174–6, 177–80, 185–7, 194, 213–14
    Labour government and, 170, 177–80, 181–2, 185–7, 192, 193–4, 213, 221
    SDLP and, 153, 154, 162, 181–2, 184–5, 188, 189, 190–2, 220–1
responses to in Ireland, 144–5, 147–8, 149, 154–5
unconstitutional methods against begin, 196–7
UWC strike and, 213, 214
UWC warning on, 196
Wilson government's attitude to, 160, 178–9
Sunningdale civil service college, 89
Sunningdale conference (November 1973)
    absence of Whitelaw, 113–14, 115, 129, 137–8
    attendees at, 116–17
    chairmanship of, 89, 105, 117–18
    Communiqué, 135, 136, 145
    final sessions, 131–5
    first session, 117–25
    Heath and, 8, 114–15, 117–18, 119
    Irish government disclosures to press at, 124–5, 126
    joint declaration on status, 129–31, 150, 151, 154, 158, 189
    procedures/agenda at, 115–16, 126
    second session, 125–30
Switzerland, 54, 269

Taylor, John, 11–12, 52, 73, 90, 94, 146, 156, 184, 260
    attempted assassination of (1972), 24
    Constitutional Convention and, 296, 308, 324
Thatcher, Margaret, 283, 315
Thorn, Gaston, 117
Trade Union Congress (TUC), 206, 217, 218
trade unions in Northern Ireland, 40, 60–1, 208, 210, 225
    Loyalist Association of Workers, 27, 40, 53, 61, 65, 69
Trevelyan, Dennis, 116, 127
Trimble, David, 321
Tully, James, 116
Twomey, Séamus, 37, 38, 161, 280, 309
Tyrie, Andy, 204, 266

Ulster Bank, 218
Ulster Defence Association (UDA), xv, 40, 47, 53–4, 65, 183, 260, 275
    barricades in Belfast, 35–6, 37–8, 39, 41–2, 217–18
    contact with republican paramilitaries, 266, 320
    Craig and, 66, 309
    talks with SDLP (August 1974), 266
    UWC strike and, 203, 204, 205, 206, 208, 209, 217–18
    Whitelaw and, 35–6, 39
Ulster Defence Regiment (UDR), 40, 211, 225, 233, 260, 262, 302, 309

loyalist paramilitary infiltration of, 53–4, 312
Ulster Freedom Fighters (UFF), 75, 98
Ulster unionism, 2, 3, 6
    'centre group' of liberal unionists, 64–5
    fear of all-Ireland government, 87, 88, 91, 97, 98, 118–19
    reaction to imposition of direct rule, 11–12, 31–2, 33, 35–6
    working-class Ulster nationalism and, 14, 246, 257, 260, 261, 298
    see also Democratic Unionist Party (DUP); Official Unionist Party; United Ulster Unionist Council (UUUC)
Ulster Volunteer Force (UVF), 53, 54, 65, 177, 183, 289, 309, 314
    decriminalisation of, 173, 177
    Dublin bombings (December 1972), 56
    sectarian violence by, 40, 299
    UWC strike and, 204, 246
    Volunteer Political Party, 260, 266
Ulster Workers' Council (UWC), xiv
    call for province-wide general strike, 210
    control over Northern Ireland, 216–17
    disowned by TUC, 206
    distrust of UUUC, 219, 243–4, 246, 266
    food and fuel distribution by, 236, 237, 239
    Hawthornden Road headquarters, xv, 203, 206
    make up of, 196
    meeting with Orme, 204–5, 209
    political motivations of, 205, 218–19, 243–4, 246
    prospect of second strike, 313–14
    responses to British Army oil plan, 242–3
    split from UUUC, 266, 309
    takes responsibility for administrative functions, 215, 218, 224, 226, 227, 229–30, 236, 237, 239
    UDA ends association with, 260
    'withdrawal' of, 242
Unionist Party of Northern Ireland, 265–6, 290
Unionist Party, Official *see* Official Unionist Party
United States of America (USA), 21, 25, 48, 57, 183
United Ulster Unionist Council (UUUC), 14
    anti-Sunningdale motion, 170, 171, 177
    attitude to power-sharing, 256
    call for early elections post-Executive, 254
    celebrates collapse of Executive, 251
    Constitutional Convention, 289, 290–1, 293, 294, 297–311, 317, 318, 319–26
    expiry of Assembly membership, 169
    extradition as wedge issue, 184
    failure to identify with SDLP leaders, 306–7
    general election (28 February 1974), 156, 157, 160
    integration option and, 290–1, 298
    meetings with SDLP, 299, 300–1
    Molyneaux becomes leader of parliamentary party, 267–8
    October 1974 election and, 267–8
    plans for civil disobedience, 179–80
    Portrush conference (April 1974), 184
    post-Executive period, 251, 254, 255, 256, 259, 260, 267–8
    reaction to government-IRA talks, 278
    softening of anti-power-sharing stance, 275
    splits in post-Executive period, 260, 267–8
    Ulster Loyalist Central Co-ordinating Committee, 308

unconstitutional methods against Sunningdale, 196–7
unconstitutional methods and, 193
unionist veto and, 259
UWC splits with, 266
UWC strike and, 202, 203–5, 206, 208, 209, 210, 213, 219, 246
UWC's distrust of, 219, 243–4, 246
voluntary coalition proposal and, 321
Wilson's views on (November 1974), 269, 271

Vanguard Unionist Progressive Party, 72, 73, 94, 121, 156, 259, 267, 275, 281–2, 310
Assembly members, 75, 81
Constitutional Convention and, 289, 307–8, 310–11

West, Harry, 73, 90, 94, 184, 229, 253, 254
Constitutional Convention and, 296, 305, 307, 309, 318, 324–5, 326
as leader of Official Unionists, 12, 151, 267
voluntary coalition proposal and, 14, 305, 309
White, John, 75
White, Kelvin, 128
Whitelaw, William
absence from Sunningdale, 113–14, 115, 129, 137–8
advisory committee, 31, 35
anti-assassination police squad, 57
anti-terrorism legislation, 57
Assembly election results and, 75–6
becomes secretary of state, 4, 31
'centre group' of liberal unionists and, 64–5
common law enforcement area issue and, 103, 106
constitutional framework, 50
Council of Ireland proposals and, 62–3, 98, 103–4, 107, 109
Craig and, 76–7, 85, 108, 109
direct rule and, 32–42, 33, 45–50, 61–2
executive by agreement proposal, 67–8, 72–3
Faulkner and, 8, 11, 51, 58, 59, 62, 64, 68, 69, 71–4, 76, 105
Heath's need for in mainland politics, 100, 101, 114
integration option and, 85, 86, 315
internment and, 32, 34, 35, 47, 106
Edward Kennedy on, 144
leaves post as secretary of state, 109–10, 113–14
legislation and, 72, 76–7
see also Constitution Act (1973)
Lynch and, 33, 36–7, 38
Northern Ireland's constitutional status issue, 128–9
Operation Folklore and, 45, 61
Operation Motorman (July 1972), 41–2, 45, 47
Paisley and, 72, 107, 108, 109
political style of, 4, 114
power-sharing proposals, 58–60, 62, 63–5, 67, 71–2
consultation process, 50–2, 53, 57

Darlington talks (September 1972), 48, 50, 51–2
mission to include SDLP, 10, 32, 34, 35, 46–8
pursuit of middle ground coalition, xv, 4, 10, 13, 32, 35–6, 46, 58–9, 64–5
referendum proposals, 47, 54, 60, 66–7
reports to Commons (22 November 1973), 109
Stormont Castle negotiations (October–November 1973), 86, 90, 93–4, 95, 96–7, 98–100, 101–5, 106–9
time constraints on, 7, 98, 99, 101, 108
power-sharing settlement, 8, 11
proscribes UFF and Red Hand Commando, 98
rolling/evolving devolution and, 59, 63–4, 67, 68
secret talks with IRA and, 36–7, 38–9, 40, 45
security policies, 32, 34–5, 40–1, 45, 47–8
special tribunals and, 41, 47–8, 49
strike (7 February 1973) and, 65–6
suspension of Stormont (1972) and, 21
shadow cabinet in opposition, 315
UDA and, 35–6, 39
value of power-sharing policy to, 7–8
warning to unconstitutional unionists, 100–1
White Paper (March 1973), 51, 54–5, 59, 60, 63–4, 67, 71
withdrawal as 'moral disgrace', 271
Whitten, Herbert, 148, 158
Widgery inquiry into Bloody Sunday, 32
Williams, Shirley, 297
Wilson, Harold, xiv, xv, xvii, xviii
anti-unionist/Northern Ireland sentiments, 157, 238–9, 261
Constitutional Convention proposals, 243, 267, 269
direct rule and, 240–1
distrust of in Dublin, 157
Faulkner and, 170, 174–5, 178
fiscal sanctions on Harland and Wolff, 224, 255–6
forms government (4 March 1974), 156–7
'hands off'/low priority approach to Northern Ireland, 157, 164, 183, 259
IRA and, 27, 39–40, 157, 193, 261, 277–8, 280, 281, 282
Northern Ireland Executive and, 181–2, 228–33, 234, 236, 262
in Opposition, 19–20, 27, 39–40, 52, 82, 85, 89
suggests Lancaster House conference, 268
talks with SDLP (10 September 1974), 266–7
televised address (25 May 1974), 212, 238–9
views on power-sharing, 178–9, 267, 269
see also Labour government (1974–9)
Wilson, Paddy, 75
Woodfield, Philip, 36–7, 116, 128, 154, 215